SKY BLADE
SWORD OF THE HEAVENS

1

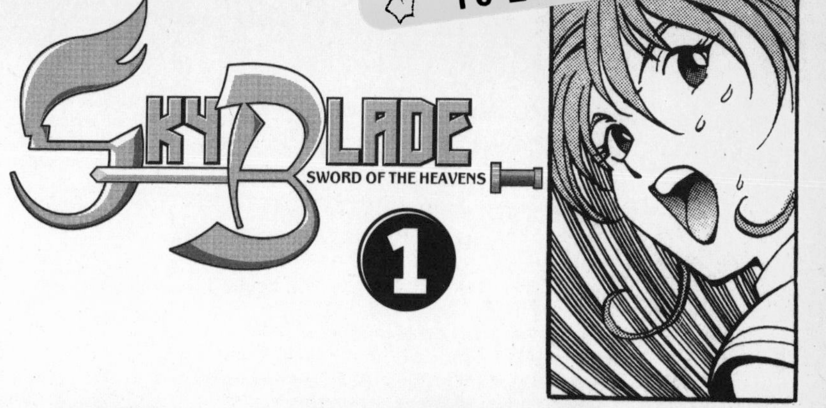

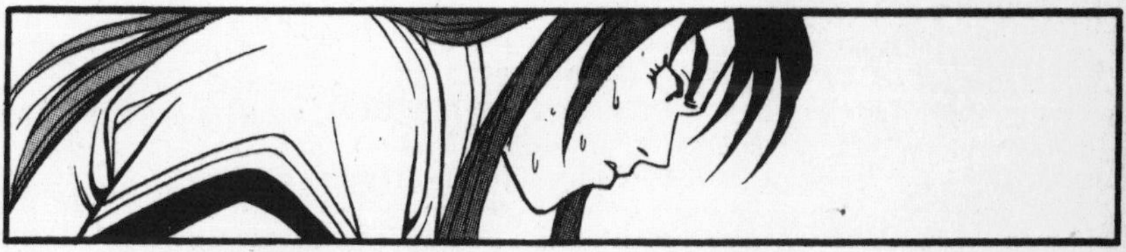

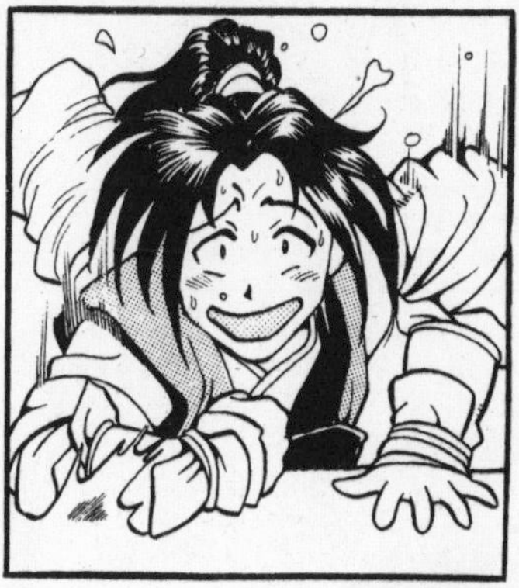

AUTHOR•HYUN KANG-SUK
ILLUSTRATOR• AH SHIN

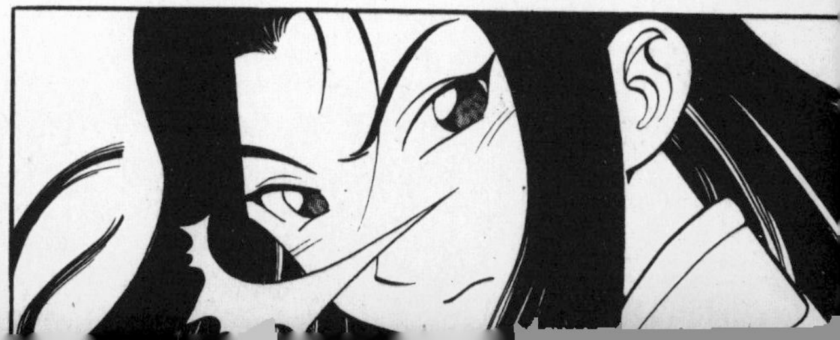

ADV Manga™
www.adv-manga.com

SKY BLADE: SWORD of the HEAVENS
VOLUME ONE

© 1998 Hyun Kang-Suk, Ah Shin/DAIWON C.I. Inc.
All Rights Reserved.
First published in Korea in 1998 by DAIWON C.I. Inc.
English translation rights in USA, Canada, UK, IRIE, NZ and Australia arranged by DAIWON C.I. Inc.

Translator **TRISHA EGGLESTON**
Lead Translator/Translation Supervisor **JAVIER LOPEZ**
ADV Manga Translation Staff **JASON AN AND SIMON JUNG**

Print Production/ Art Studio Manager **LISA PUCKETT**
Pre-press Manager **KLYS REEDYK**
Art Production Manager **RYAN MASON**
Sr. Designer/Creative Manager **JORGE ALVARADO**
Graphic Designer/Group Leader **SHANNON RASBERRY**
Graphic Artists **CHRIS LAPP AND LISA RAPER**
Graphic Intern **MARK MEZA**

Publishing Editor **SUSAN ITIN**
Assistant Editor **MARGARET SCHAROLD**
Editorial Assistant **VARSHA BHUCHAR**
Proofreaders **SHERIDAN JACOBS AND STEVEN REED**

Research/ Traffic Coordinator **MARSHA ARNOLD**

Executive VP, CFO, COO **KEVIN CORCORAN**

President, CEO & Publisher **JOHN LEDFORD**

Email: editor@adv-manga.com
www.adv-manga.com
www.advfilms.com

For sales and distribution inquiries please call 1.800.282.7202

ADV MANGA™ is a division of A.D. Vision, Inc.
10114 W. Sam Houston Parkway, Suite 200, Houston, Texas 77099

English text © 2004 published by A.D. Vision, Inc. under exclusive license.
ADV MANGA is a trademark of A.D. Vision, Inc.

ISBN: 1-4139-0081-X
First printing, June 2004
10 9 8 7 6 5 4 3 2 1
Printed in Canada

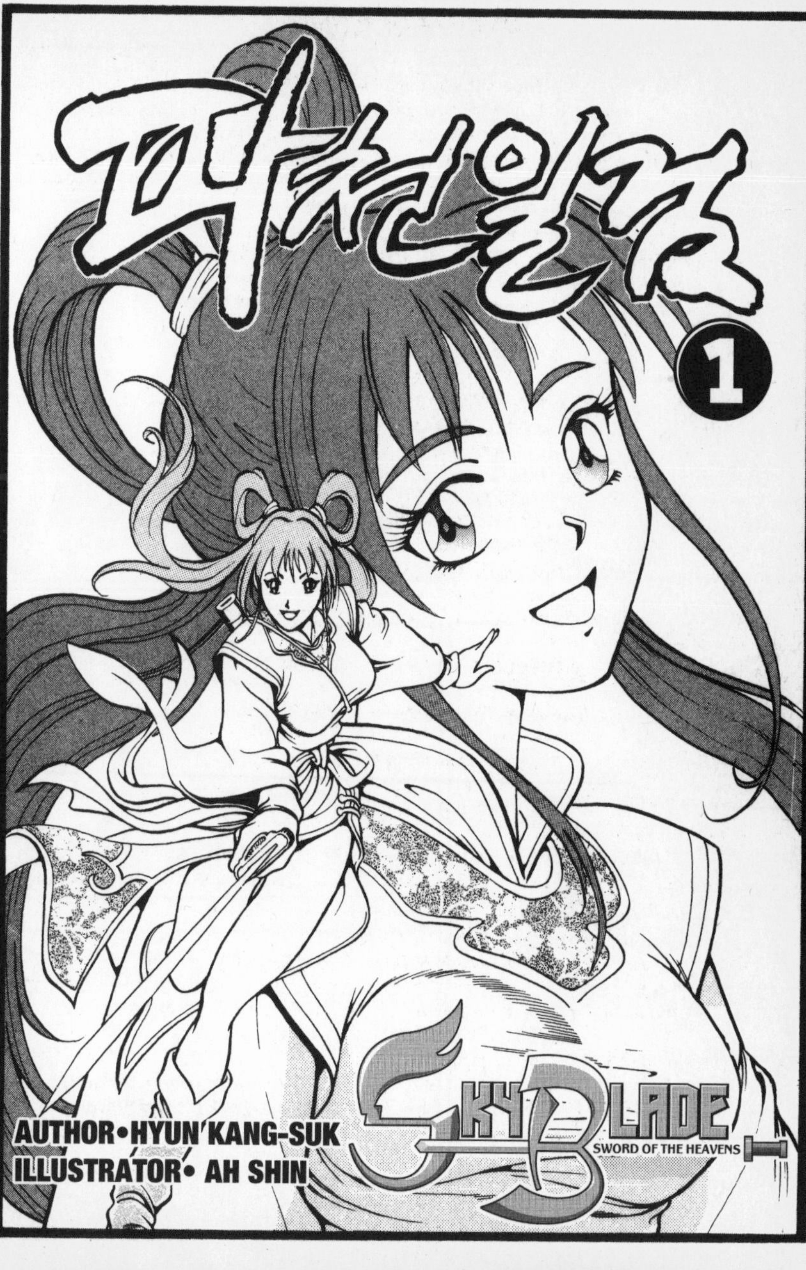
파천일검
1
SKY BLADE
SWORD OF THE HEAVENS
AUTHOR•HYUN KANG-SUK
ILLUSTRATOR• AH SHIN

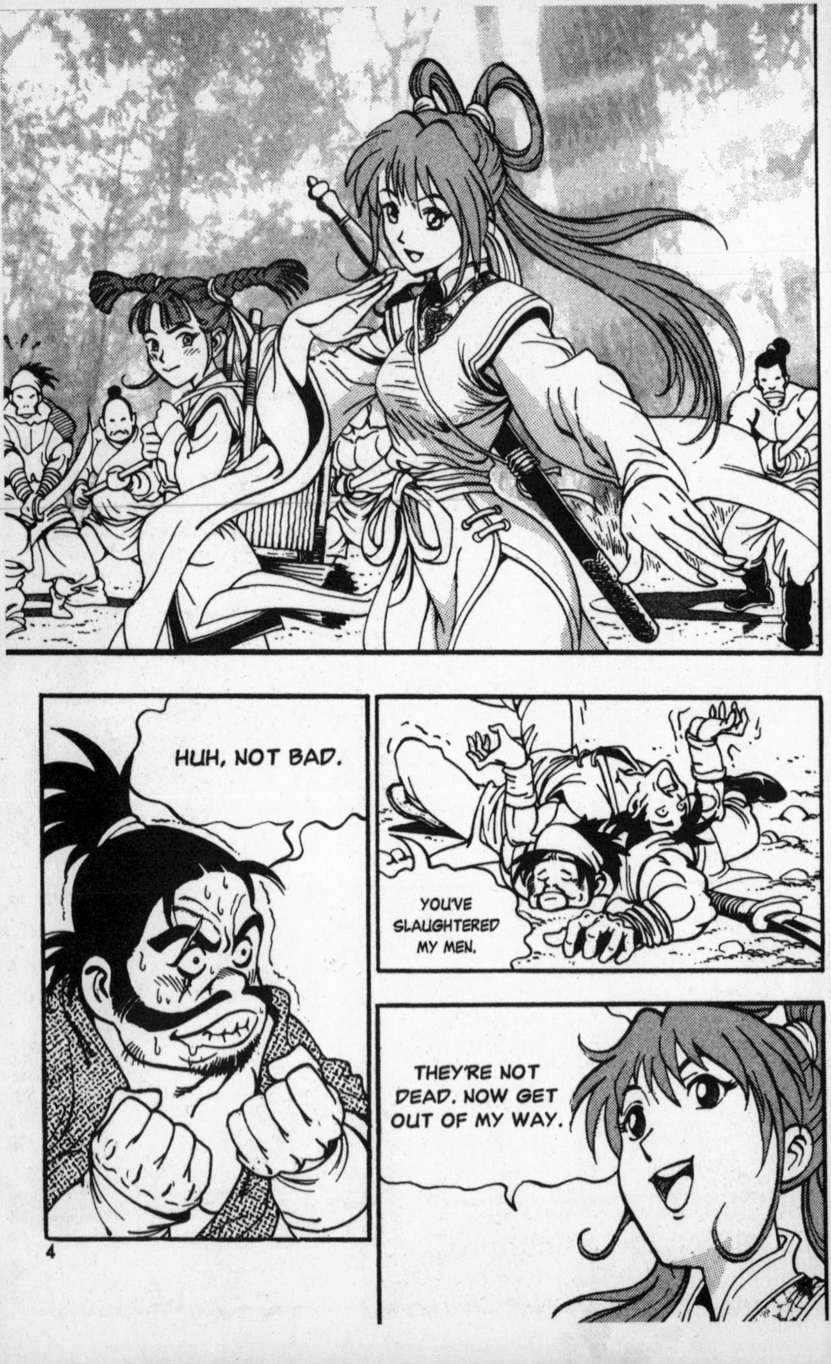
HUH, NOT BAD.
YOU'VE SLAUGHTERED MY MEN.
THEY'RE NOT DEAD. NOW GET OUT OF MY WAY.

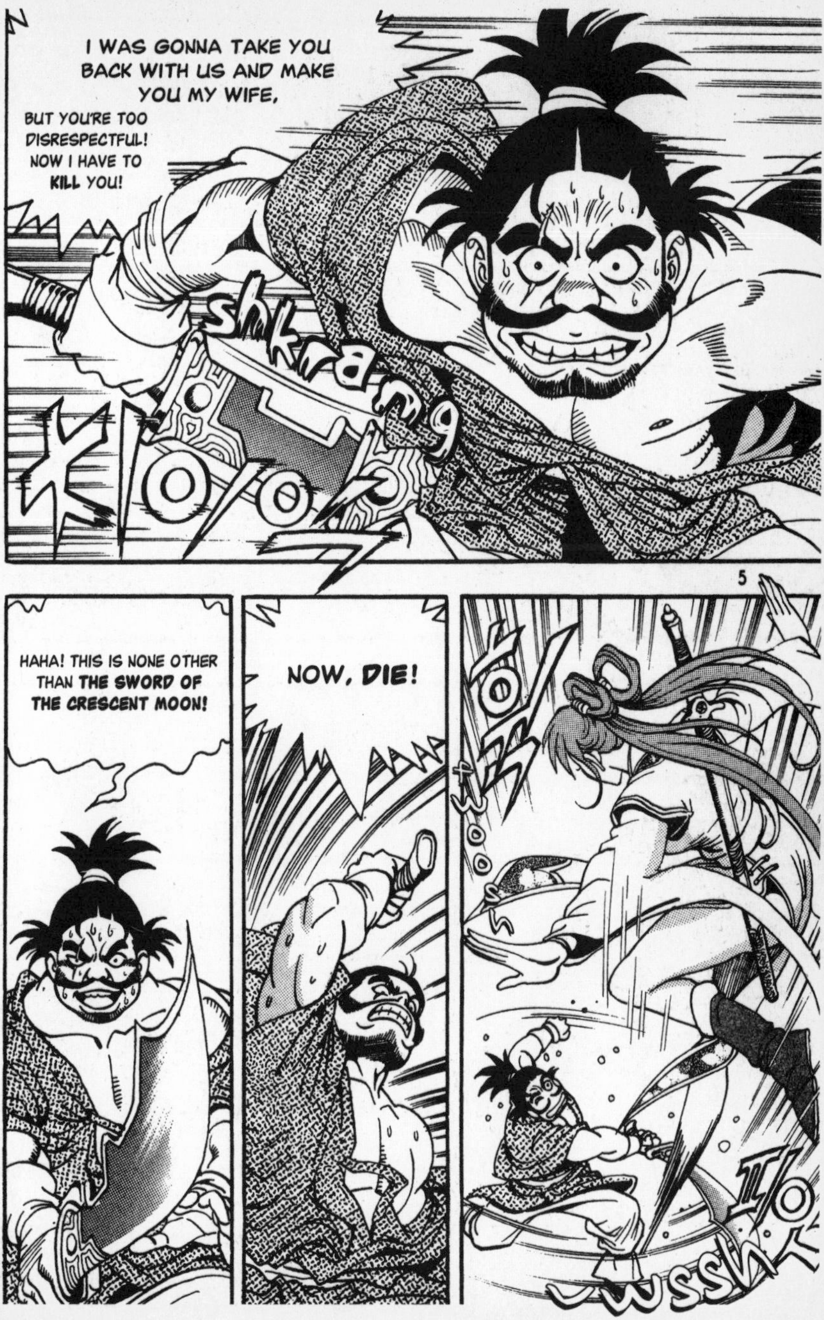
I WAS GONNA TAKE YOU BACK WITH US AND MAKE YOU MY WIFE,
BUT YOU'RE TOO DISRESPECTFUL! NOW I HAVE TO KILL YOU!
shkrang
HAHA! THIS IS NONE OTHER THAN THE SWORD OF THE CRESCENT MOON!
NOW, DIE!
WSSSH

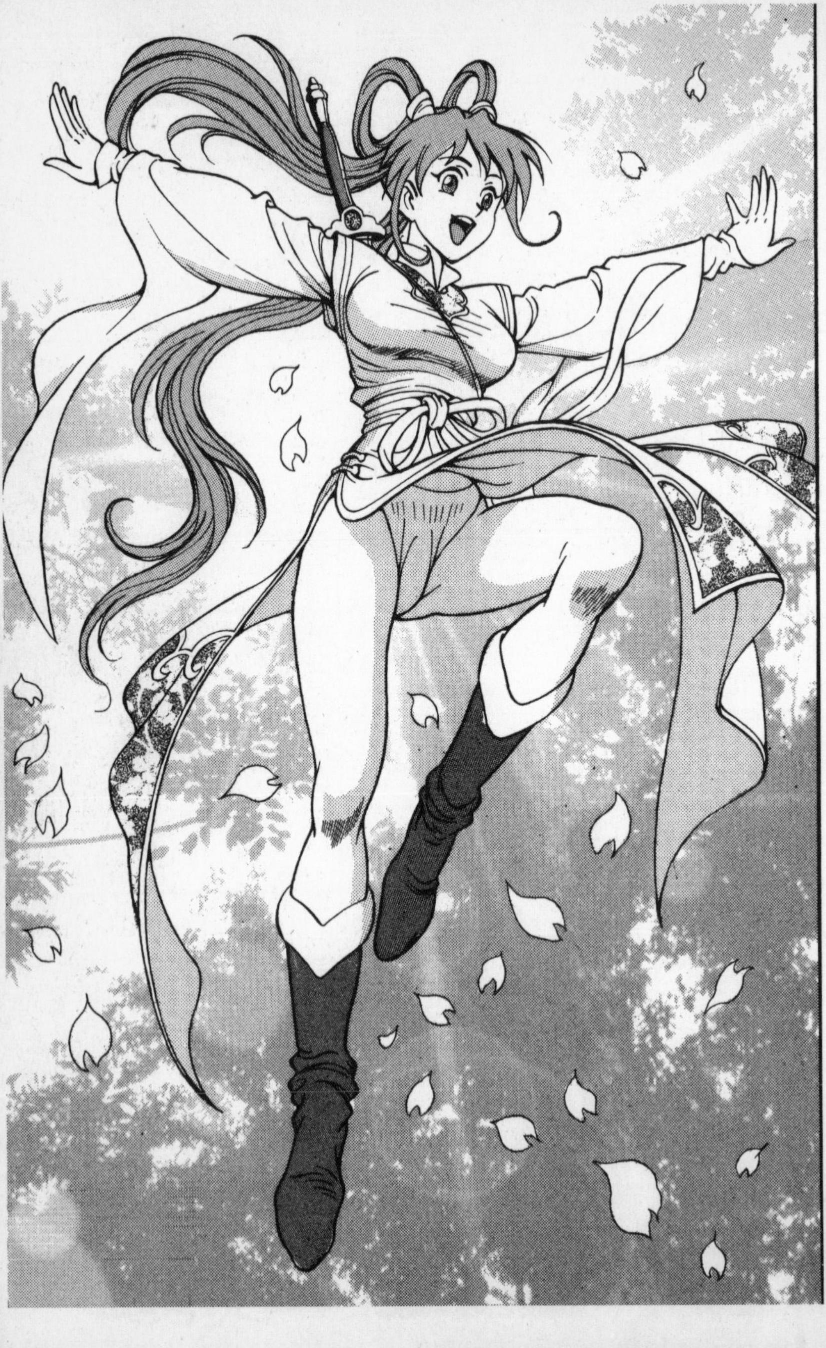

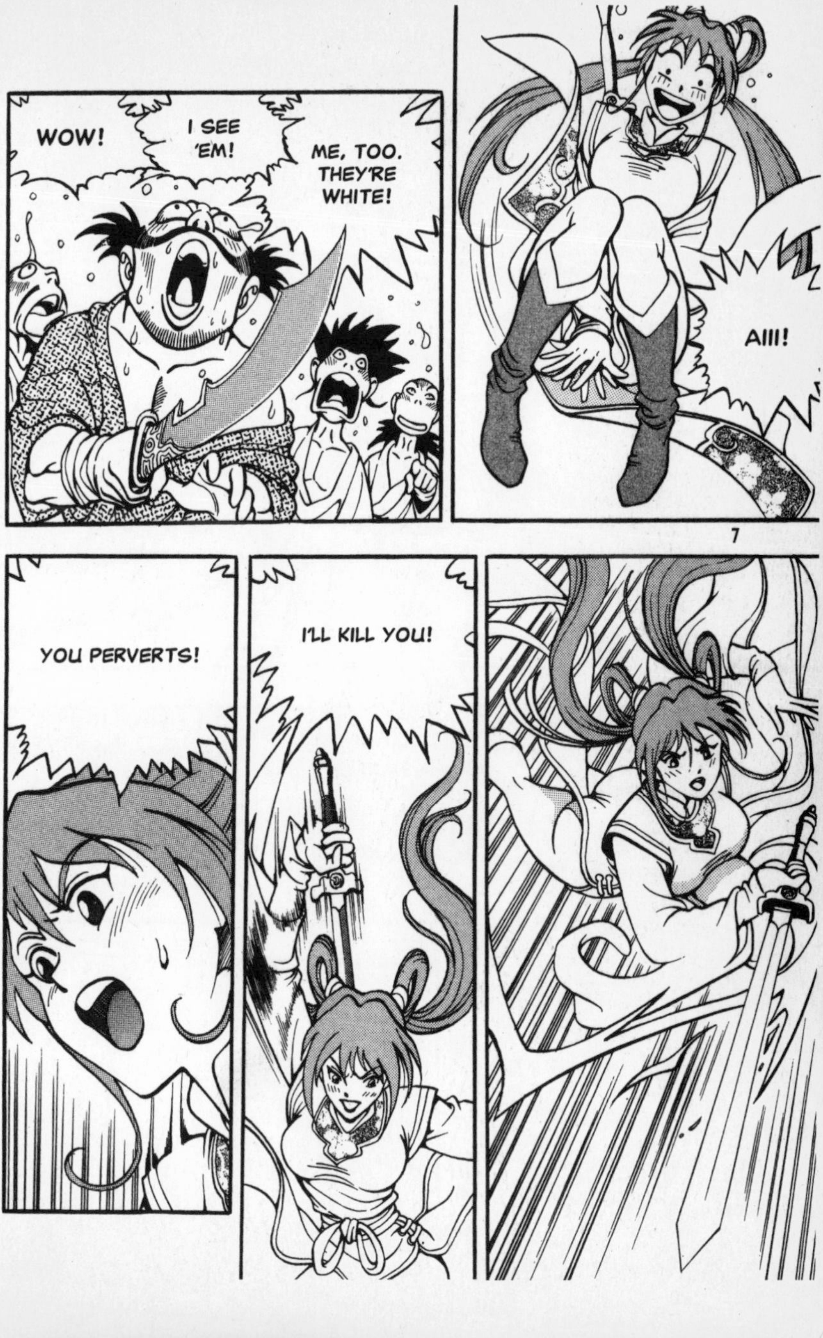
WOW!
I SEE 'EM!
ME, TOO. THEY'RE WHITE!
AIII!
YOU PERVERTS!
I'LL KILL YOU!

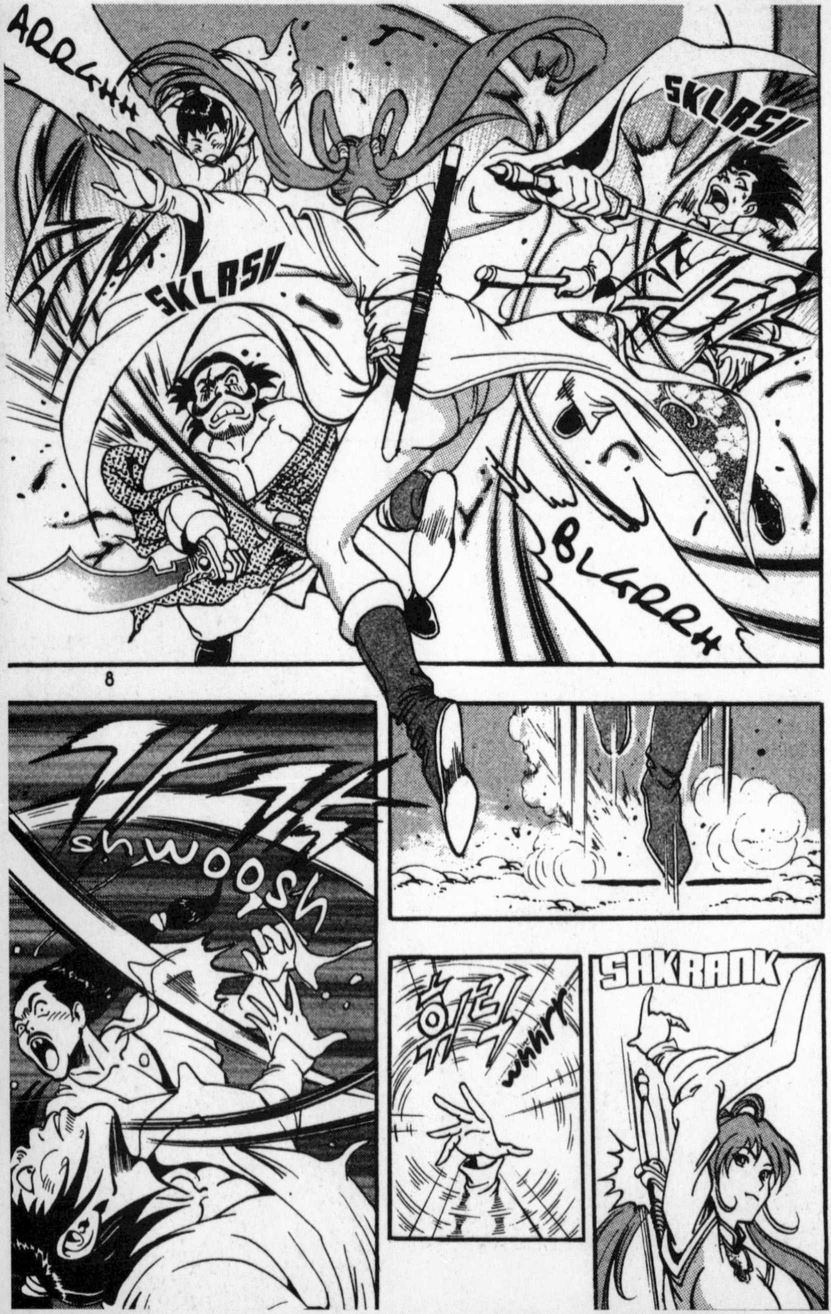
ARRGHHH
SKLASH
SKLASH
BLGRRH
shWOOSH
휘리릭
whhrr
SHKRANK

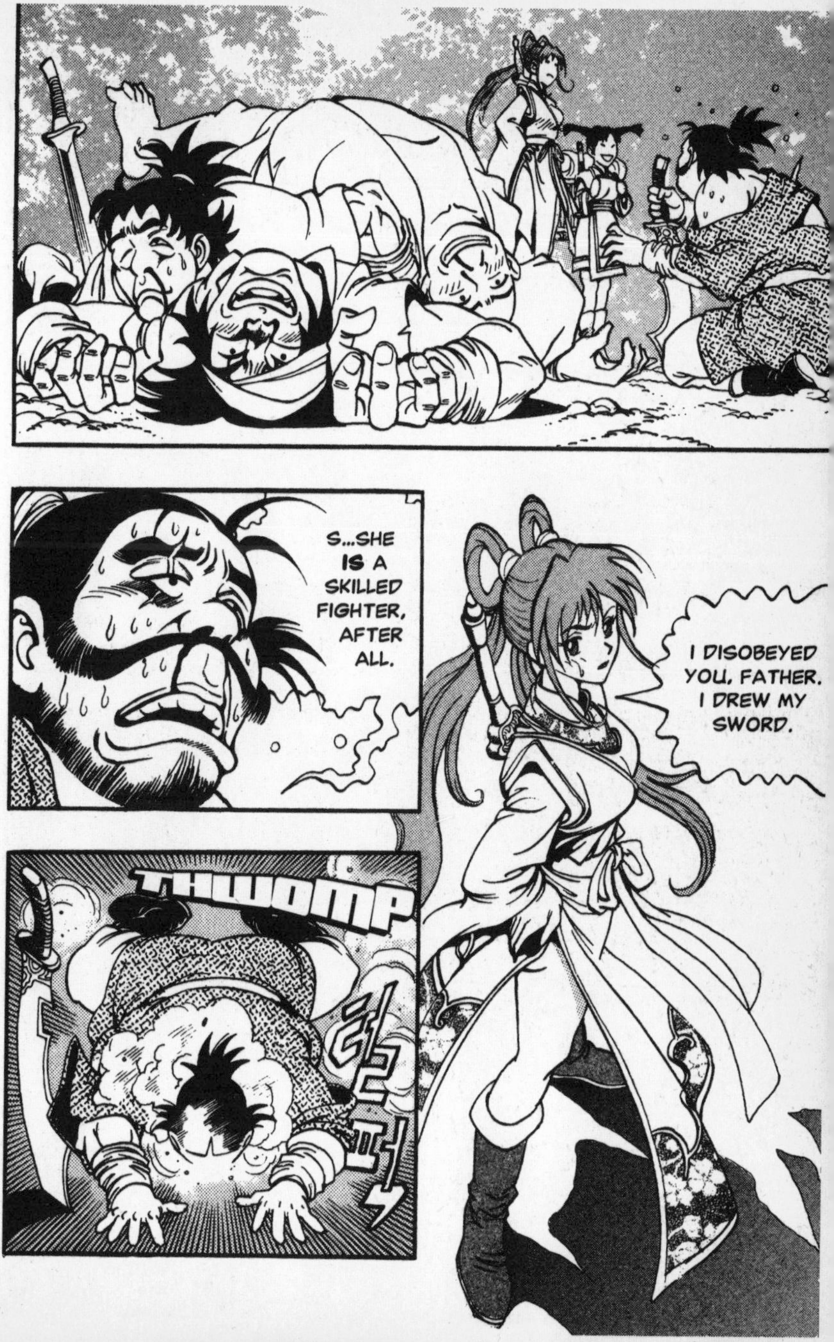
S...SHE IS A SKILLED FIGHTER, AFTER ALL.
I DISOBEYED YOU, FATHER. I DREW MY SWORD.
THWOMP

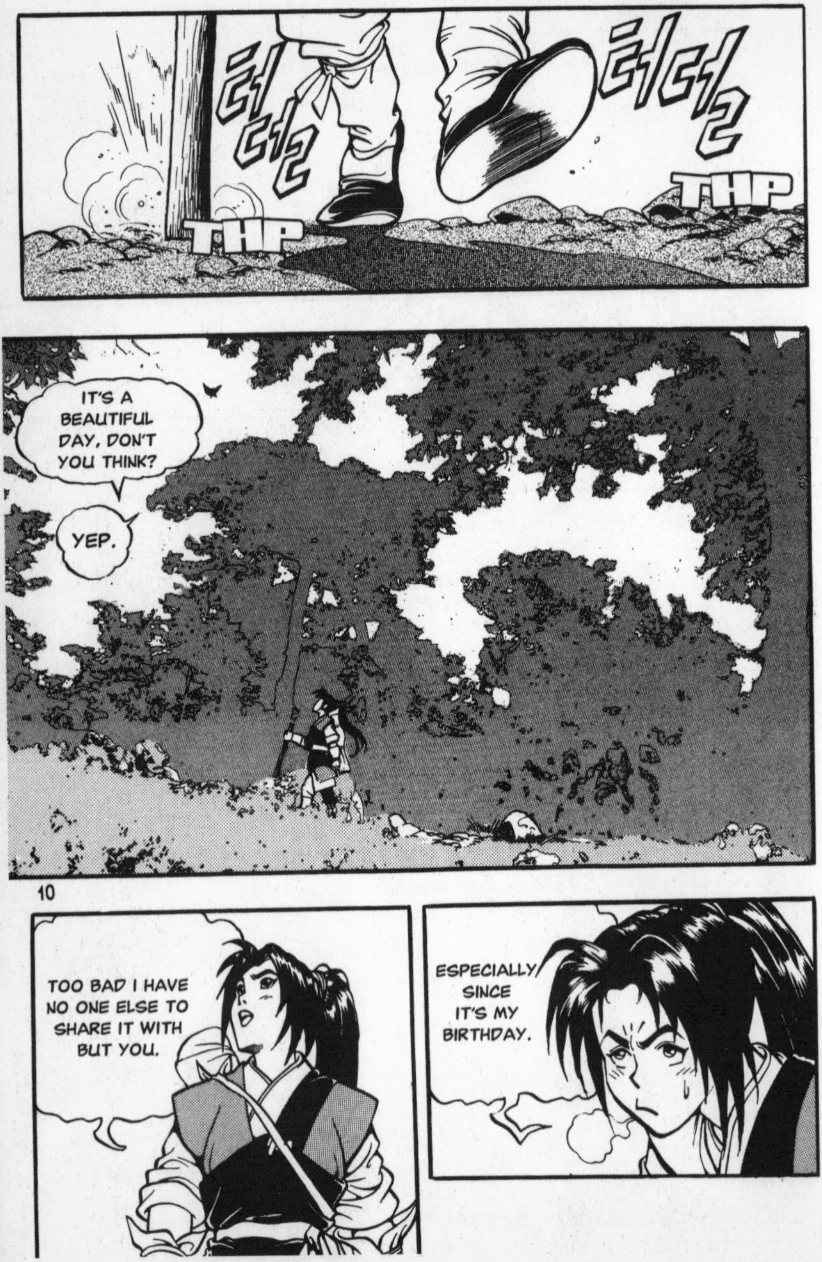
THP
THP
IT'S A BEAUTIFUL DAY, DON'T YOU THINK?
YEP.
TOO BAD I HAVE NO ONE ELSE TO SHARE IT WITH BUT YOU.
ESPECIALLY SINCE IT'S MY BIRTHDAY.

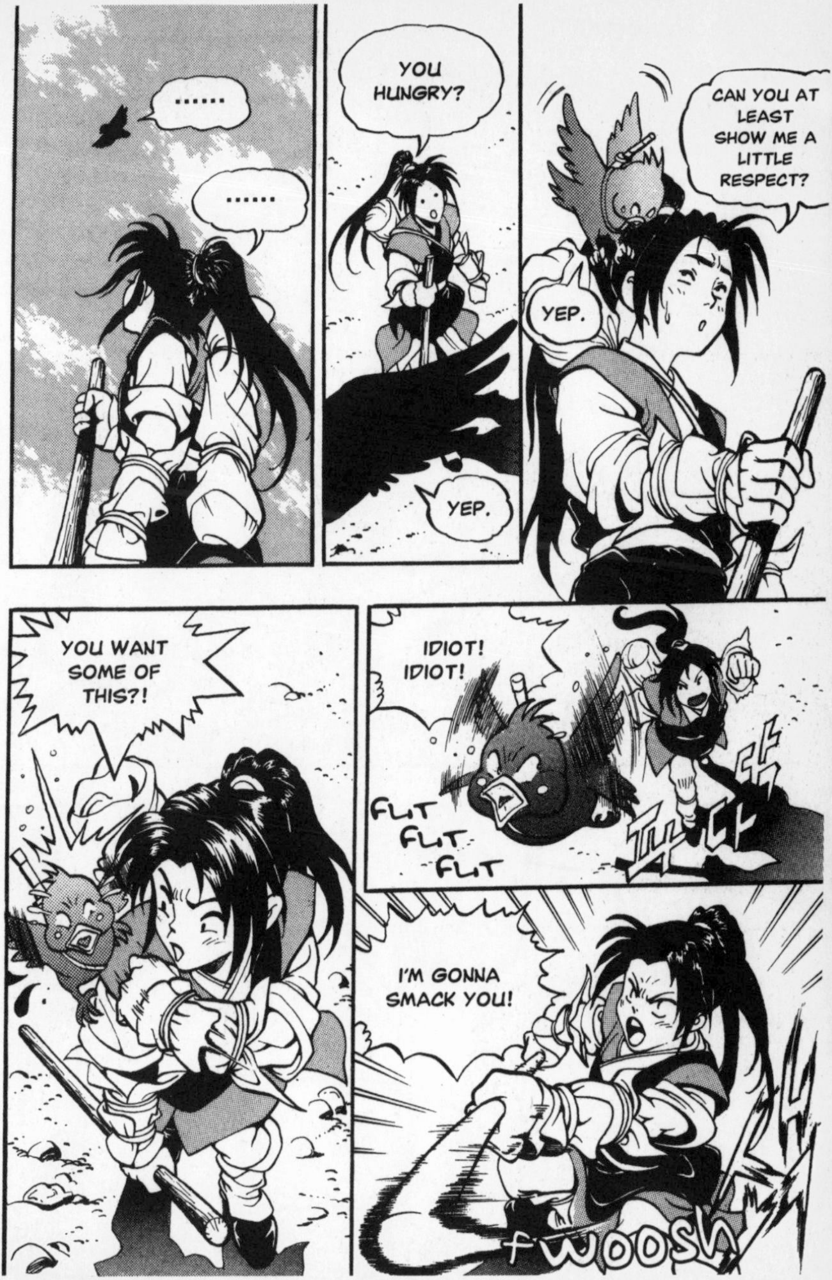
......
......
YOU HUNGRY?
YEP.
CAN YOU AT LEAST SHOW ME A LITTLE RESPECT?
YEP.
YOU WANT SOME OF THIS?!
IDIOT! IDIOT!
FLIT FLIT FLIT
I'M GONNA SMACK YOU!
FWOOSH

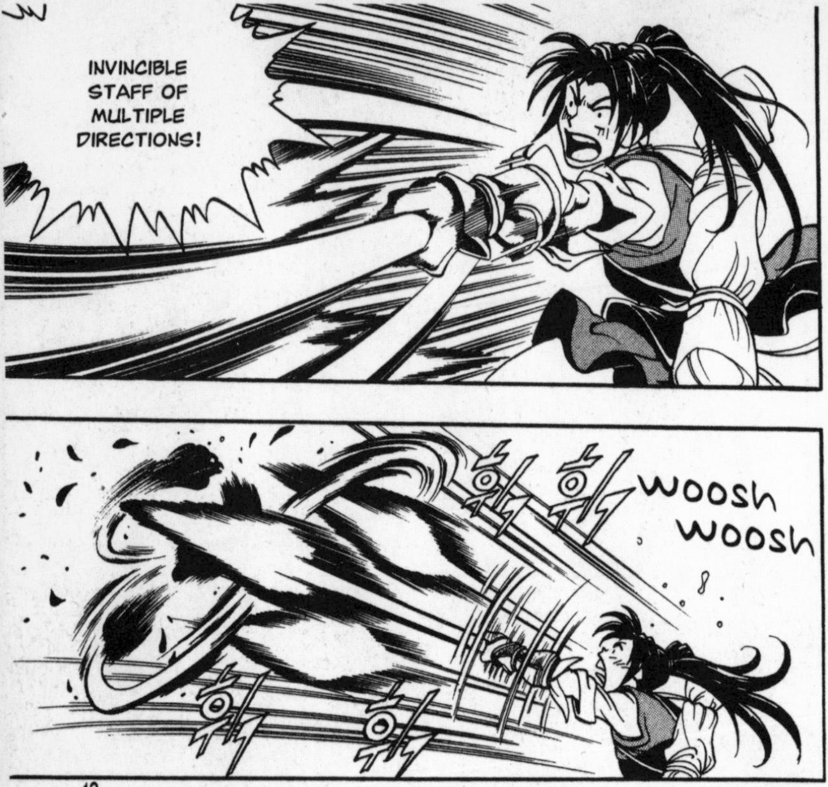
INVINCIBLE STAFF OF MULTIPLE DIRECTIONS!
woosh woosh

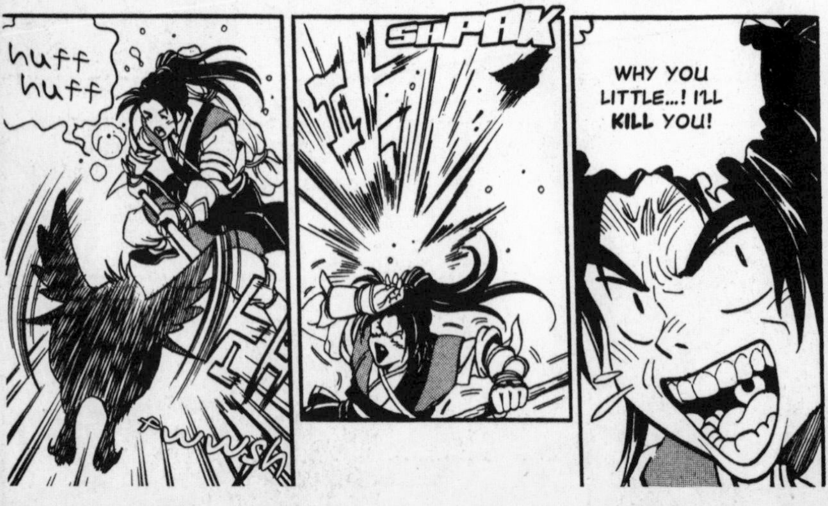
huff huff
fwwsh
SHPAK
WHY YOU LITTLE...! I'LL KILL YOU!

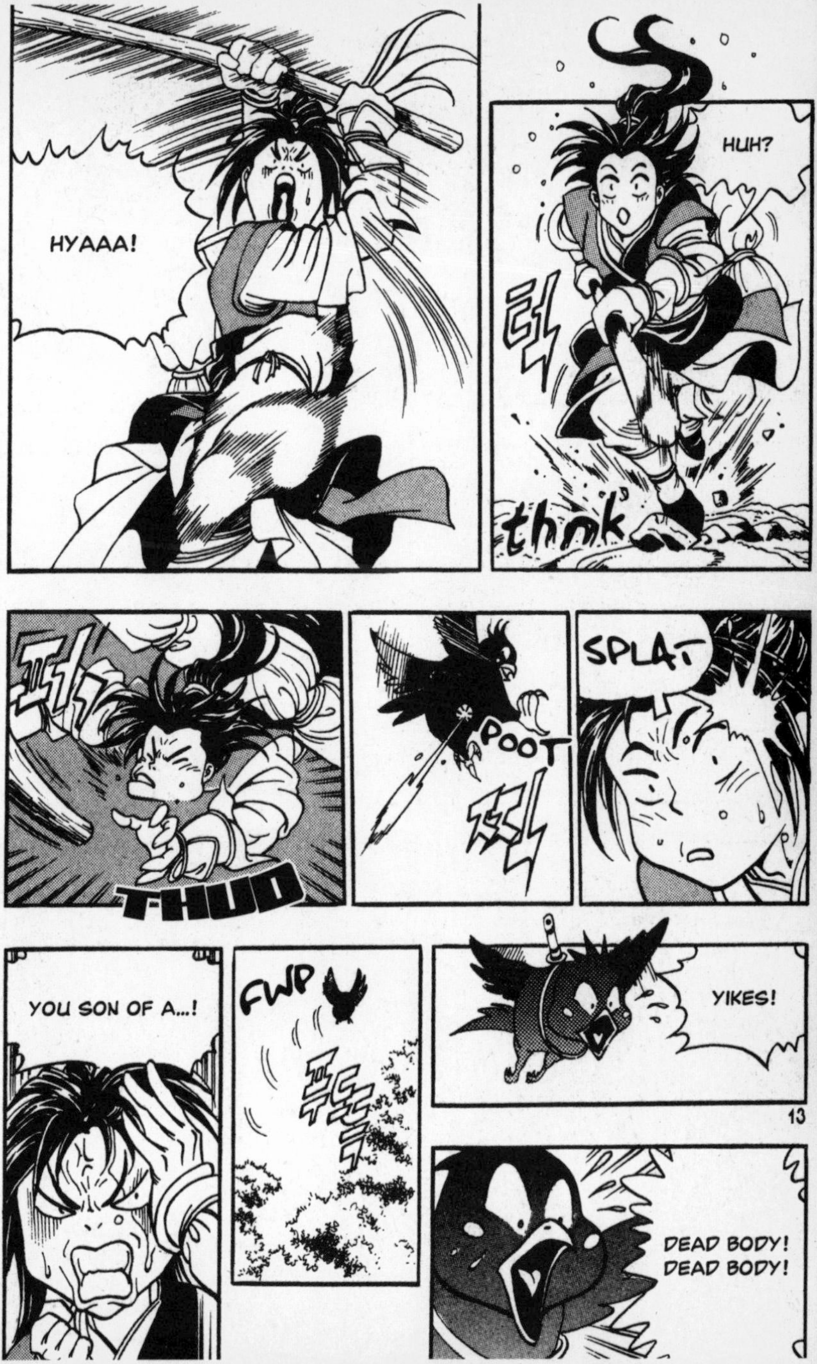
HYAAA!
HUH?
thnk
THUD
POOT
SPLAT
YOU SON OF A...!
FWP
YIKES!
DEAD BODY!
DEAD BODY!

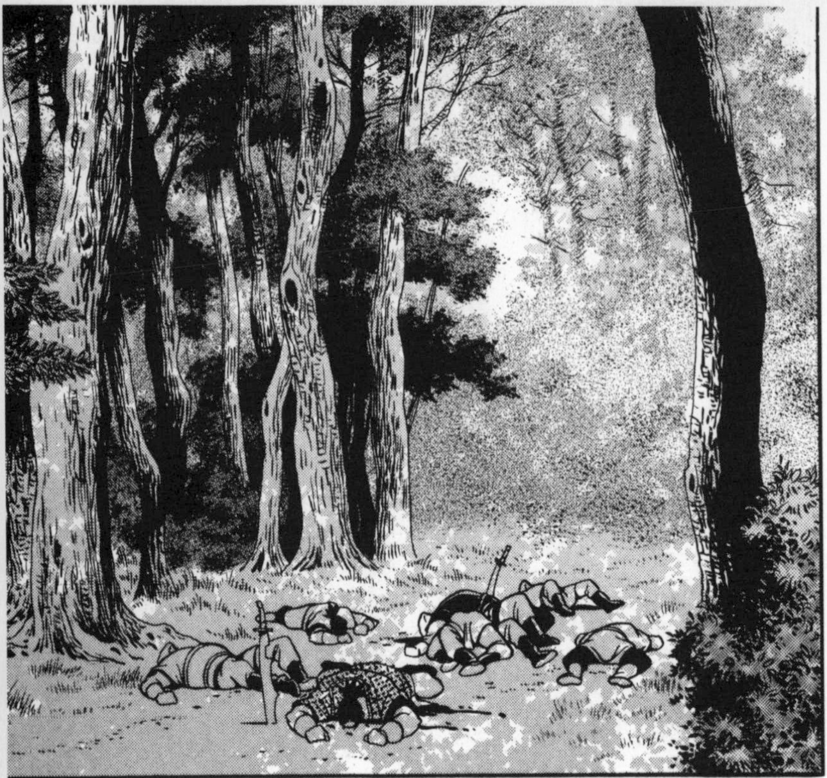

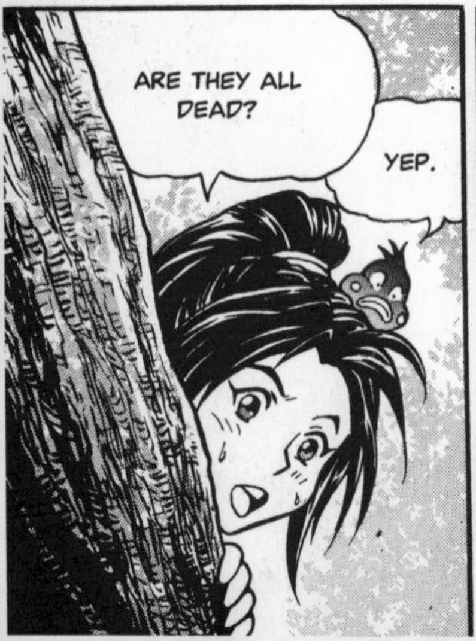
ARE THEY ALL DEAD?
YEP.

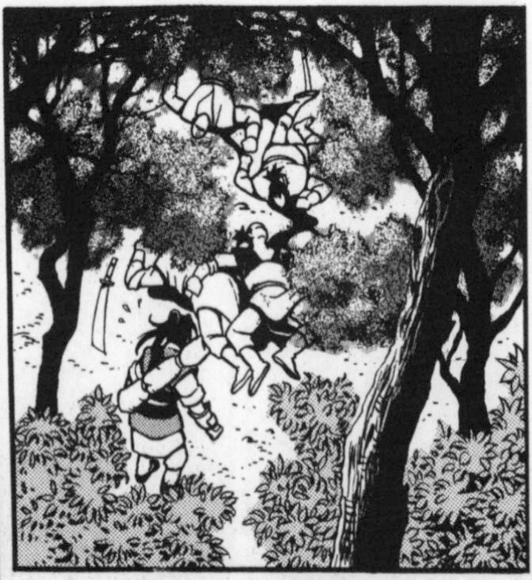

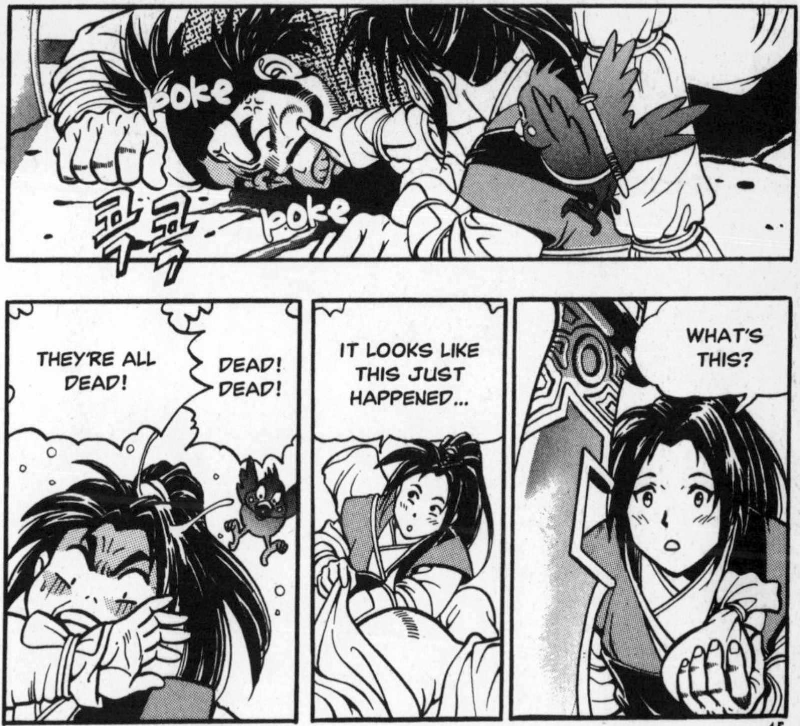
poke
콕콕
poke
THEY'RE ALL DEAD!
DEAD! DEAD!
IT LOOKS LIKE THIS JUST HAPPENED...
WHAT'S THIS?

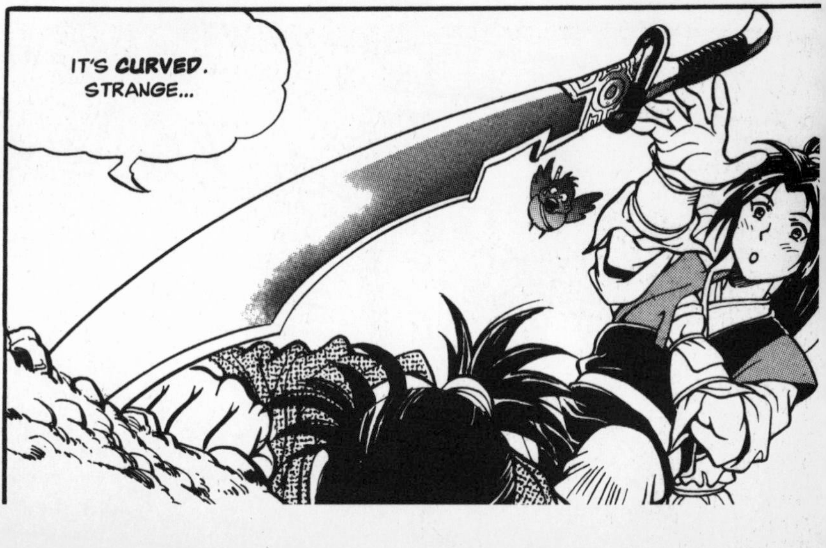
IT'S **CURVED**. STRANGE...

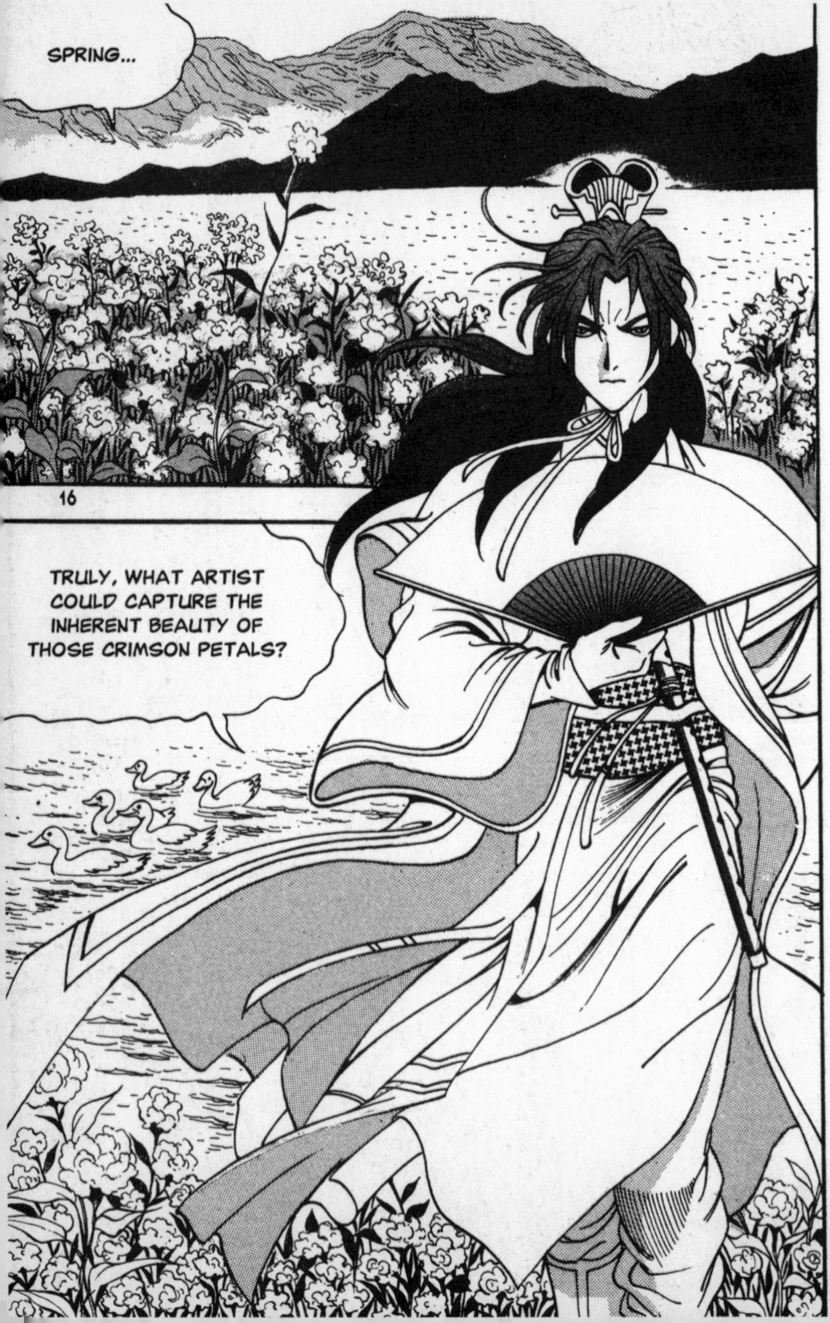
SPRING...
TRULY, WHAT ARTIST COULD CAPTURE THE INHERENT BEAUTY OF THOSE CRIMSON PETALS?

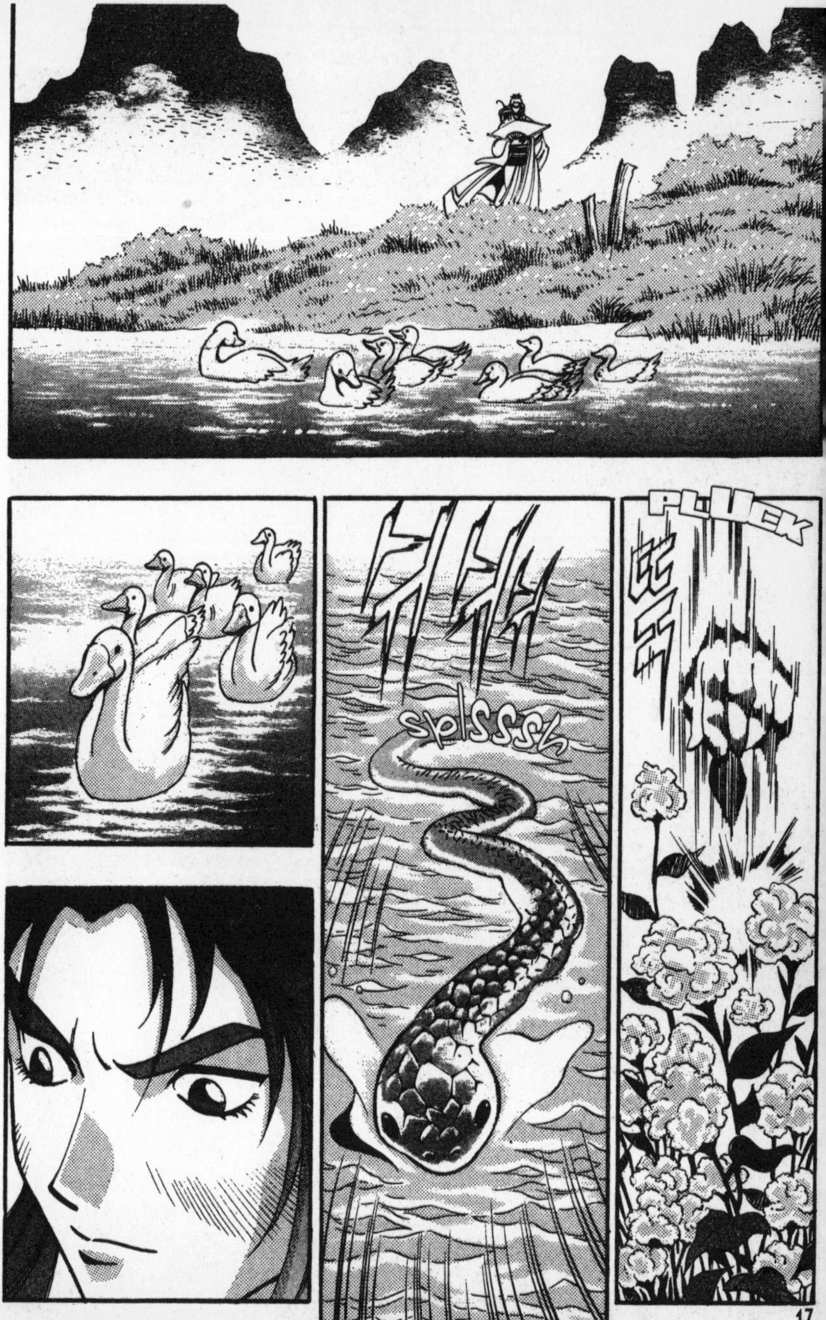
splsssh
PLUCK

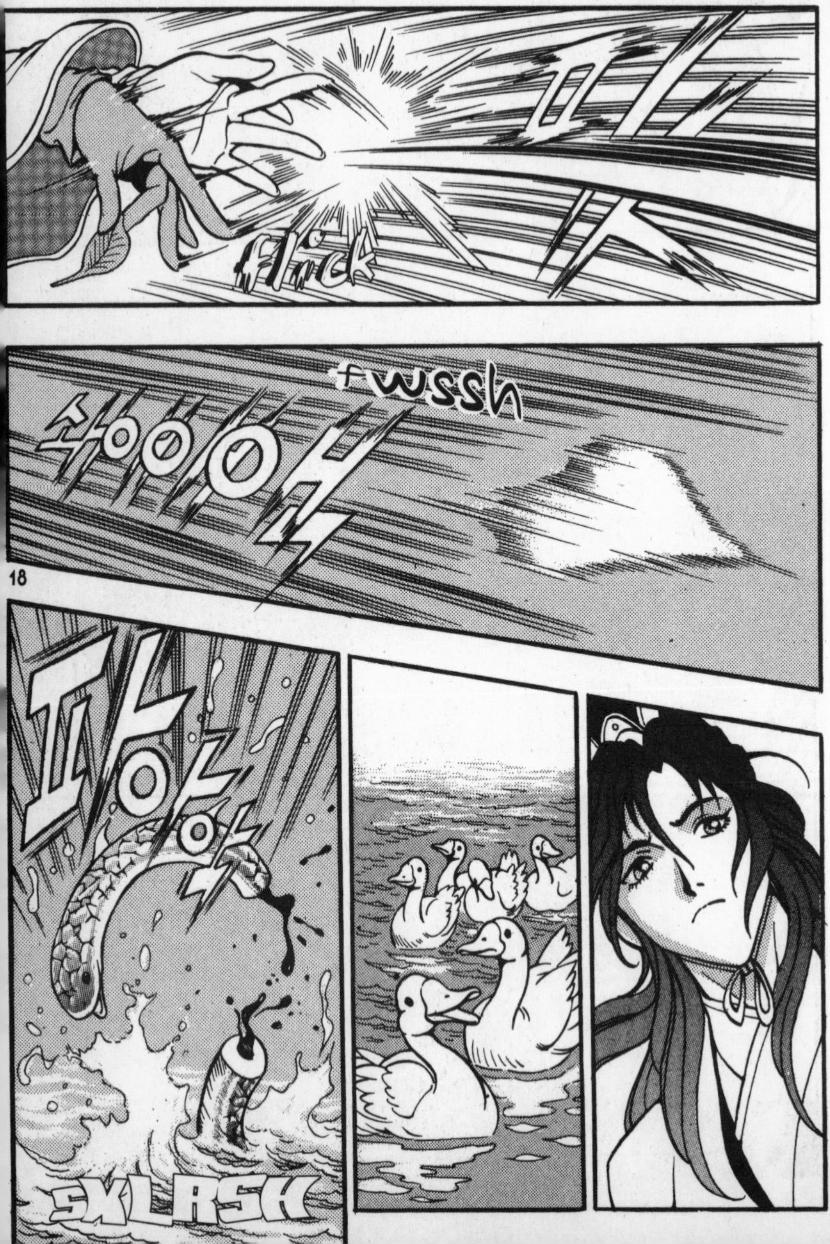
flick
fwssh

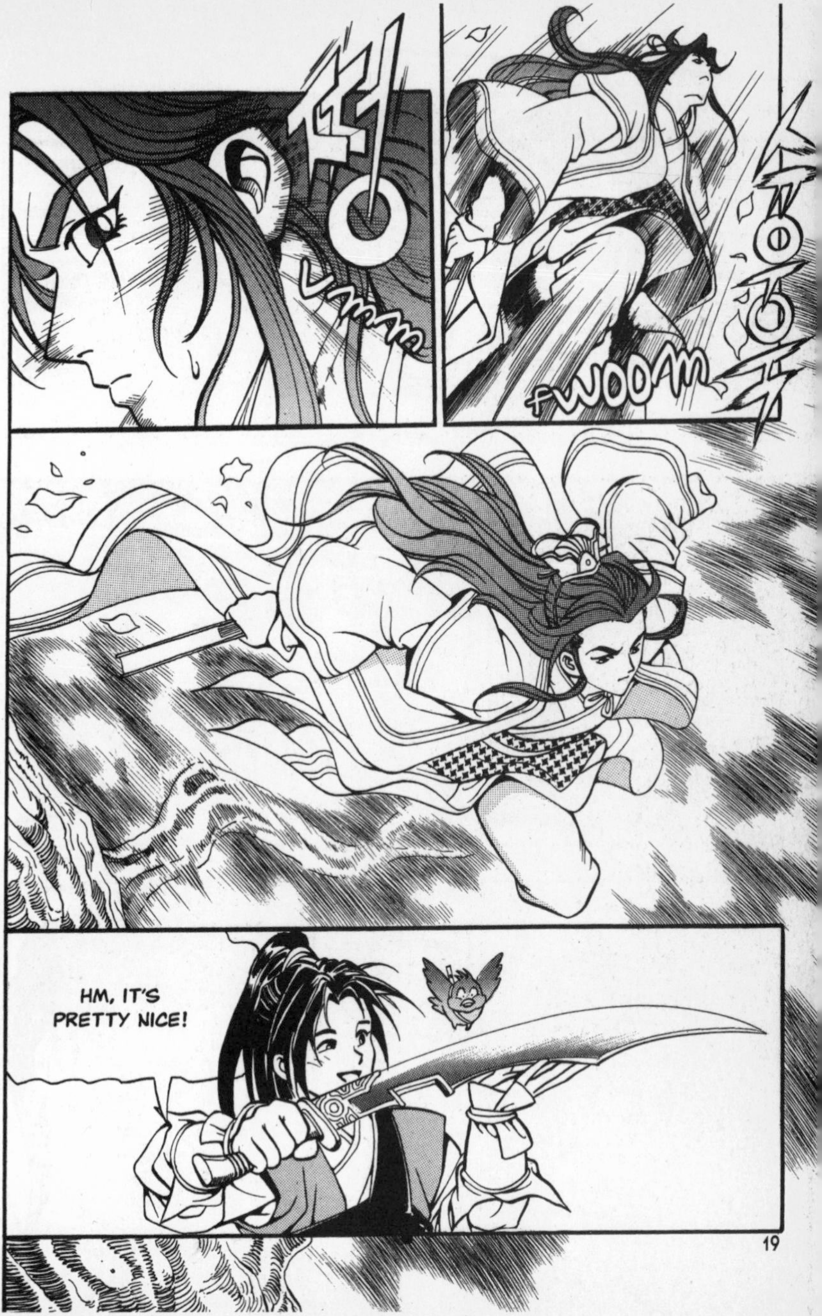
VMMM
FWOOM
HM, IT'S PRETTY NICE!

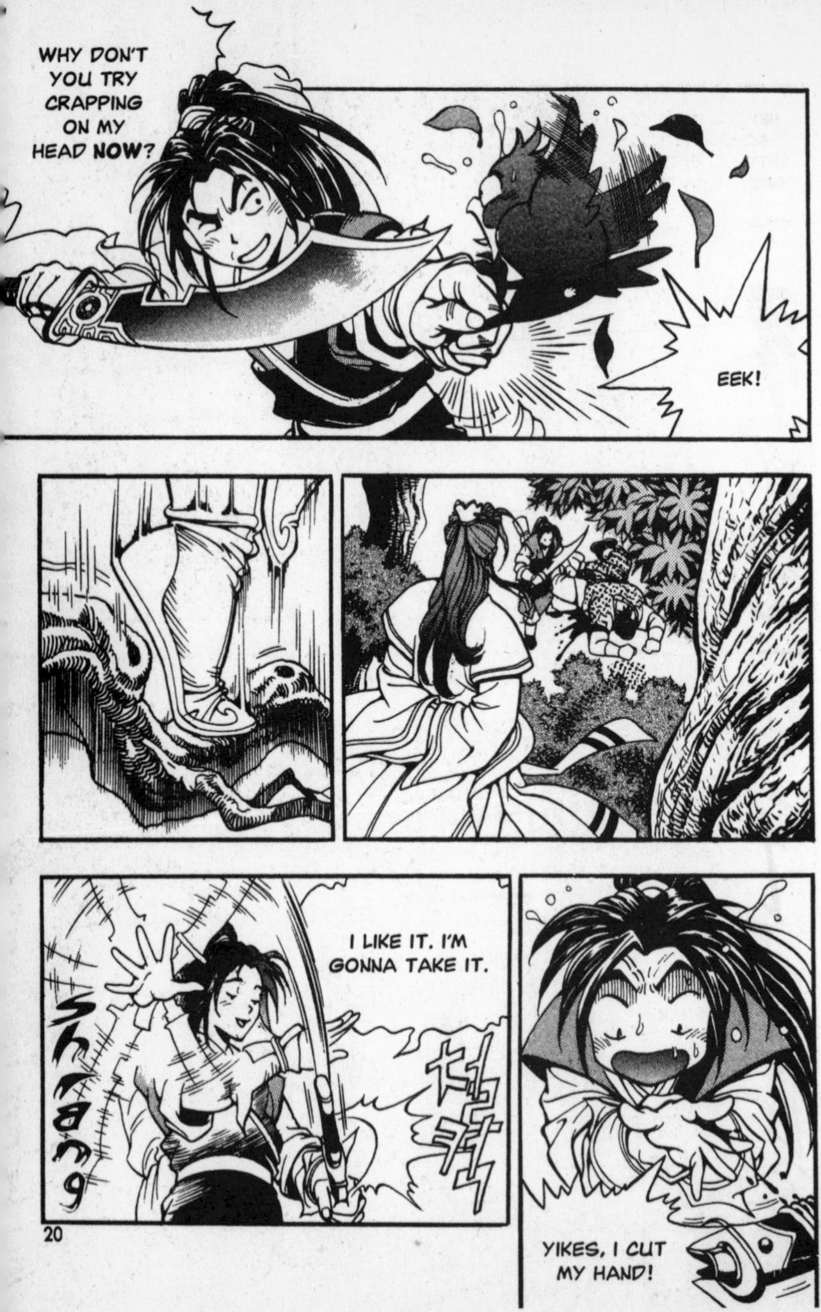
WHY DON'T YOU TRY CRAPPING ON MY HEAD NOW?
EEK!
I LIKE IT. I'M GONNA TAKE IT.
YIKES, I CUT MY HAND!

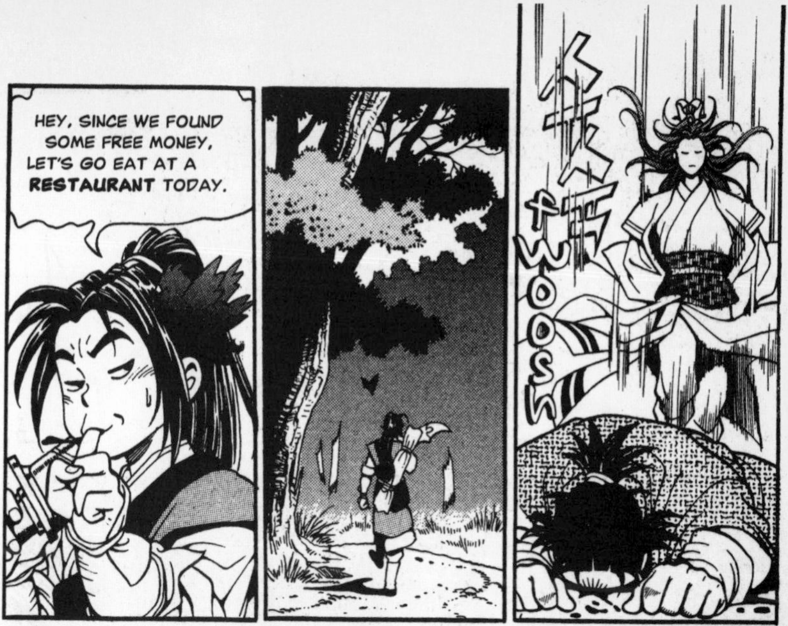
WOOSH
HEY, SINCE WE FOUND SOME FREE MONEY, LET'S GO EAT AT A **RESTAURANT** TODAY.

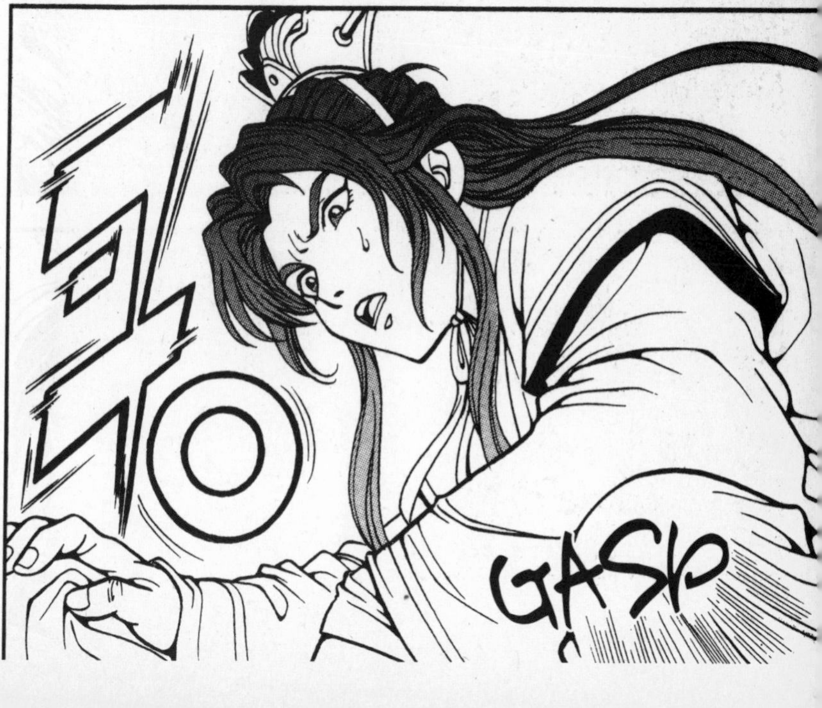
GASP

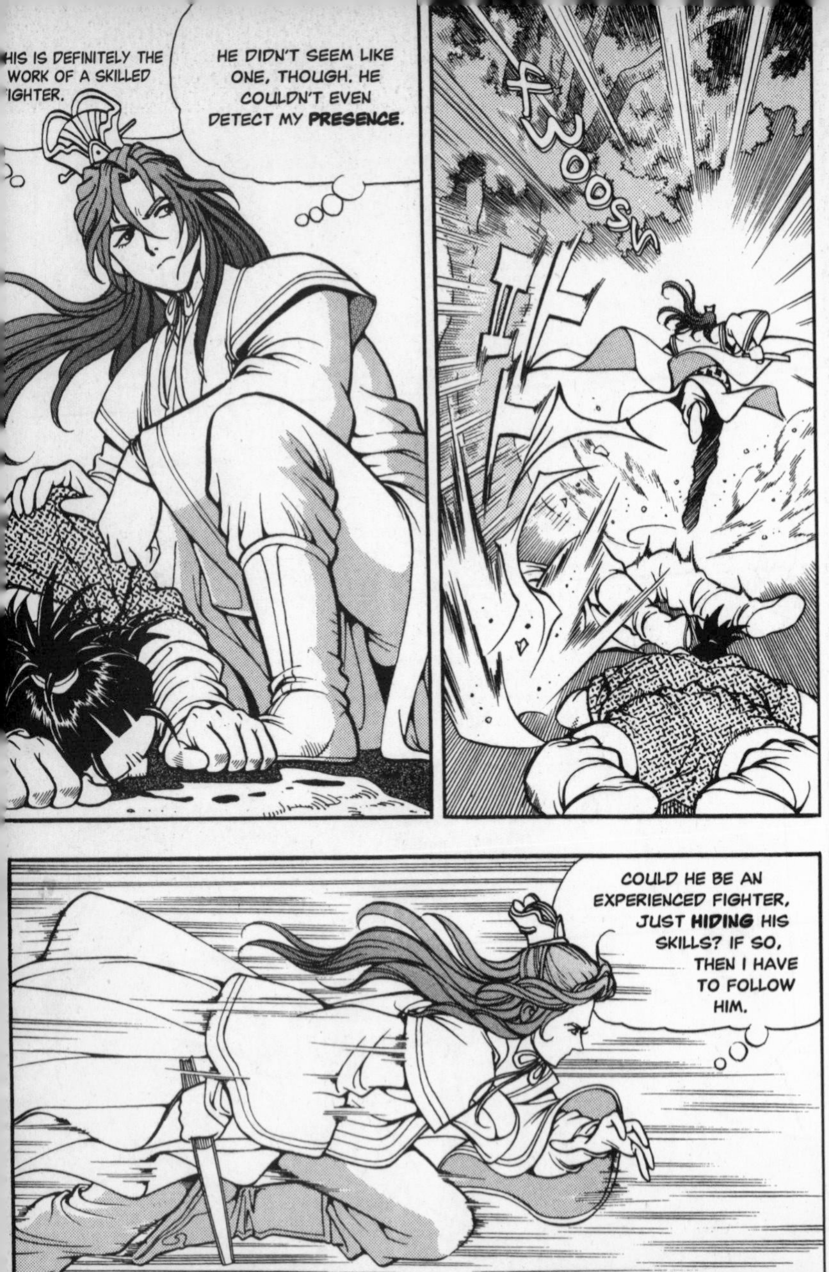
HIS IS DEFINITELY THE WORK OF A SKILLED FIGHTER.
HE DIDN'T SEEM LIKE ONE, THOUGH. HE COULDN'T EVEN DETECT MY **PRESENCE**.
FWOOSH
COULD HE BE AN EXPERIENCED FIGHTER, JUST **HIDING** HIS SKILLS? IF SO, THEN I HAVE TO FOLLOW HIM.

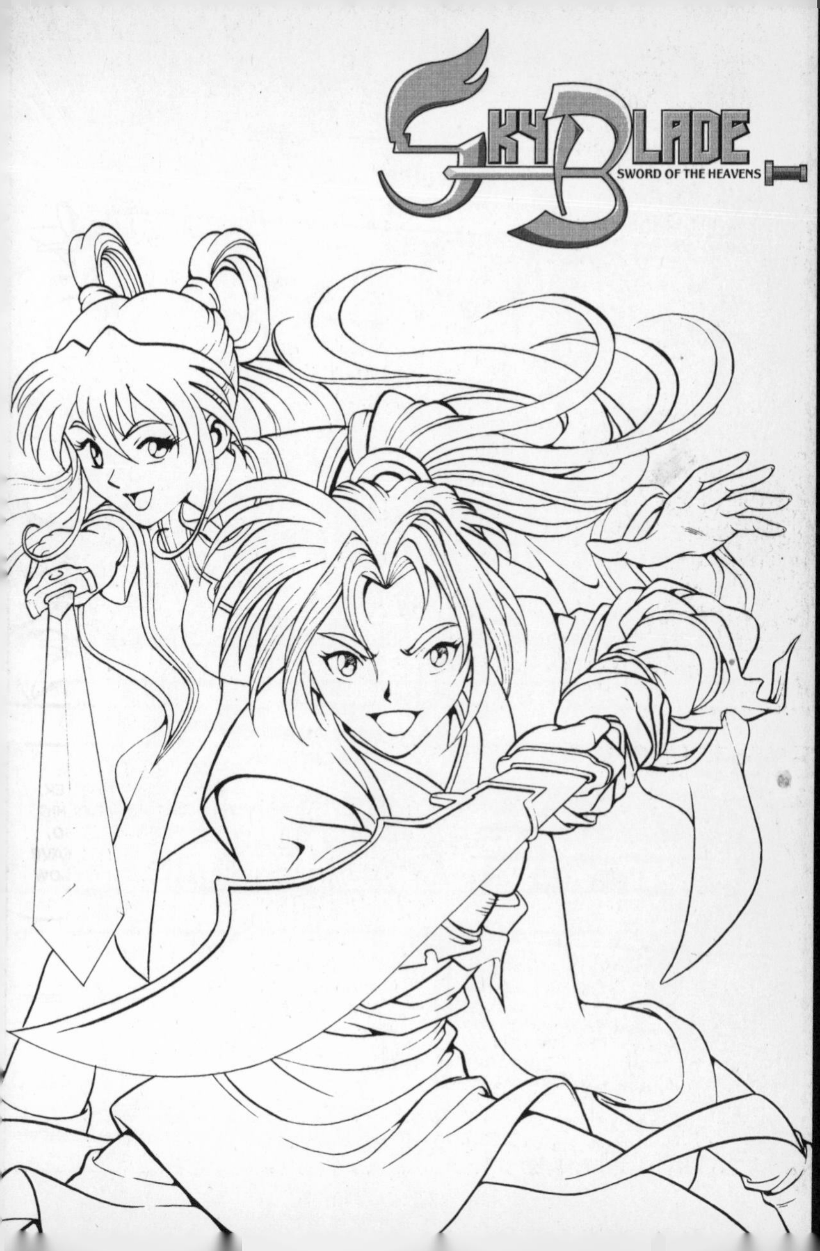
SKY BLADE
SWORD OF THE HEAVENS

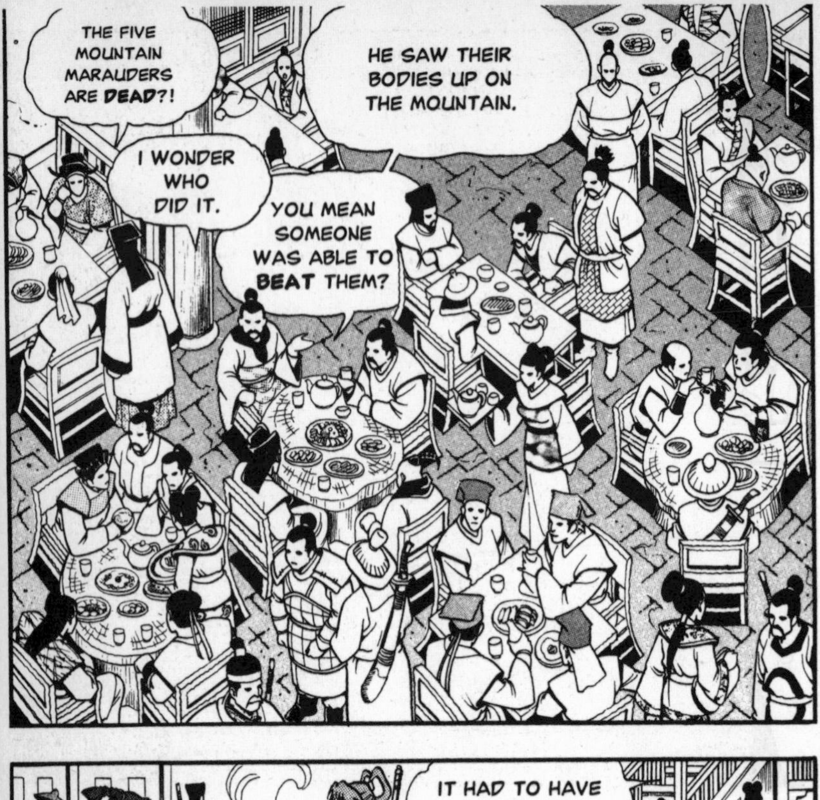

THE FIVE MOUNTAIN MARAUDERS ARE DEAD?!
HE SAW THEIR BODIES UP ON THE MOUNTAIN.
I WONDER WHO DID IT.
YOU MEAN SOMEONE WAS ABLE TO BEAT THEM?

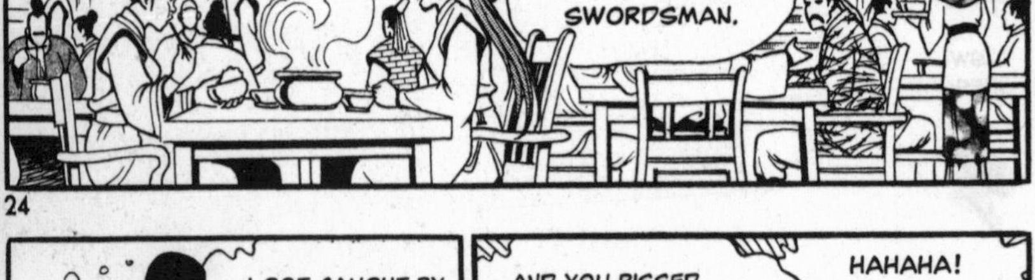

IT HAD TO HAVE BEEN AN EXPERT SWORDSMAN.

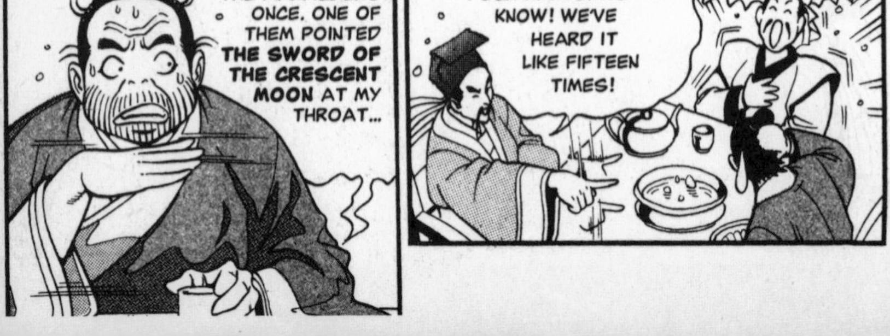

I GOT CAUGHT BY THE MARAUDERS ONCE. ONE OF THEM POINTED THE SWORD OF THE CRESCENT MOON AT MY THROAT...
AND YOU PISSED YOUR PANTS. WE KNOW! WE'VE HEARD IT LIKE FIFTEEN TIMES!
HAHAHA!

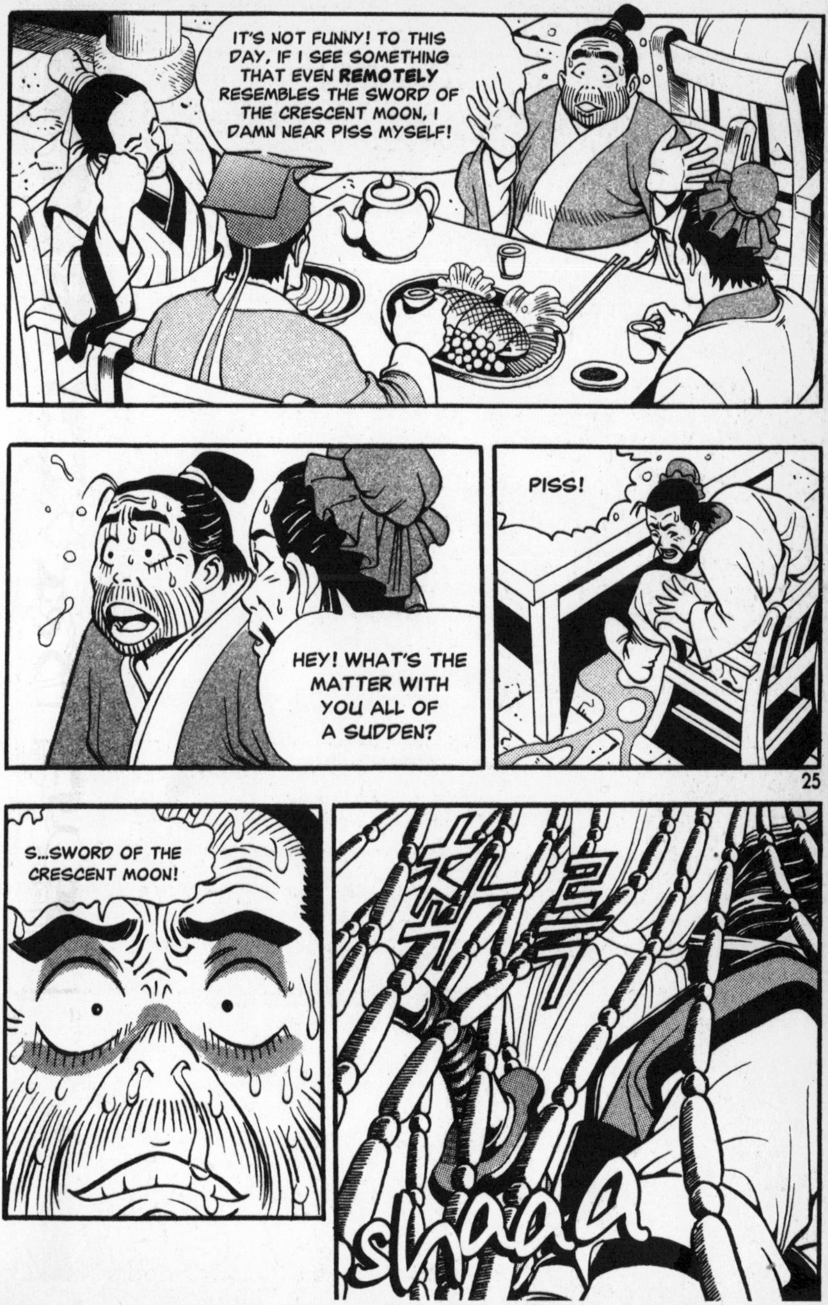
IT'S NOT FUNNY! TO THIS DAY, IF I SEE SOMETHING THAT EVEN **REMOTELY** RESEMBLES THE SWORD OF THE CRESCENT MOON, I DAMN NEAR PISS MYSELF!
HEY! WHAT'S THE MATTER WITH YOU ALL OF A SUDDEN?
PISS!
S...SWORD OF THE CRESCENT MOON!
shaaa

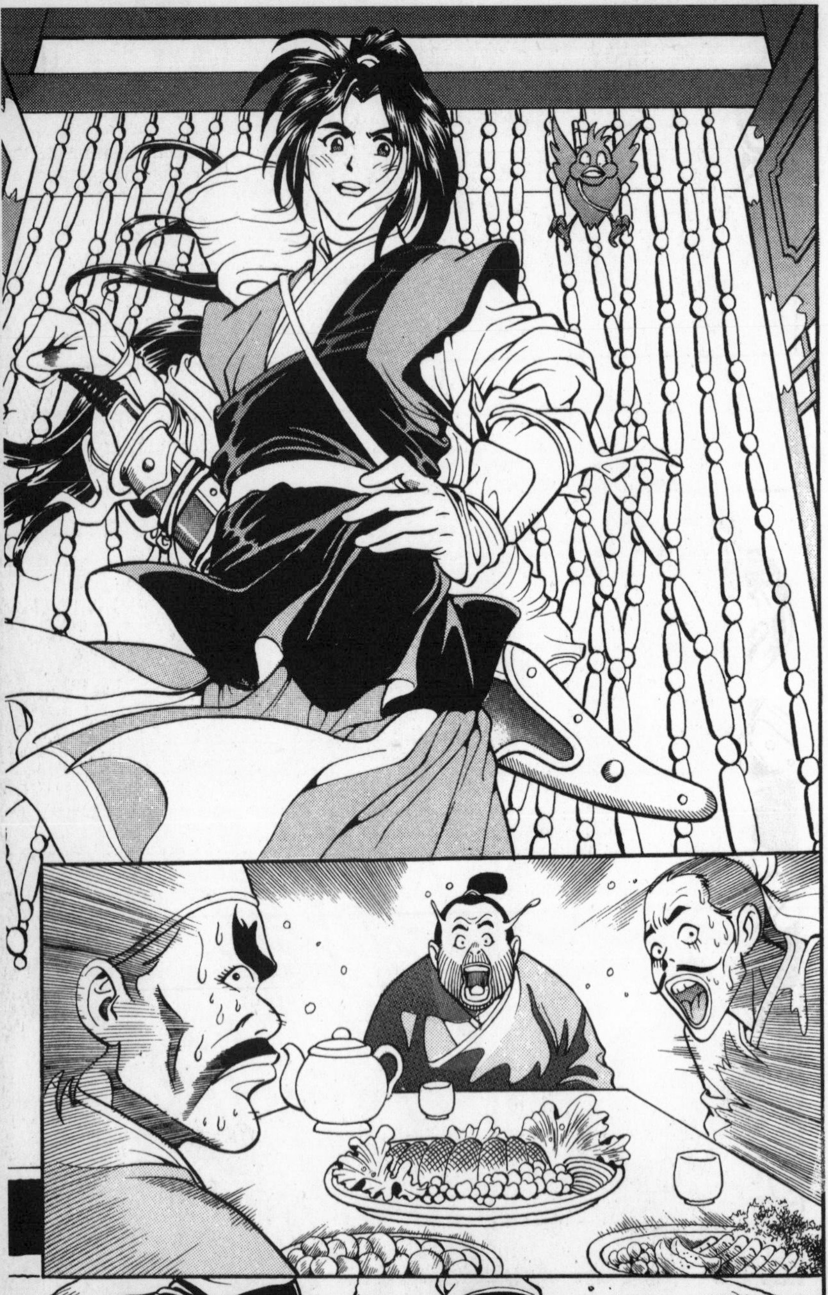

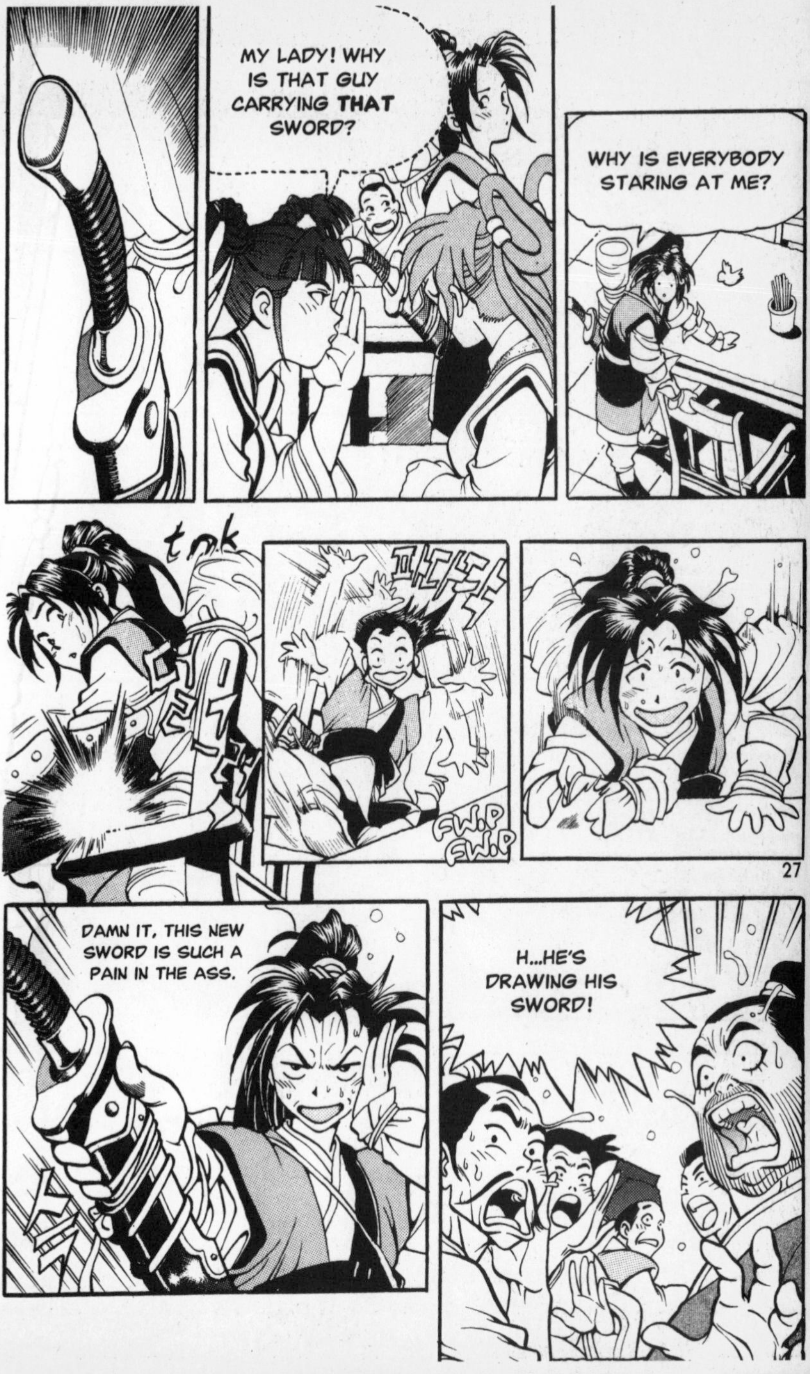

MY LADY! WHY IS THAT GUY CARRYING THAT SWORD?
WHY IS EVERYBODY STARING AT ME?
tnk
FWIP FWIP
DAMN IT, THIS NEW SWORD IS SUCH A PAIN IN THE ASS.
H...HE'S DRAWING HIS SWORD!

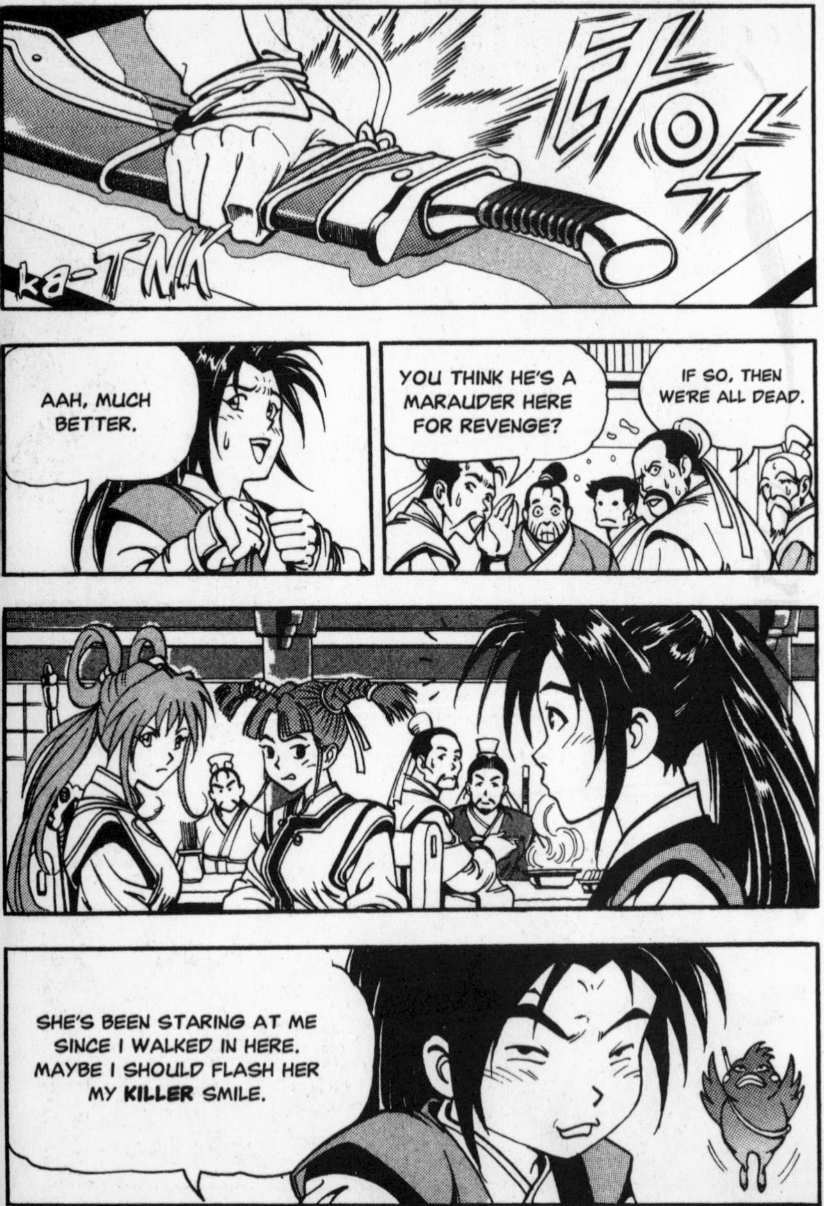
KA-TNK
AAH, MUCH BETTER.
YOU THINK HE'S A MARAUDER HERE FOR REVENGE?
IF SO, THEN WE'RE ALL DEAD.
SHE'S BEEN STARING AT ME SINCE I WALKED IN HERE. MAYBE I SHOULD FLASH HER MY **KILLER** SMILE.

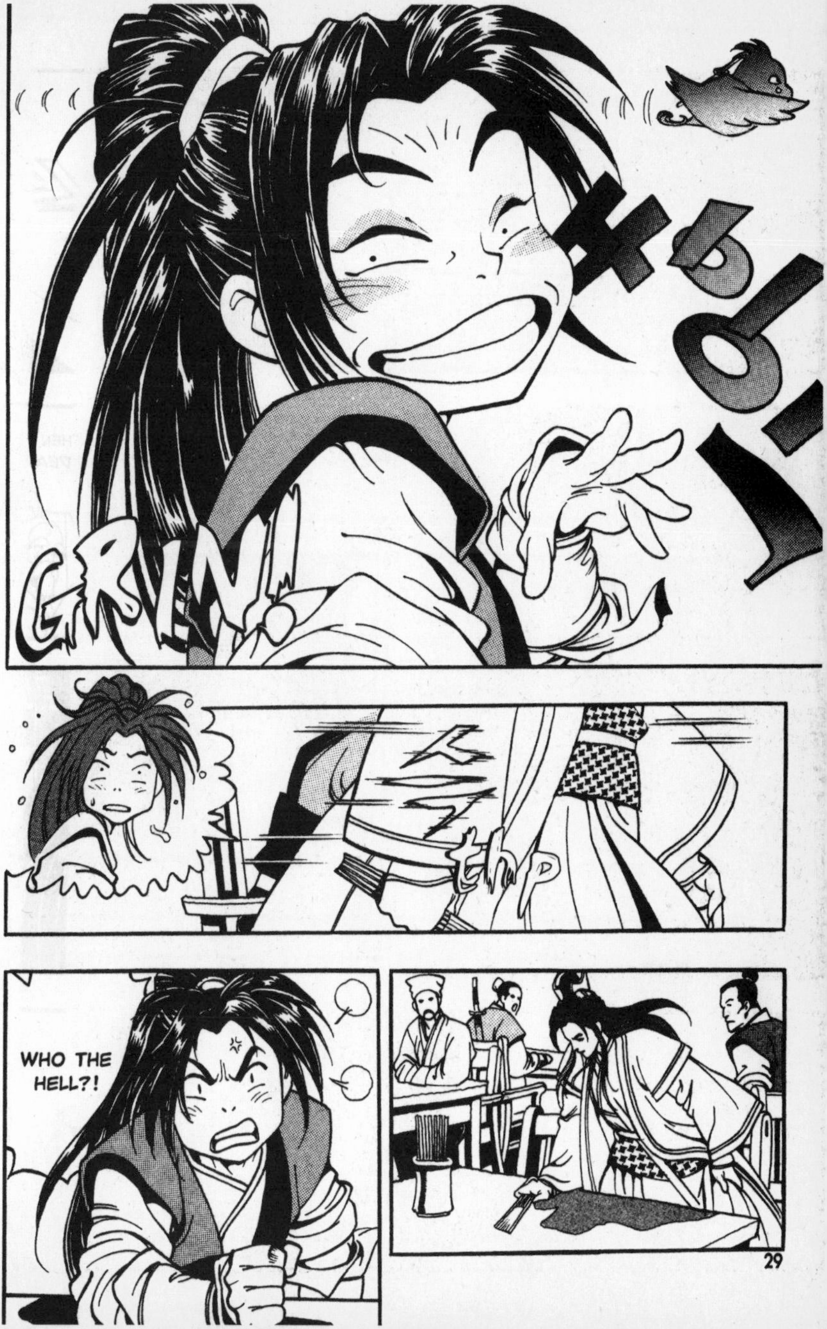

GRIN!
WHO THE HELL?!

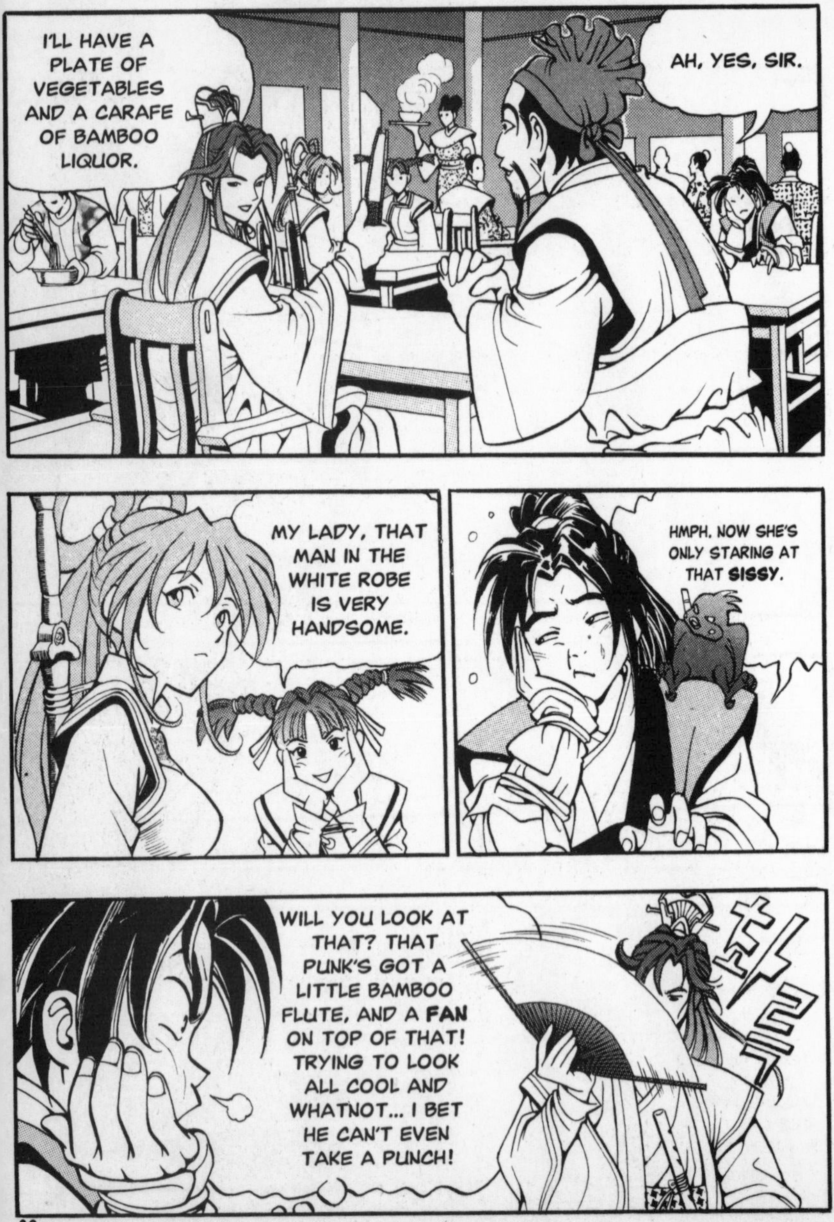
I'LL HAVE A PLATE OF VEGETABLES AND A CARAFE OF BAMBOO LIQUOR.
AH, YES, SIR.
MY LADY, THAT MAN IN THE WHITE ROBE IS VERY HANDSOME.
HMPH. NOW SHE'S ONLY STARING AT THAT SISSY.
WILL YOU LOOK AT THAT? THAT PUNK'S GOT A LITTLE BAMBOO FLUTE, AND A FAN ON TOP OF THAT! TRYING TO LOOK ALL COOL AND WHATNOT... I BET HE CAN'T EVEN TAKE A PUNCH!

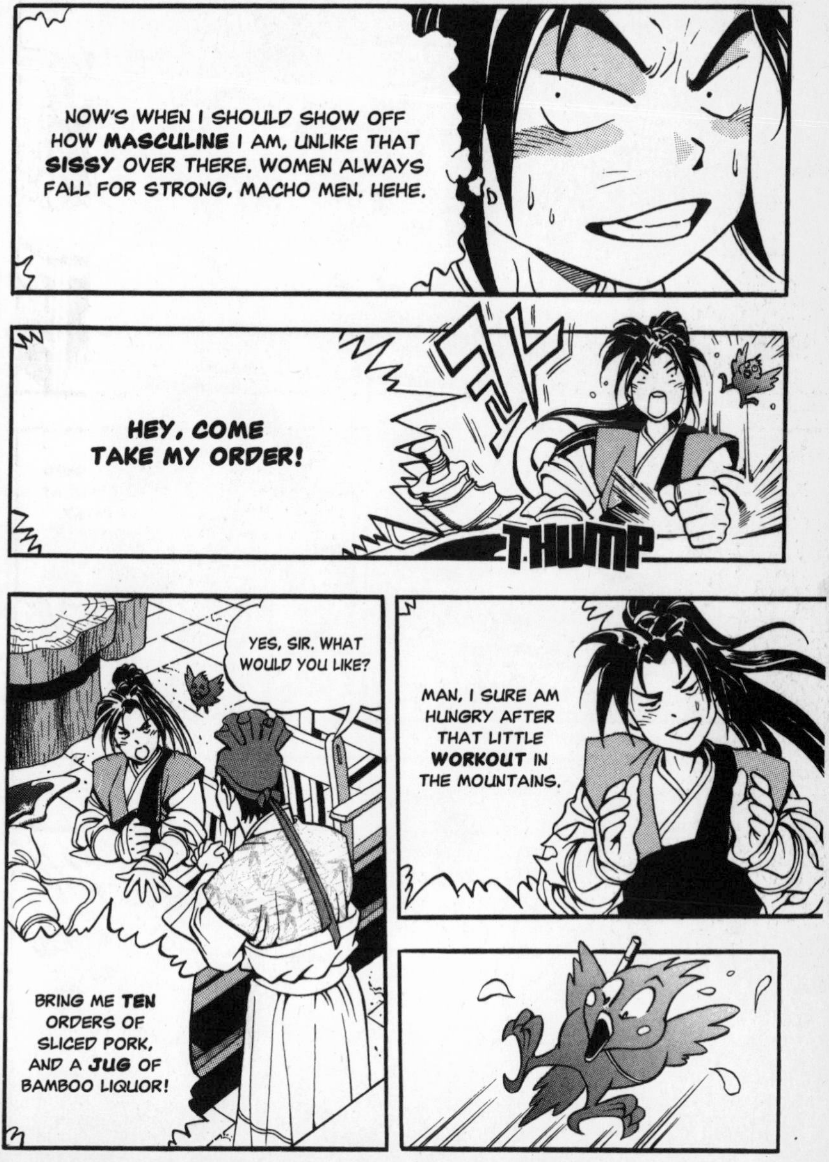
NOW'S WHEN I SHOULD SHOW OFF HOW **MASCULINE** I AM, UNLIKE THAT **SISSY** OVER THERE. WOMEN ALWAYS FALL FOR STRONG, MACHO MEN. HEHE.
HEY, COME TAKE MY ORDER!
THUMP
YES, SIR. WHAT WOULD YOU LIKE?
MAN, I SURE AM HUNGRY AFTER THAT LITTLE **WORKOUT** IN THE MOUNTAINS.
BRING ME **TEN** ORDERS OF SLICED PORK, AND A **JUG** OF BAMBOO LIQUOR!

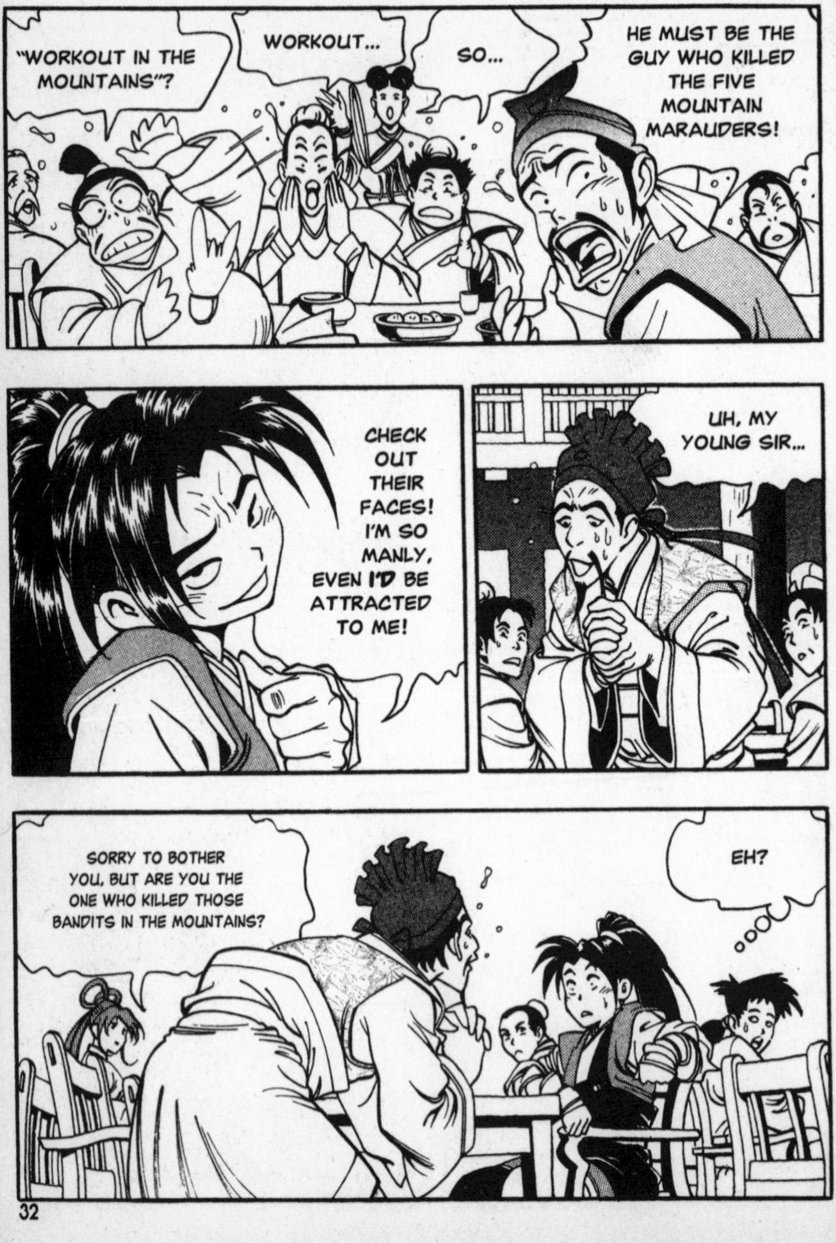
"WORKOUT IN THE MOUNTAINS"?
WORKOUT...
SO...
HE MUST BE THE GUY WHO KILLED THE FIVE MOUNTAIN MARAUDERS!
CHECK OUT THEIR FACES! I'M SO MANLY, EVEN I'D BE ATTRACTED TO ME!
UH, MY YOUNG SIR...
SORRY TO BOTHER YOU, BUT ARE YOU THE ONE WHO KILLED THOSE BANDITS IN THE MOUNTAINS?
EH?

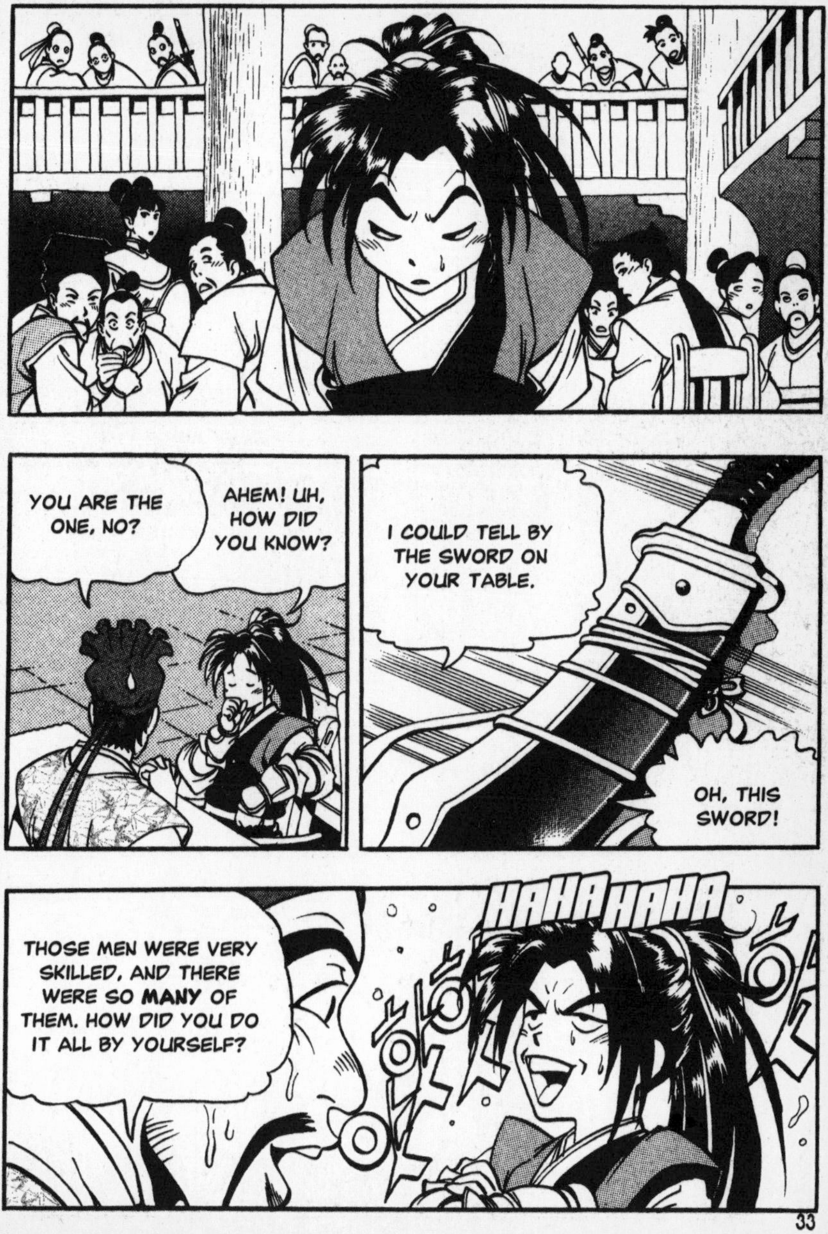
YOU ARE THE ONE, NO?
AHEM! UH, HOW DID YOU KNOW?
I COULD TELL BY THE SWORD ON YOUR TABLE.
OH, THIS SWORD!
THOSE MEN WERE VERY SKILLED, AND THERE WERE SO **MANY** OF THEM. HOW DID YOU DO IT ALL BY YOURSELF?
HAHA HAHA

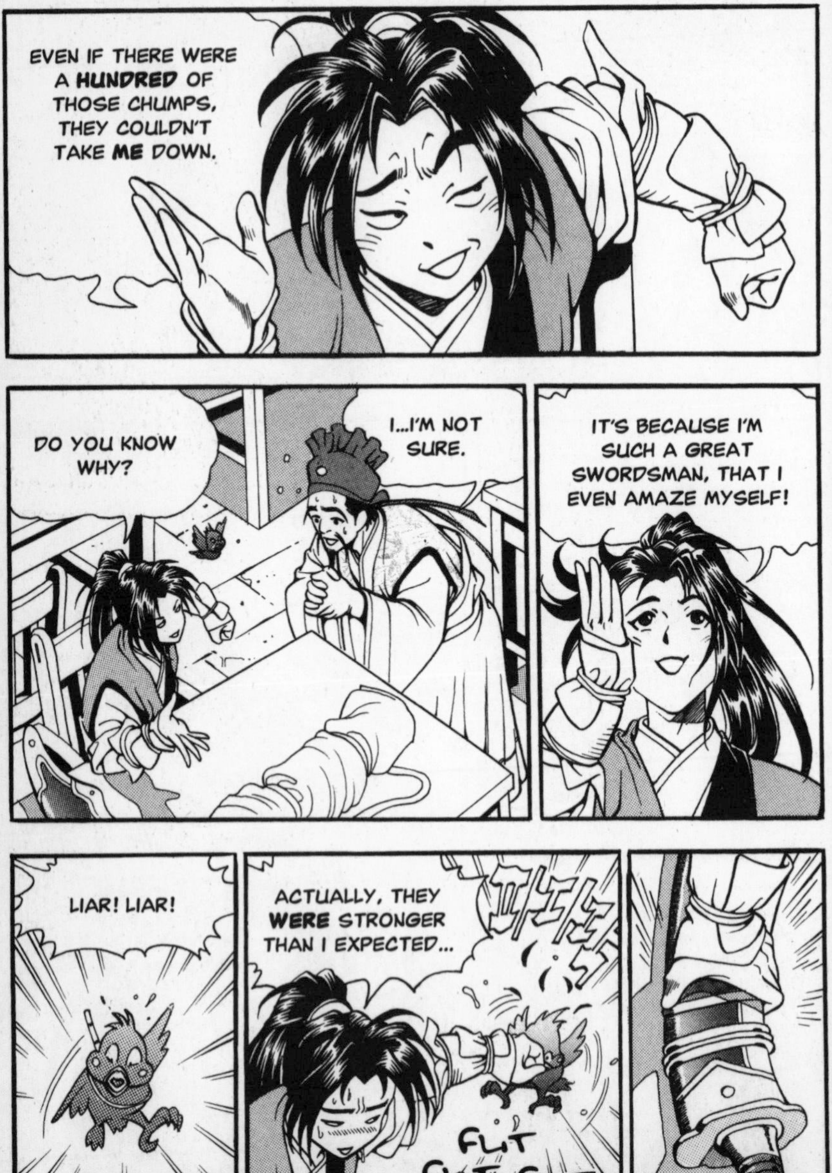
EVEN IF THERE WERE A HUNDRED OF THOSE CHUMPS, THEY COULDN'T TAKE ME DOWN.
DO YOU KNOW WHY?
I...I'M NOT SURE.
IT'S BECAUSE I'M SUCH A GREAT SWORDSMAN, THAT I EVEN AMAZE MYSELF!
LIAR! LIAR!
ACTUALLY, THEY WERE STRONGER THAN I EXPECTED...
FLIT
FLIT FLIT

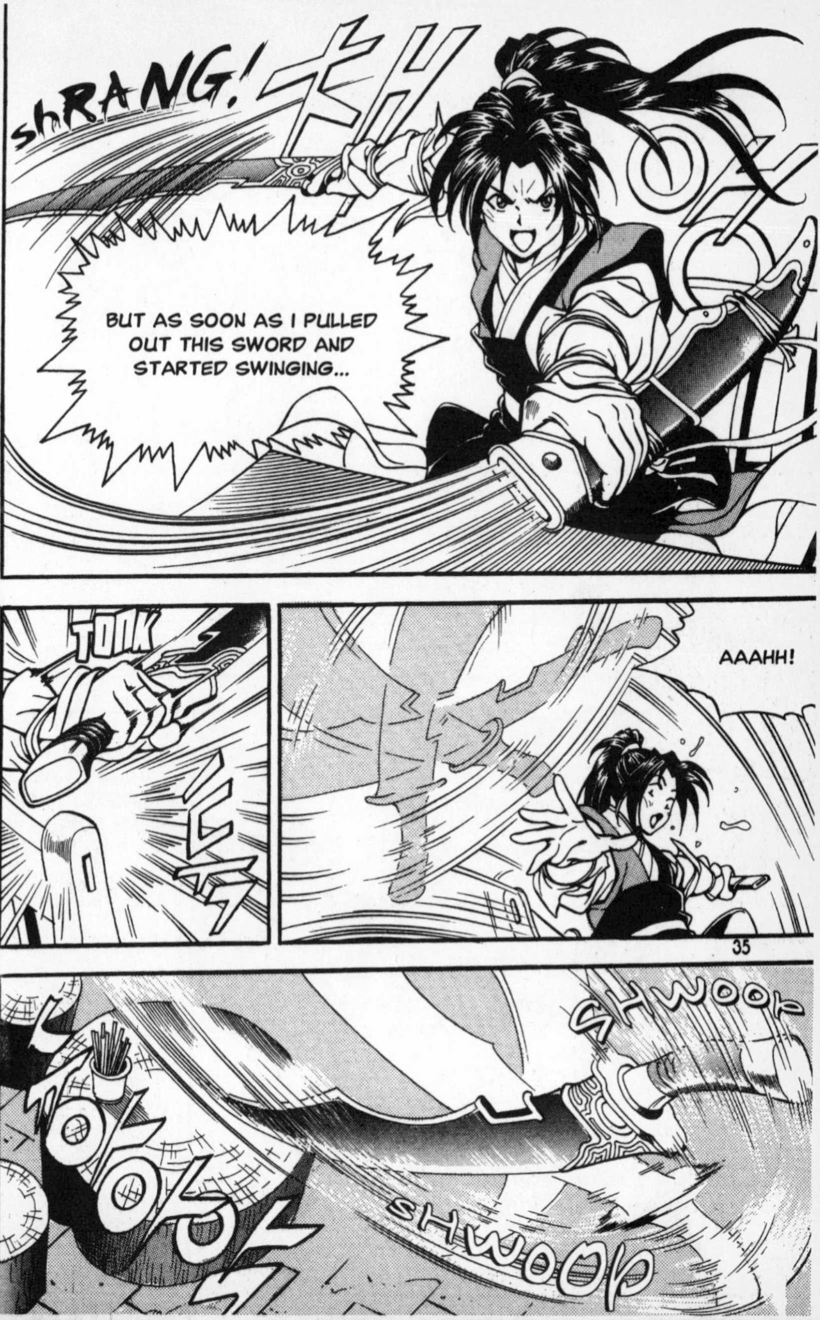
shRANG!
BUT AS SOON AS I PULLED OUT THIS SWORD AND STARTED SWINGING...
TONK
AAAHH!
SHWOOP
SHWOOP

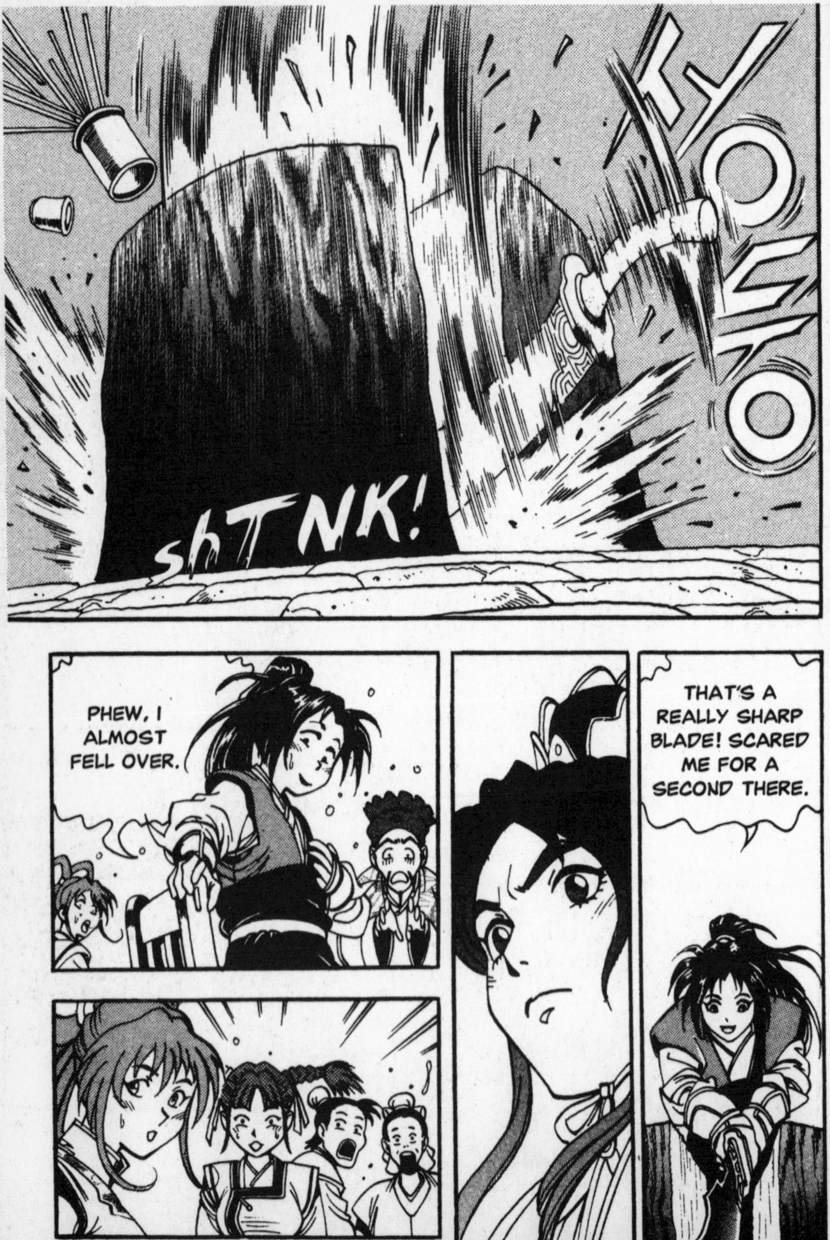
SHTNK!
PHEW, I ALMOST FELL OVER.
THAT'S A REALLY SHARP BLADE! SCARED ME FOR A SECOND THERE.

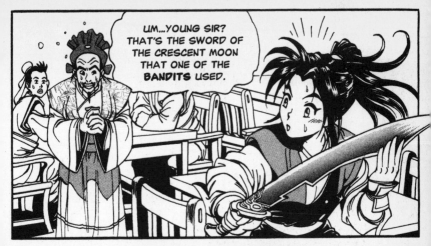

UM...YOUNG SIR? THAT'S THE SWORD OF THE CRESCENT MOON THAT ONE OF THE **BANDITS** USED.

AHAHA! YOU'RE ABSOLUTELY RIGHT! FIRST I FOUGHT THEM WITH MY BARE HANDS, AND THEN I SNATCHED THIS SWORD AND USED IT AGAINST THEM!

What a nosy old man.

I DON'T BELIEVE THIS. HE'S NOTHING BUT A FRAUD!

But he showed such skill...he sliced through that tree stump like it was TOFU.

37

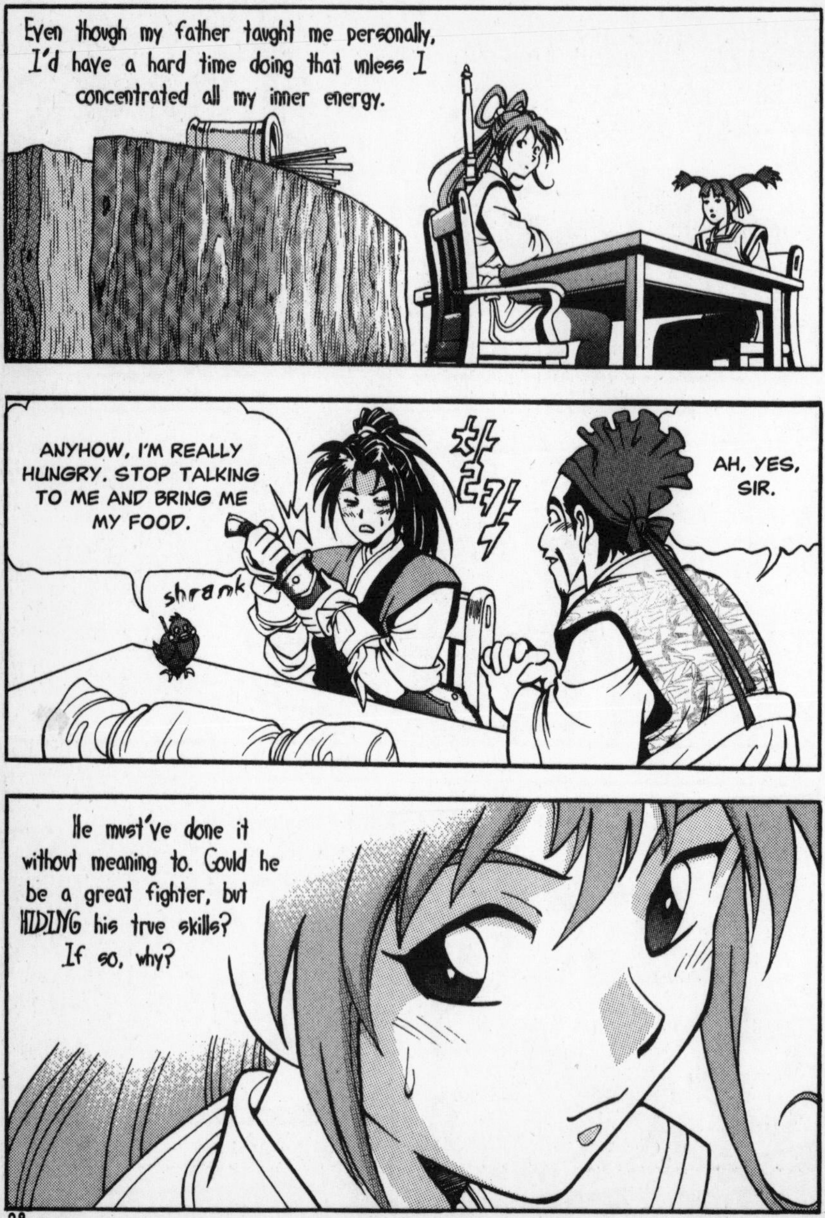
Even though my father taught me personally, I'd have a hard time doing that unless I concentrated all my inner energy.
ANYHOW, I'M REALLY HUNGRY. STOP TALKING TO ME AND BRING ME MY FOOD.
shrank
AH, YES, SIR.
He must've done it without meaning to. Could he be a great fighter, but HIDING his true skills? If so, why?

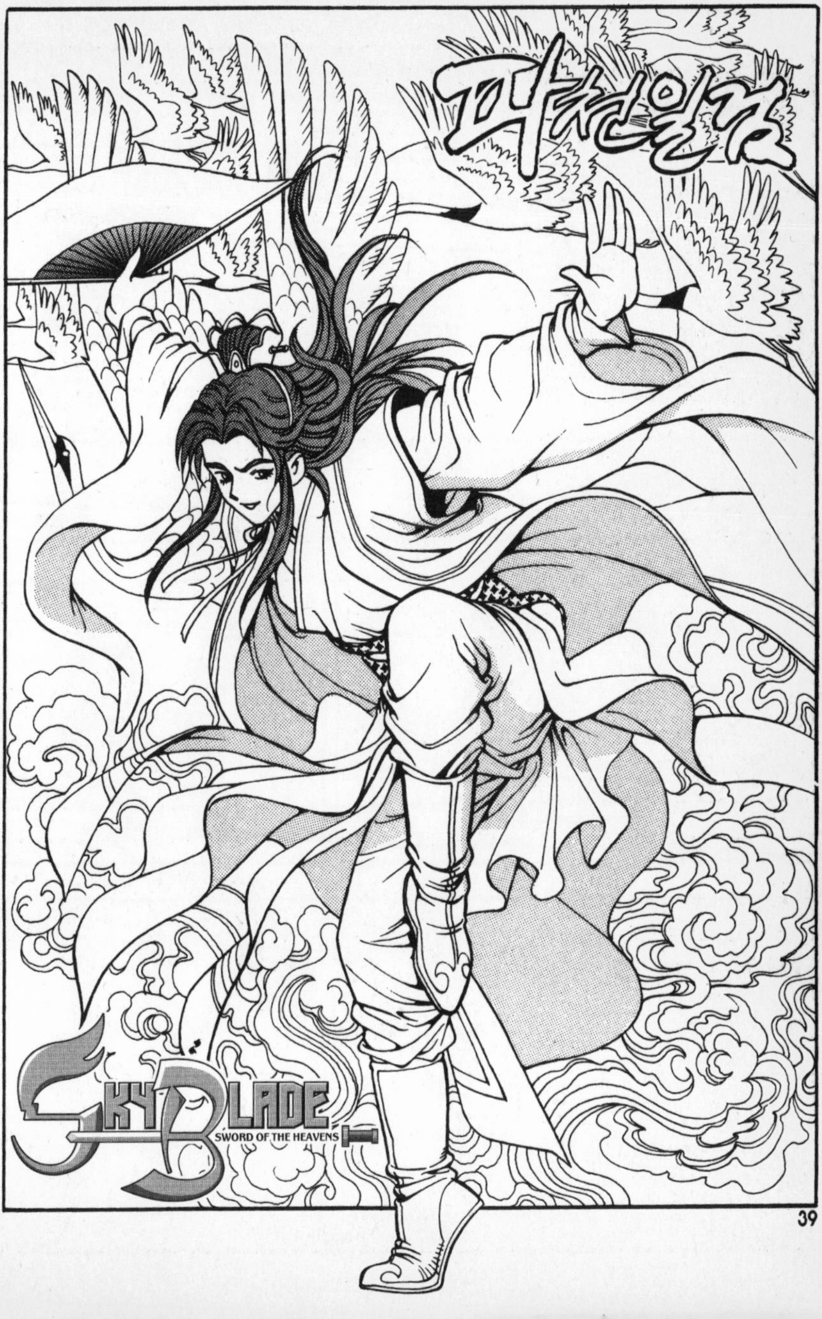
파천일검
SKY BLADE
SWORD OF THE HEAVENS

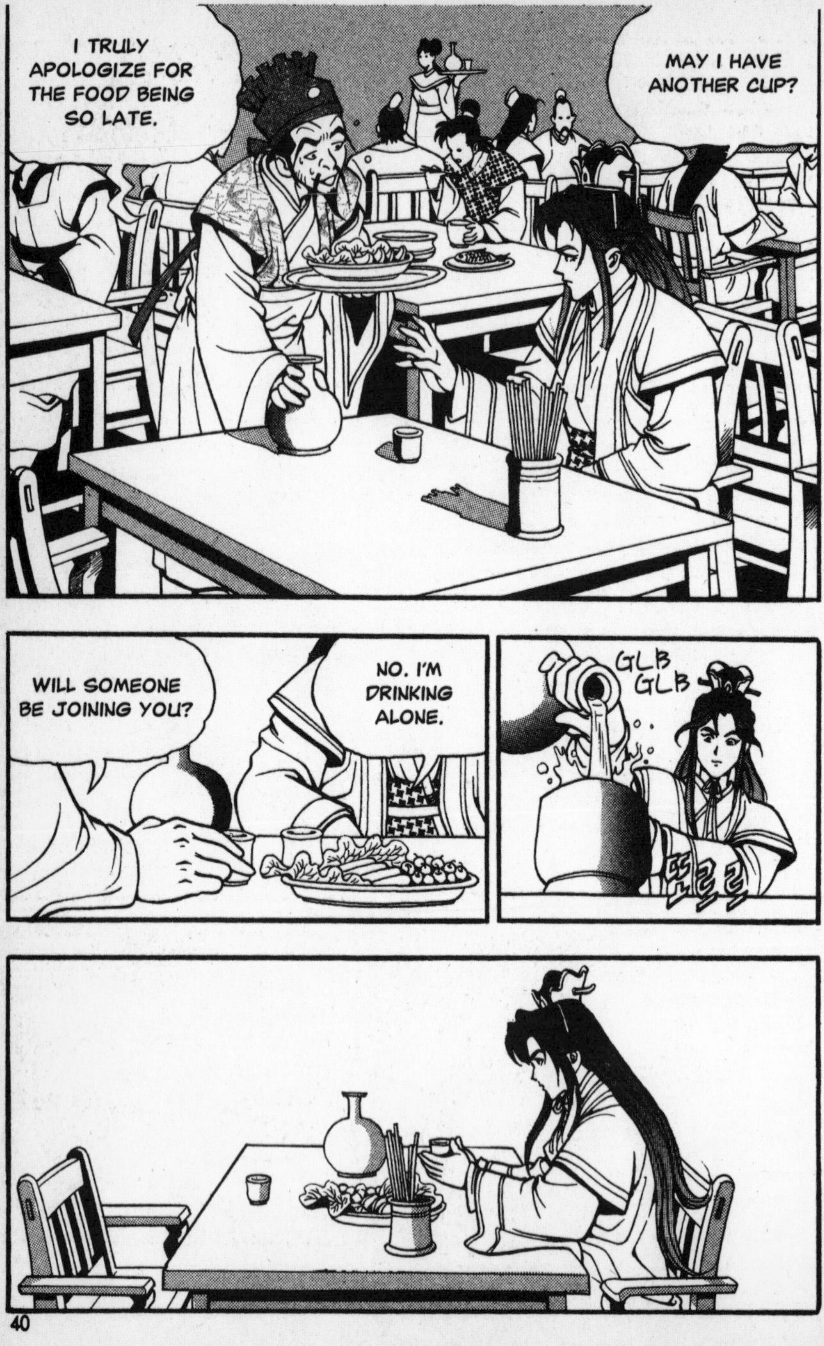
I TRULY APOLOGIZE FOR THE FOOD BEING SO LATE.
MAY I HAVE ANOTHER CUP?
WILL SOMEONE BE JOINING YOU?
NO. I'M DRINKING ALONE.
GLB GLB

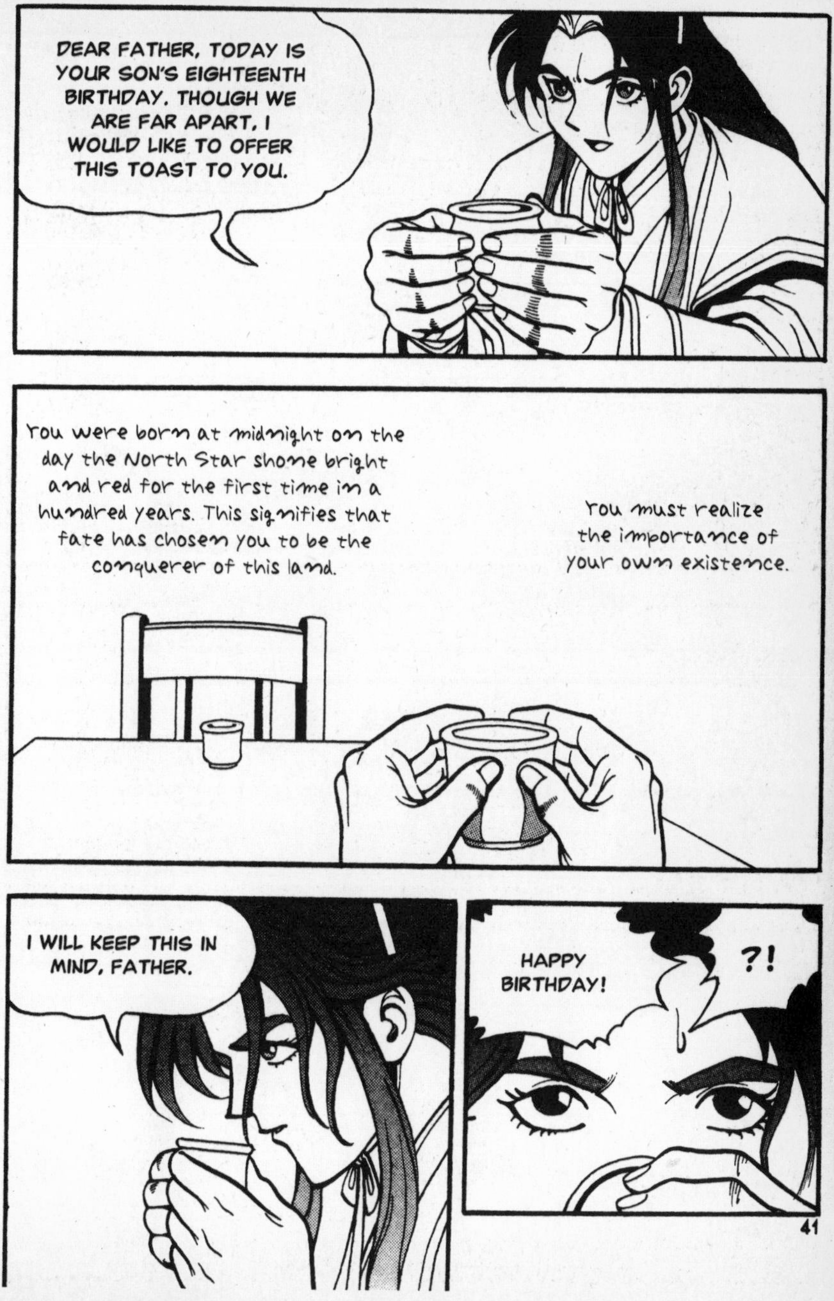
DEAR FATHER, TODAY IS YOUR SON'S EIGHTEENTH BIRTHDAY. THOUGH WE ARE FAR APART, I WOULD LIKE TO OFFER THIS TOAST TO YOU.
You were born at midnight on the day the North Star shone bright and red for the first time in a hundred years. This signifies that fate has chosen you to be the conquerer of this land.
You must realize the importance of your own existence.
I WILL KEEP THIS IN MIND, FATHER.
HAPPY BIRTHDAY!
?!

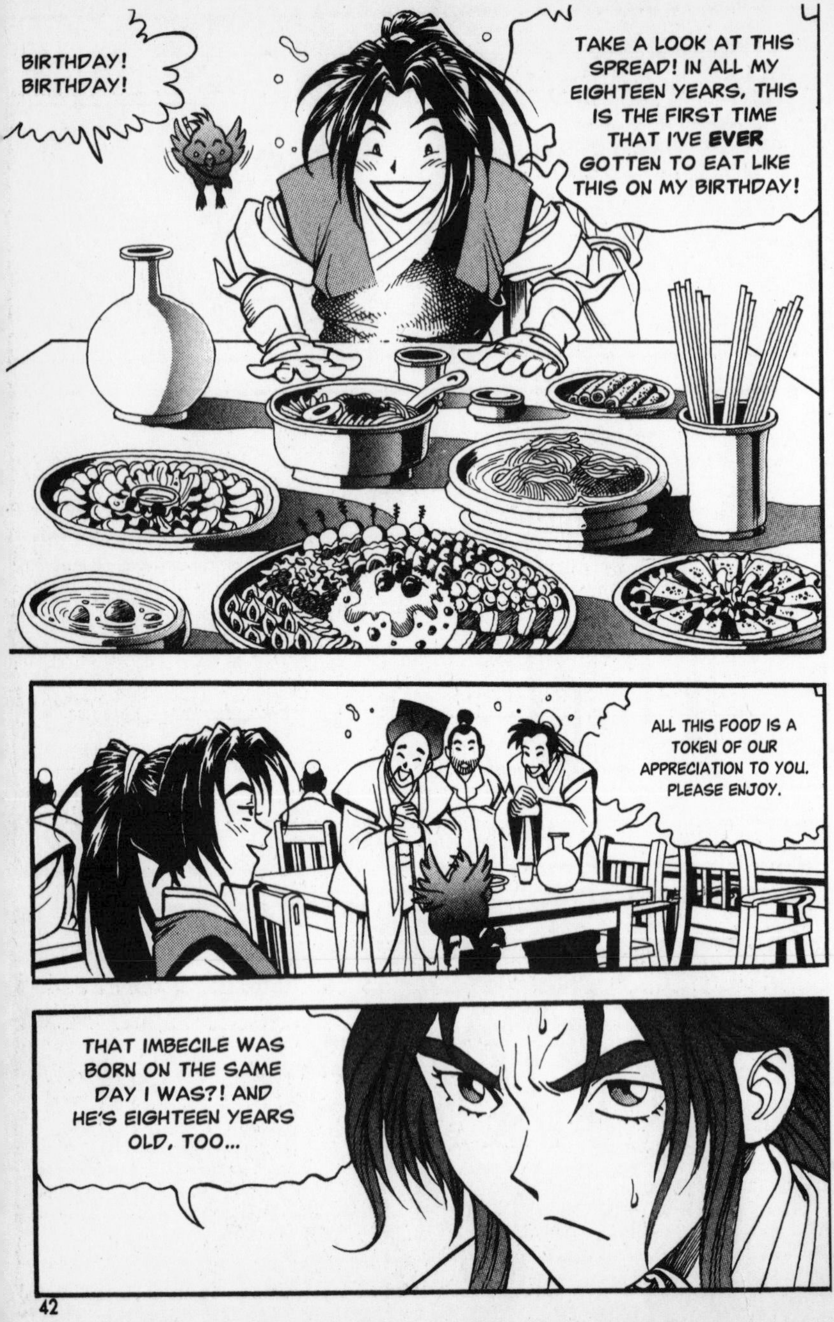
BIRTHDAY! BIRTHDAY!
TAKE A LOOK AT THIS SPREAD! IN ALL MY EIGHTEEN YEARS, THIS IS THE FIRST TIME THAT I'VE **EVER** GOTTEN TO EAT LIKE THIS ON MY BIRTHDAY!
ALL THIS FOOD IS A TOKEN OF OUR APPRECIATION TO YOU. PLEASE ENJOY.
THAT IMBECILE WAS BORN ON THE SAME DAY I WAS?! AND HE'S EIGHTEEN YEARS OLD, TOO...

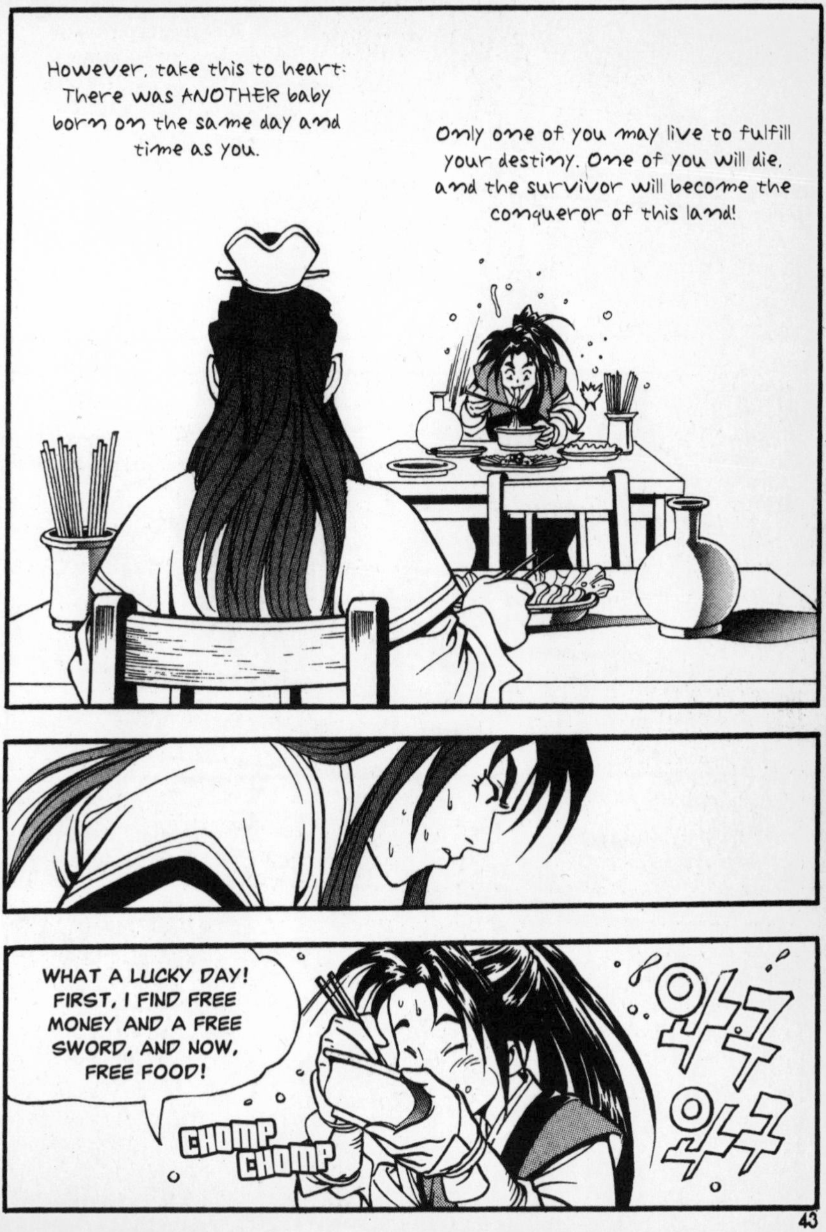
However, take this to heart: There was ANOTHER baby born on the same day and time as you.
Only one of you may live to fulfill your destiny. One of you will die, and the survivor will become the conqueror of this land!
WHAT A LUCKY DAY! FIRST, I FIND FREE MONEY AND A FREE SWORD, AND NOW, FREE FOOD!
CHOMP CHOMP

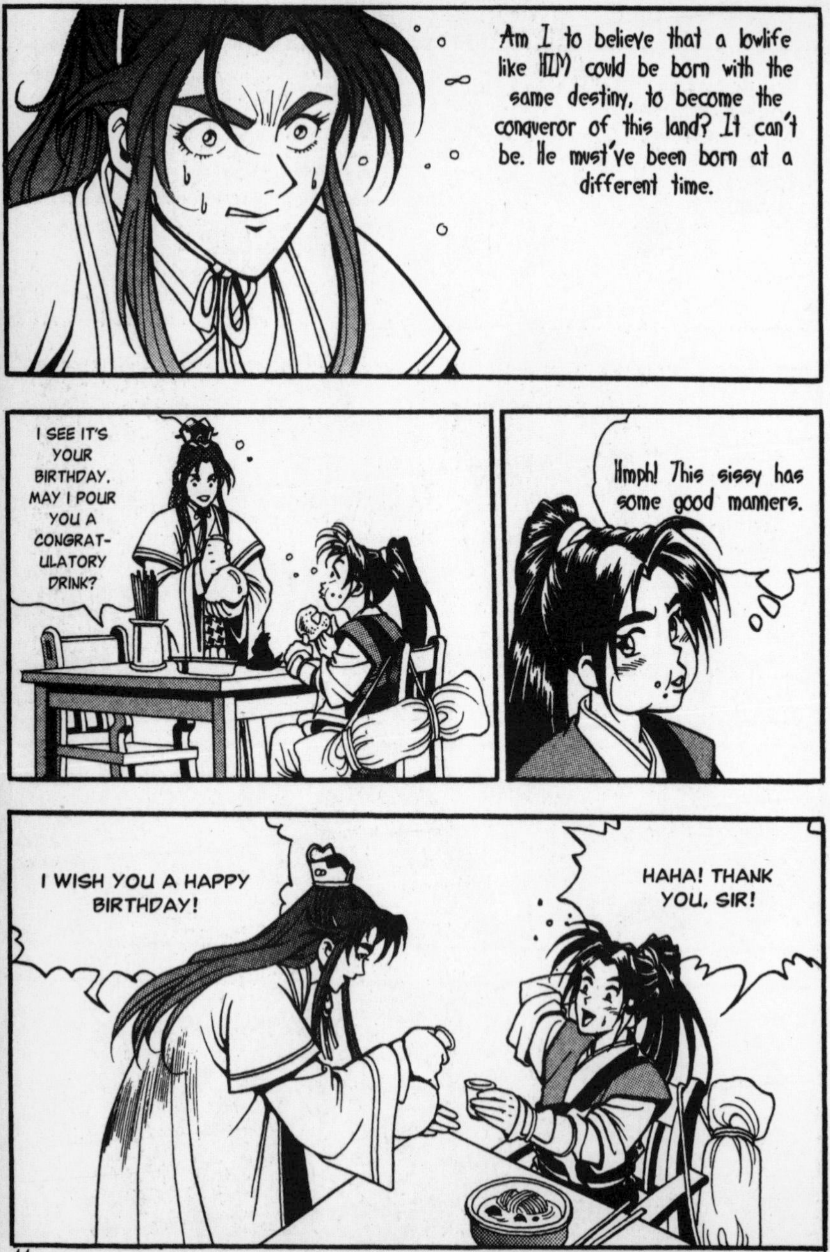
Am I to believe that a lowlife like HIM could be born with the same destiny, to become the conqueror of this land? It can't be. He must've been born at a different time.
I SEE IT'S YOUR BIRTHDAY. MAY I POUR YOU A CONGRAT-ULATORY DRINK?
Hmph! This sissy has some good manners.
I WISH YOU A HAPPY BIRTHDAY!
HAHA! THANK YOU, SIR!

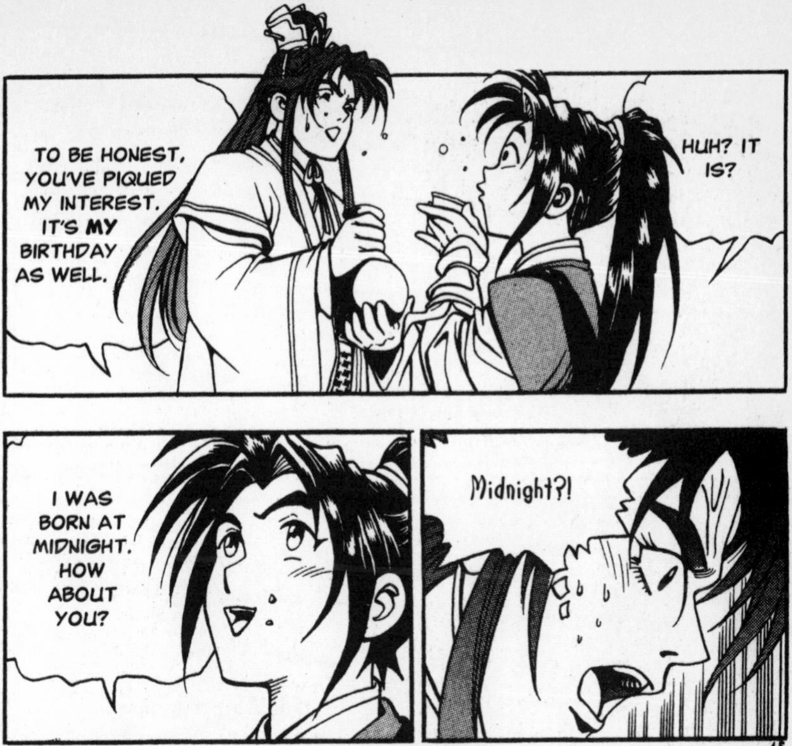
TO BE HONEST, YOU'VE PIQUED MY INTEREST. IT'S MY BIRTHDAY AS WELL.
HUH? IT IS?
I WAS BORN AT MIDNIGHT. HOW ABOUT YOU?
Midnight?!

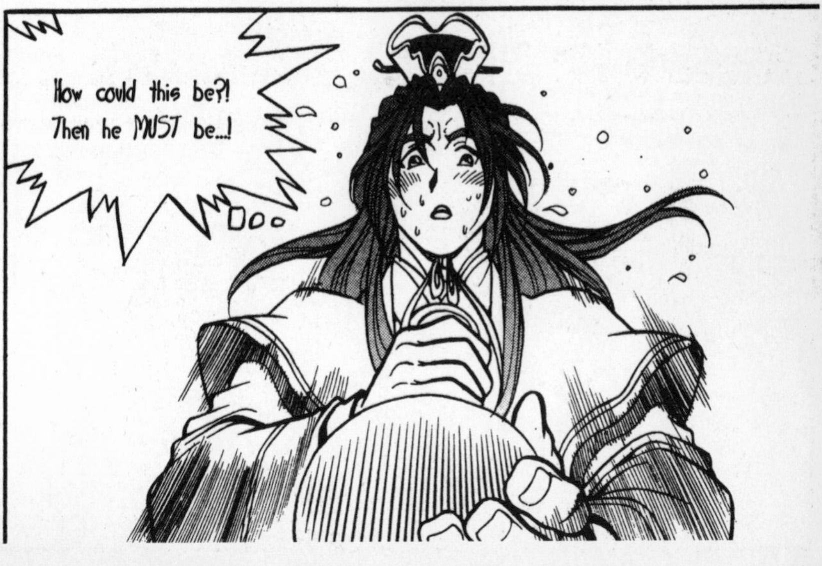
How could this be?! Then he MUST be...!

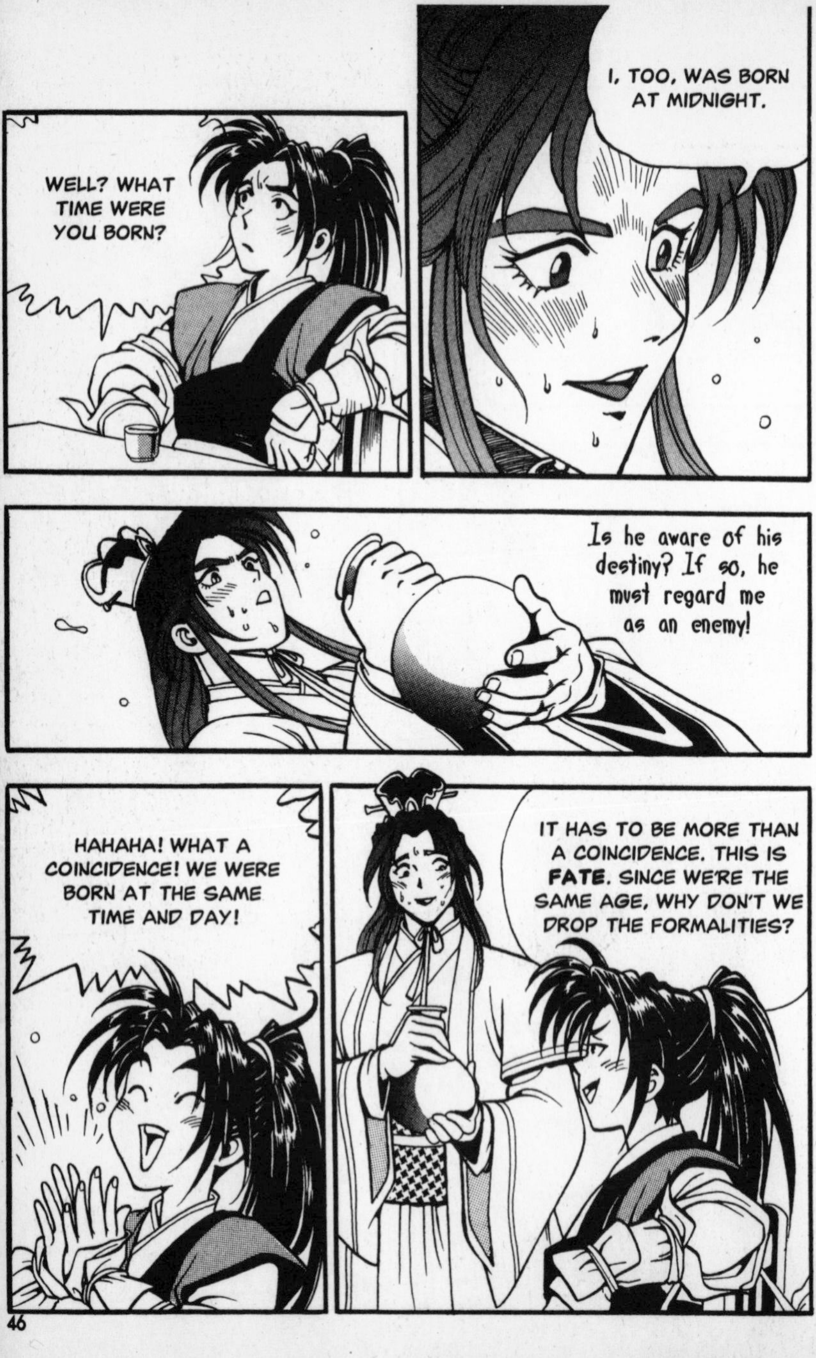
WELL? WHAT TIME WERE YOU BORN?
I, TOO, WAS BORN AT MIDNIGHT.
Is he aware of his destiny? If so, he must regard me as an enemy!
HAHAHA! WHAT A COINCIDENCE! WE WERE BORN AT THE SAME TIME AND DAY!
IT HAS TO BE MORE THAN A COINCIDENCE. THIS IS FATE. SINCE WE'RE THE SAME AGE, WHY DON'T WE DROP THE FORMALITIES?

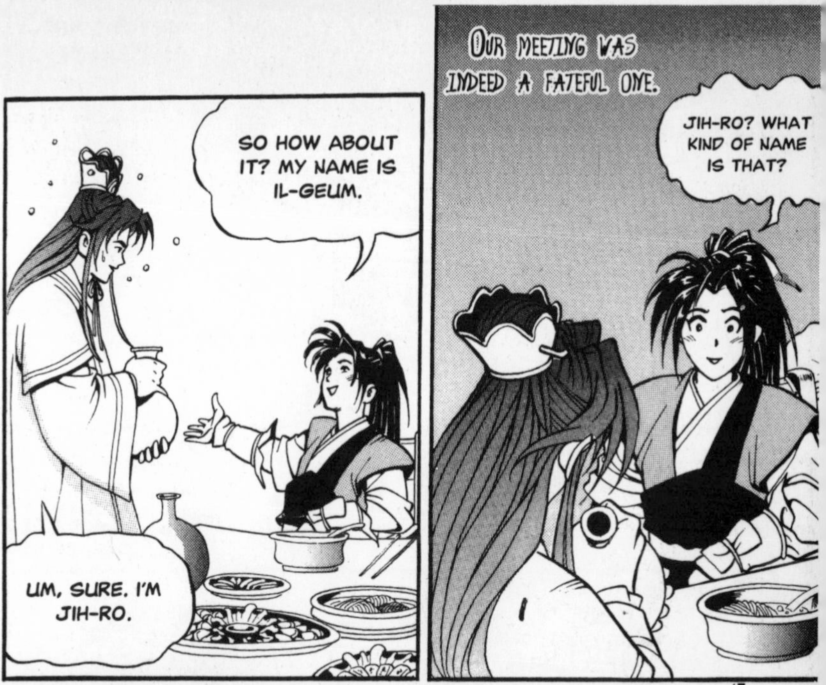
SO HOW ABOUT IT? MY NAME IS IL-GEUM.
UM, SURE. I'M JIH-RO.
OUR MEETING WAS INDEED A FATEFUL ONE.
JIH-RO? WHAT KIND OF NAME IS THAT?

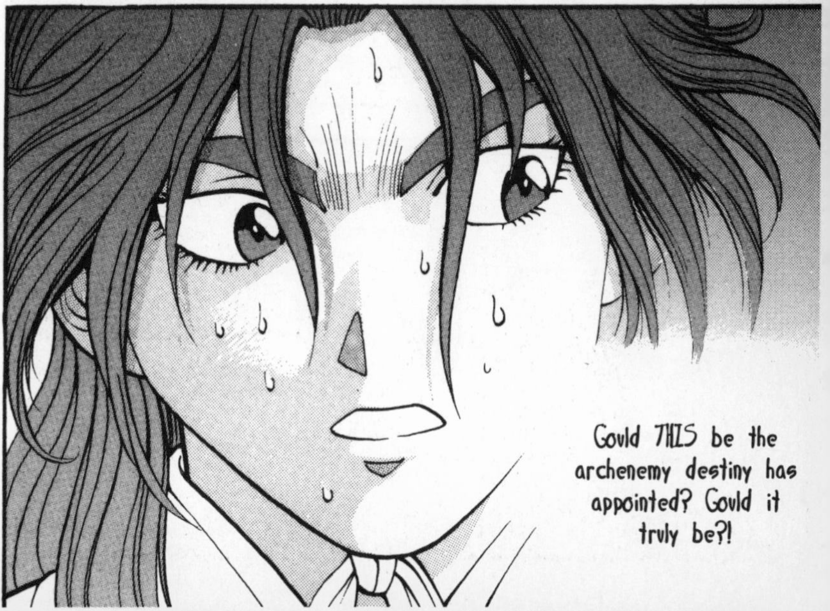
Could THIS be the archenemy destiny has appointed? Could it truly be?!

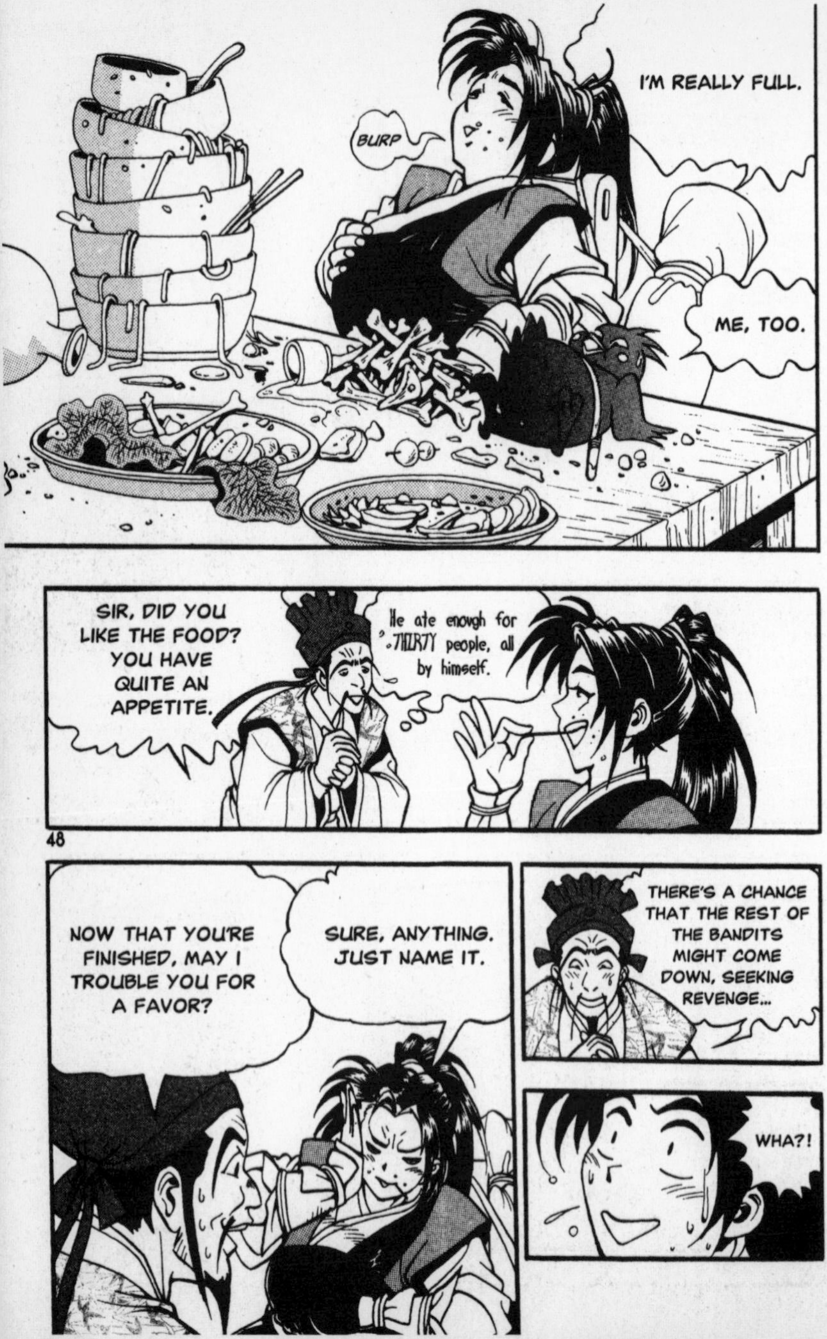
BURP
I'M REALLY FULL.
ME, TOO.
SIR, DID YOU LIKE THE FOOD? YOU HAVE QUITE AN APPETITE.
He ate enough for THIRTY people, all by himself.
NOW THAT YOU'RE FINISHED, MAY I TROUBLE YOU FOR A FAVOR?
SURE, ANYTHING. JUST NAME IT.
THERE'S A CHANCE THAT THE REST OF THE BANDITS MIGHT COME DOWN, SEEKING REVENGE...
WHA?!

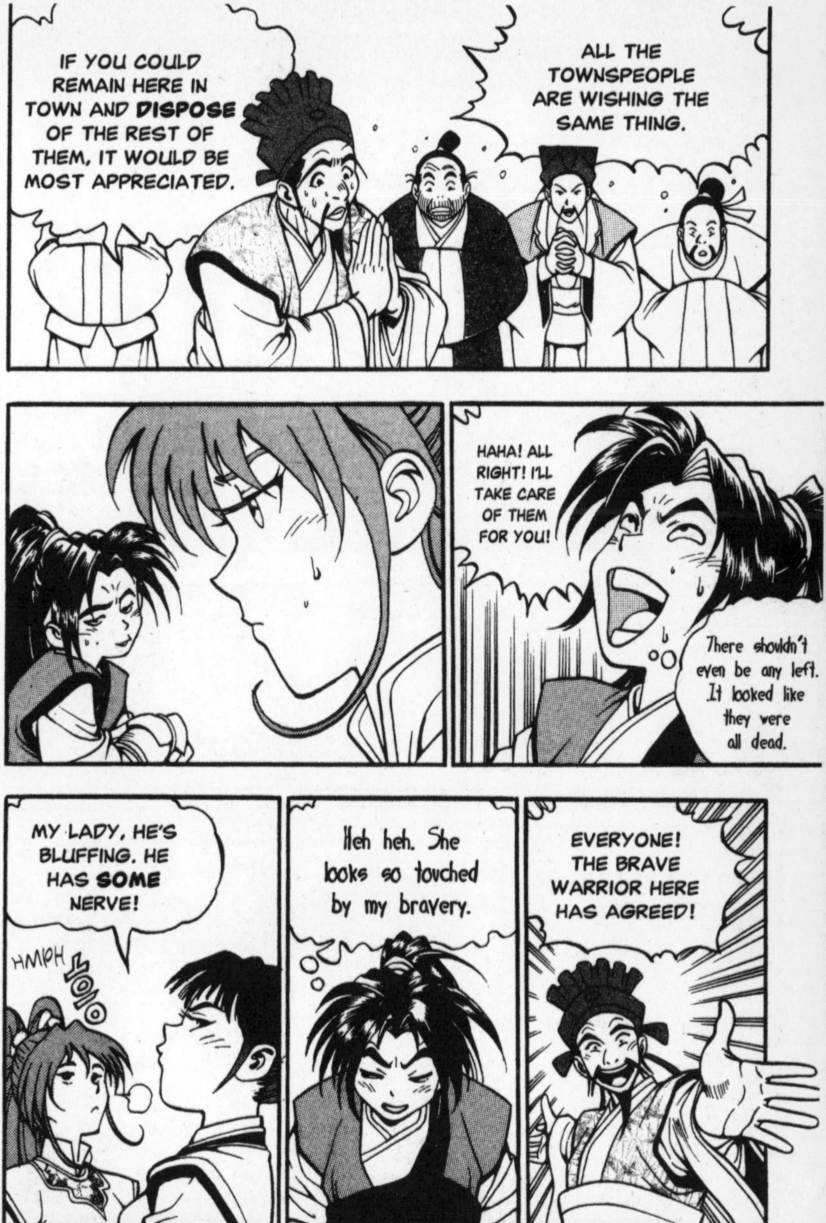
IF YOU COULD REMAIN HERE IN TOWN AND DISPOSE OF THE REST OF THEM, IT WOULD BE MOST APPRECIATED.
ALL THE TOWNSPEOPLE ARE WISHING THE SAME THING.
HAHA! ALL RIGHT! I'LL TAKE CARE OF THEM FOR YOU!
There shouldn't even be any left. It looked like they were all dead.
MY LADY, HE'S BLUFFING. HE HAS SOME NERVE!
HMPH
Heh heh. She looks so touched by my bravery.
EVERYONE! THE BRAVE WARRIOR HERE HAS AGREED!

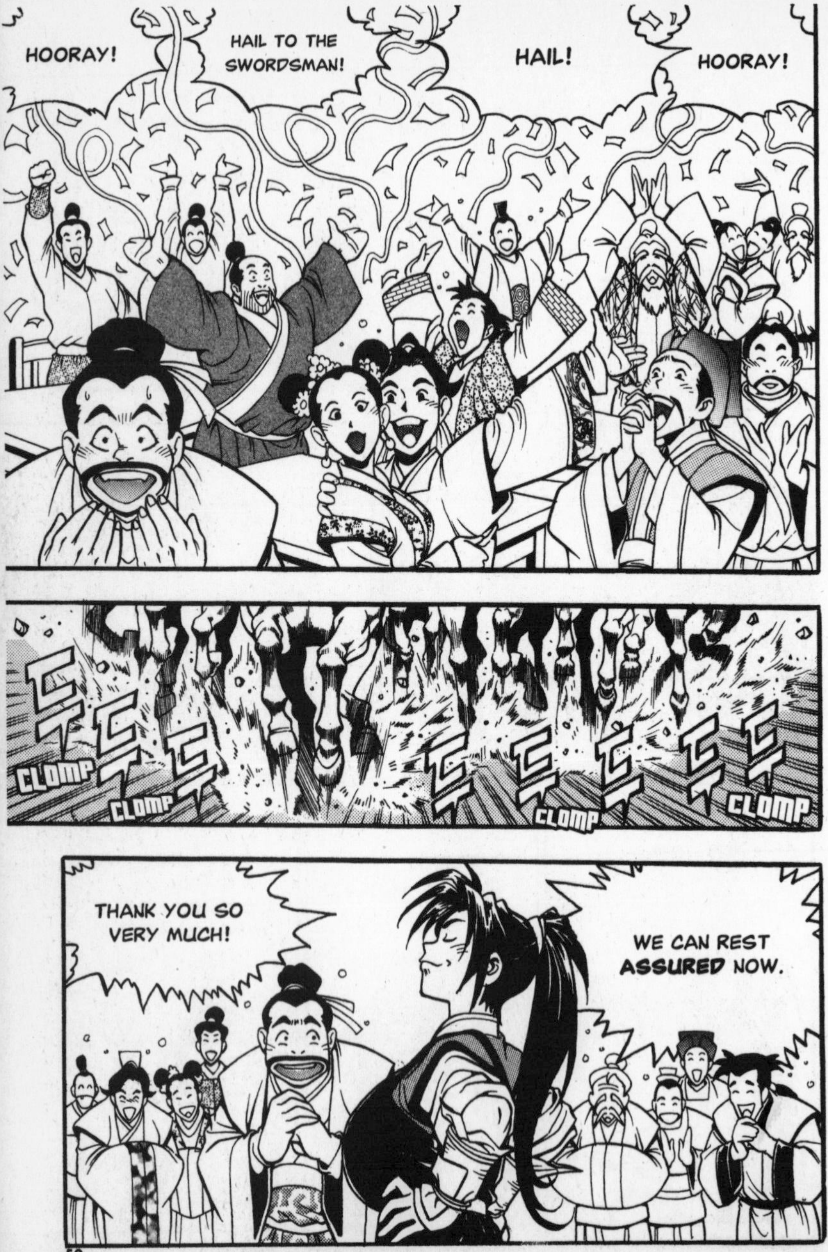
HOORAY!
HAIL TO THE SWORDSMAN!
HAIL!
HOORAY!
CLOMP
CLOMP
CLOMP
CLOMP
THANK YOU SO VERY MUCH!
WE CAN REST ASSURED NOW.

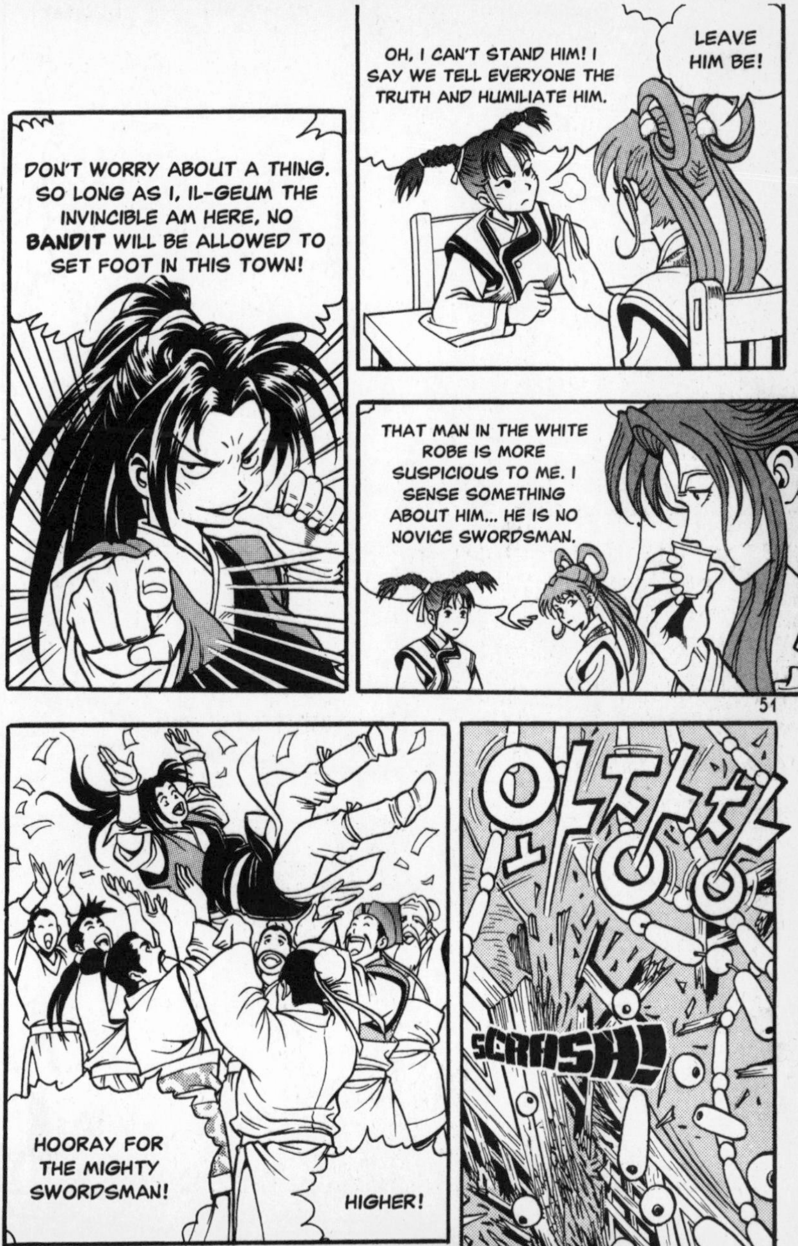
DON'T WORRY ABOUT A THING. SO LONG AS I, IL-GEUM THE INVINCIBLE AM HERE, NO **BANDIT** WILL BE ALLOWED TO SET FOOT IN THIS TOWN!
OH, I CAN'T STAND HIM! I SAY WE TELL EVERYONE THE TRUTH AND HUMILIATE HIM.
LEAVE HIM BE!
THAT MAN IN THE WHITE ROBE IS MORE SUSPICIOUS TO ME. I SENSE SOMETHING ABOUT HIM... HE IS NO NOVICE SWORDSMAN.
HOORAY FOR THE MIGHTY SWORDSMAN!
HIGHER!
SCRASH!

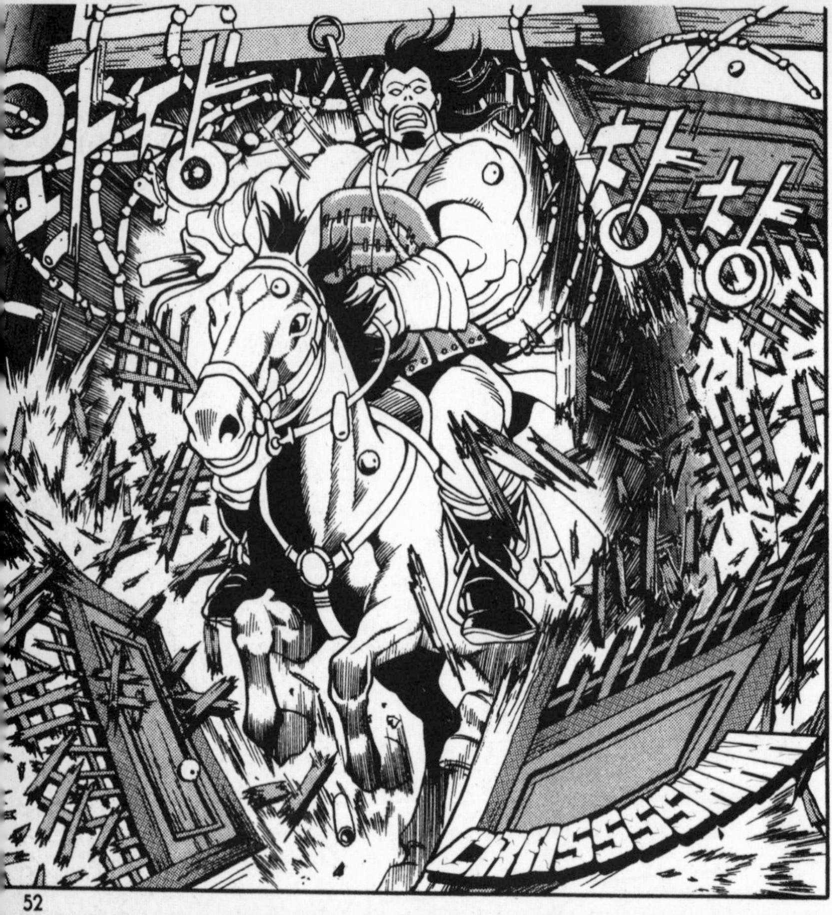
CRASSSSH

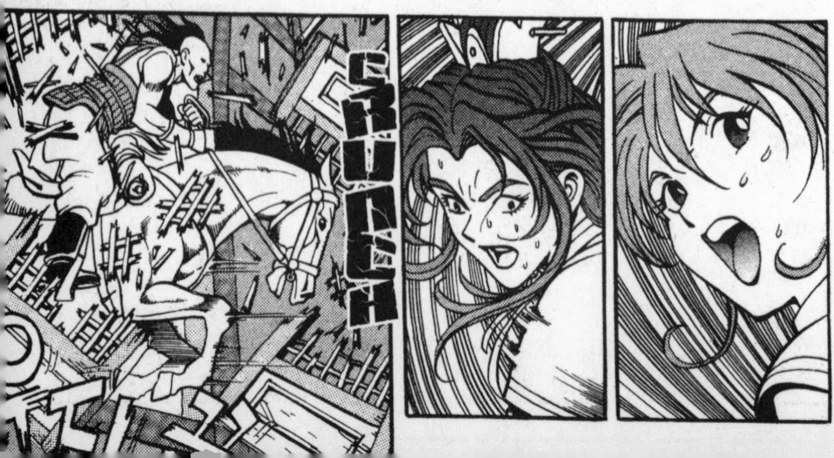
GRUNCH

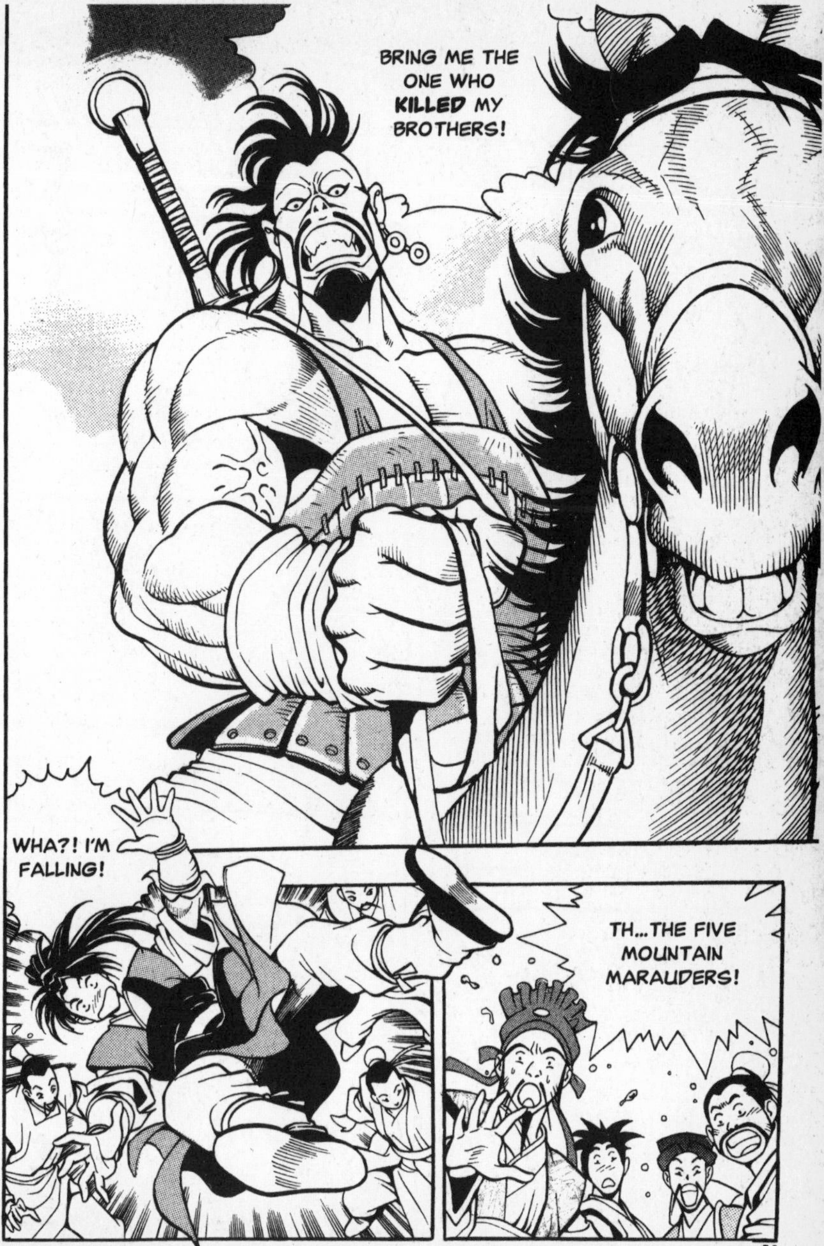
BRING ME THE ONE WHO KILLED MY BROTHERS!
WHA?! I'M FALLING!
TH...THE FIVE MOUNTAIN MARAUDERS!

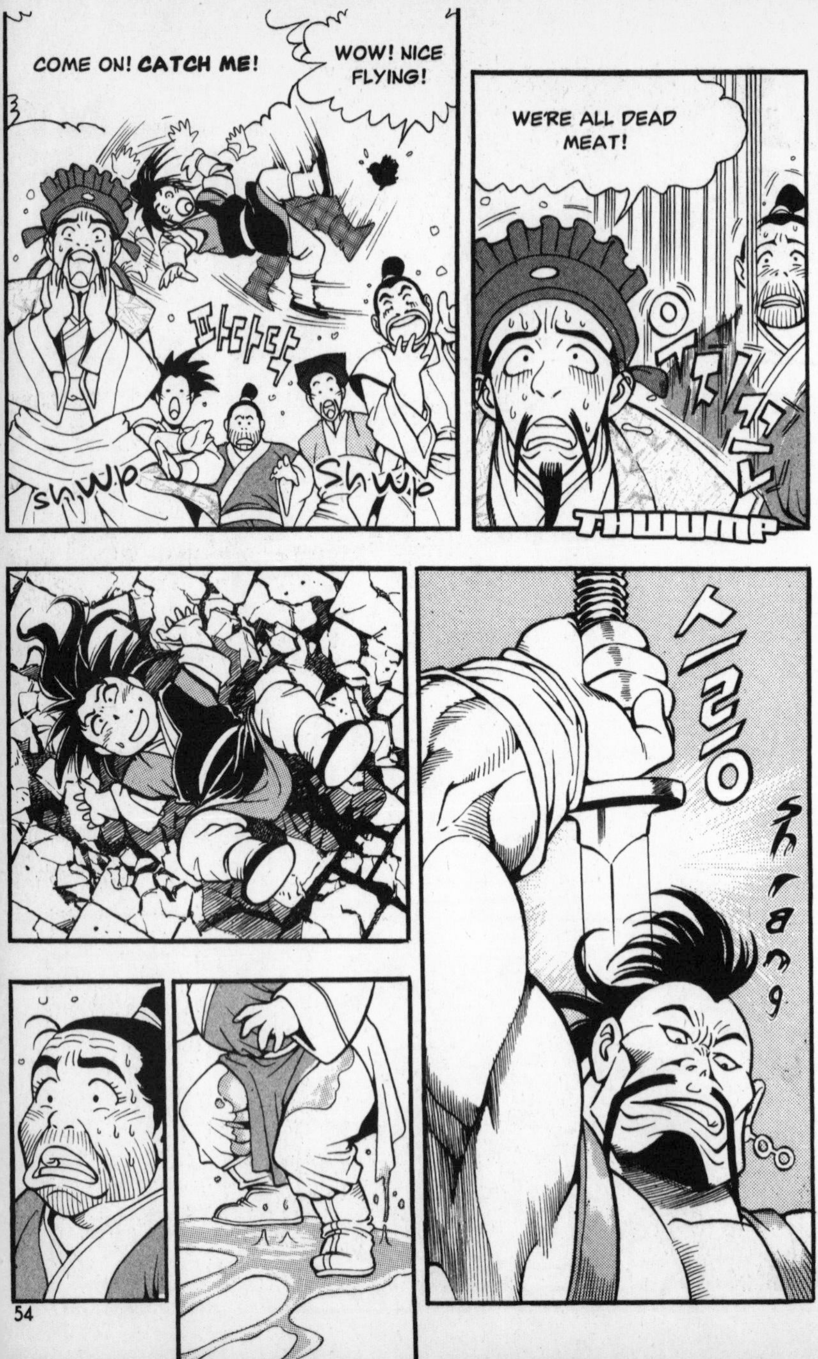
COME ON! CATCH ME!
WOW! NICE FLYING!
SHWIP
SHWIP
WE'RE ALL DEAD MEAT!
THWUMP

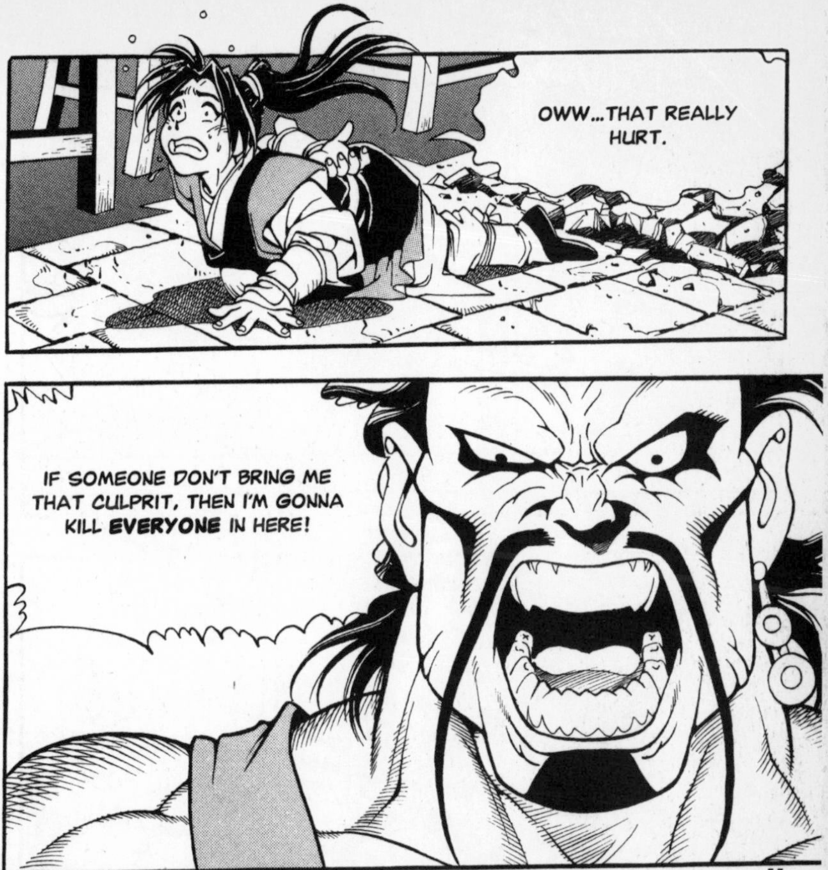
OWW...THAT REALLY HURT.
IF SOMEONE DON'T BRING ME THAT CULPRIT, THEN I'M GONNA KILL EVERYONE IN HERE!

55

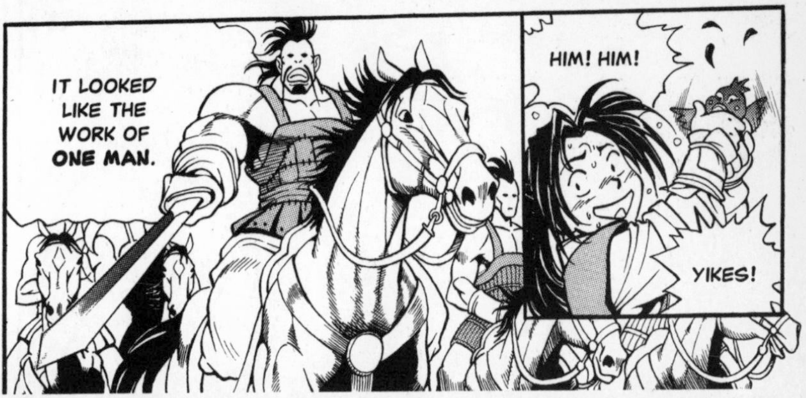
IT LOOKED LIKE THE WORK OF ONE MAN.
HIM! HIM!
YIKES!

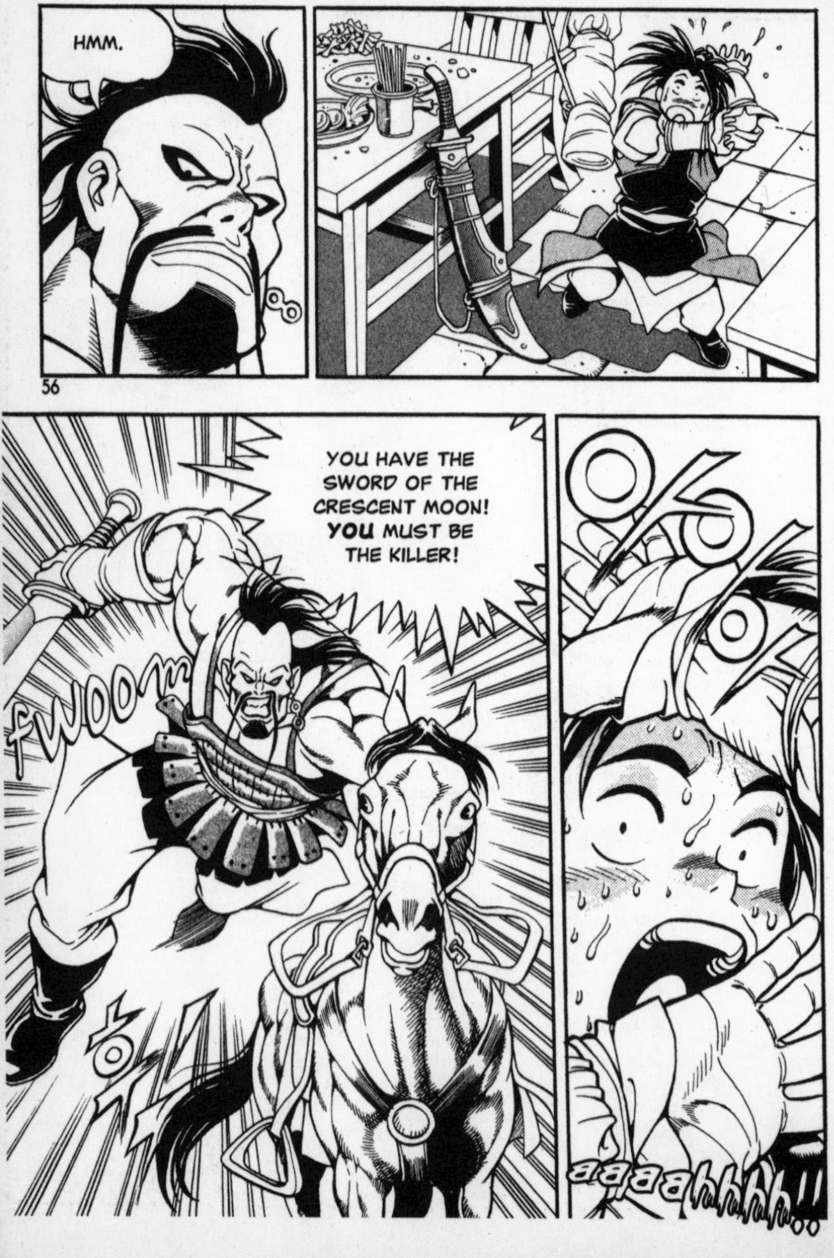
HMM.
YOU HAVE THE SWORD OF THE CRESCENT MOON! YOU MUST BE THE KILLER!
fwoom
aaaahhhhh!!

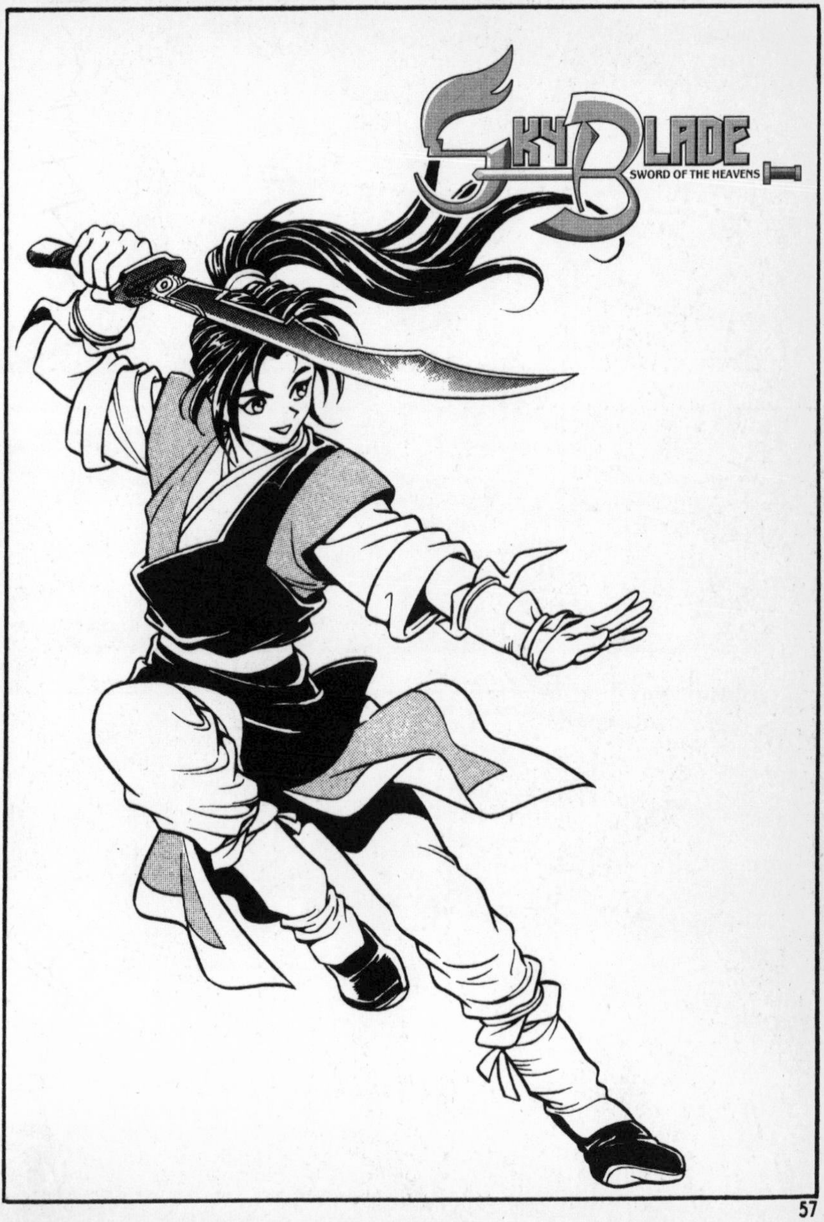
SKY BLADE
SWORD OF THE HEAVENS

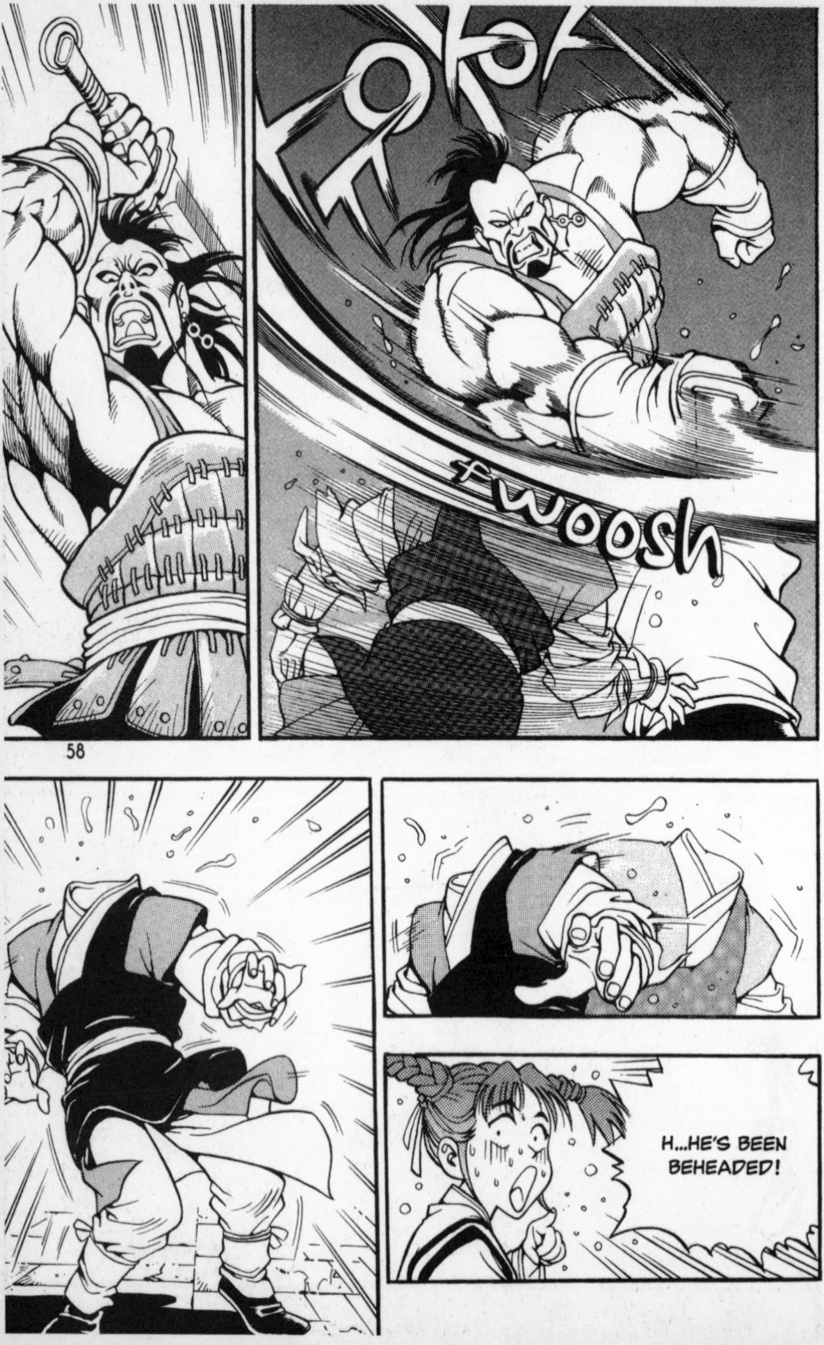
WOOSH
H...HE'S BEEN BEHEADED!

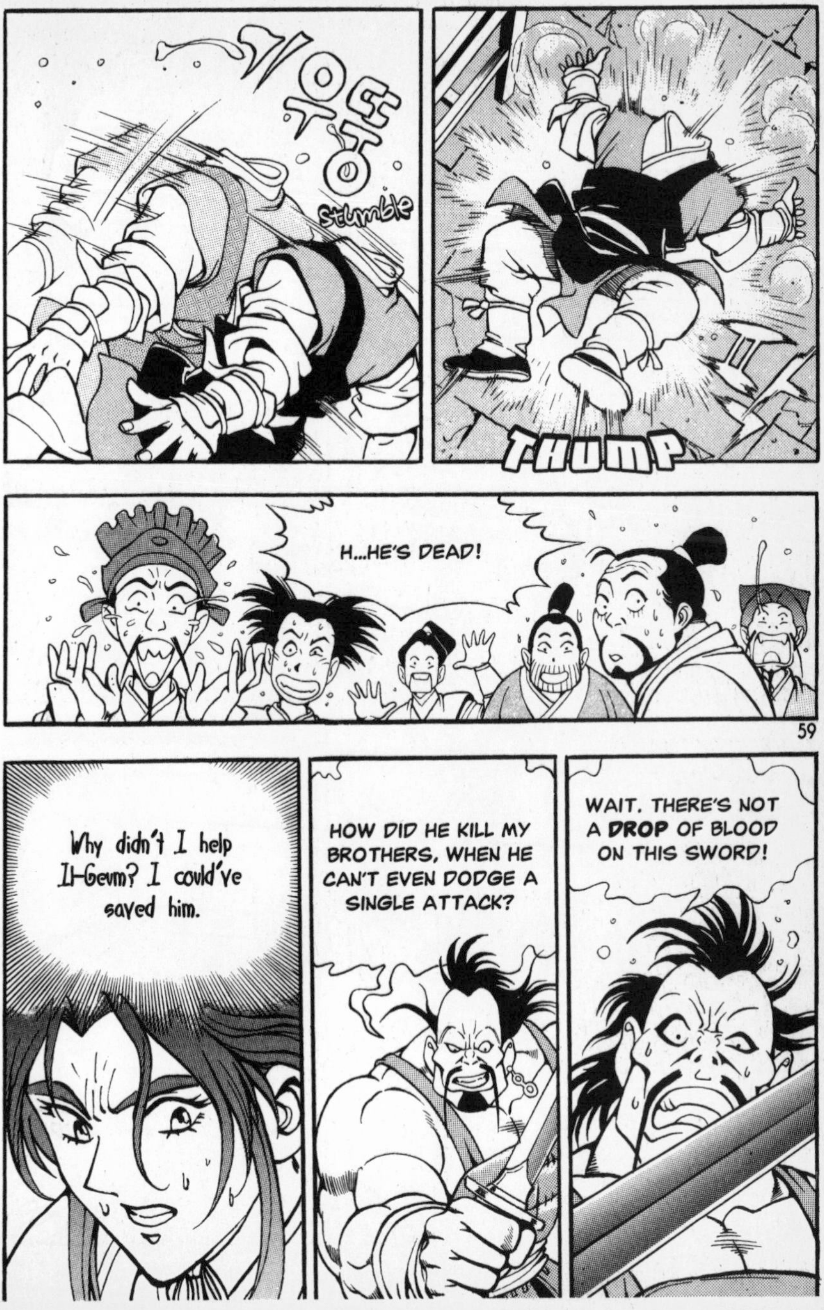
기우뚱
Stumble
THUMP
H...HE'S DEAD!
Why didn't I help Il-Geum? I could've saved him.
HOW DID HE KILL MY BROTHERS, WHEN HE CAN'T EVEN DODGE A SINGLE ATTACK?
WAIT. THERE'S NOT A **DROP** OF BLOOD ON THIS SWORD!

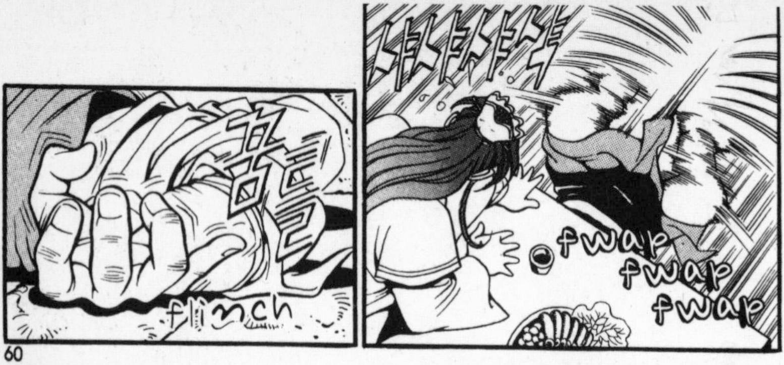

flinch
fwap
fwap
fwap

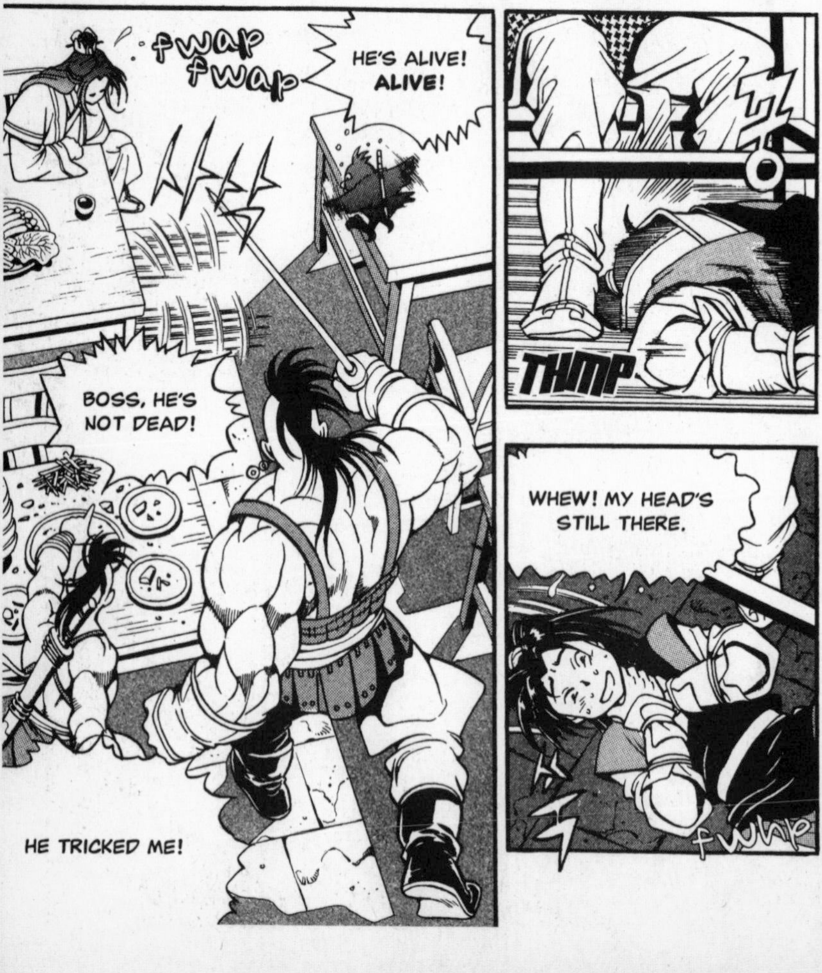

fwap
fwap
HE'S ALIVE! ALIVE!
BOSS, HE'S NOT DEAD!
HE TRICKED ME!
THUMP
WHEW! MY HEAD'S STILL THERE.

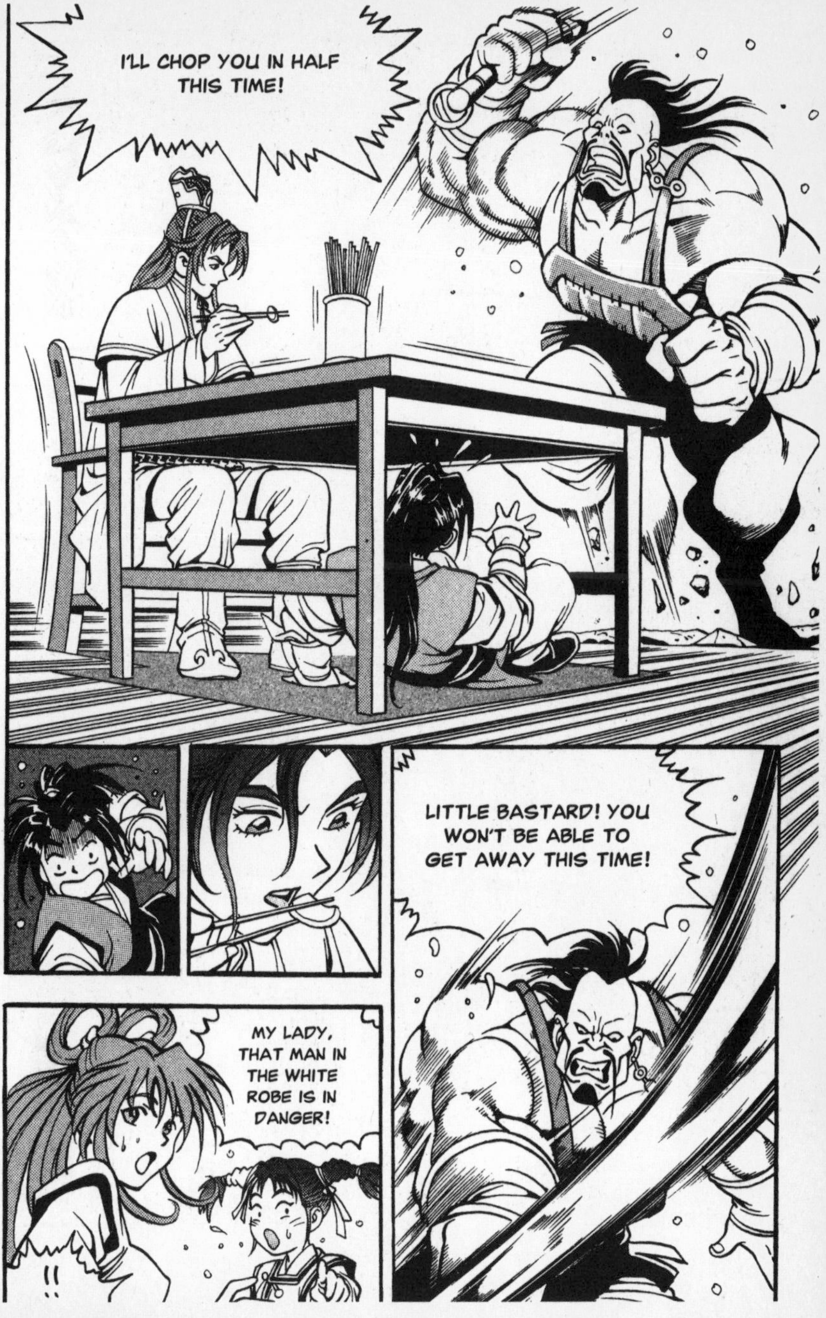
I'LL CHOP YOU IN HALF THIS TIME!
LITTLE BASTARD! YOU WON'T BE ABLE TO GET AWAY THIS TIME!
MY LADY, THAT MAN IN THE WHITE ROBE IS IN DANGER!
!!

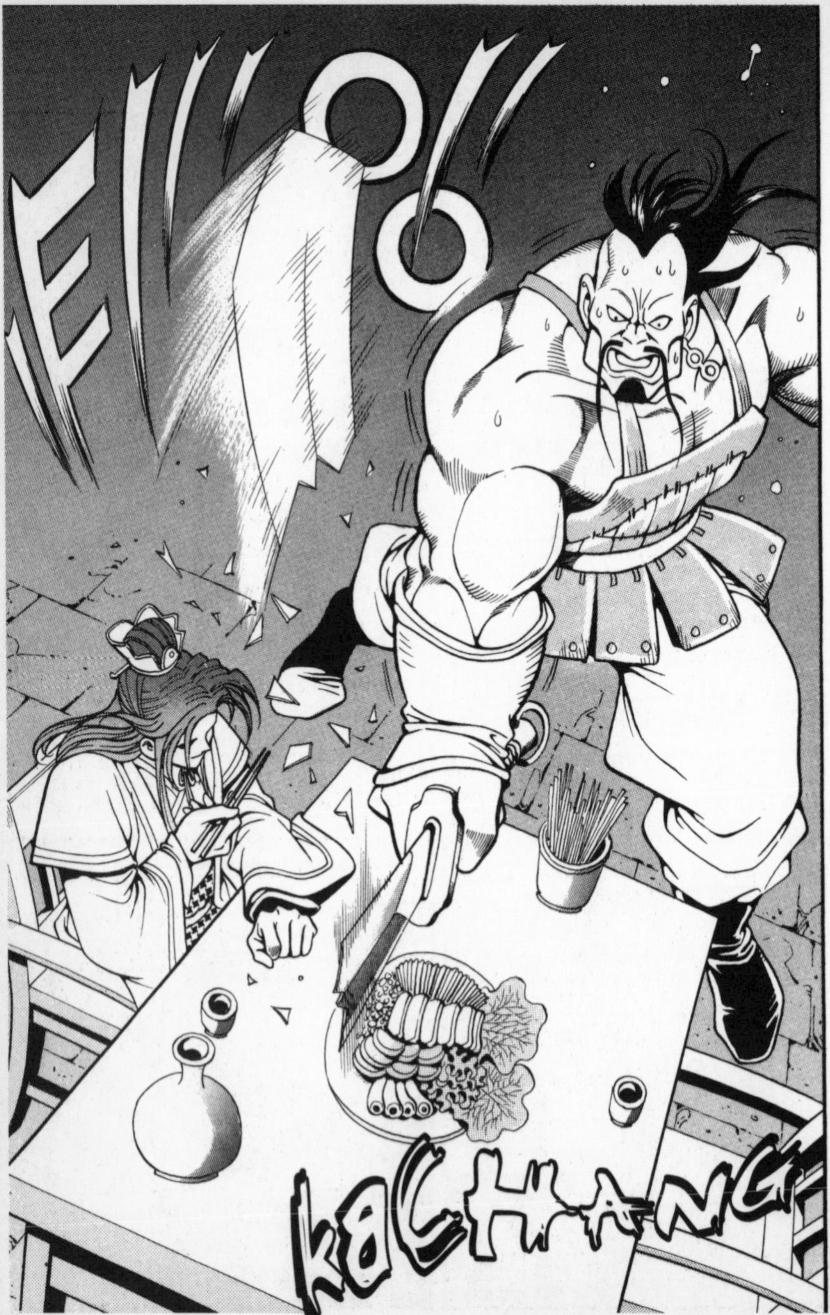
KACHANG

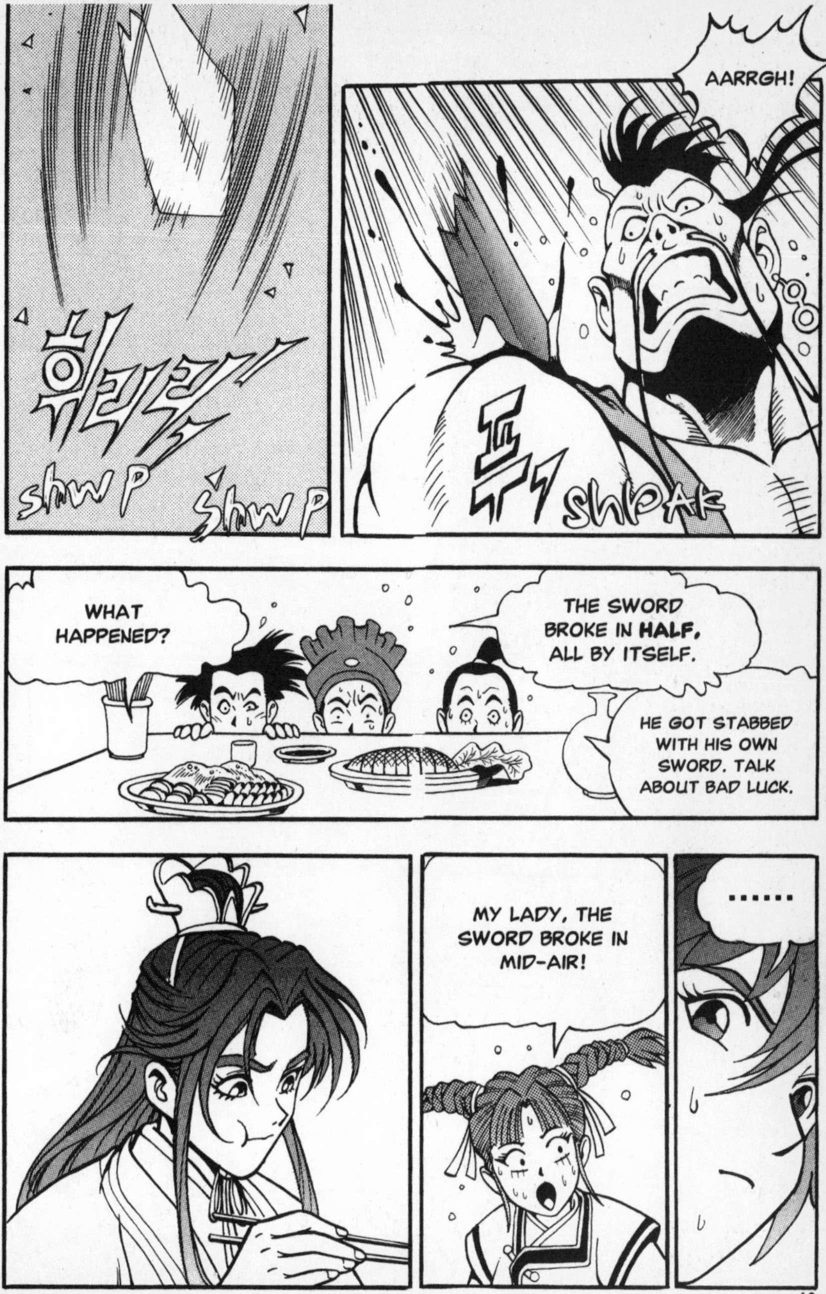

shwp
shwp
AARRGH!
SHPAK
WHAT HAPPENED?
THE SWORD BROKE IN **HALF,** ALL BY ITSELF.
HE GOT STABBED WITH HIS OWN SWORD. TALK ABOUT BAD LUCK.
MY LADY, THE SWORD BROKE IN MID-AIR!
......

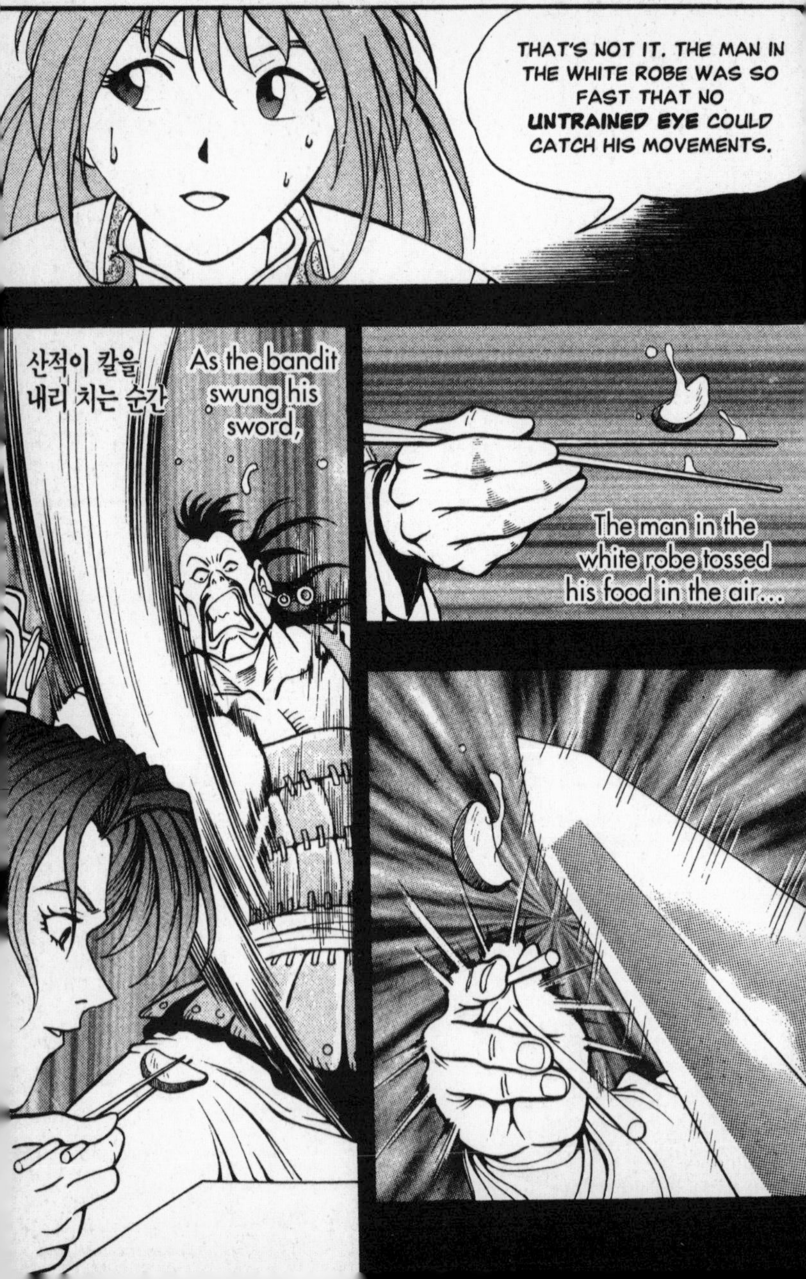

THAT'S NOT IT. THE MAN IN THE WHITE ROBE WAS SO FAST THAT NO **UNTRAINED EYE** COULD CATCH HIS MOVEMENTS.
산적이 칼을 내리 치는 순간
As the bandit swung his sword,
The man in the white robe tossed his food in the air...

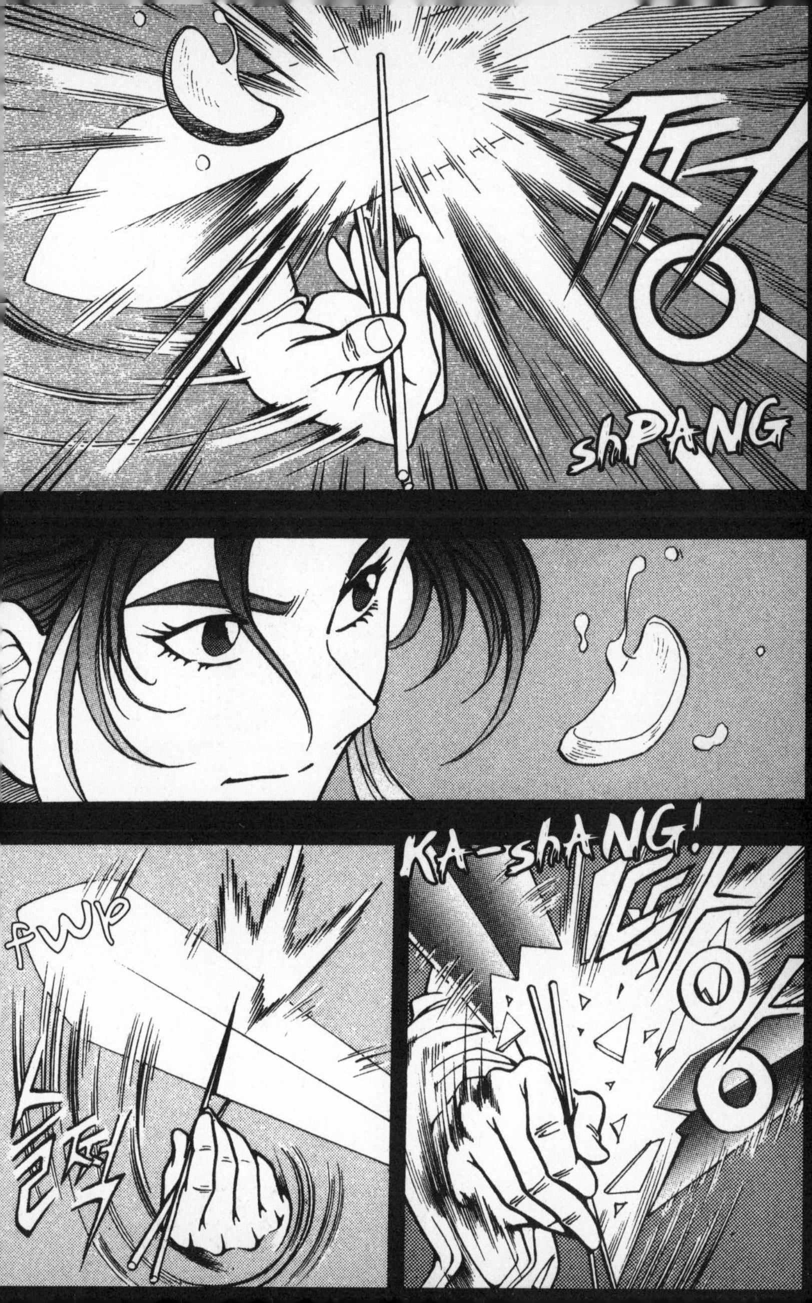
shPANG
fwp
KA-shANG!

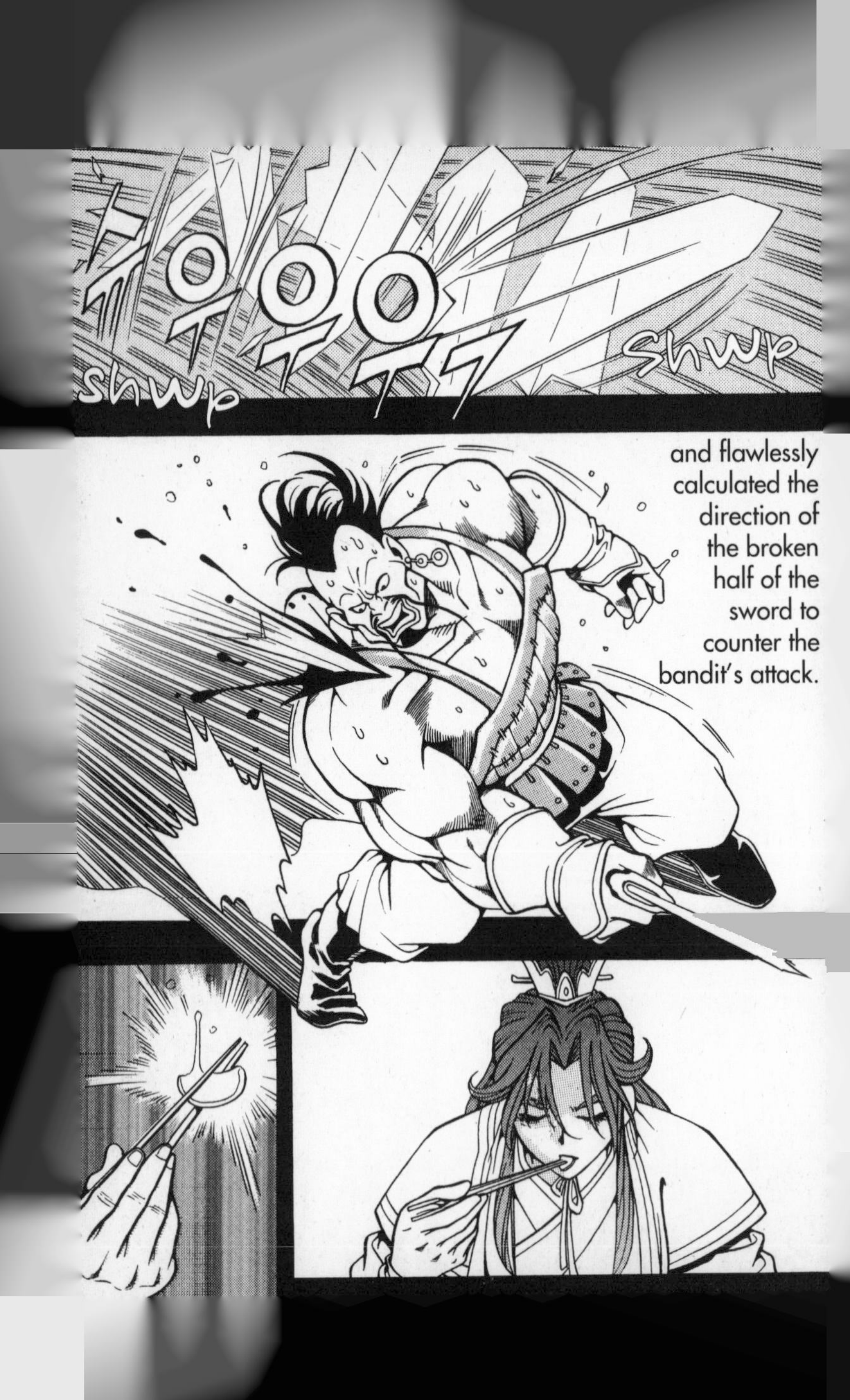

TOOOTT
shwp
shwp
and flawlessly calculated the direction of the broken half of the sword to counter the bandit's attack.

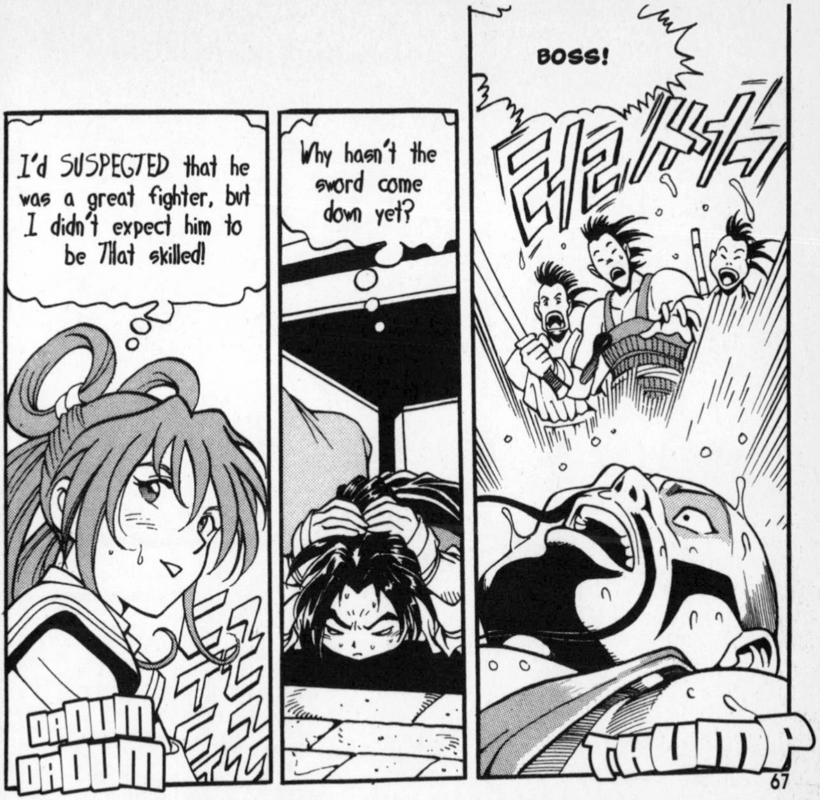
I'd SUSPECTED that he was a great fighter, but I didn't expect him to be THat skilled!
DADUM DADUM
Why hasn't the sword come down yet?
BOSS!
THUMP

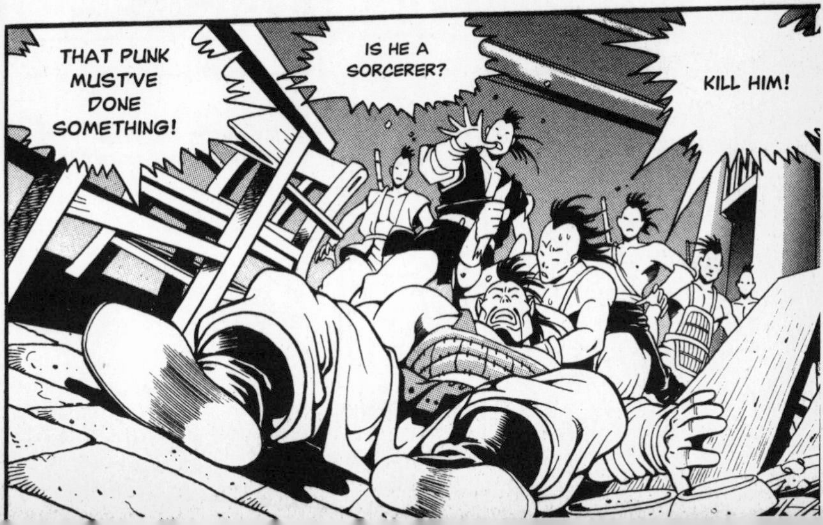
THAT PUNK MUST'VE DONE SOMETHING!
IS HE A SORCERER?
KILL HIM!

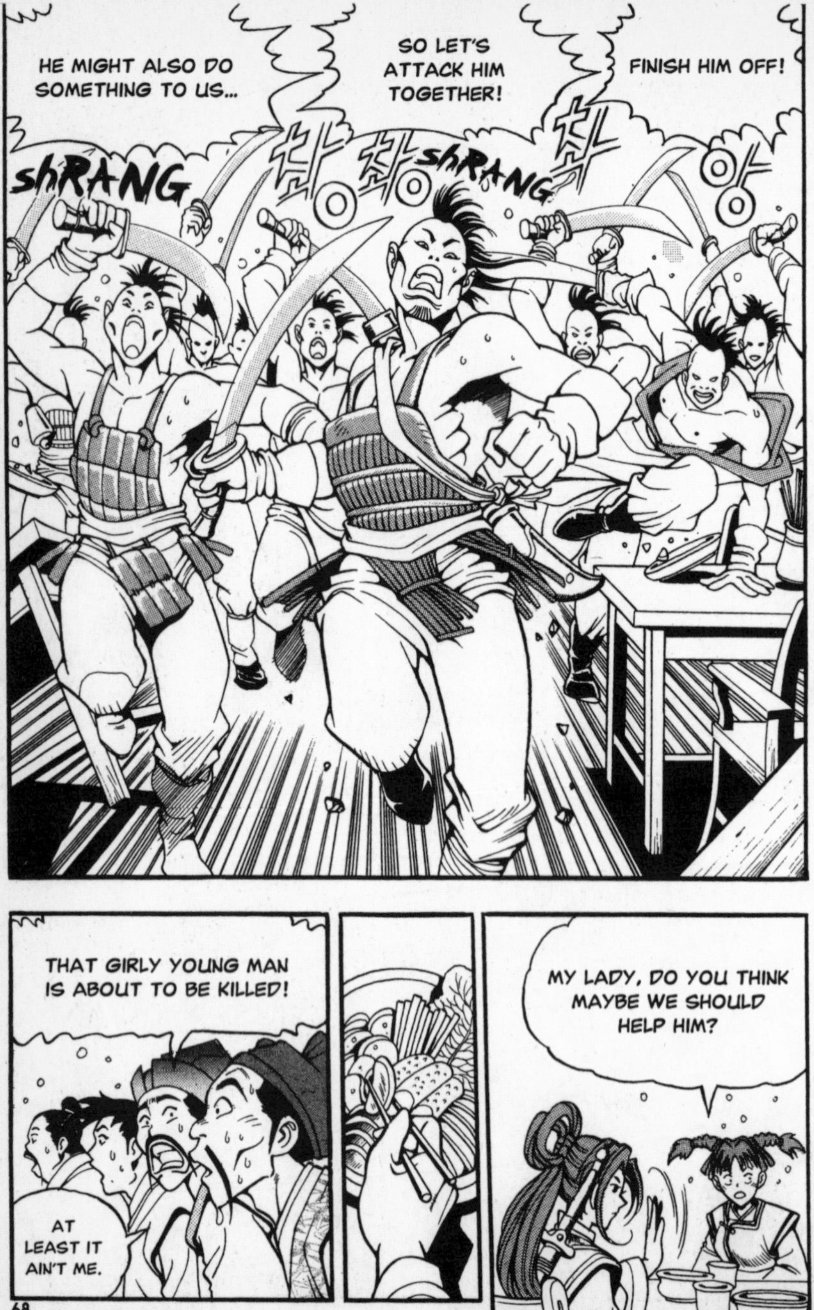
HE MIGHT ALSO DO SOMETHING TO US...
SO LET'S ATTACK HIM TOGETHER!
FINISH HIM OFF!
shRANG
shRANG
THAT GIRLY YOUNG MAN IS ABOUT TO BE KILLED!
AT LEAST IT AIN'T ME.
MY LADY, DO YOU THINK MAYBE WE SHOULD HELP HIM?

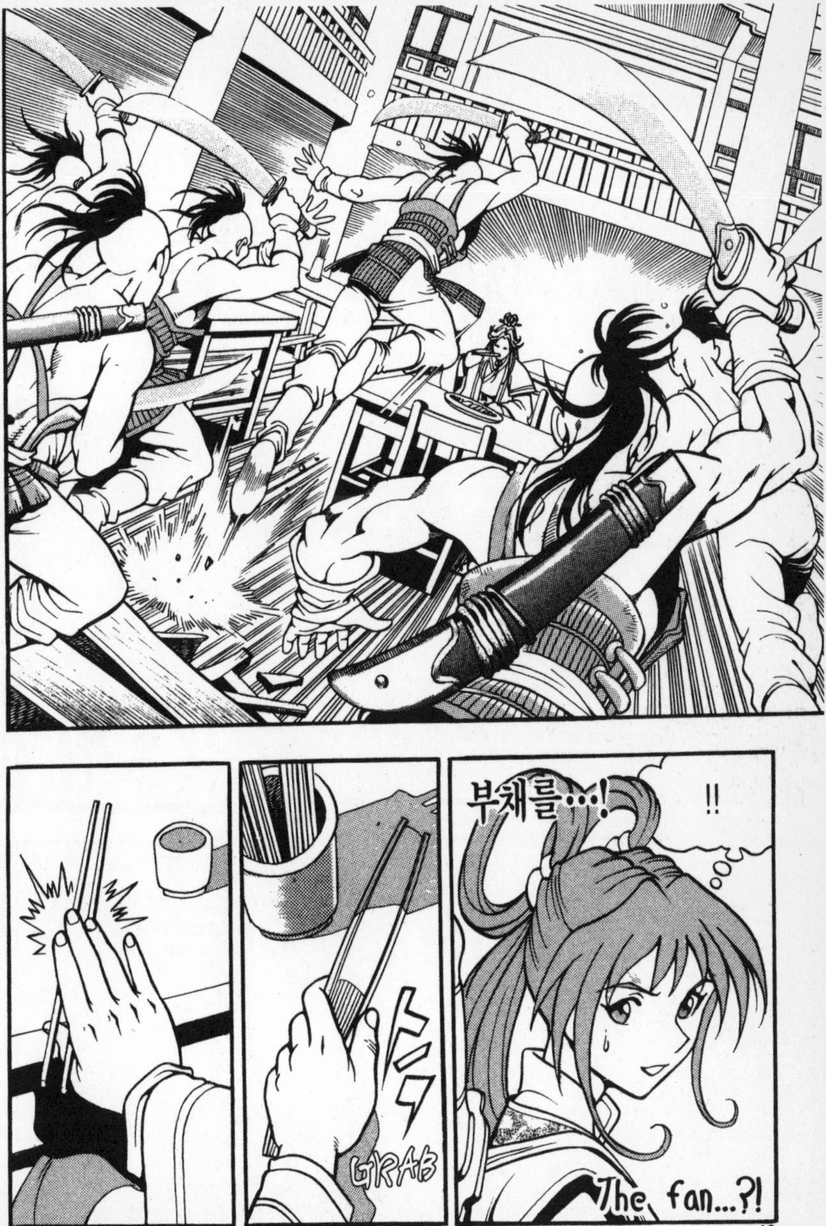
GRAB
부채를…!
!!
The fan...?!

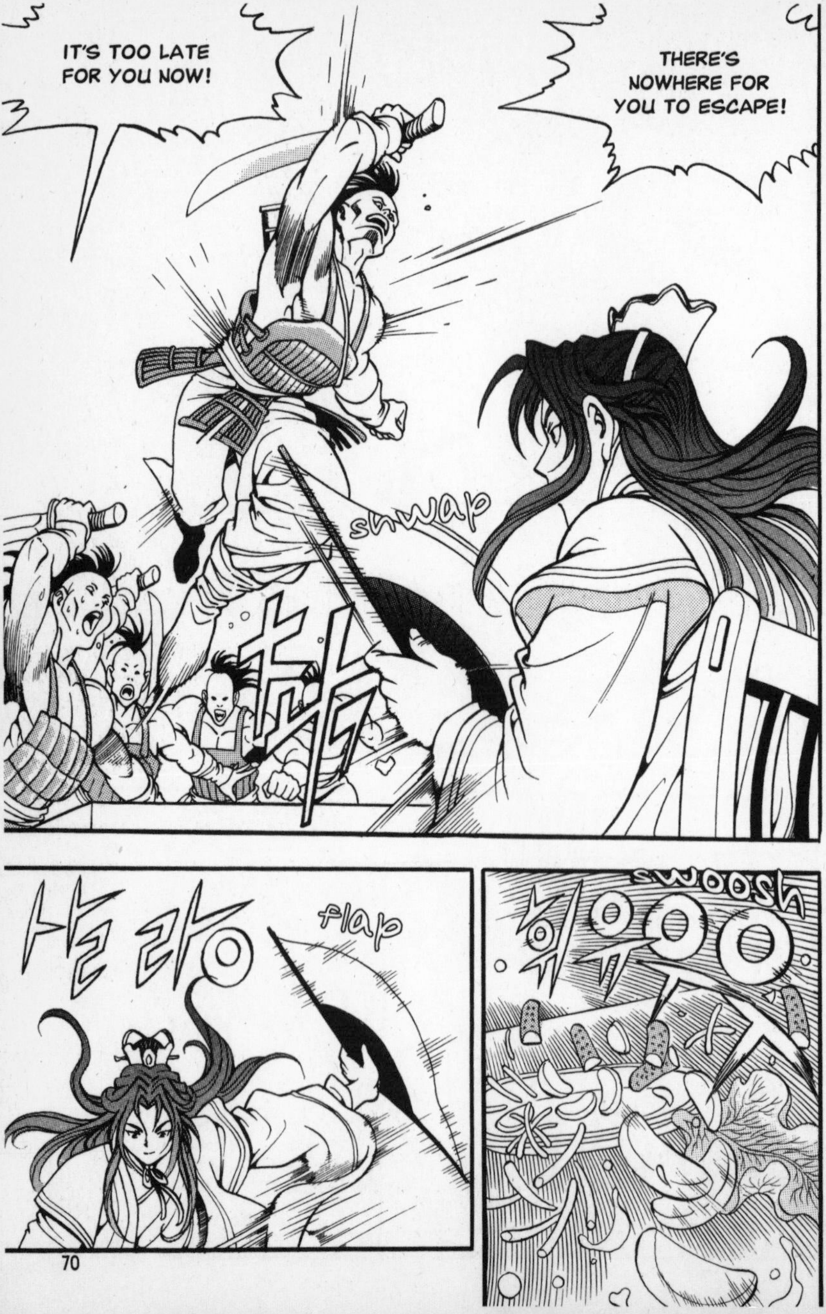
IT'S TOO LATE FOR YOU NOW!
THERE'S NOWHERE FOR YOU TO ESCAPE!
shwap
flap
swoosh

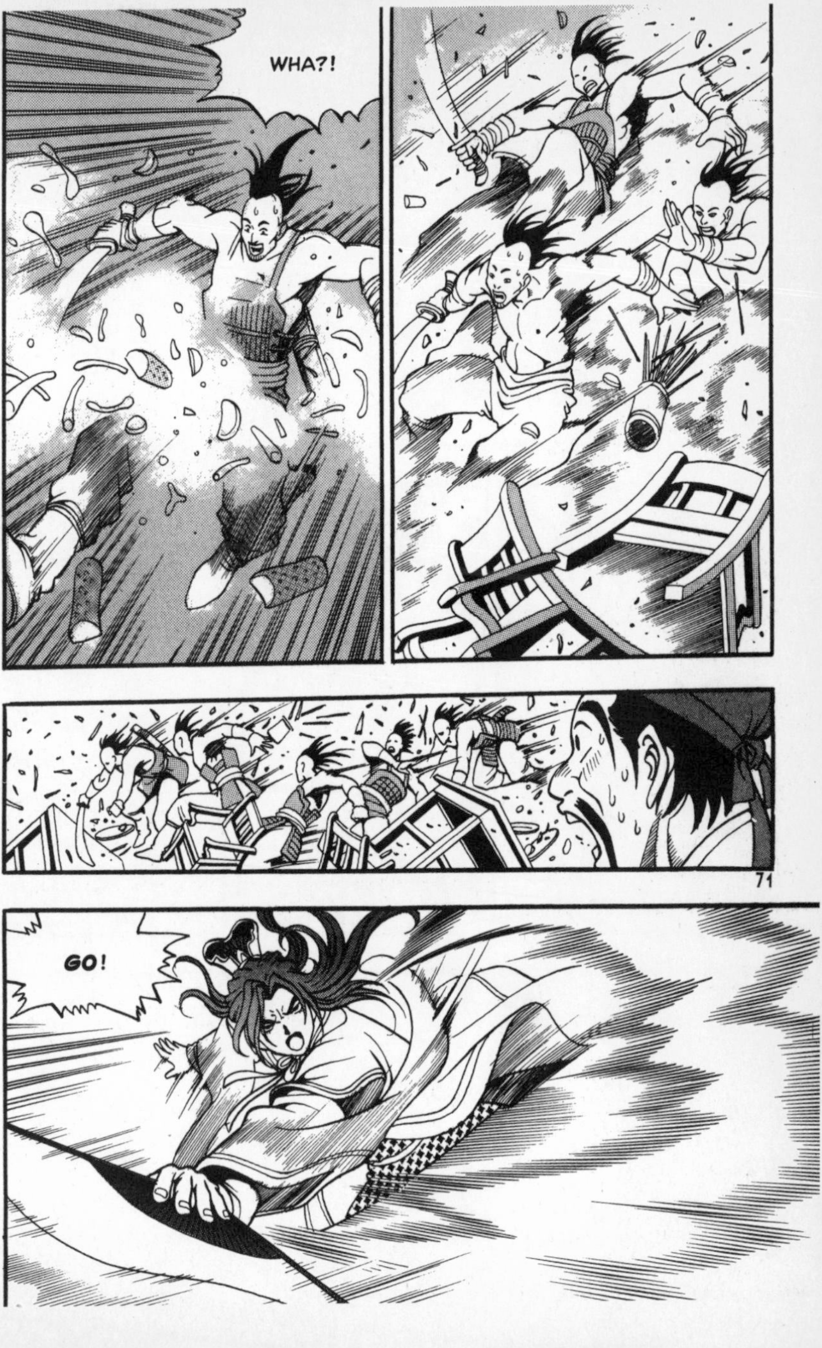
WHA?!
GO!

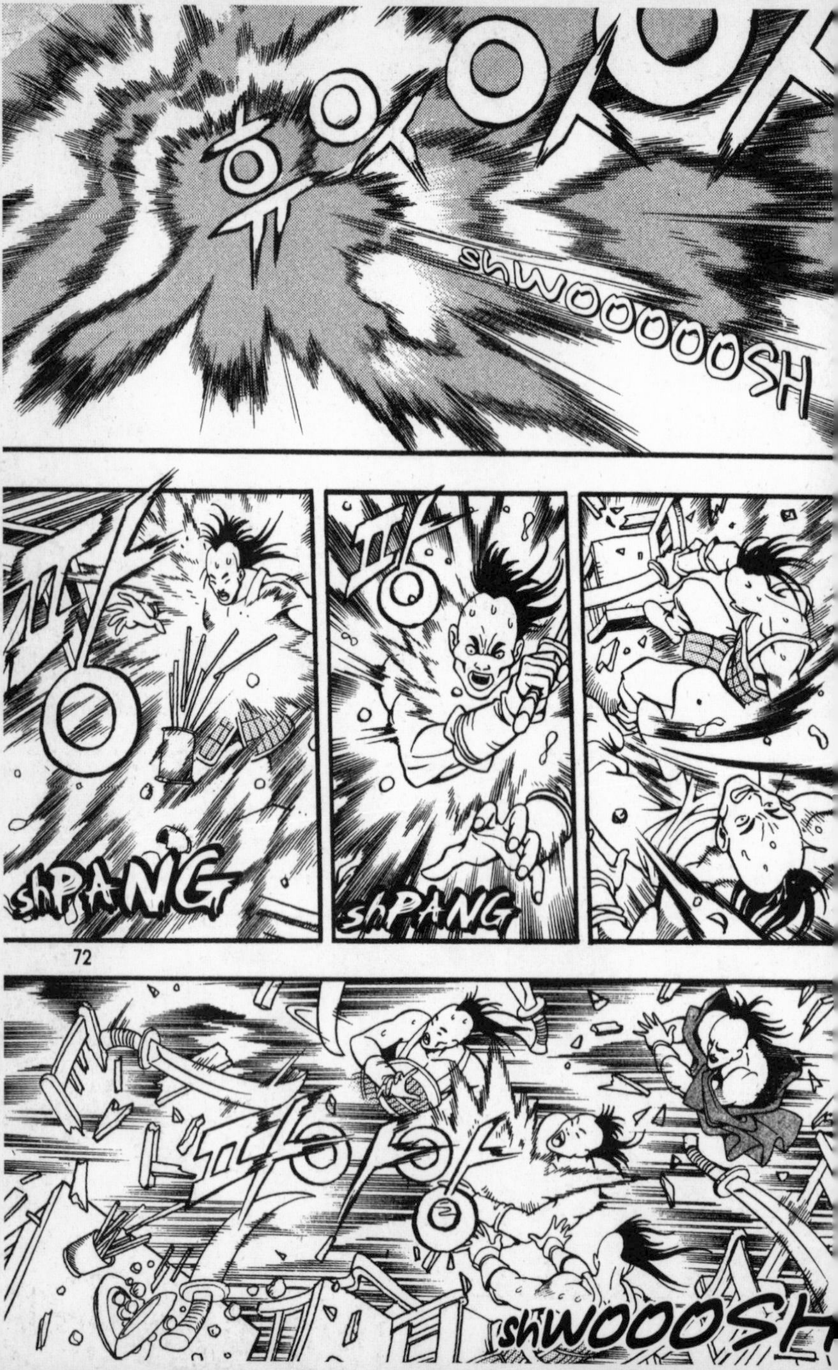
shWOOOOOOSH
shPANG
shPANG
shWOOOSH

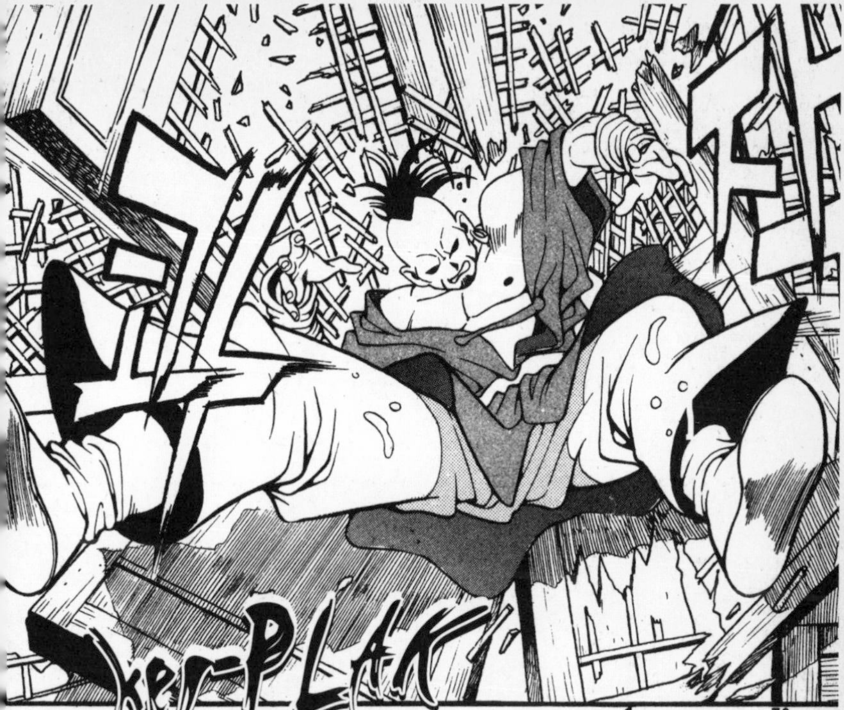
ker-PLAK

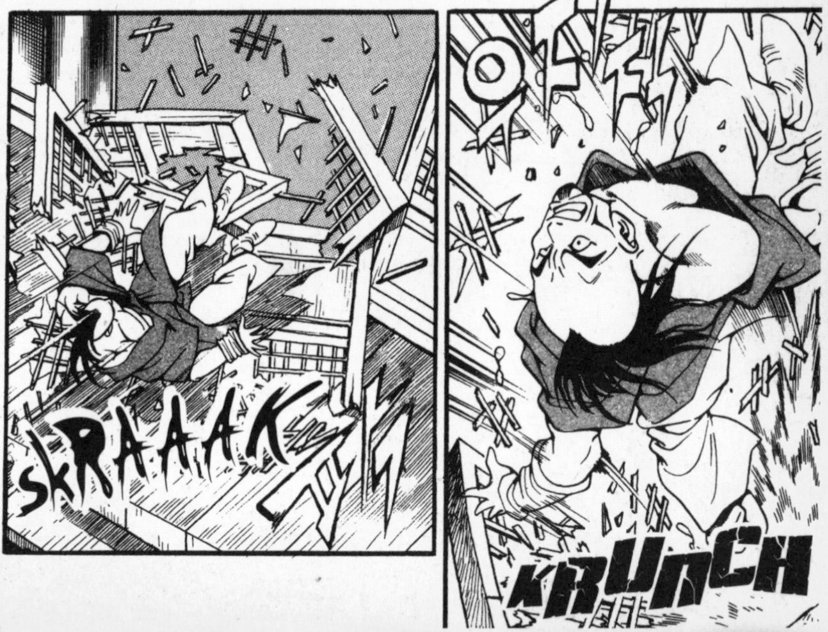
SKRAAAK
KRUNCH

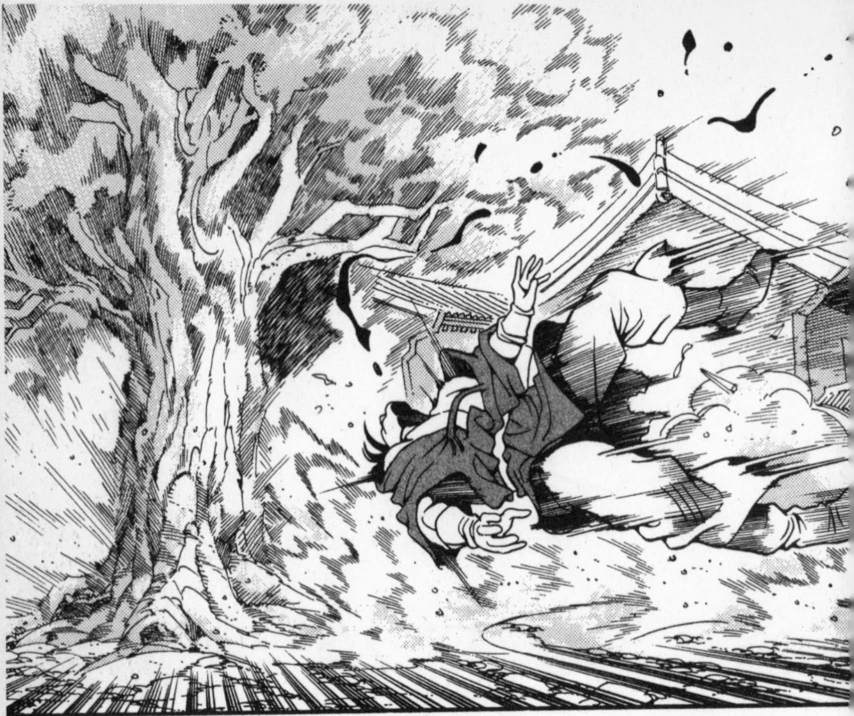

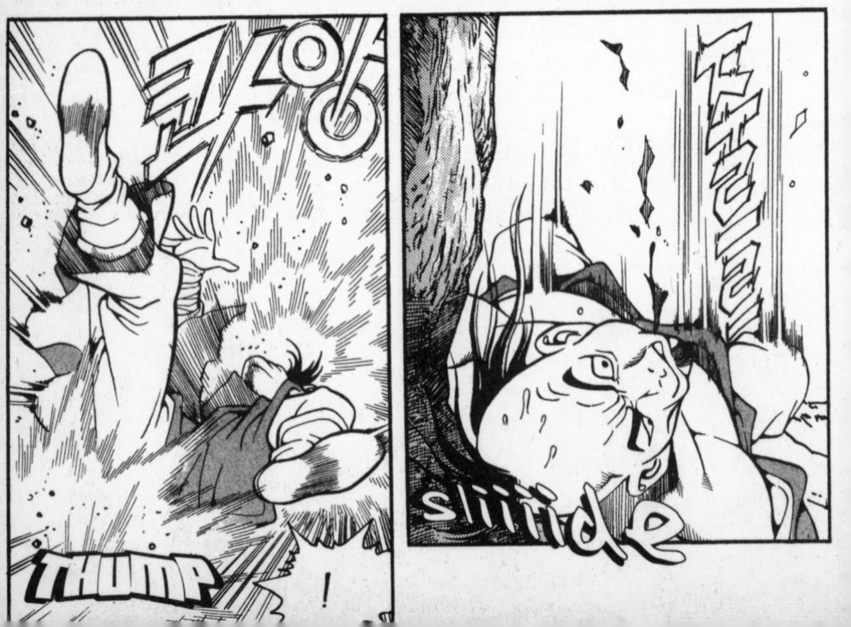
THUMP
!
sliiiide

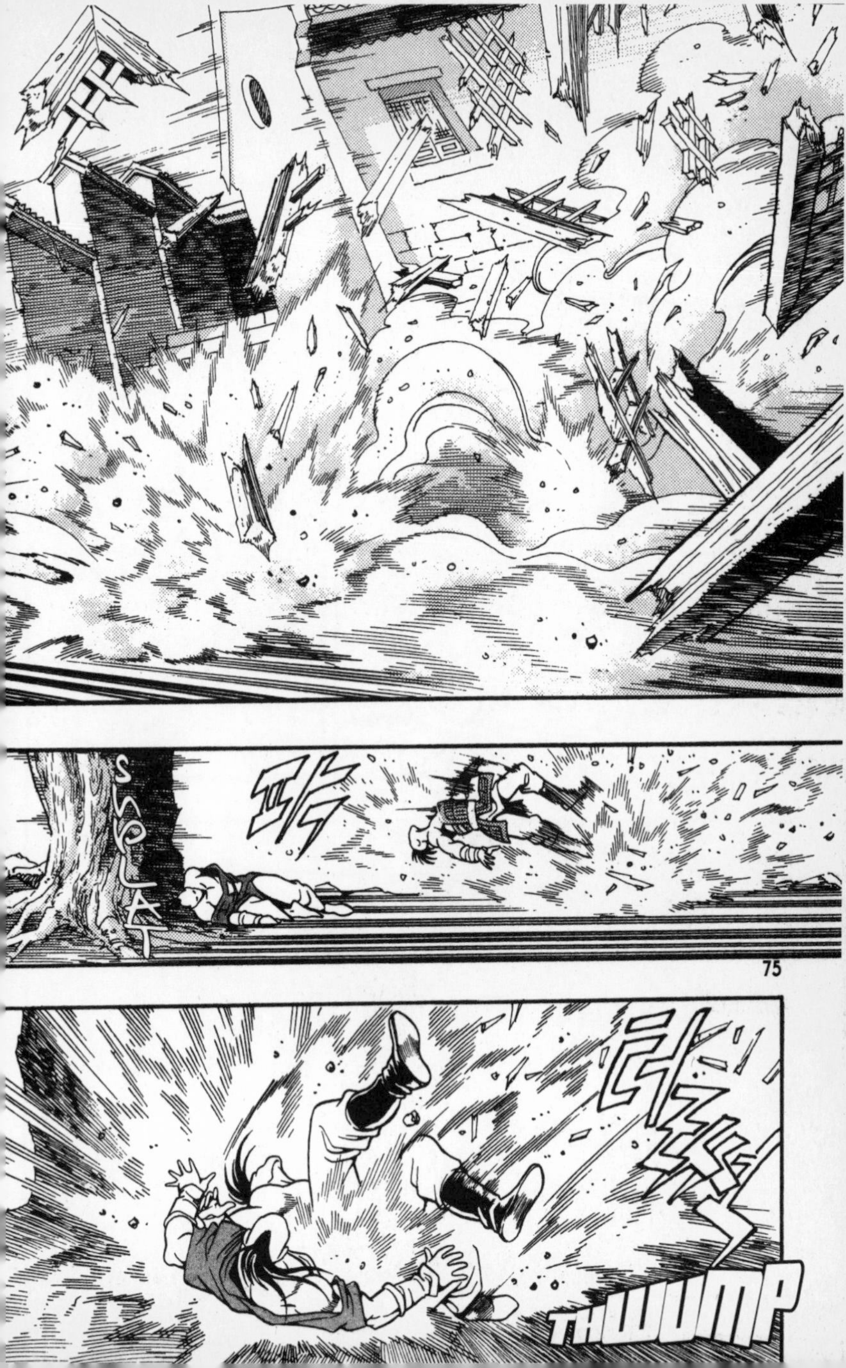
SPLAT
THWUMP

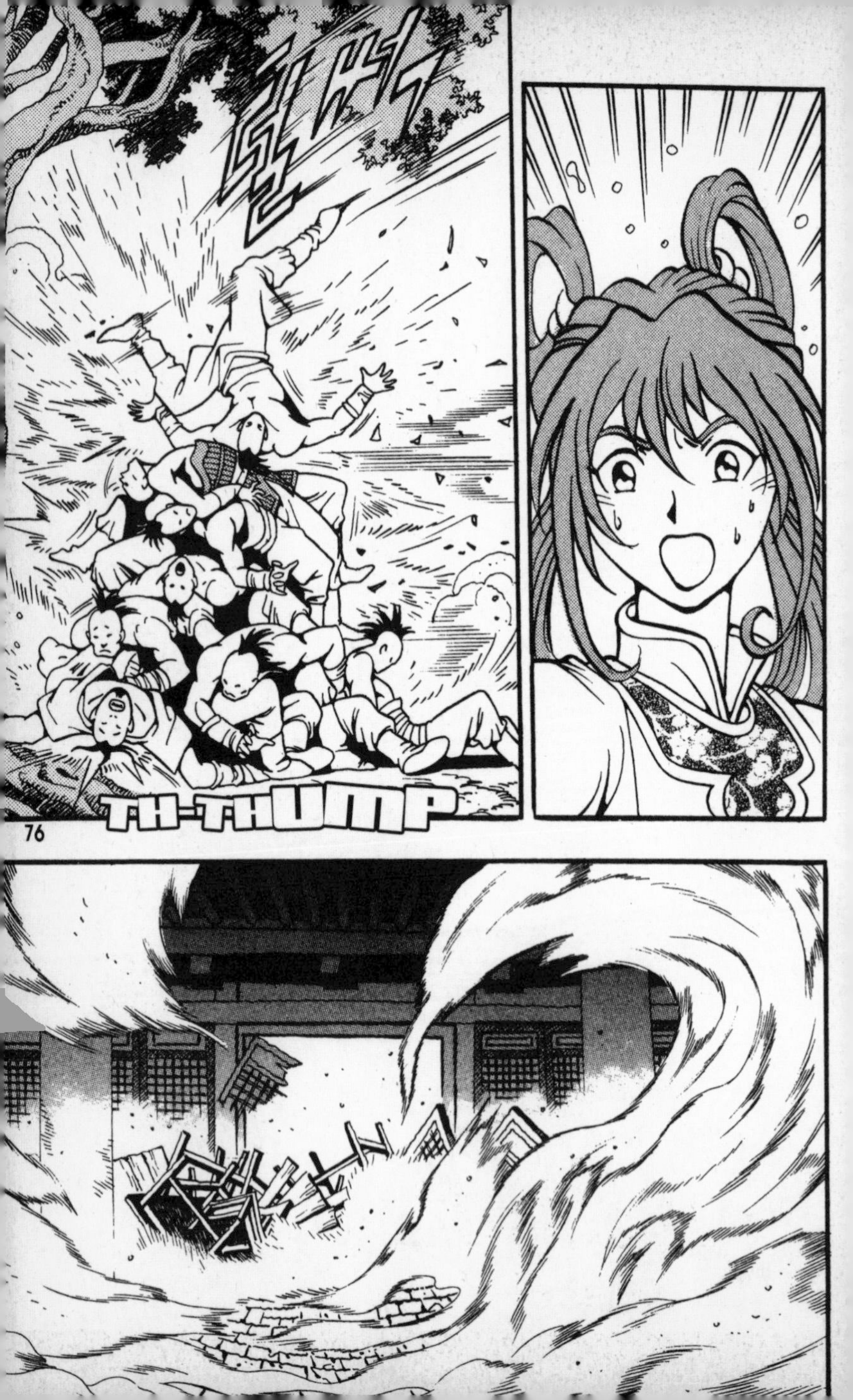
TH-THUMP

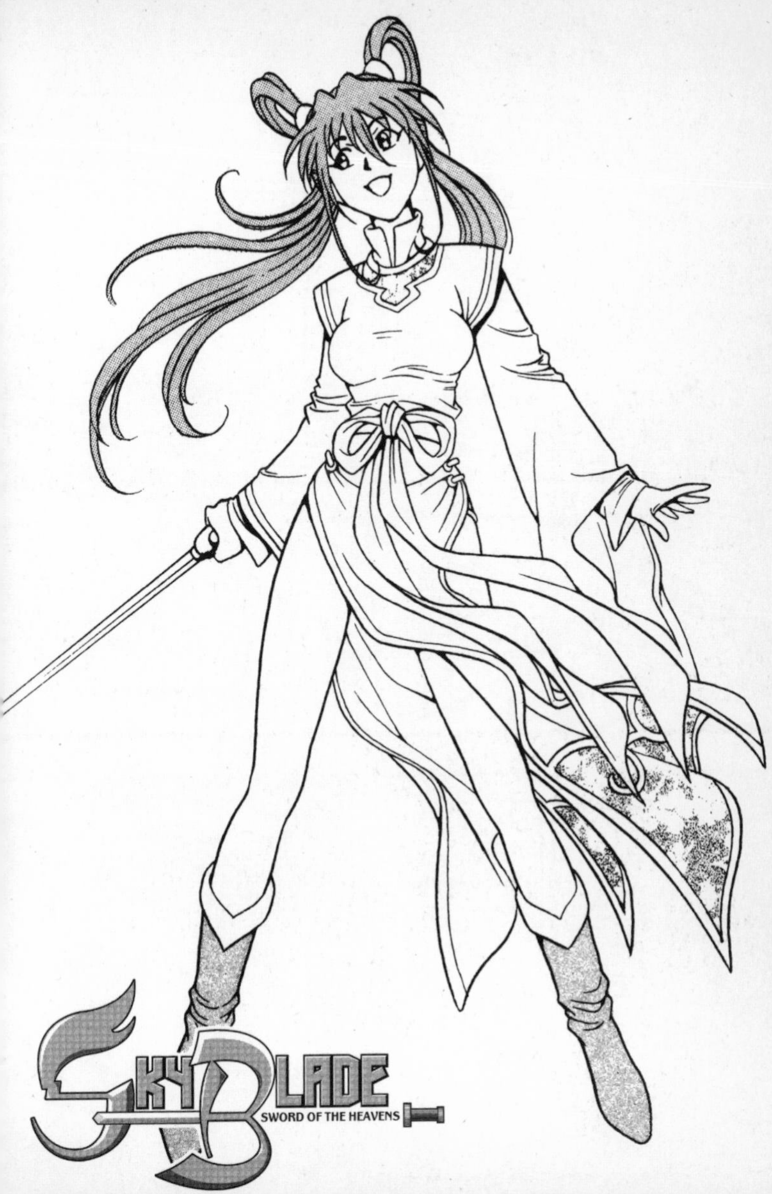
SKY BLADE
SWORD OF THE HEAVENS

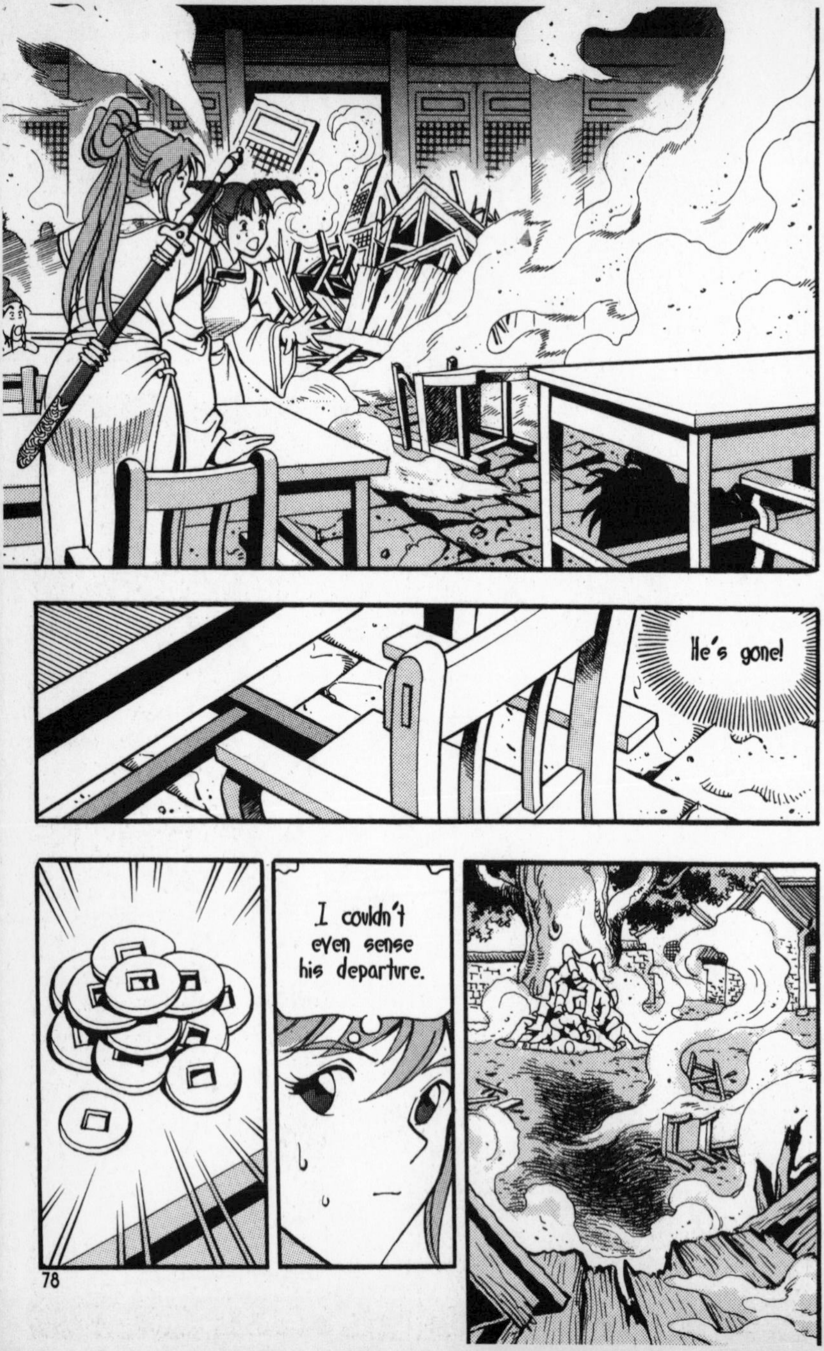
He's gone!
I couldn't even sense his departure.

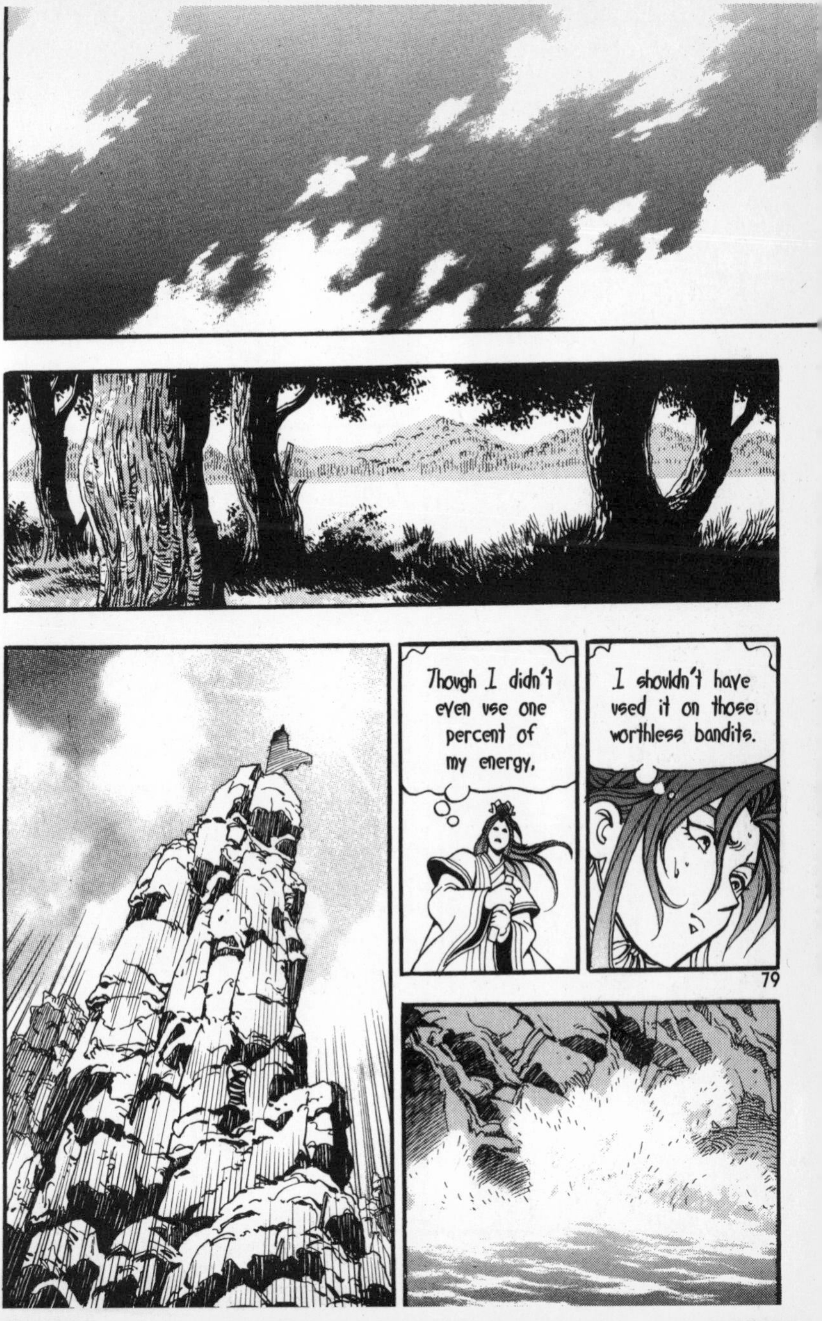

I shouldn't have used it on those worthless bandits.
Though I didn't even use one percent of my energy.

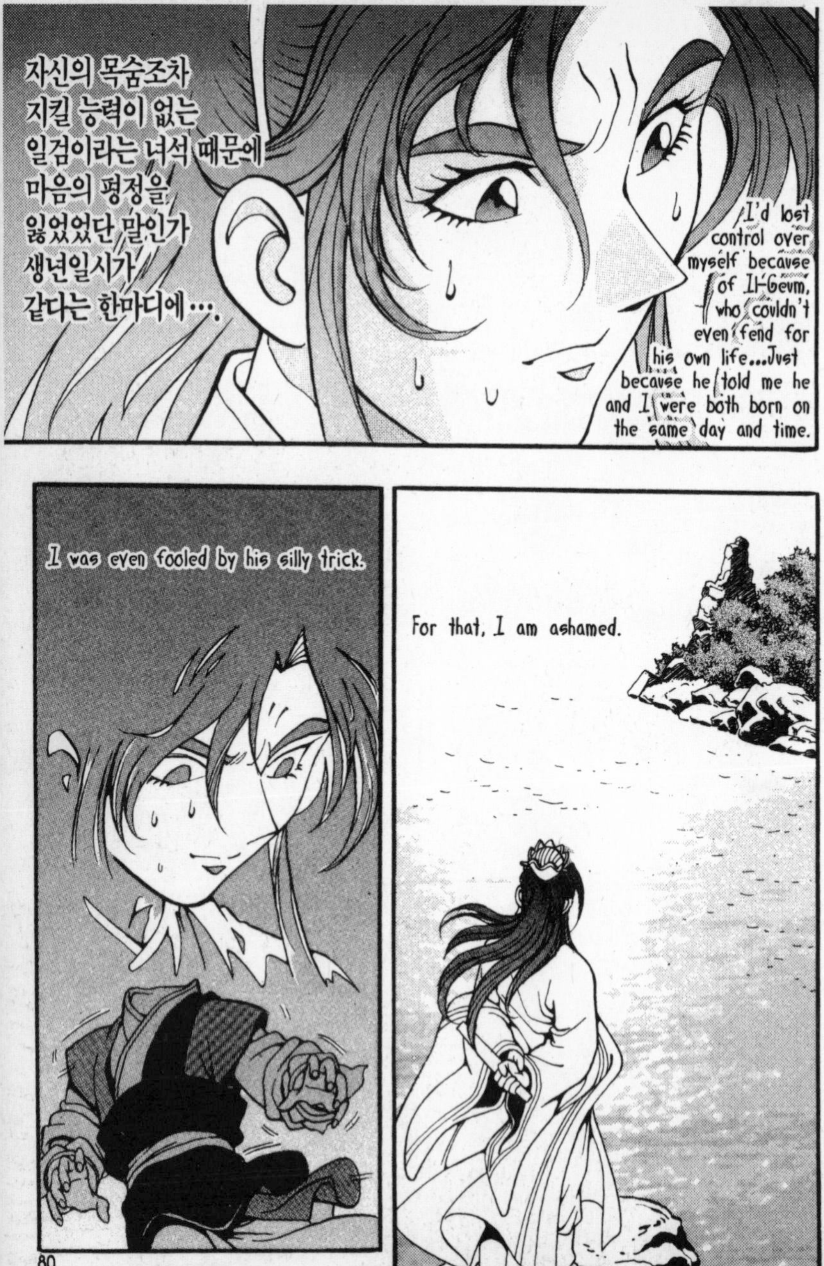
자신의 목숨조차 지킬 능력이 없는 일검이라는 녀석 때문에 마음의 평정을 잃었었단 말인가 생년일시가 같다는 한마디에….
I'd lost control over myself because of Il-Geum, who couldn't even fend for his own life...Just because he told me he and I were both born on the same day and time.
I was even fooled by his silly trick.
For that, I am ashamed.

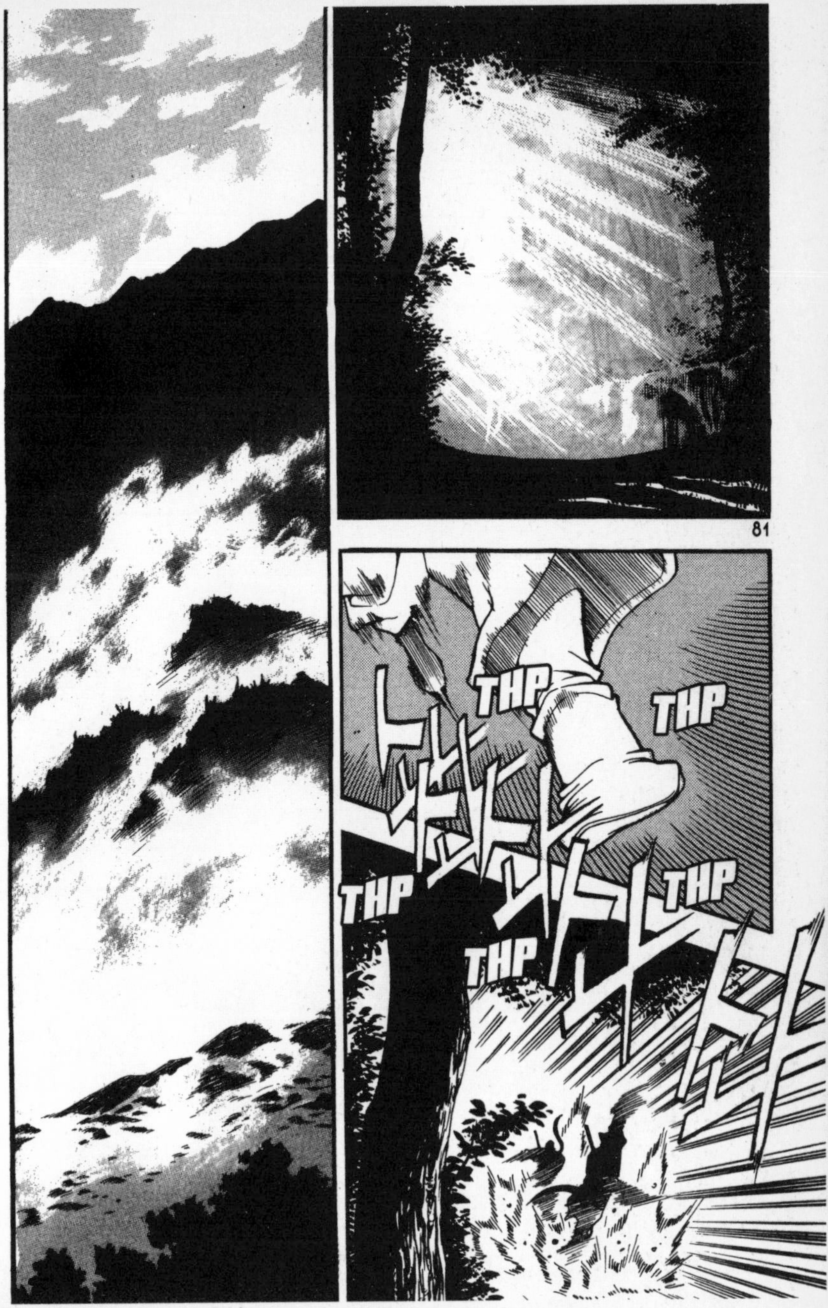
THP
THP
THP
THP
THP

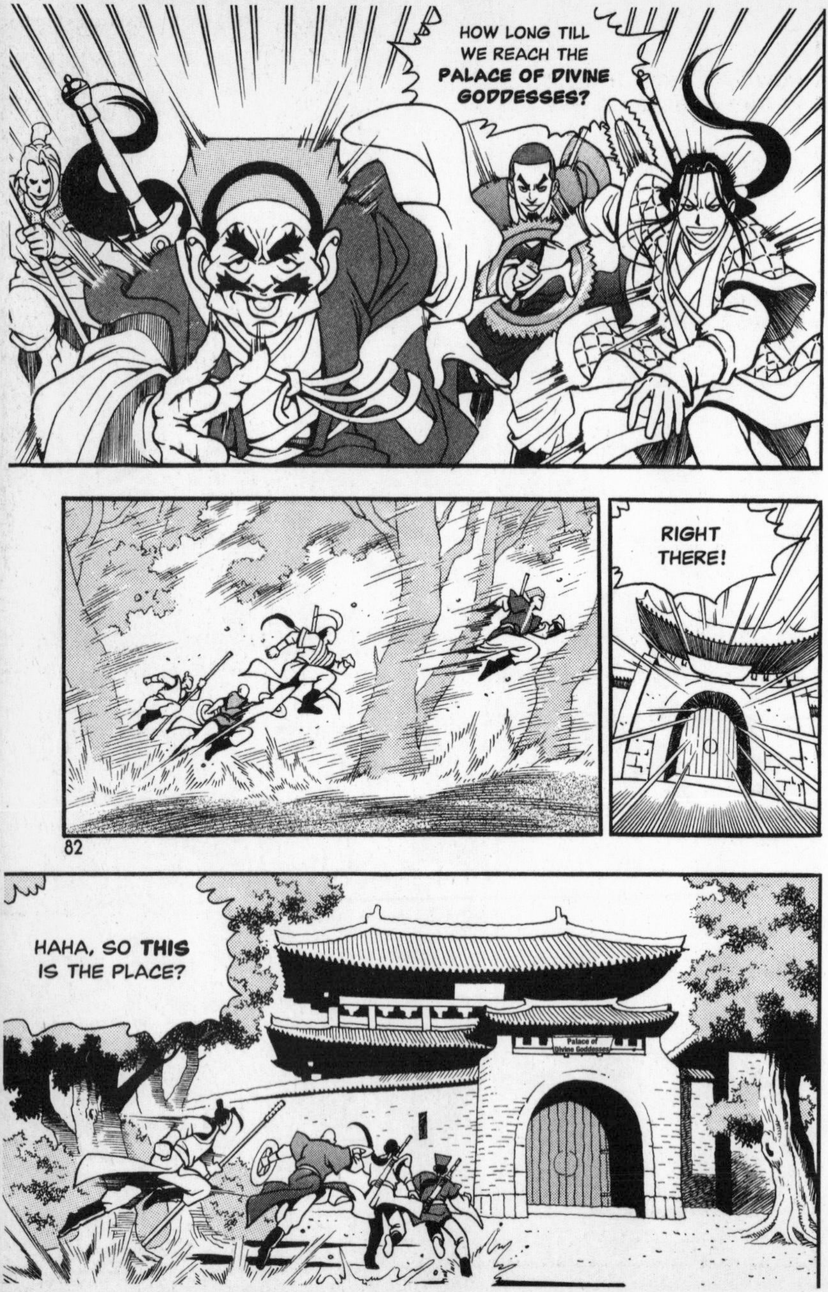
HOW LONG TILL WE REACH THE PALACE OF DIVINE GODDESSES?
RIGHT THERE!
HAHA, SO THIS IS THE PLACE?
Palace of Divine Goddesses

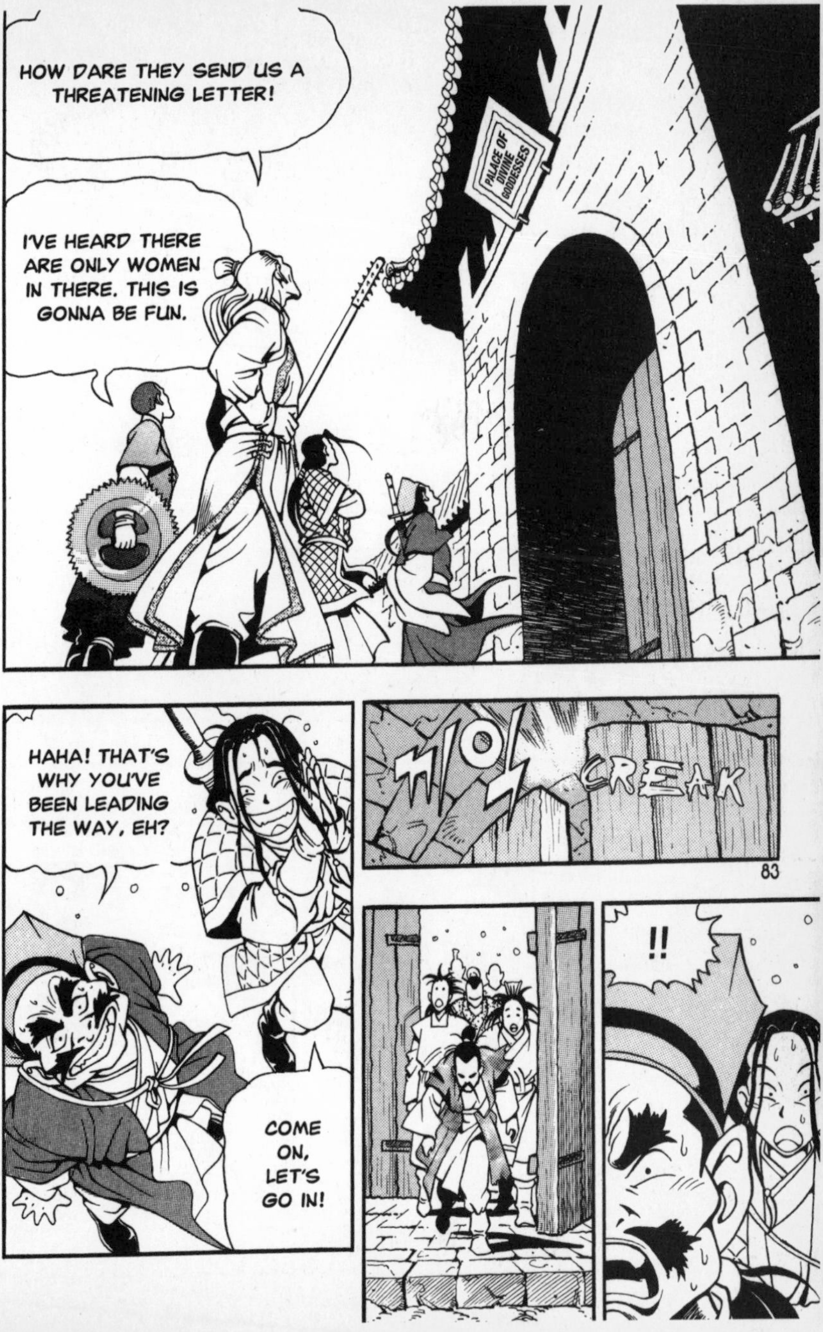
HOW DARE THEY SEND US A THREATENING LETTER!
PALACE OF DIVINE GODDESSES
I'VE HEARD THERE ARE ONLY WOMEN IN THERE. THIS IS GONNA BE FUN.
HAHA! THAT'S WHY YOU'VE BEEN LEADING THE WAY, EH?
COME ON, LET'S GO IN!
CREAK
!!

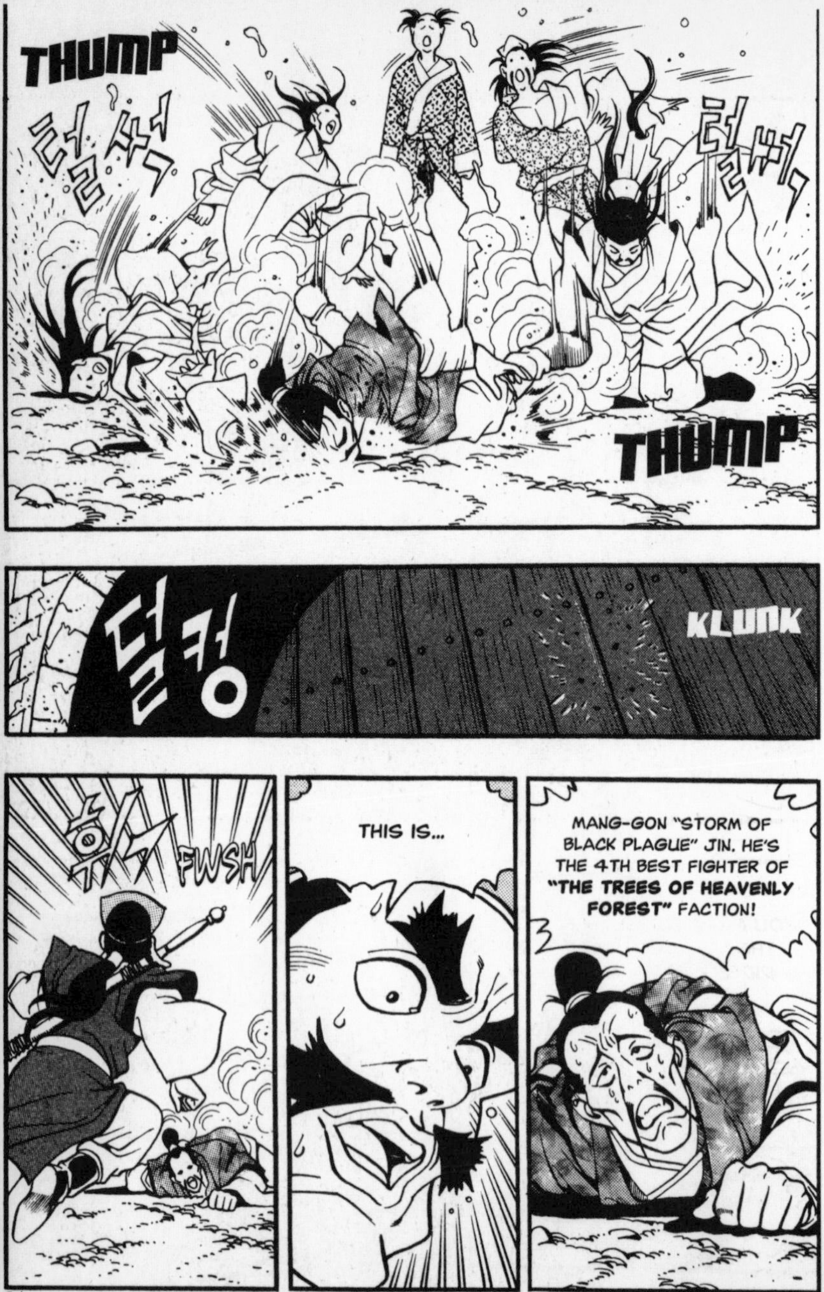
THUMP
THUMP
덜컹
KLUNK
FWSH
THIS IS...
MANG-GON "STORM OF BLACK PLAGUE" JIN. HE'S THE 4TH BEST FIGHTER OF "THE TREES OF HEAVENLY FOREST" FACTION!

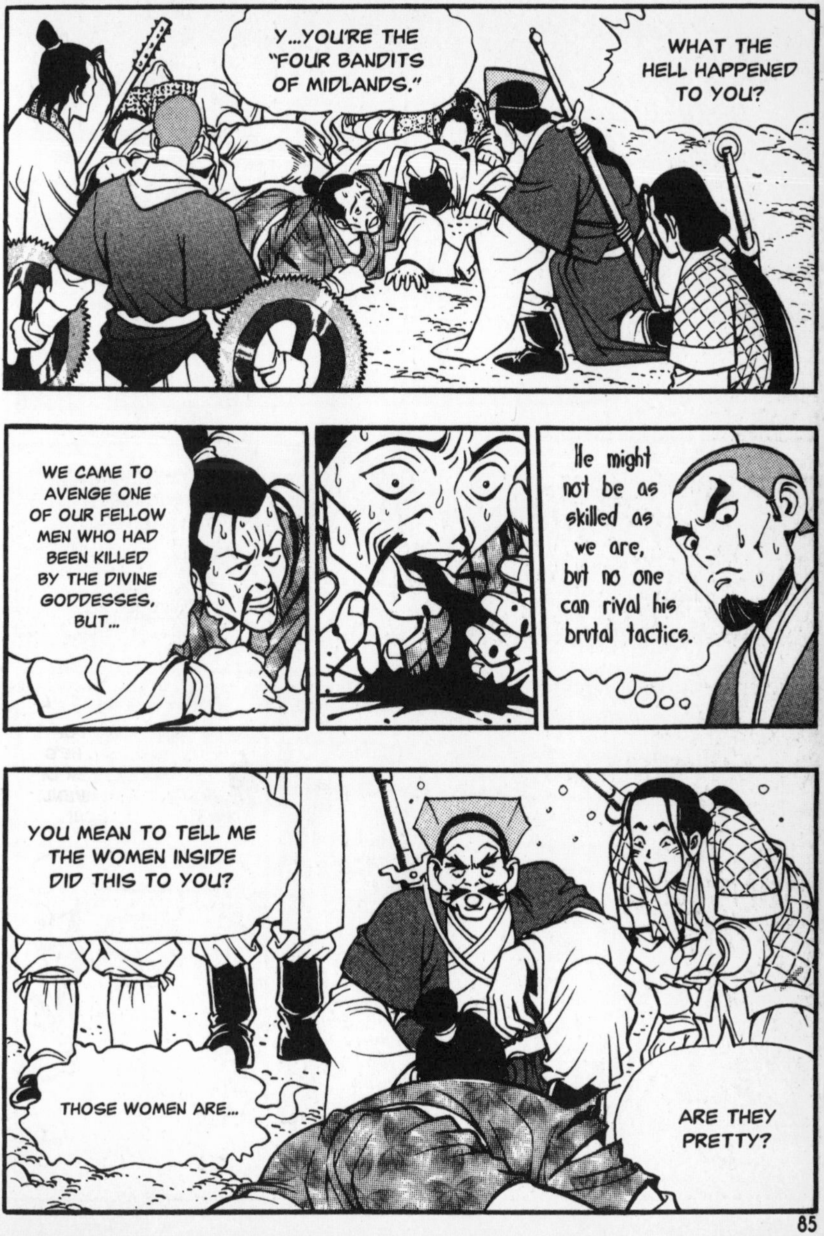
Y...YOU'RE THE "FOUR BANDITS OF MIDLANDS."
WHAT THE HELL HAPPENED TO YOU?
WE CAME TO AVENGE ONE OF OUR FELLOW MEN WHO HAD BEEN KILLED BY THE DIVINE GODDESSES, BUT...
He might not be as skilled as we are, but no one can rival his brutal tactics.
YOU MEAN TO TELL ME THE WOMEN INSIDE DID THIS TO YOU?
THOSE WOMEN ARE...
ARE THEY PRETTY?

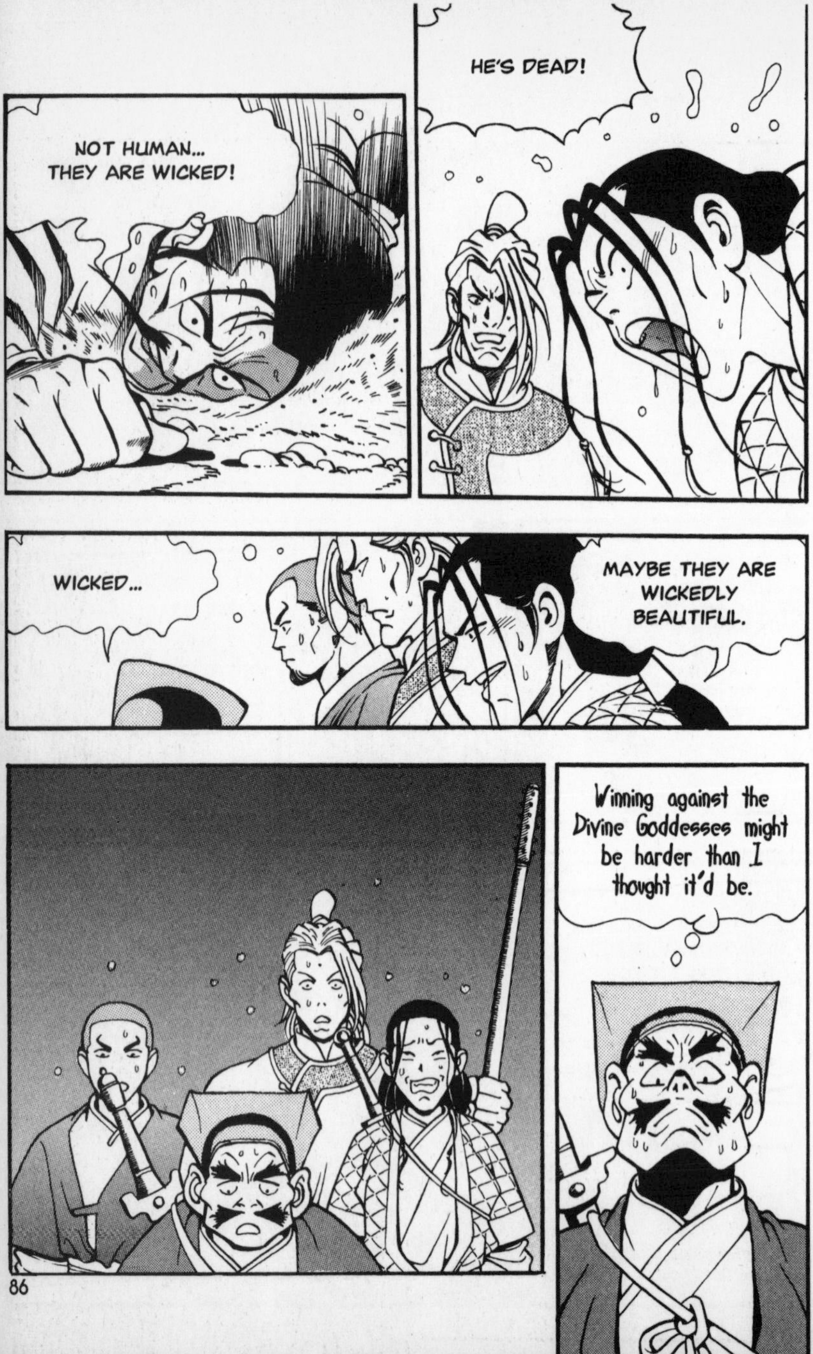
NOT HUMAN... THEY ARE WICKED!
HE'S DEAD!
WICKED...
MAYBE THEY ARE WICKEDLY BEAUTIFUL.
Winning against the Divine Goddesses might be harder than I thought it'd be.

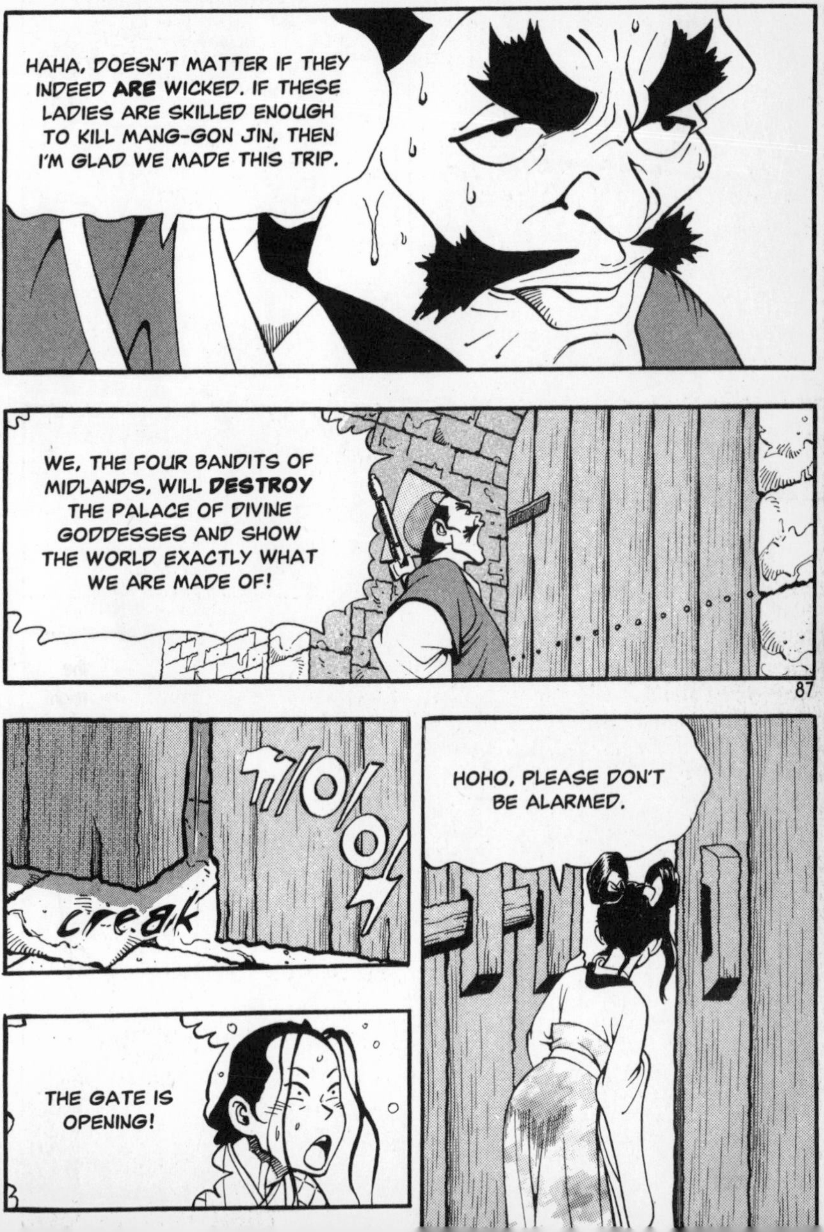
HAHA, DOESN'T MATTER IF THEY INDEED **ARE** WICKED. IF THESE LADIES ARE SKILLED ENOUGH TO KILL MANG-GON JIN, THEN I'M GLAD WE MADE THIS TRIP.
WE, THE FOUR BANDITS OF MIDLANDS, WILL **DESTROY** THE PALACE OF DIVINE GODDESSES AND SHOW THE WORLD EXACTLY WHAT WE ARE MADE OF!
creak
THE GATE IS OPENING!
HOHO, PLEASE DON'T BE ALARMED.

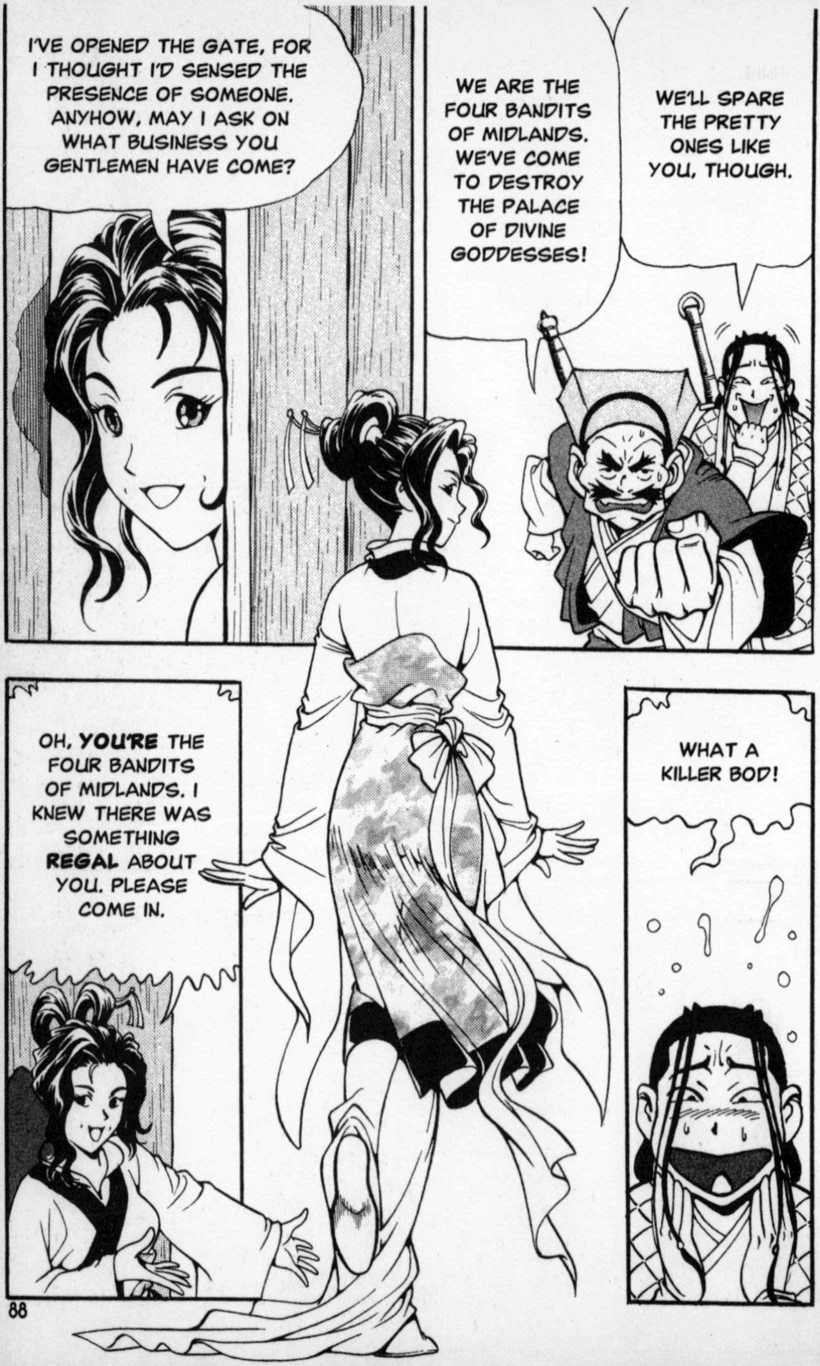
I'VE OPENED THE GATE, FOR I THOUGHT I'D SENSED THE PRESENCE OF SOMEONE. ANYHOW, MAY I ASK ON WHAT BUSINESS YOU GENTLEMEN HAVE COME?
WE ARE THE FOUR BANDITS OF MIDLANDS. WE'VE COME TO DESTROY THE PALACE OF DIVINE GODDESSES!
WE'LL SPARE THE PRETTY ONES LIKE YOU, THOUGH.
OH, **YOU'RE** THE FOUR BANDITS OF MIDLANDS. I KNEW THERE WAS SOMETHING **REGAL** ABOUT YOU. PLEASE COME IN.
WHAT A KILLER BOD!

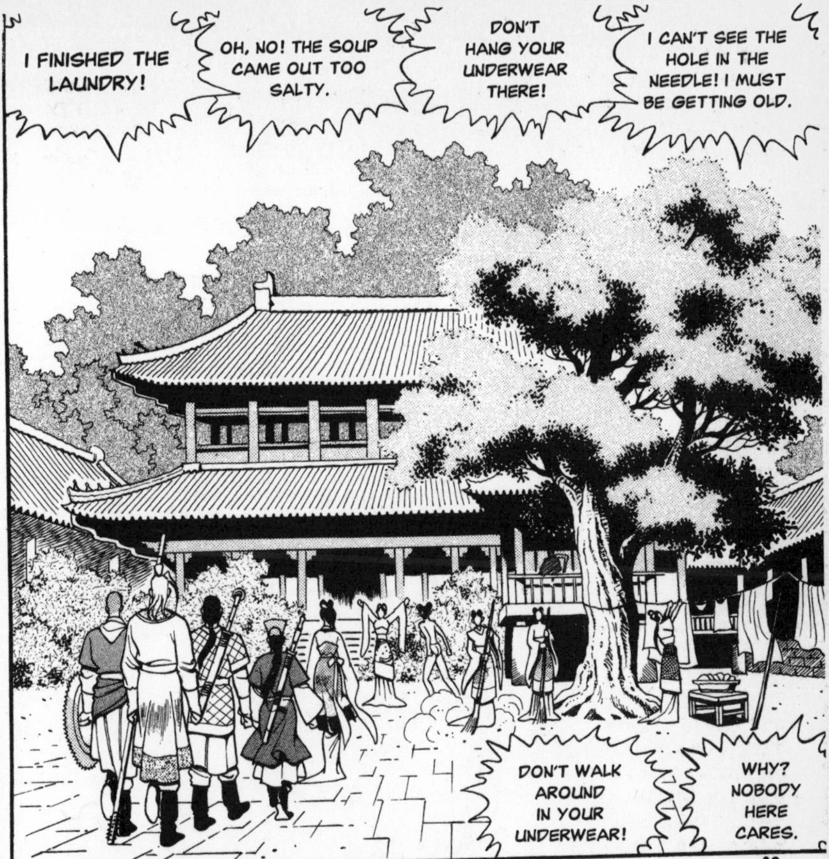
I FINISHED THE LAUNDRY!
OH, NO! THE SOUP CAME OUT TOO SALTY.
DON'T HANG YOUR UNDERWEAR THERE!
I CAN'T SEE THE HOLE IN THE NEEDLE! I MUST BE GETTING OLD.
DON'T WALK AROUND IN YOUR UNDERWEAR!
WHY? NOBODY HERE CARES.

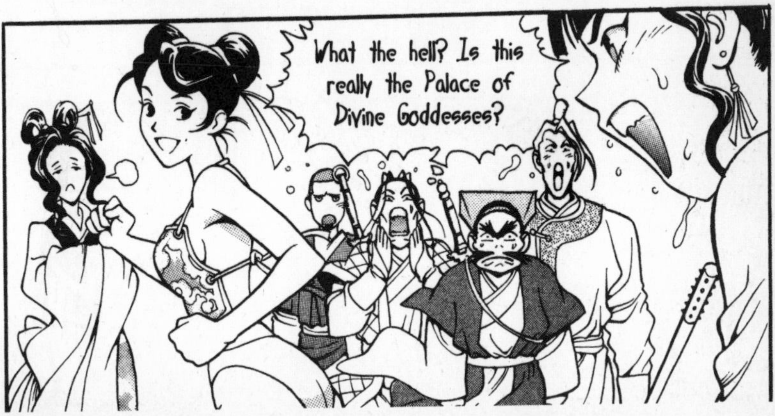
What the hell? Is this really the Palace of Divine Goddesses?

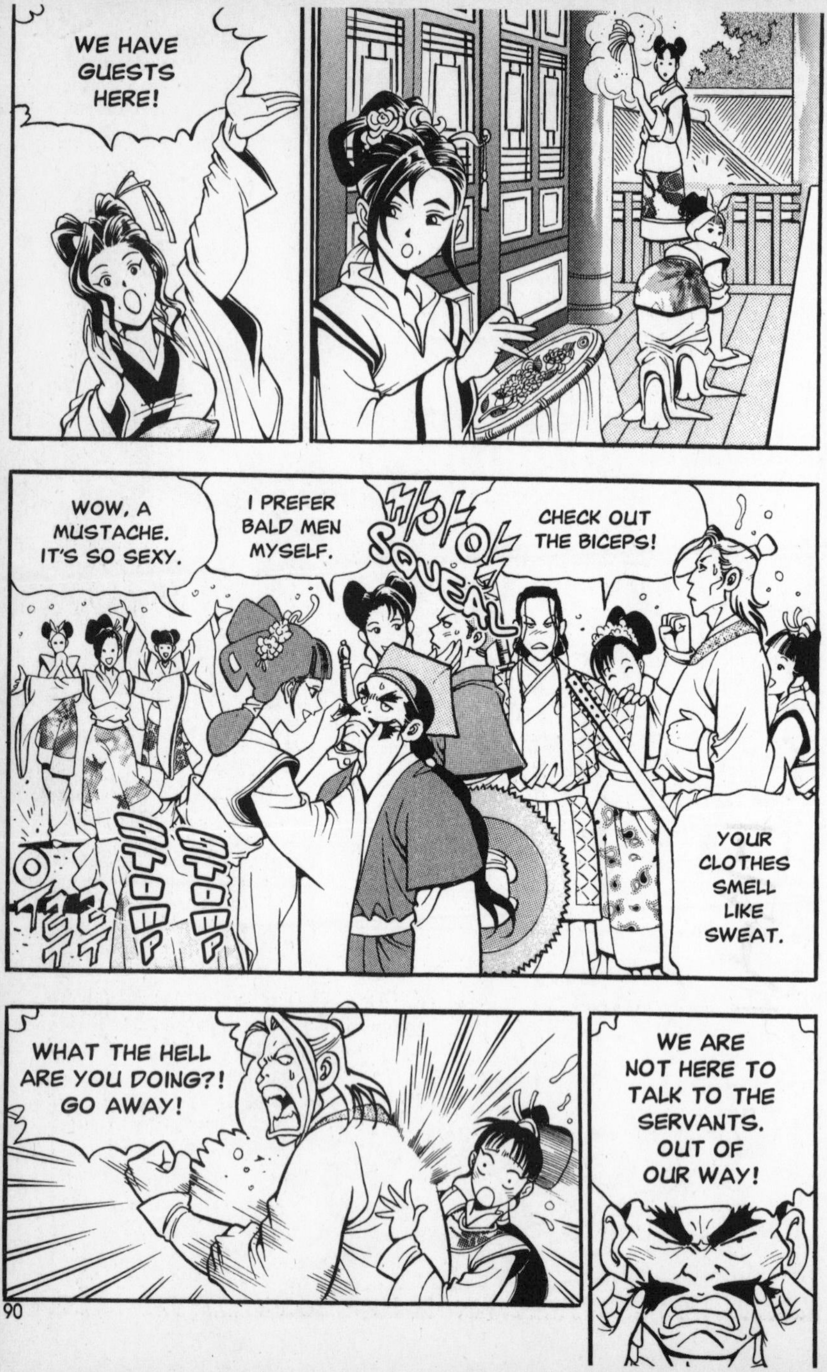
WE HAVE GUESTS HERE!
WOW, A MUSTACHE. IT'S SO SEXY.
I PREFER BALD MEN MYSELF.
SQUEAL
CHECK OUT THE BICEPS!
YOUR CLOTHES SMELL LIKE SWEAT.
STOMP STOMP
WHAT THE HELL ARE YOU DOING?! GO AWAY!
WE ARE NOT HERE TO TALK TO THE SERVANTS. OUT OF OUR WAY!

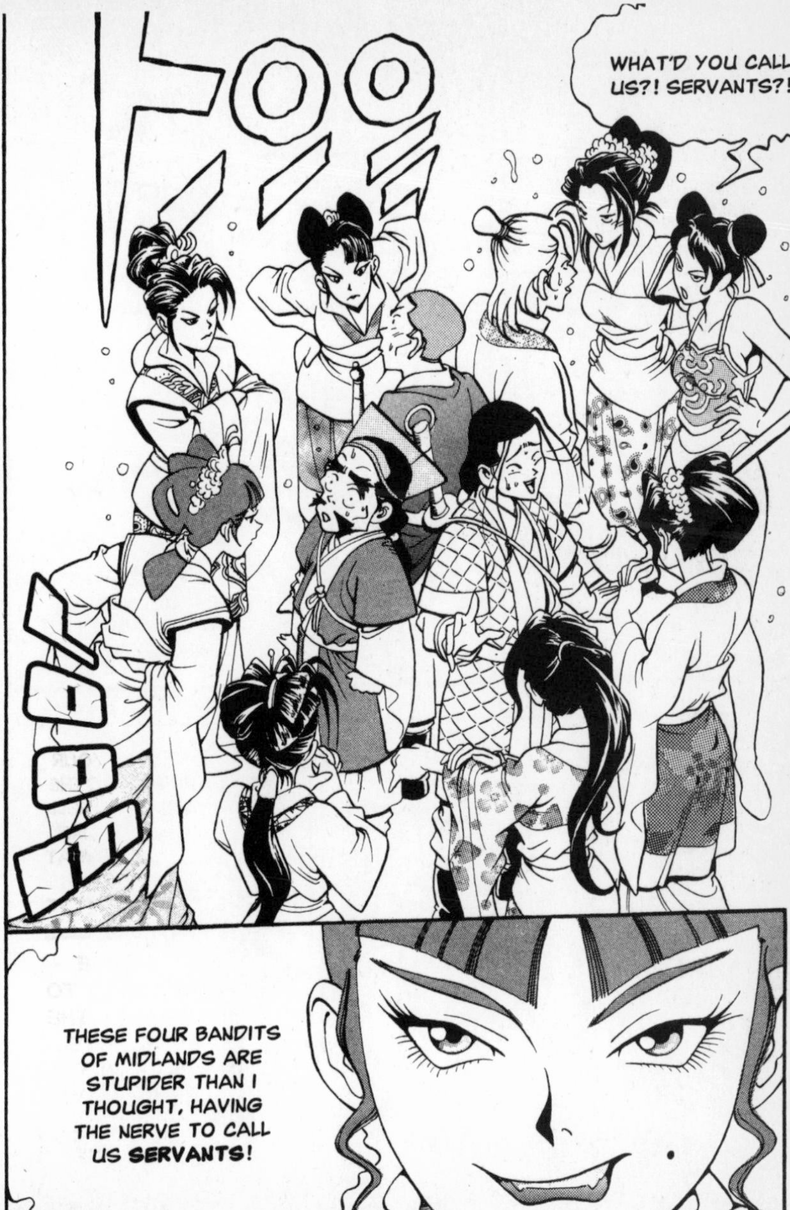
WHAT'D YOU CALL US?! SERVANTS?!
THESE FOUR BANDITS OF MIDLANDS ARE STUPIDER THAN I THOUGHT, HAVING THE NERVE TO CALL US **SERVANTS**!

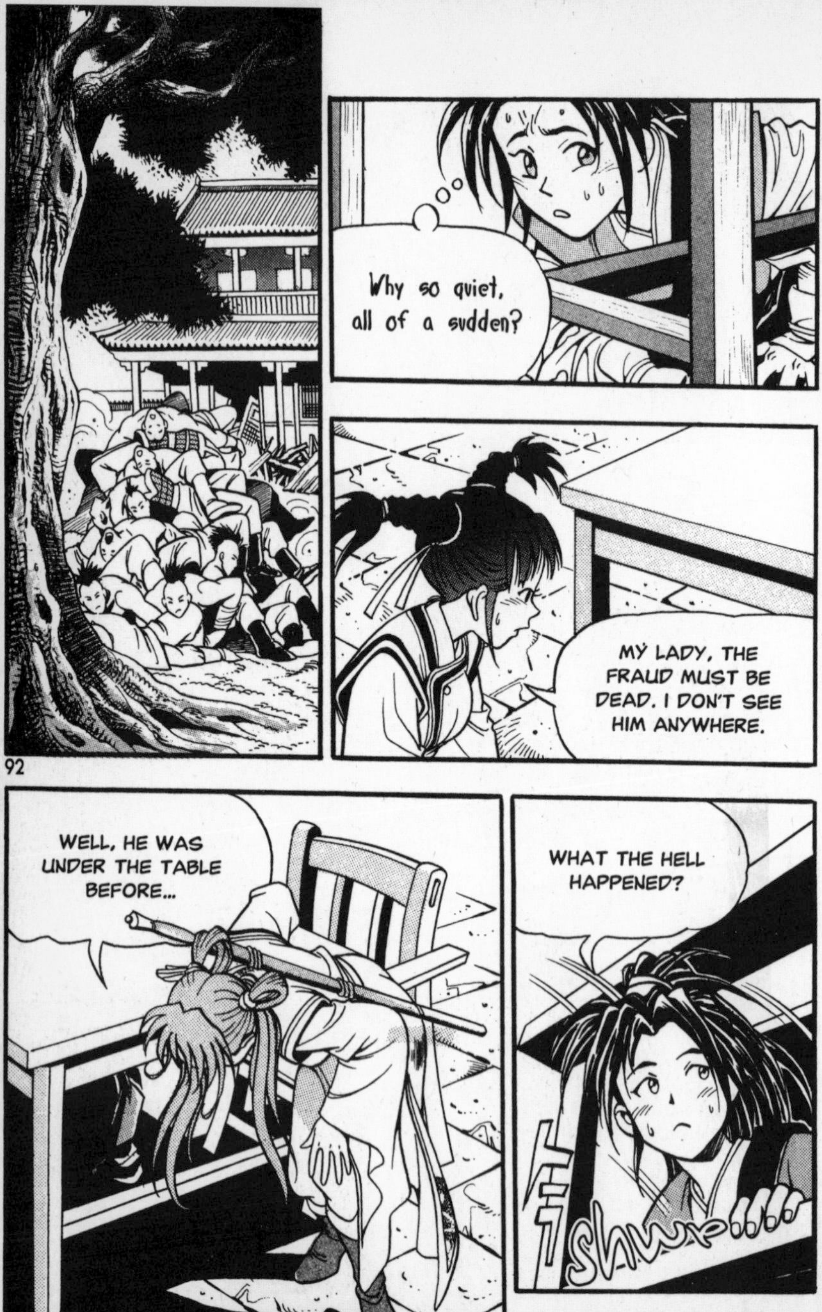
Why so quiet, all of a sudden?
MY LADY, THE FRAUD MUST BE DEAD. I DON'T SEE HIM ANYWHERE.
WELL, HE WAS UNDER THE TABLE BEFORE...
WHAT THE HELL HAPPENED?

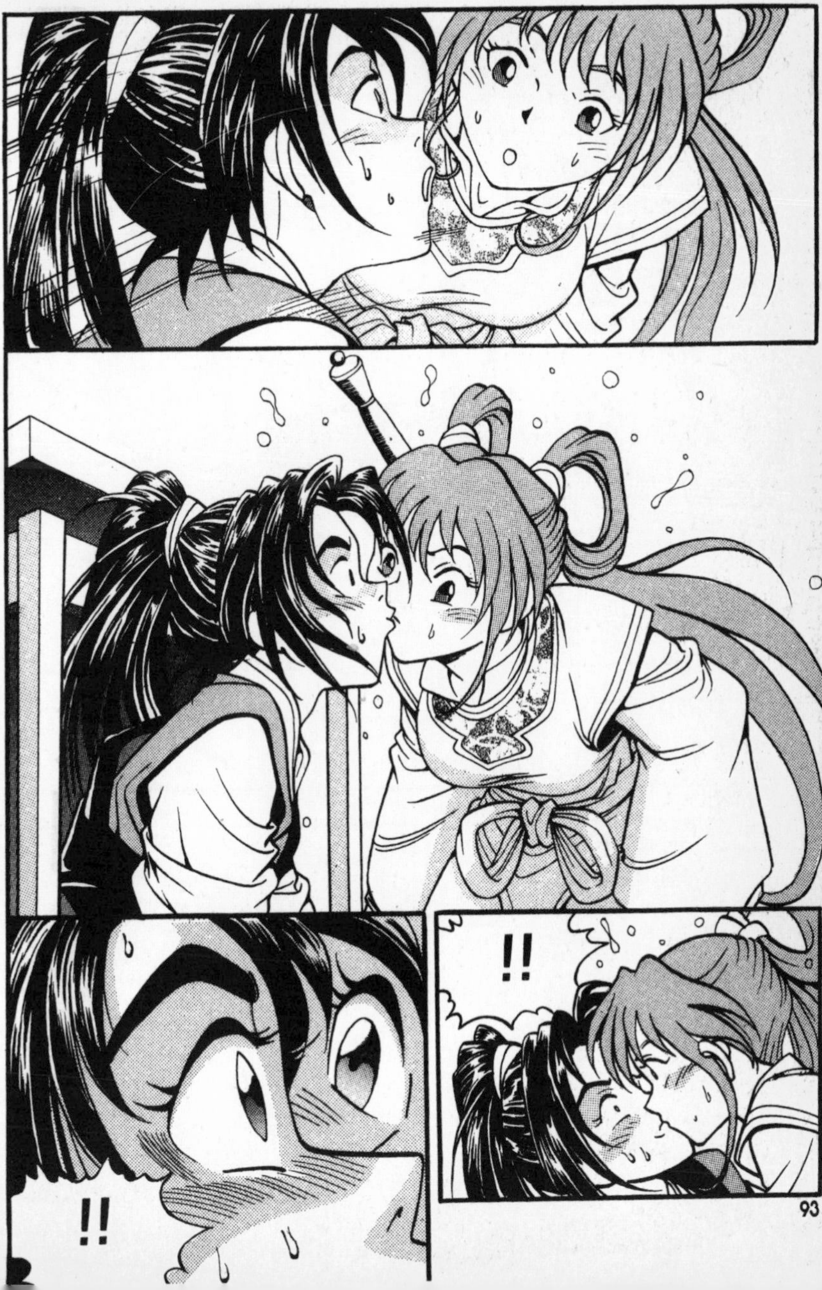
!!
!!

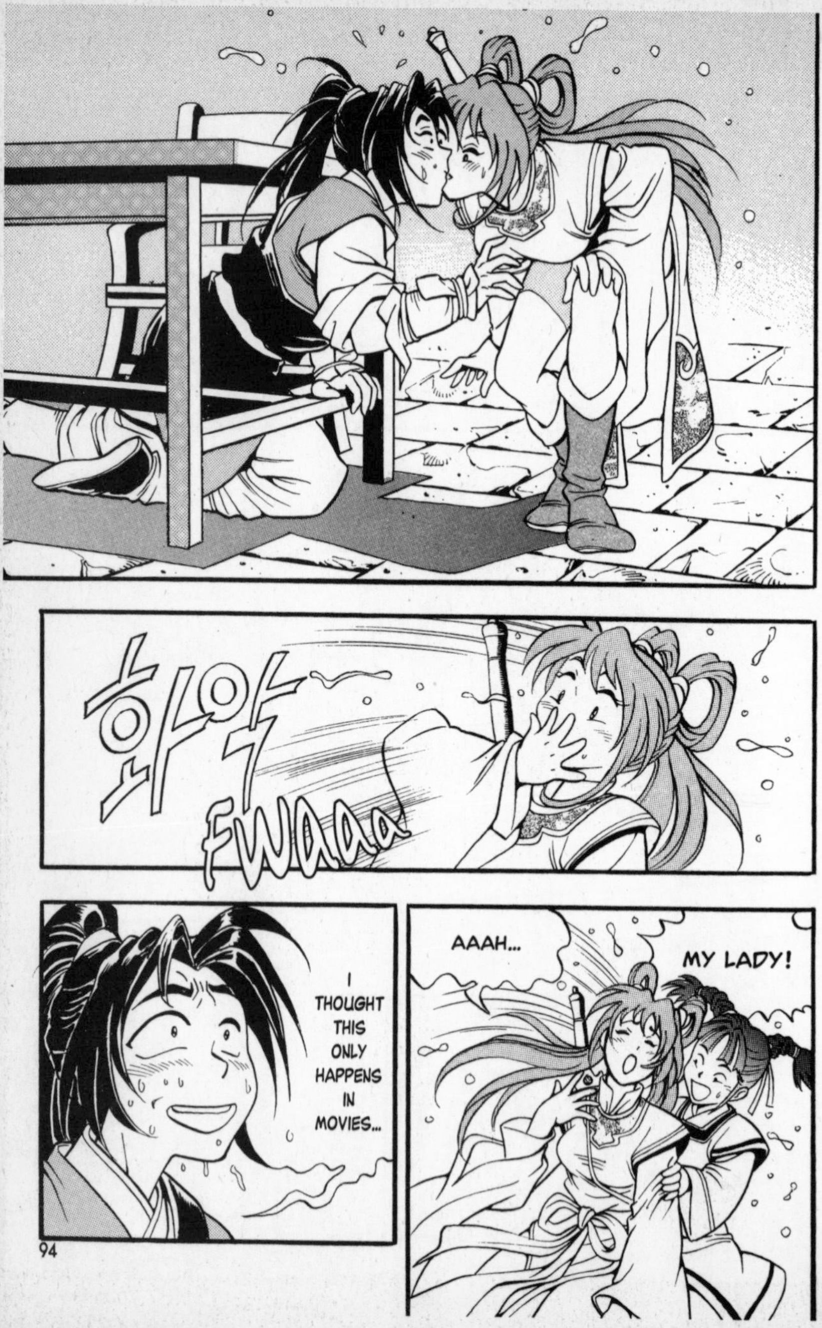
화악
FWAAa
I THOUGHT THIS ONLY HAPPENS IN MOVIES...
AAAH...
MY LADY!

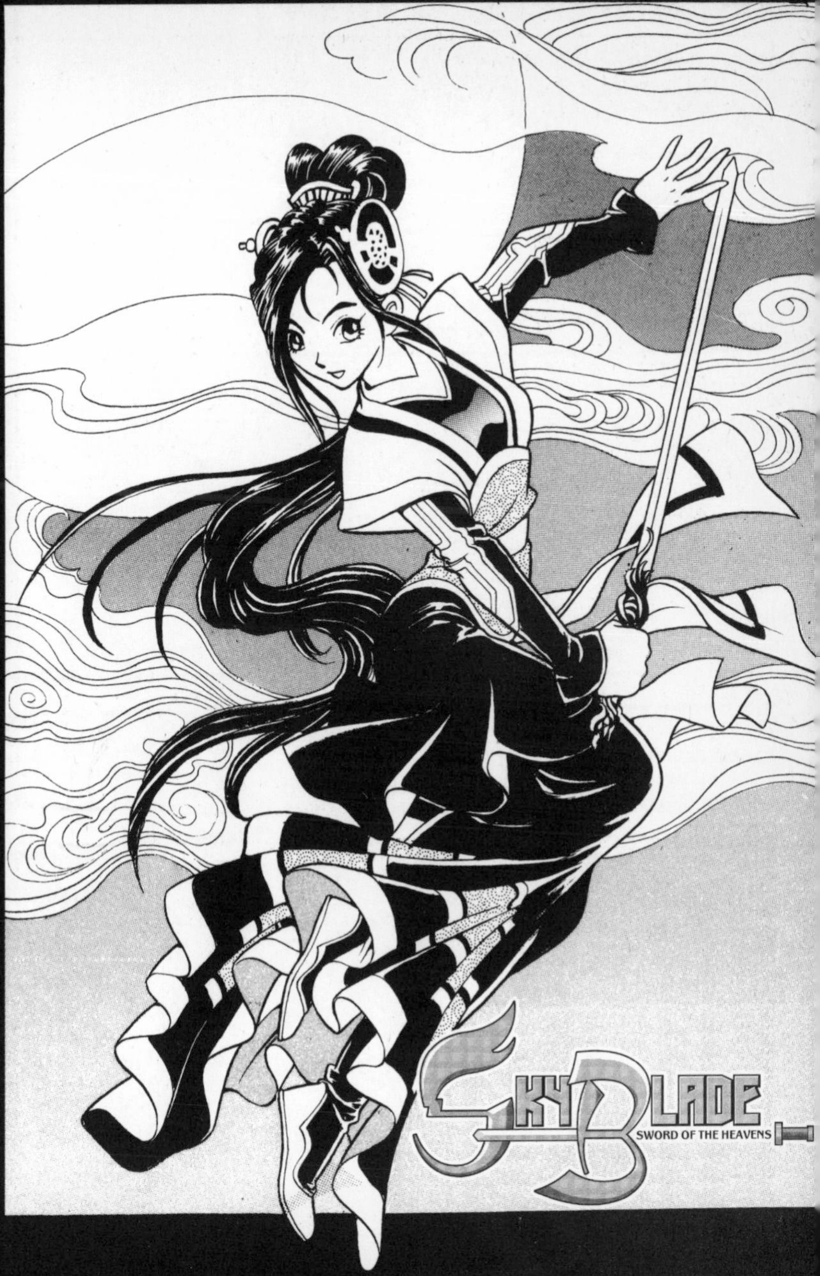
SKY BLADE
SWORD OF THE HEAVENS

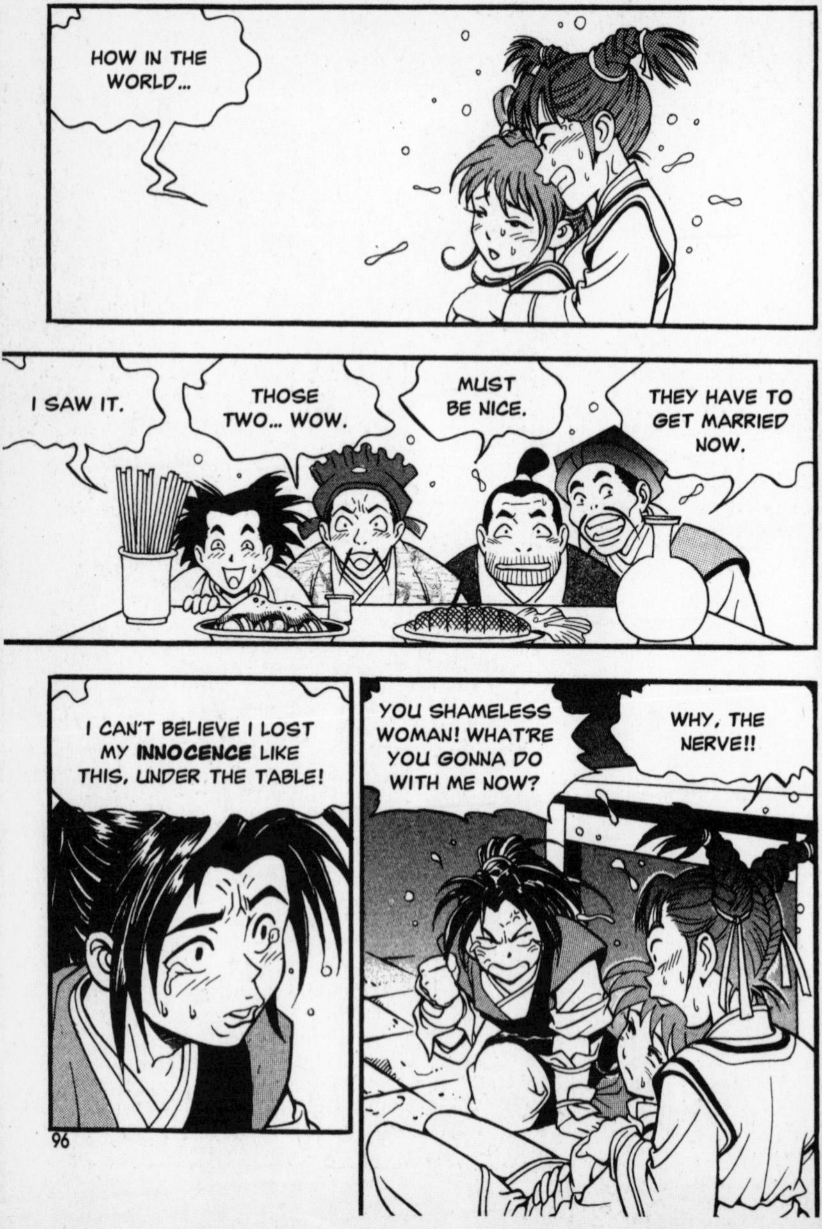
HOW IN THE WORLD...
THEY HAVE TO GET MARRIED NOW.
MUST BE NICE.
THOSE TWO... WOW.
I SAW IT.
WHY, THE NERVE!!
YOU SHAMELESS WOMAN! WHAT'RE YOU GONNA DO WITH ME NOW?
I CAN'T BELIEVE I LOST MY **INNOCENCE** LIKE THIS, UNDER THE TABLE!

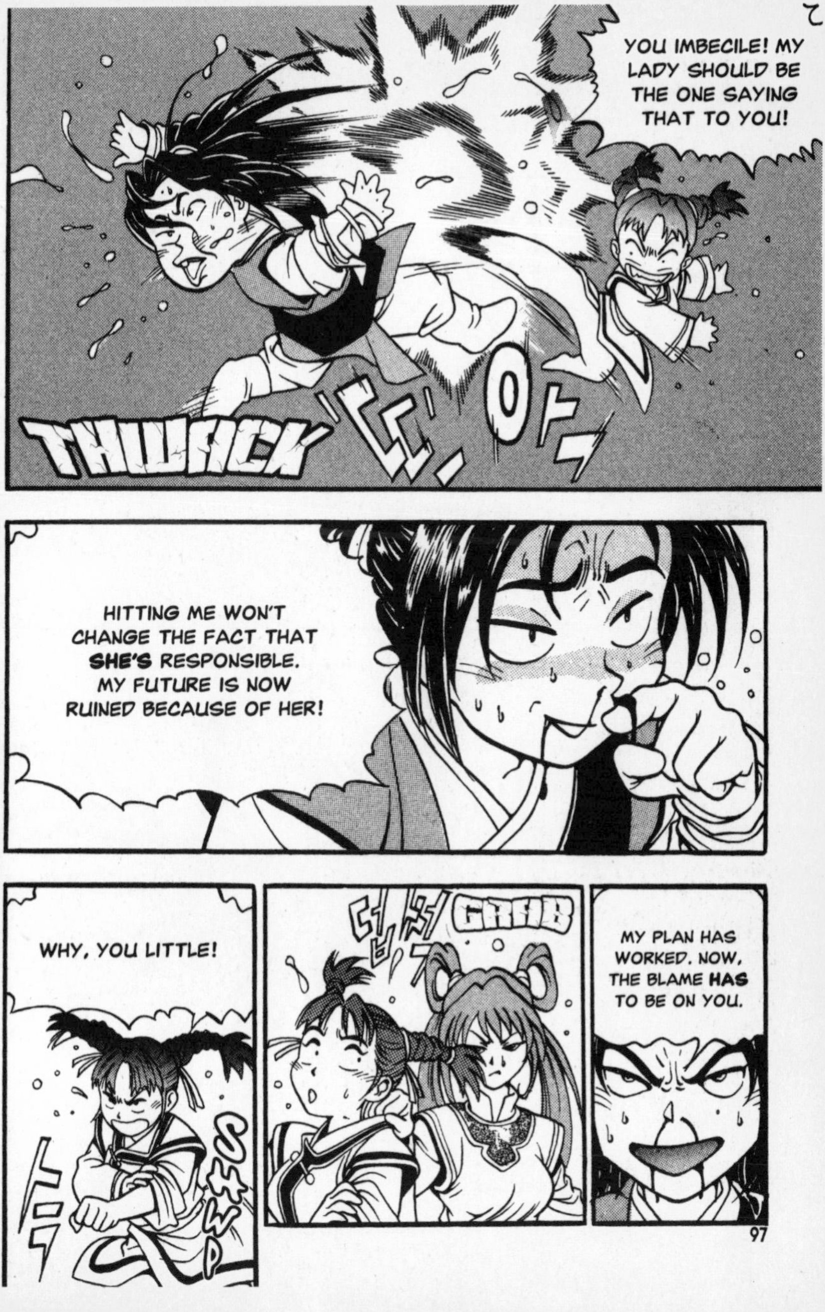
YOU IMBECILE! MY LADY SHOULD BE THE ONE SAYING THAT TO YOU!
THWACK
HITTING ME WON'T CHANGE THE FACT THAT SHE'S RESPONSIBLE. MY FUTURE IS NOW RUINED BECAUSE OF HER!
WHY, YOU LITTLE!
SHWP
GRAB
MY PLAN HAS WORKED. NOW, THE BLAME HAS TO BE ON YOU.

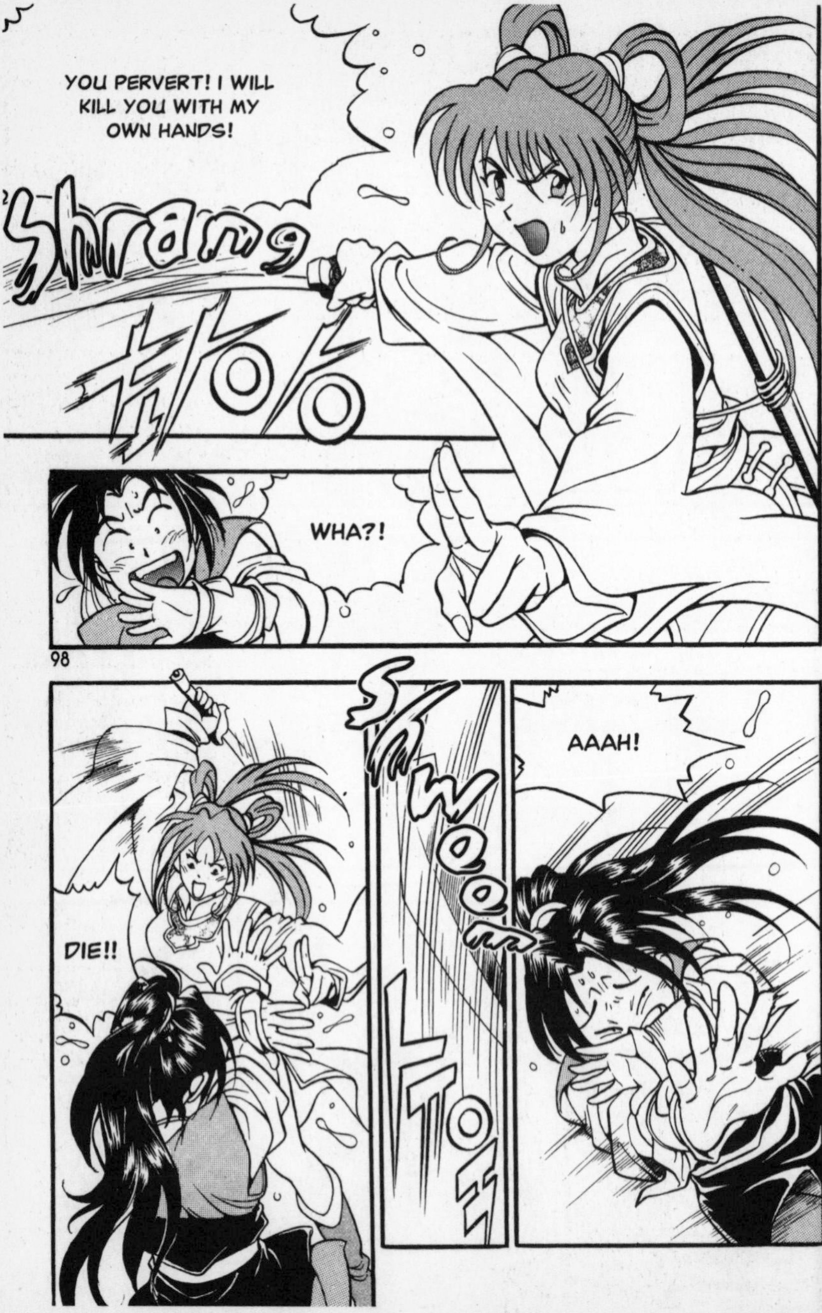
YOU PERVERT! I WILL KILL YOU WITH MY OWN HANDS!
Shrang
WHA?!
DIE!!
Shwoom
AAAH!

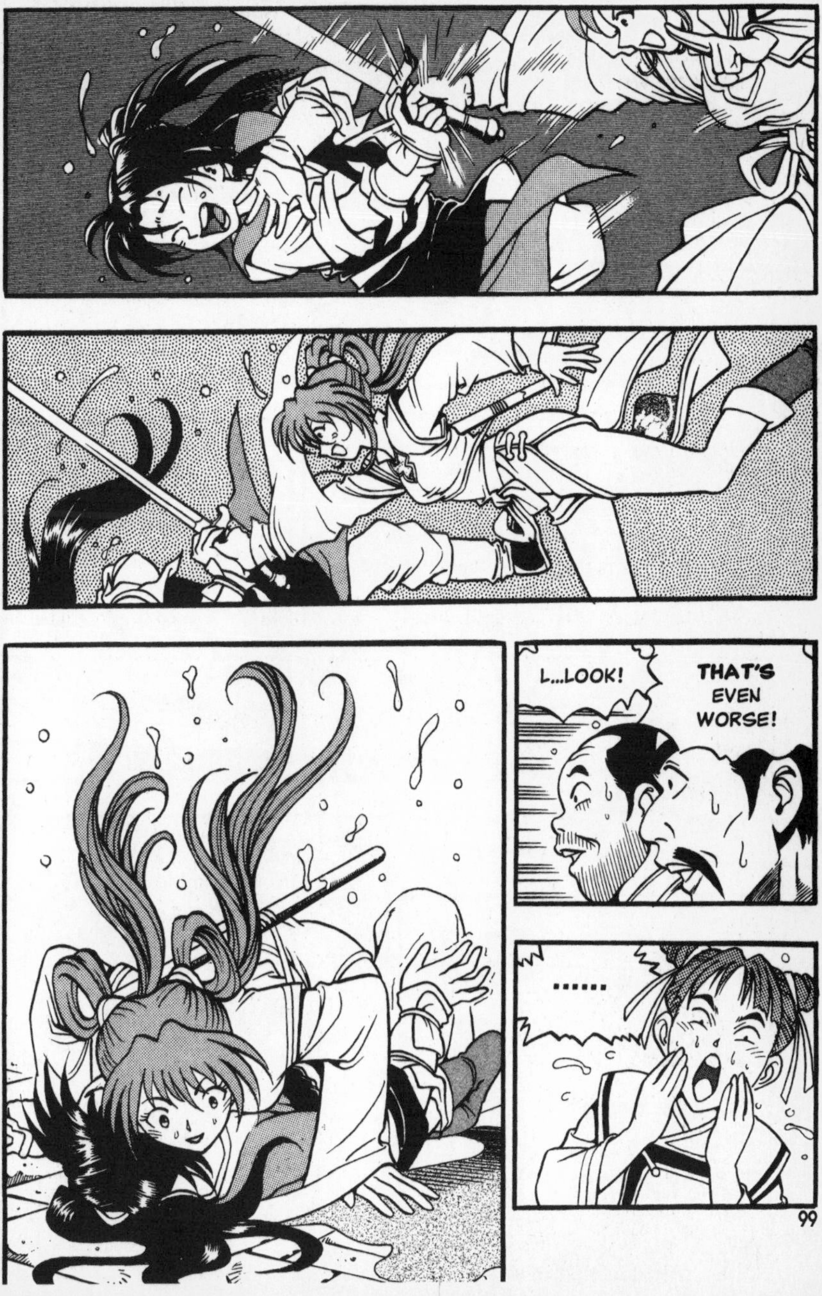
THAT'S EVEN WORSE!
L...LOOK!
......

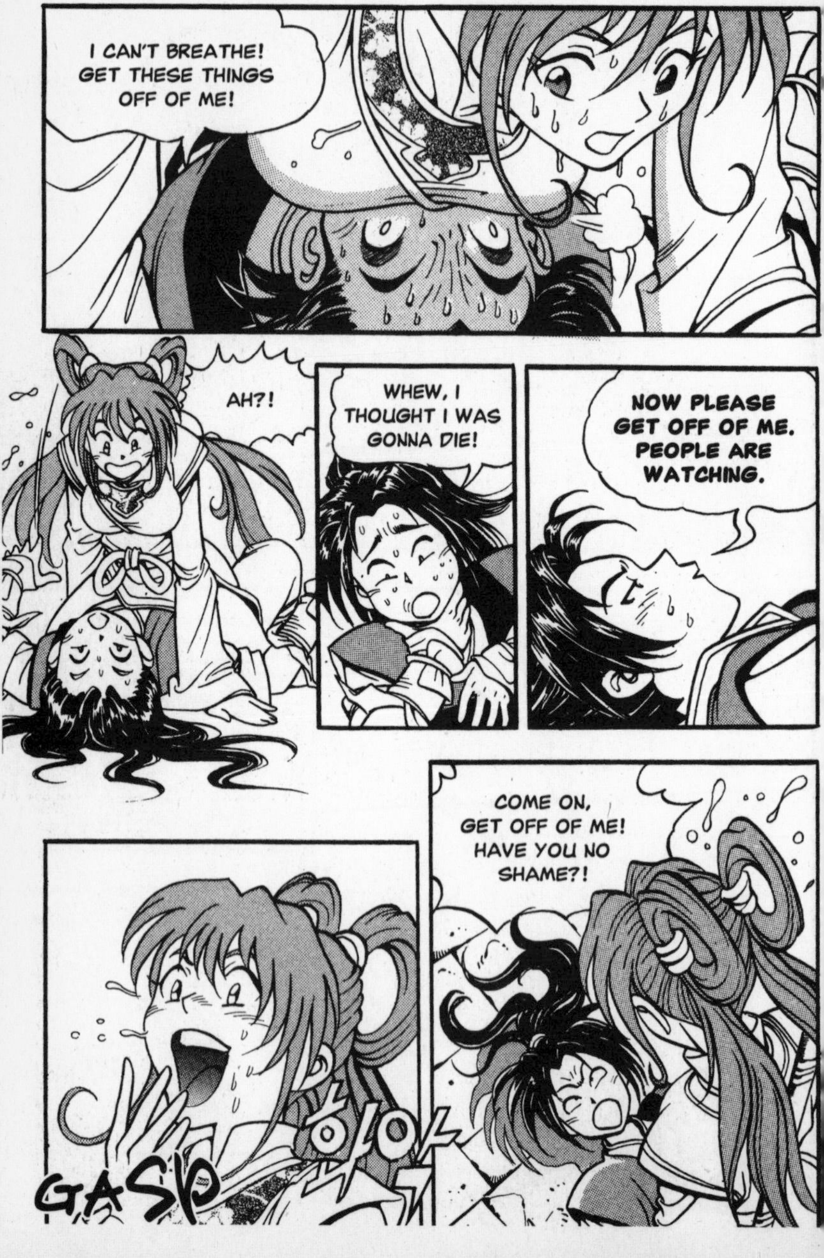
I CAN'T BREATHE! GET THESE THINGS OFF OF ME!
AH?!
WHEW, I THOUGHT I WAS GONNA DIE!
NOW PLEASE GET OFF OF ME. PEOPLE ARE WATCHING.
COME ON, GET OFF OF ME! HAVE YOU NO SHAME?!
GASP

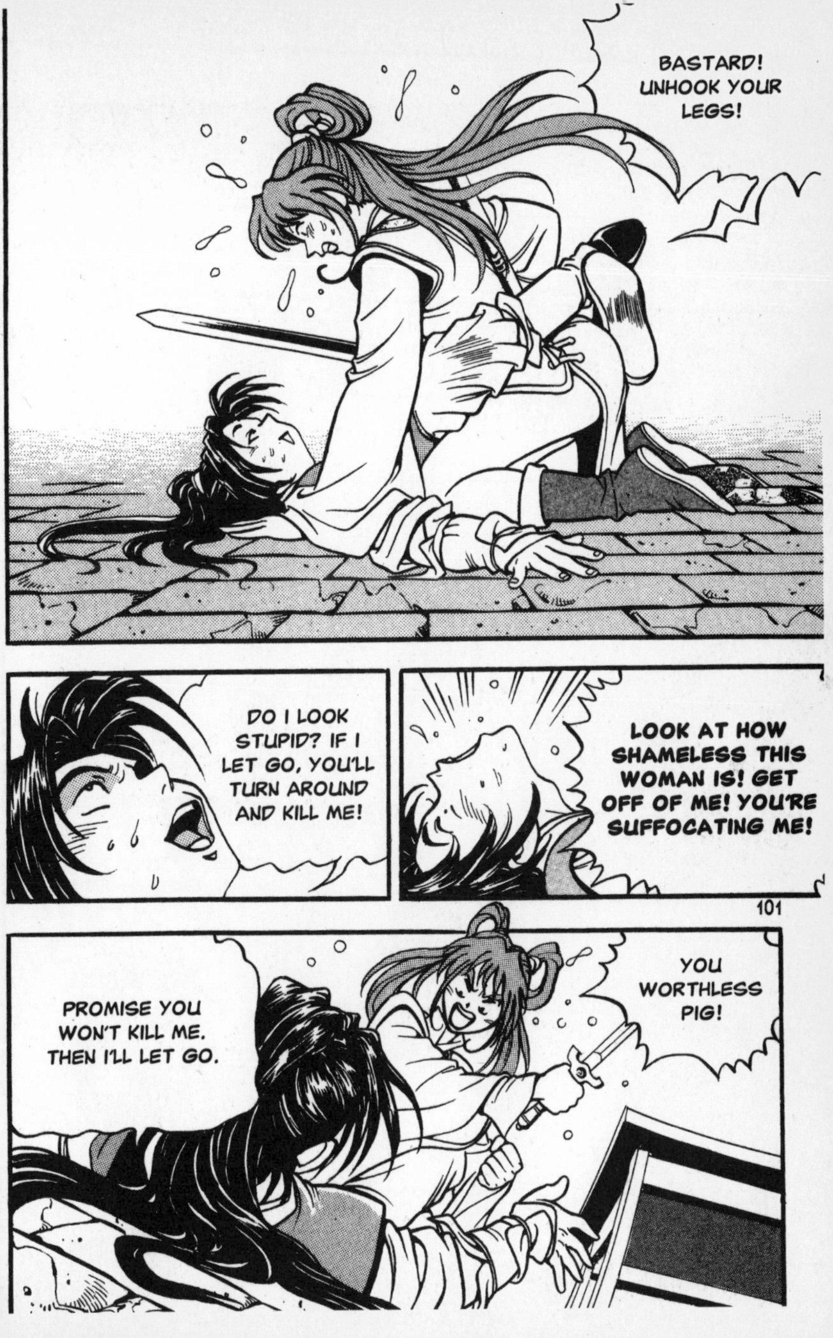
BASTARD! UNHOOK YOUR LEGS!
DO I LOOK STUPID? IF I LET GO, YOU'LL TURN AROUND AND KILL ME!
LOOK AT HOW SHAMELESS THIS WOMAN IS! GET OFF OF ME! YOU'RE SUFFOCATING ME!
PROMISE YOU WON'T KILL ME. THEN I'LL LET GO.
YOU WORTHLESS PIG!

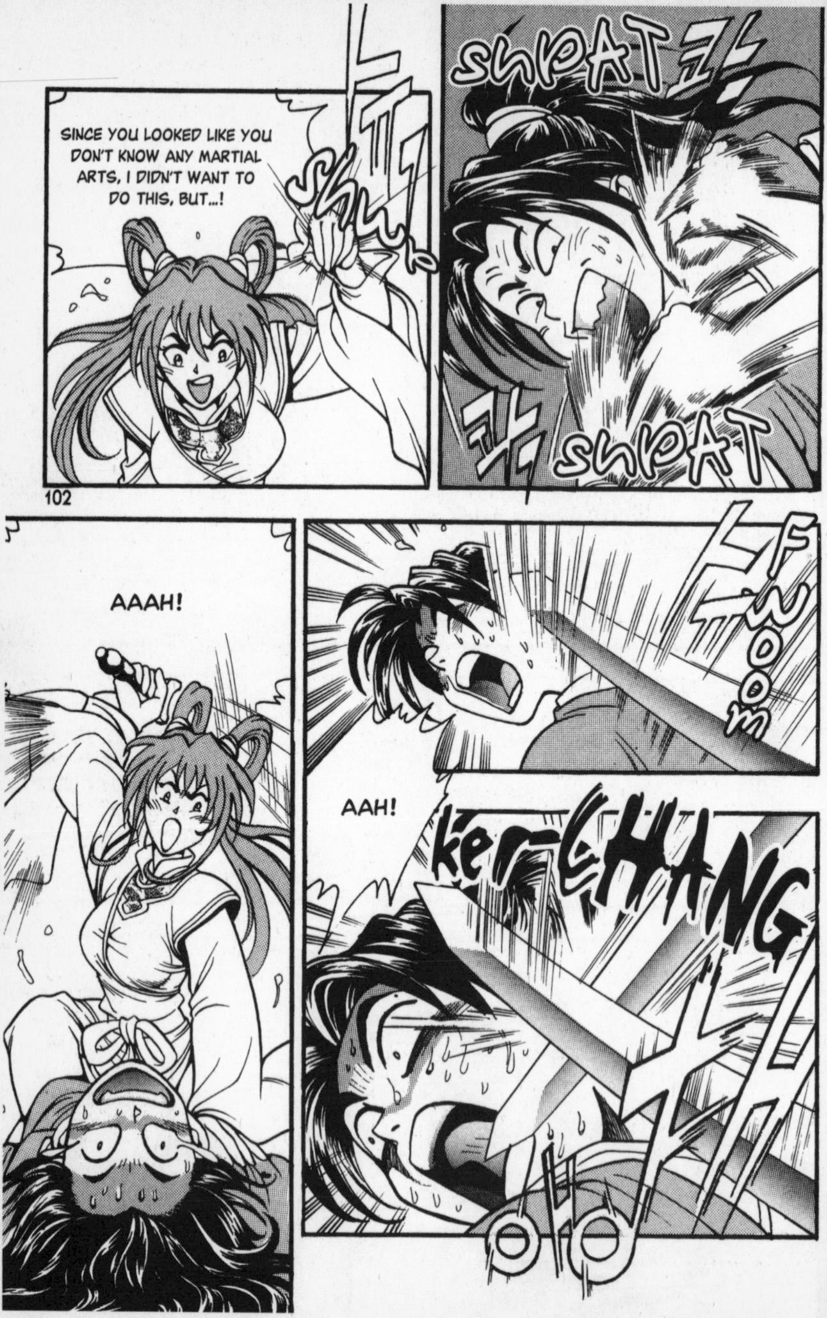

SINCE YOU LOOKED LIKE YOU DON'T KNOW ANY MARTIAL ARTS, I DIDN'T WANT TO DO THIS, BUT...!
SHUP
SHPAT
SHPAT
AAAH!
FWOOM
AAH!
KER-CHANG

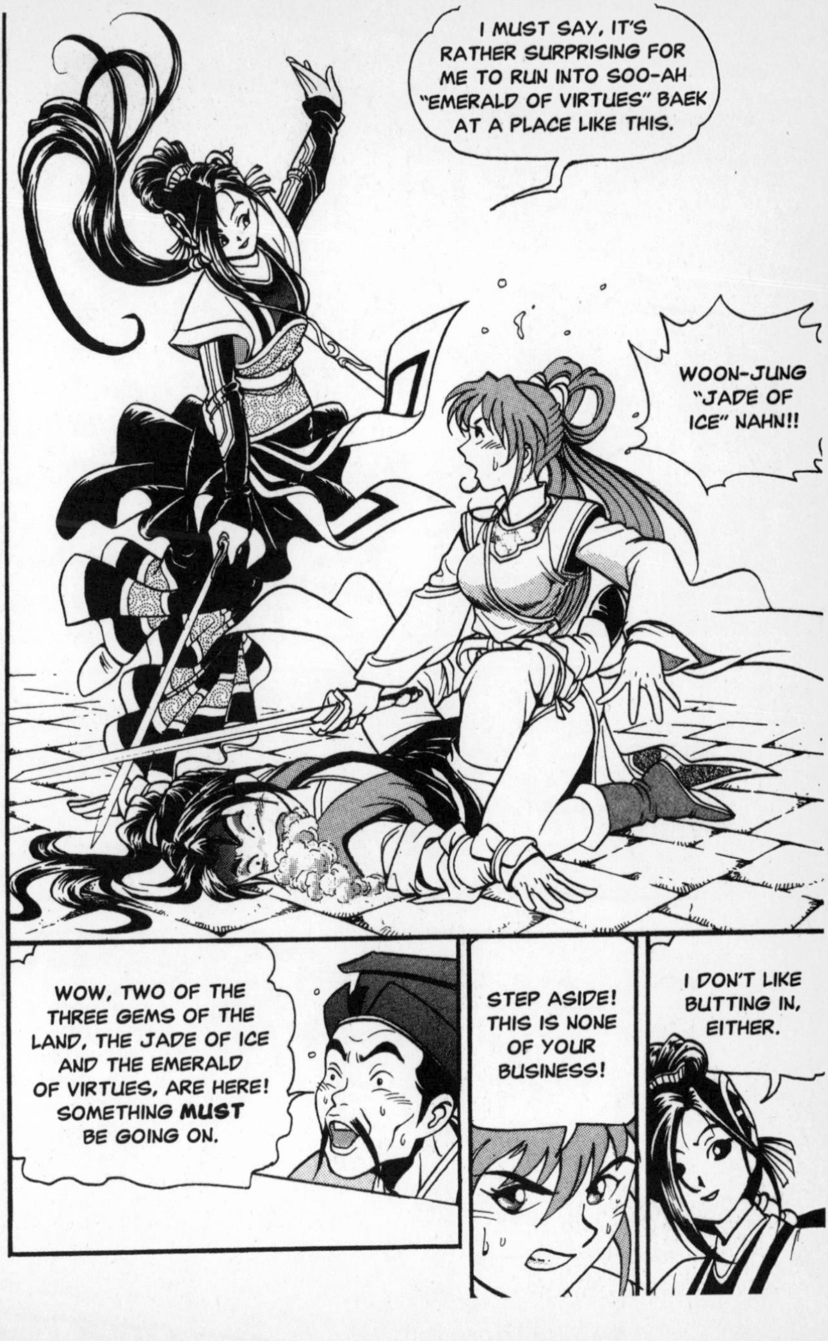
I MUST SAY, IT'S RATHER SURPRISING FOR ME TO RUN INTO SOO-AH "EMERALD OF VIRTUES" BAEK AT A PLACE LIKE THIS.
WOON-JUNG "JADE OF ICE" NAHN!!
WOW, TWO OF THE THREE GEMS OF THE LAND, THE JADE OF ICE AND THE EMERALD OF VIRTUES, ARE HERE! SOMETHING **MUST** BE GOING ON.
STEP ASIDE! THIS IS NONE OF YOUR BUSINESS!
I DON'T LIKE BUTTING IN, EITHER.

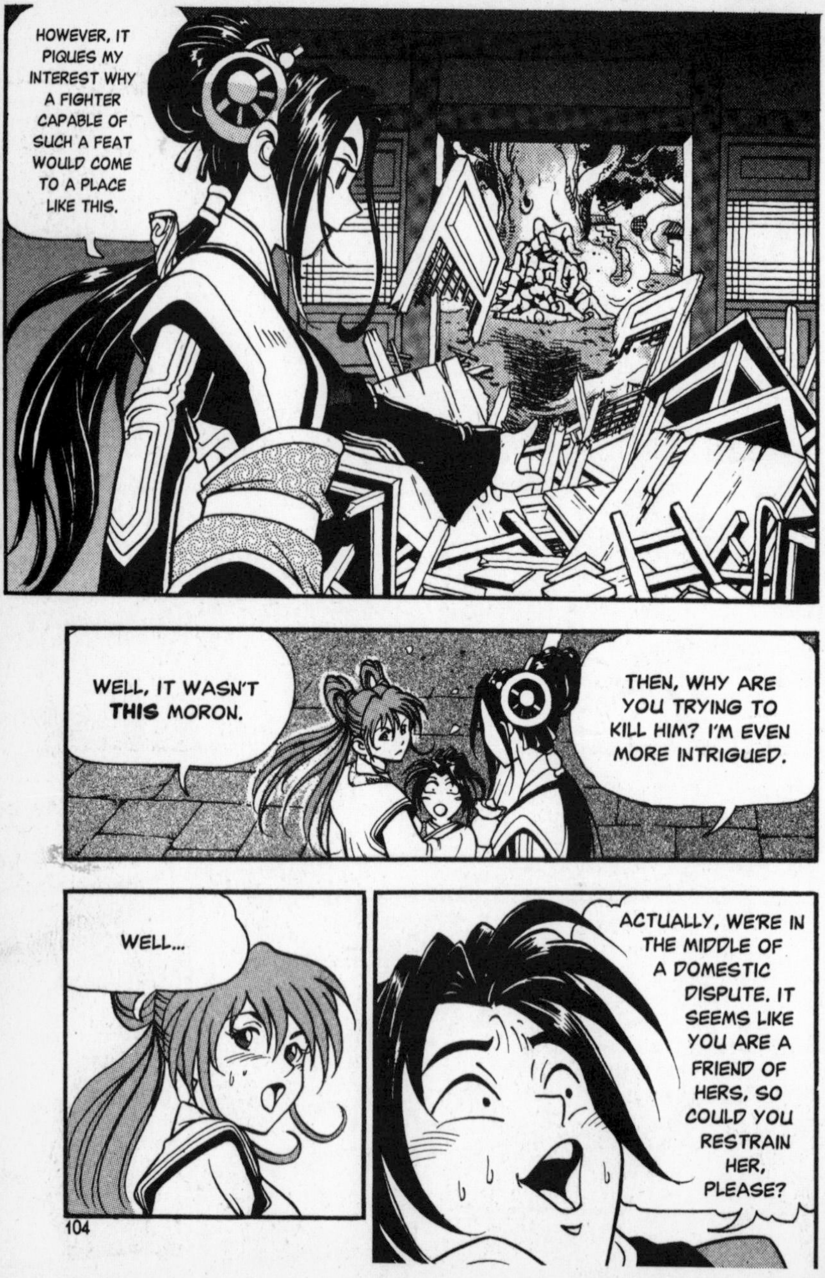
HOWEVER, IT PIQUES MY INTEREST WHY A FIGHTER CAPABLE OF SUCH A FEAT WOULD COME TO A PLACE LIKE THIS.
WELL, IT WASN'T **THIS** MORON.
THEN, WHY ARE YOU TRYING TO KILL HIM? I'M EVEN MORE INTRIGUED.
WELL...
ACTUALLY, WE'RE IN THE MIDDLE OF A DOMESTIC DISPUTE. IT SEEMS LIKE YOU ARE A FRIEND OF HERS, SO COULD YOU RESTRAIN HER, PLEASE?

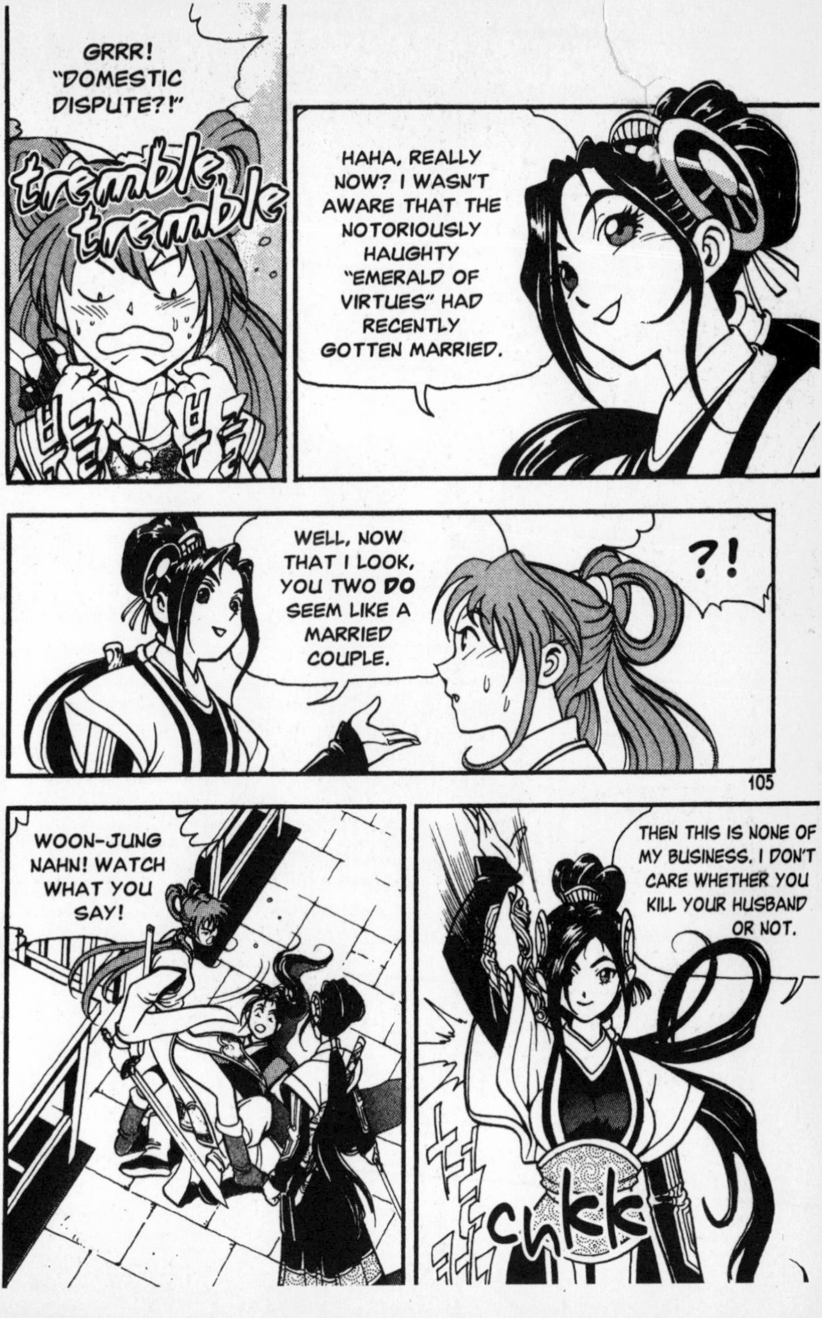
GRRR! "DOMESTIC DISPUTE?!"
tremble tremble
HAHA, REALLY NOW? I WASN'T AWARE THAT THE NOTORIOUSLY HAUGHTY "EMERALD OF VIRTUES" HAD RECENTLY GOTTEN MARRIED.
WELL, NOW THAT I LOOK, YOU TWO **DO** SEEM LIKE A MARRIED COUPLE.
?!
WOON-JUNG NAHN! WATCH WHAT YOU SAY!
THEN THIS IS NONE OF MY BUSINESS. I DON'T CARE WHETHER YOU KILL YOUR HUSBAND OR NOT.
chkk

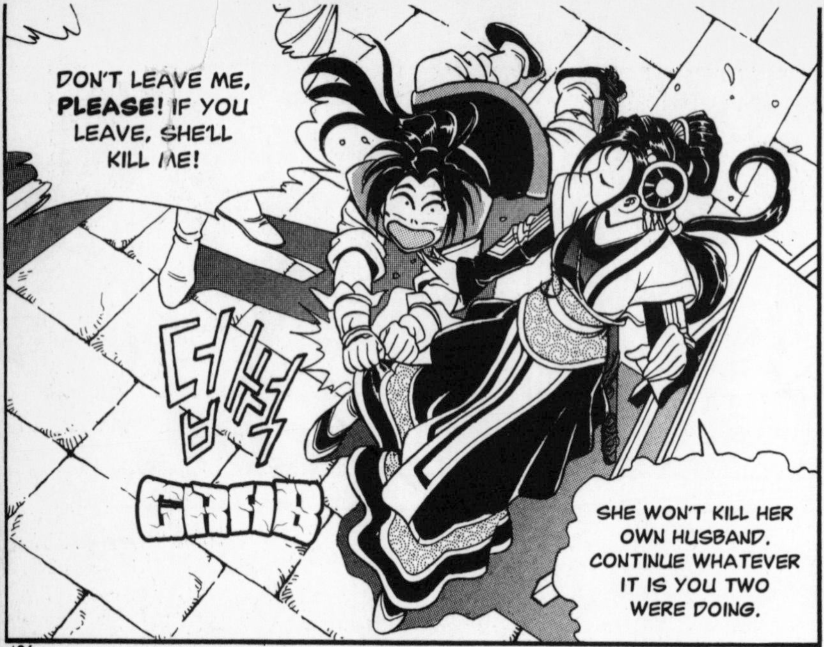
DON'T LEAVE ME, PLEASE! IF YOU LEAVE, SHE'LL KILL ME!
GRAB
SHE WON'T KILL HER OWN HUSBAND. CONTINUE WHATEVER IT IS YOU TWO WERE DOING.

106

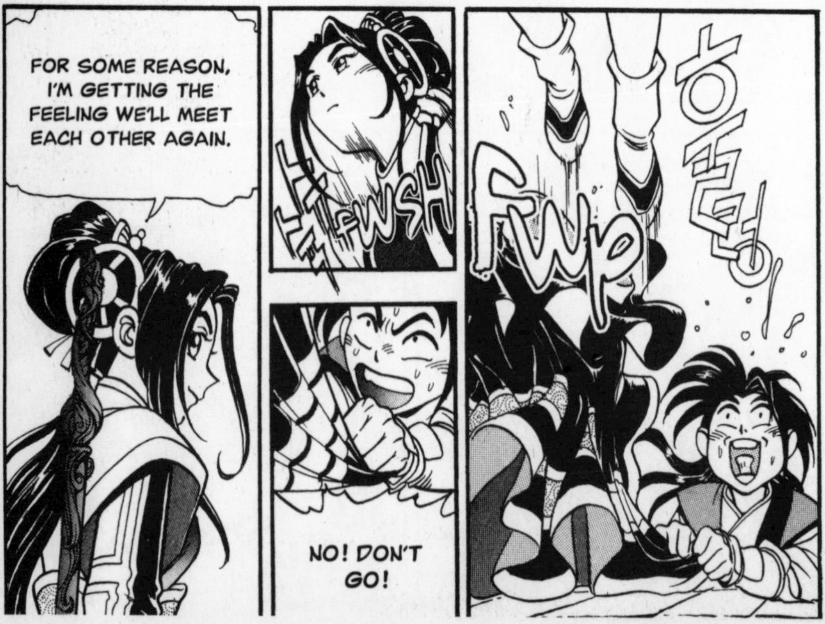
FOR SOME REASON, I'M GETTING THE FEELING WE'LL MEET EACH OTHER AGAIN.
FWSH
FWP
NO! DON'T GO!

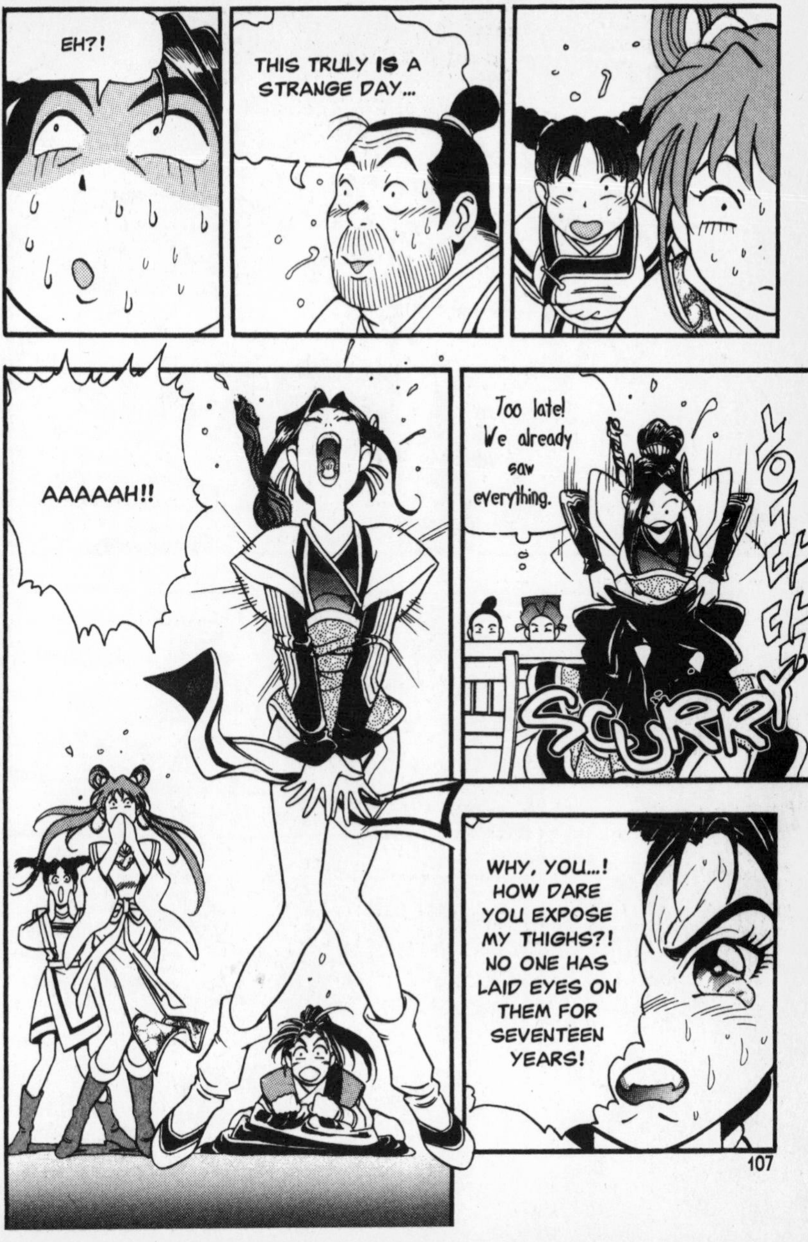

EH?!
THIS TRULY IS A STRANGE DAY...
AAAAAH!!
Too late! We already saw everything.
SCURRY
WHY, YOU...! HOW DARE YOU EXPOSE MY THIGHS?! NO ONE HAS LAID EYES ON THEM FOR SEVENTEEN YEARS!

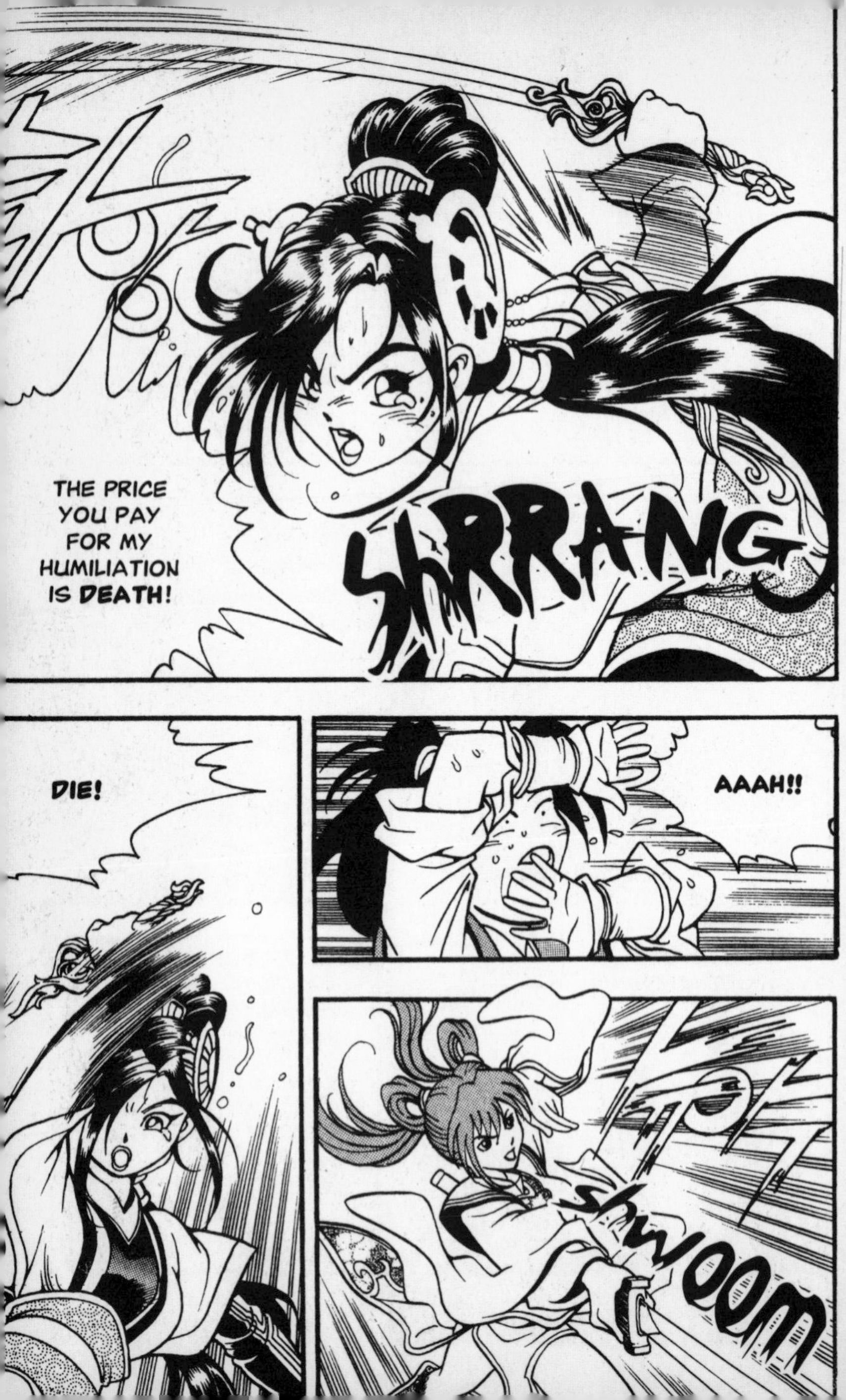
THE PRICE YOU PAY FOR MY HUMILIATION IS DEATH!
SHRRANG
DIE!
AAAH!!
SHWOOM

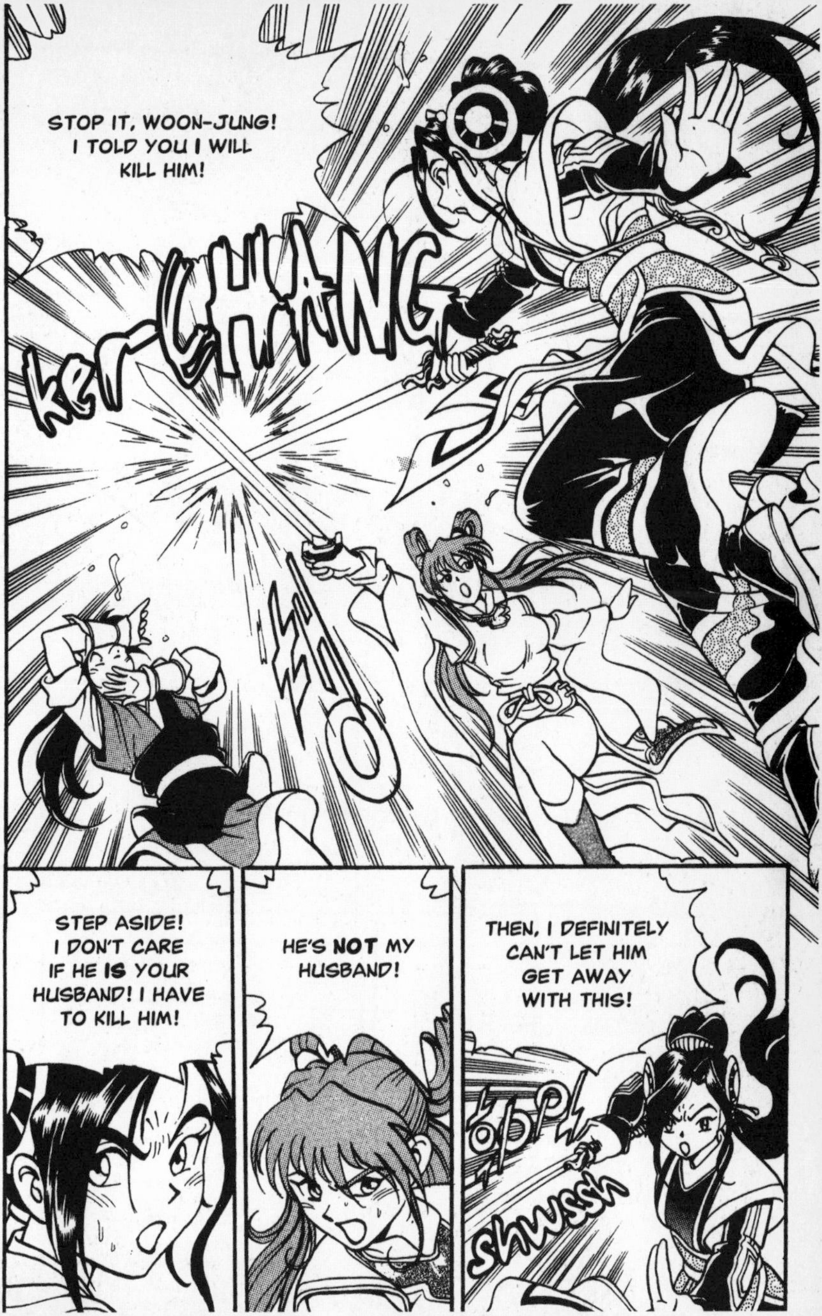
STOP IT, WOON-JUNG! I TOLD YOU I WILL KILL HIM!
ker-CHANG
STEP ASIDE! I DON'T CARE IF HE **IS** YOUR HUSBAND! I HAVE TO KILL HIM!
HE'S **NOT** MY HUSBAND!
THEN, I DEFINITELY CAN'T LET HIM GET AWAY WITH THIS!
shussh

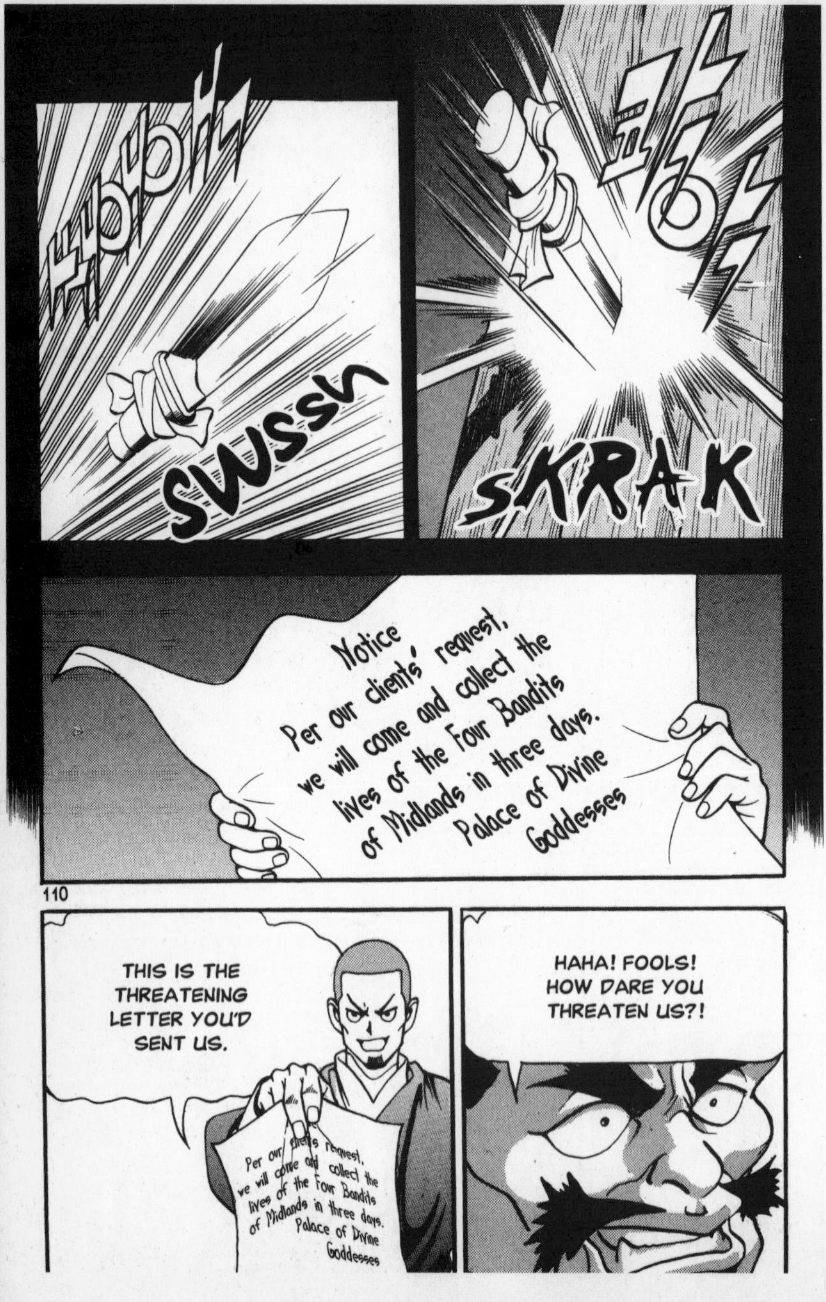
SWUSSH
SKRAK
Notice
Per our clients' request,
we will come and collect the
lives of the Four Bandits
of Midlands in three days.
Palace of Divine
Goddesses
THIS IS THE THREATENING LETTER YOU'D SENT US.
Per our clients request,
we will come and collect the
lives of the Four Bandits
of Midlands in three days.
Palace of Divine
Goddesses
HAHA! FOOLS! HOW DARE YOU THREATEN US?!

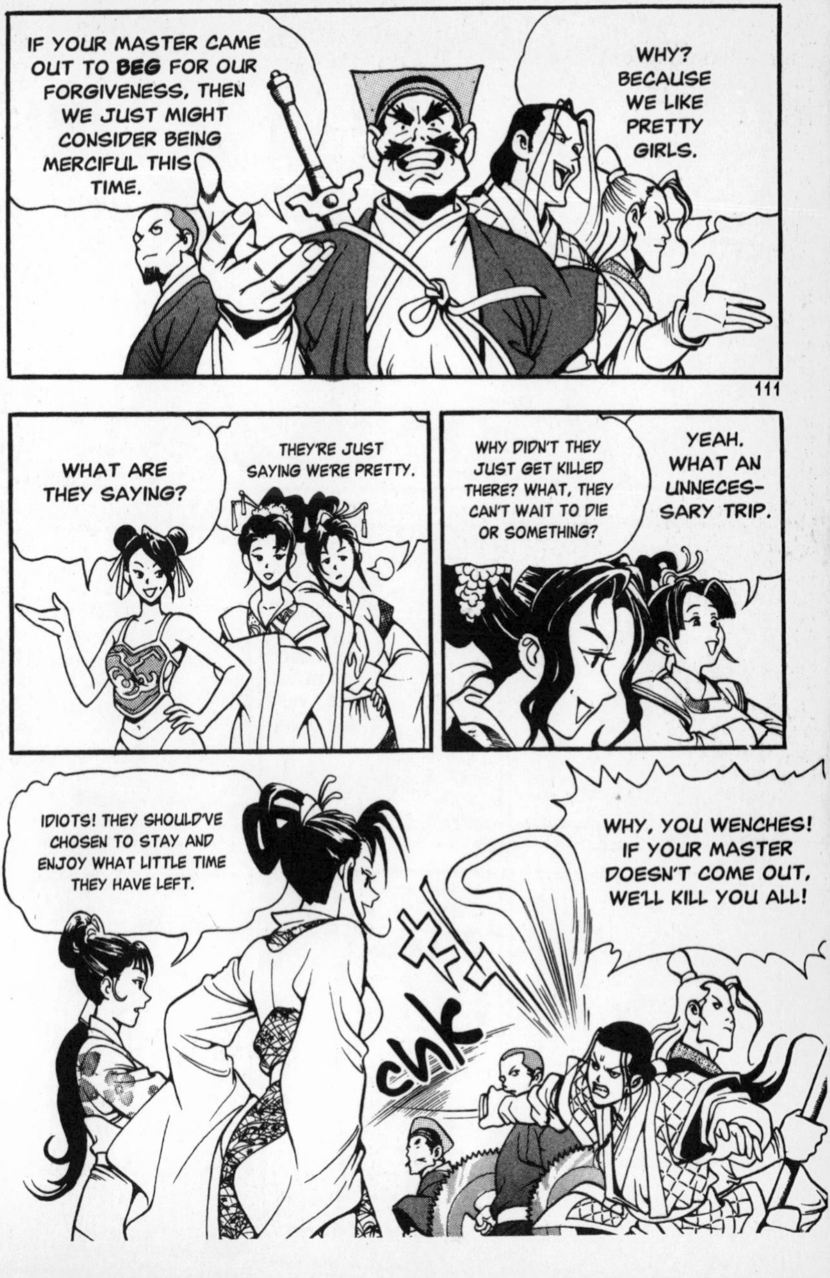
IF YOUR MASTER CAME OUT TO BEG FOR OUR FORGIVENESS, THEN WE JUST MIGHT CONSIDER BEING MERCIFUL THIS TIME.
WHY? BECAUSE WE LIKE PRETTY GIRLS.
WHAT ARE THEY SAYING?
THEY'RE JUST SAYING WE'RE PRETTY.
WHY DIDN'T THEY JUST GET KILLED THERE? WHAT, THEY CAN'T WAIT TO DIE OR SOMETHING?
YEAH. WHAT AN UNNECES-SARY TRIP.
IDIOTS! THEY SHOULD'VE CHOSEN TO STAY AND ENJOY WHAT LITTLE TIME THEY HAVE LEFT.
WHY, YOU WENCHES! IF YOUR MASTER DOESN'T COME OUT, WE'LL KILL YOU ALL!
chk

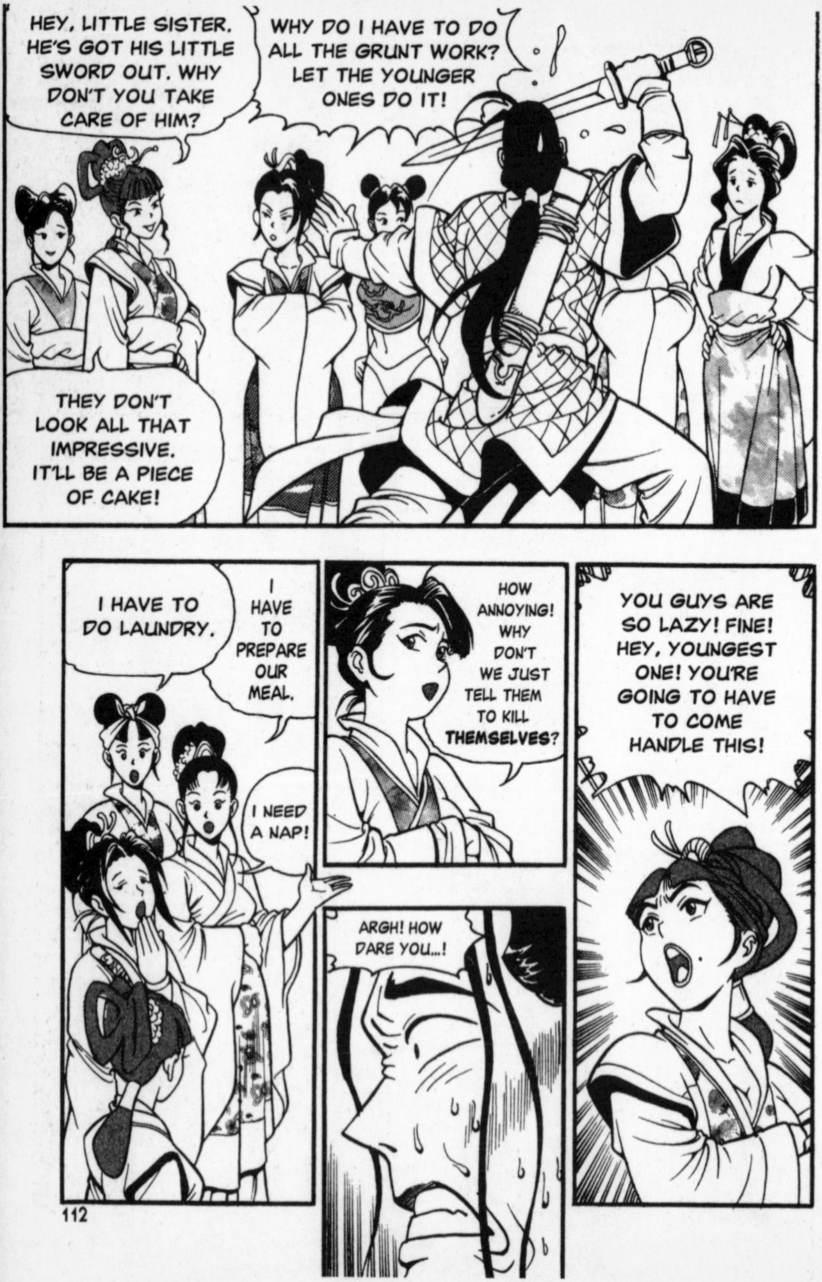
HEY, LITTLE SISTER. HE'S GOT HIS LITTLE SWORD OUT. WHY DON'T YOU TAKE CARE OF HIM?
WHY DO I HAVE TO DO ALL THE GRUNT WORK? LET THE YOUNGER ONES DO IT!
THEY DON'T LOOK ALL THAT IMPRESSIVE. IT'LL BE A PIECE OF CAKE!
I HAVE TO DO LAUNDRY.
I HAVE TO PREPARE OUR MEAL.
I NEED A NAP!
HOW ANNOYING! WHY DON'T WE JUST TELL THEM TO KILL THEMSELVES?
ARGH! HOW DARE YOU...!
YOU GUYS ARE SO LAZY! FINE! HEY, YOUNGEST ONE! YOU'RE GOING TO HAVE TO COME HANDLE THIS!

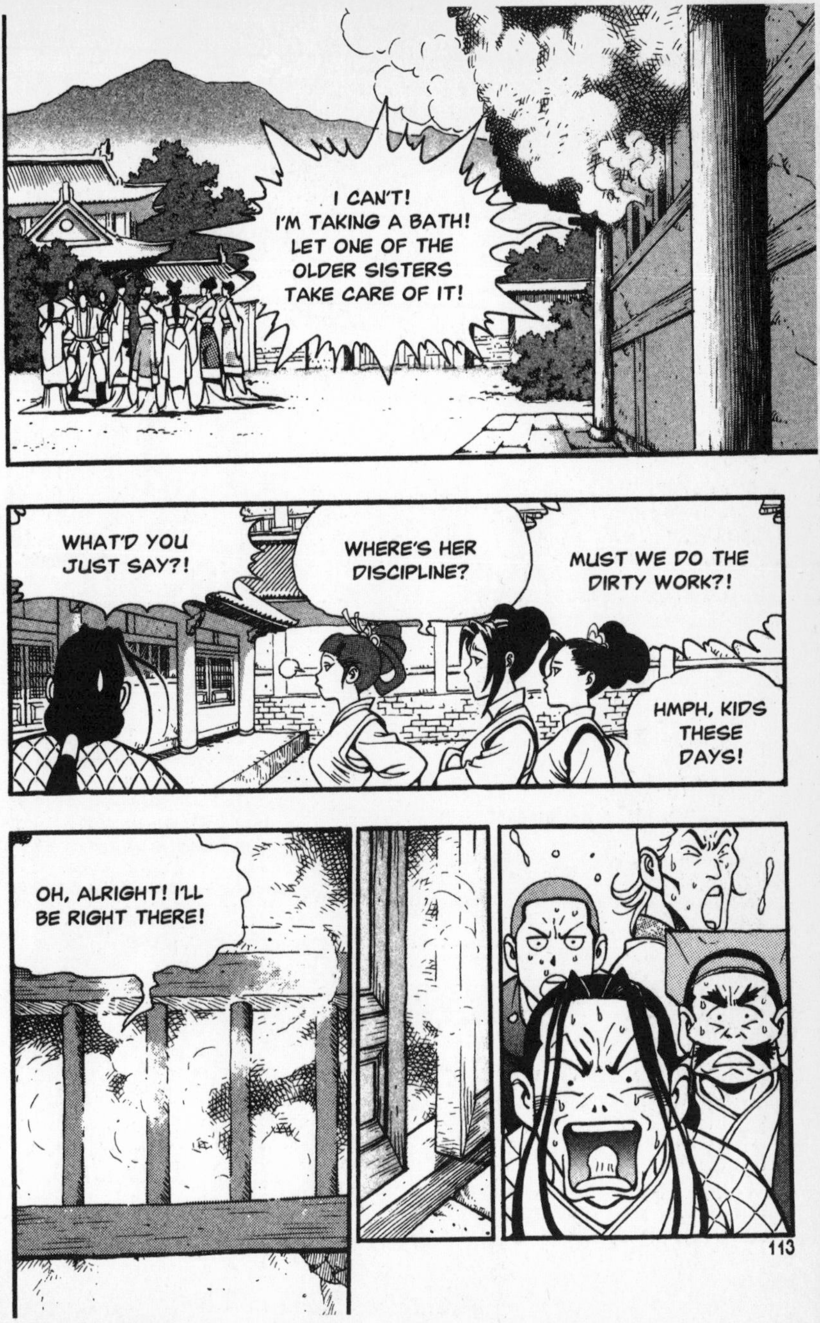
I CAN'T! I'M TAKING A BATH! LET ONE OF THE OLDER SISTERS TAKE CARE OF IT!
WHAT'D YOU JUST SAY?!
WHERE'S HER DISCIPLINE?
MUST WE DO THE DIRTY WORK?!
HMPH, KIDS THESE DAYS!
OH, ALRIGHT! I'LL BE RIGHT THERE!

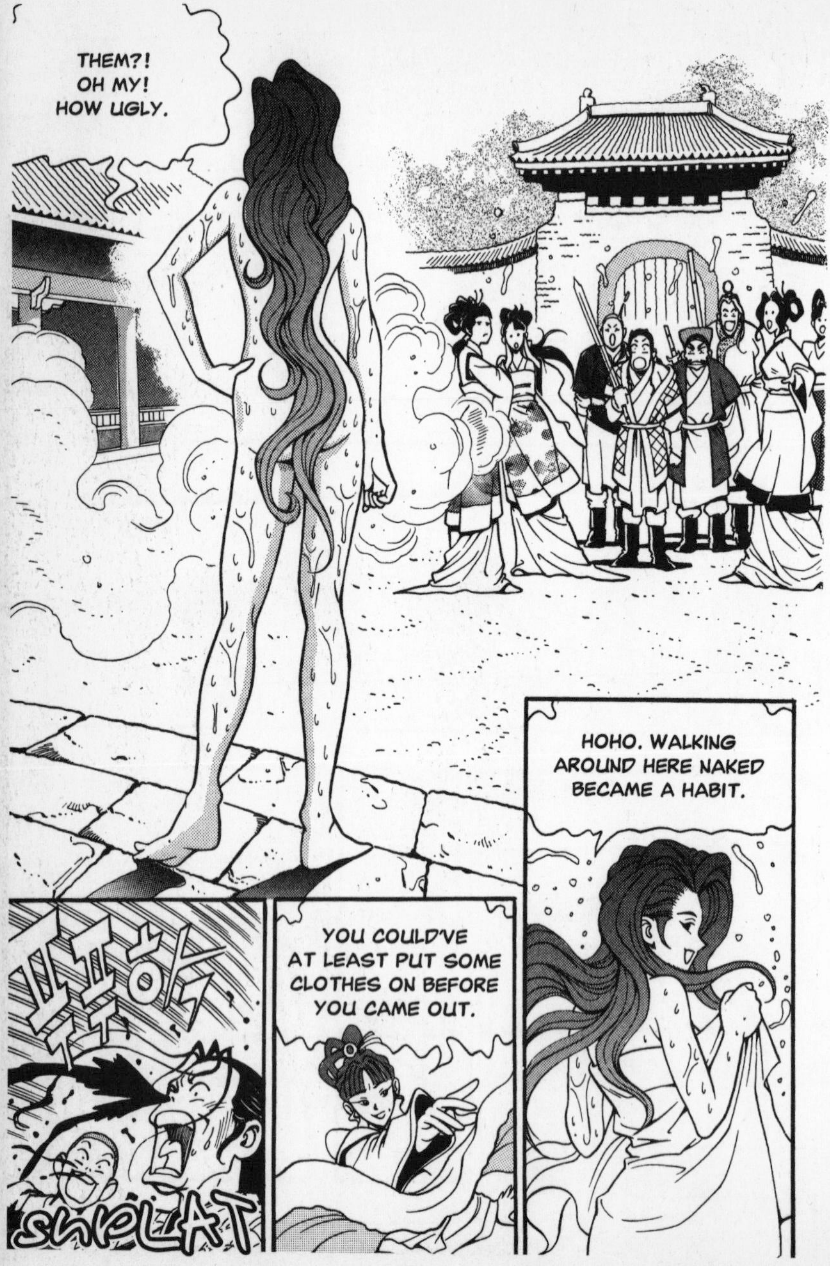
THEM?! OH MY! HOW UGLY.
SHPLAT
YOU COULD'VE AT LEAST PUT SOME CLOTHES ON BEFORE YOU CAME OUT.
HOHO. WALKING AROUND HERE NAKED BECAME A HABIT.

SKY BLADE
SWORD OF THE HEAVENS

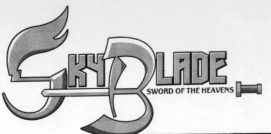

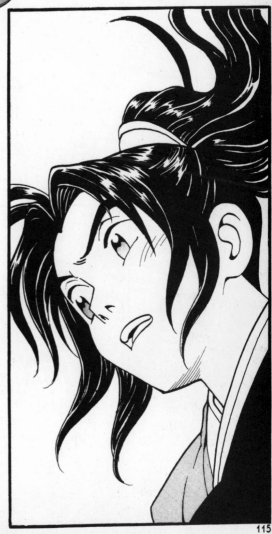

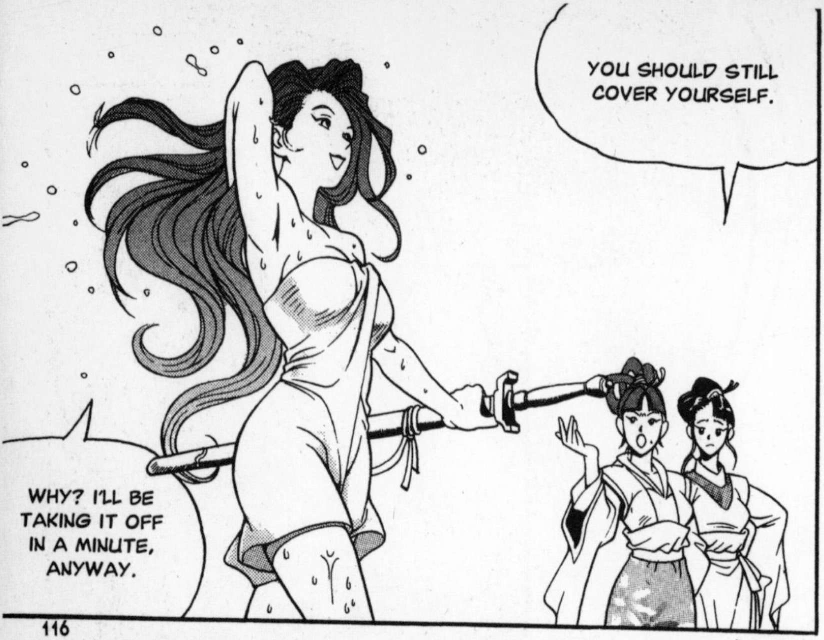
YOU SHOULD STILL COVER YOURSELF.
WHY? I'LL BE TAKING IT OFF IN A MINUTE, ANYWAY.

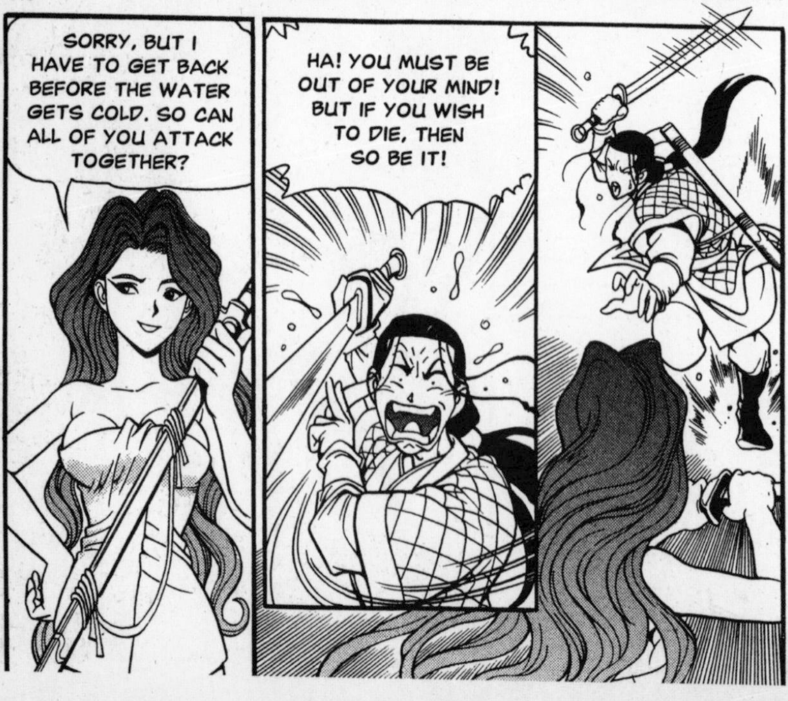
SORRY, BUT I HAVE TO GET BACK BEFORE THE WATER GETS COLD. SO CAN ALL OF YOU ATTACK TOGETHER?
HA! YOU MUST BE OUT OF YOUR MIND! BUT IF YOU WISH TO DIE, THEN SO BE IT!

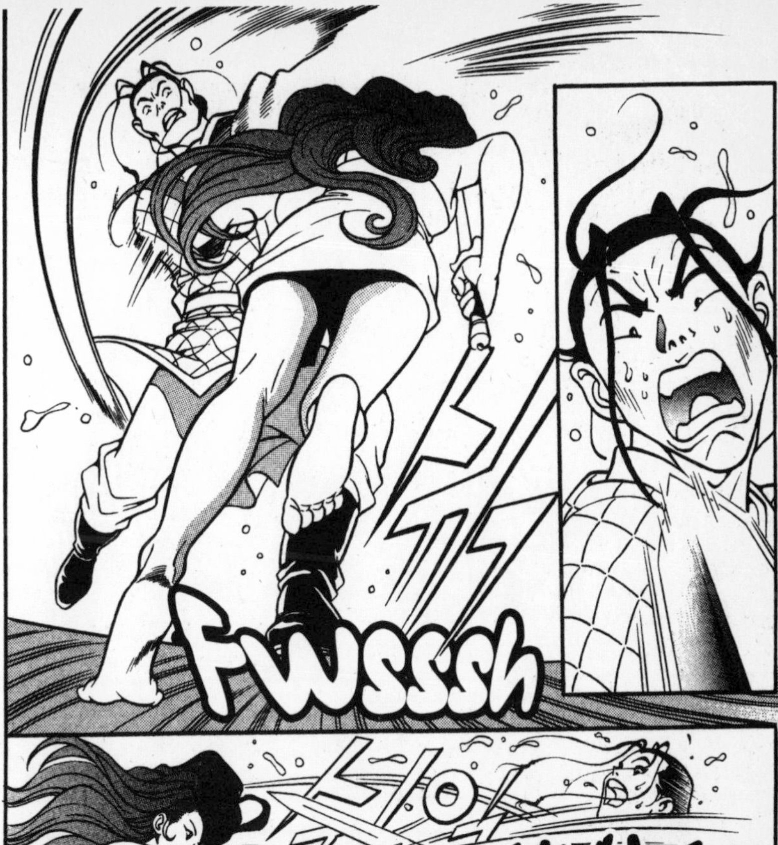
Fwsssh
shWACK

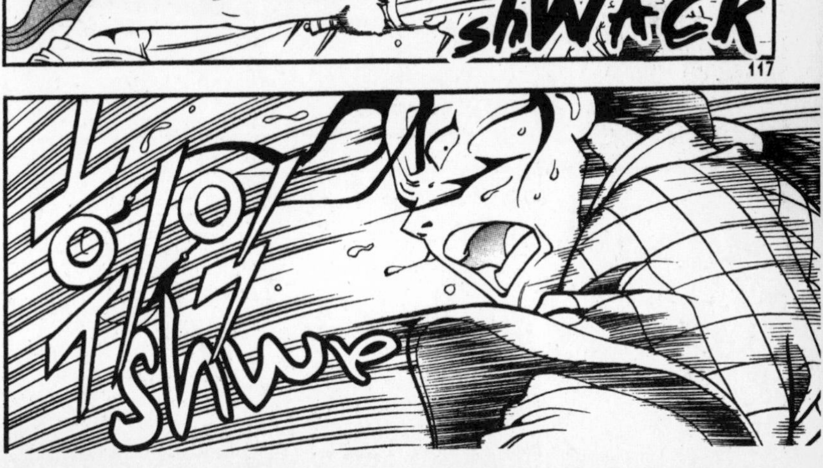
shwe

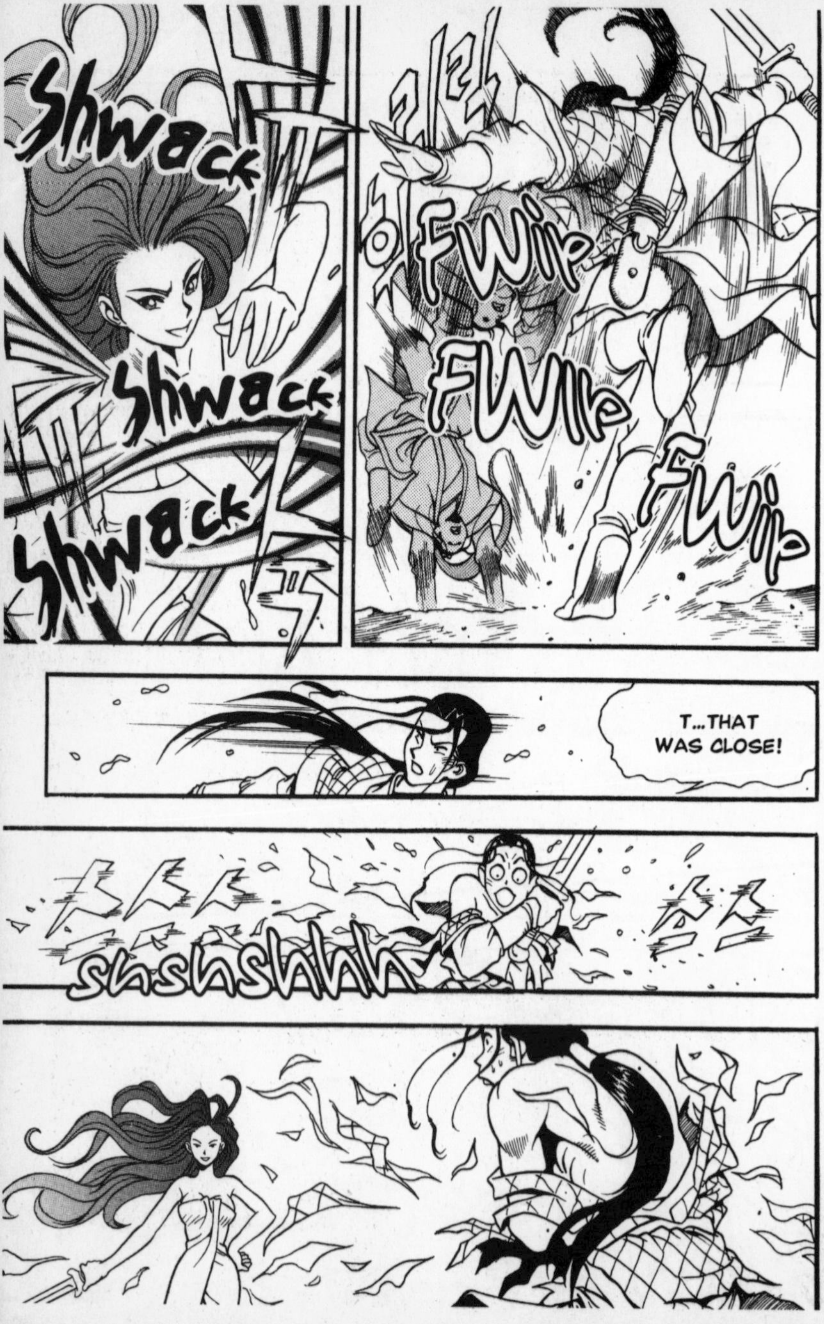
Shwack
Shwack
Shwack
Fwip
Fwip
Fwip
T...THAT WAS CLOSE!
shshshhh

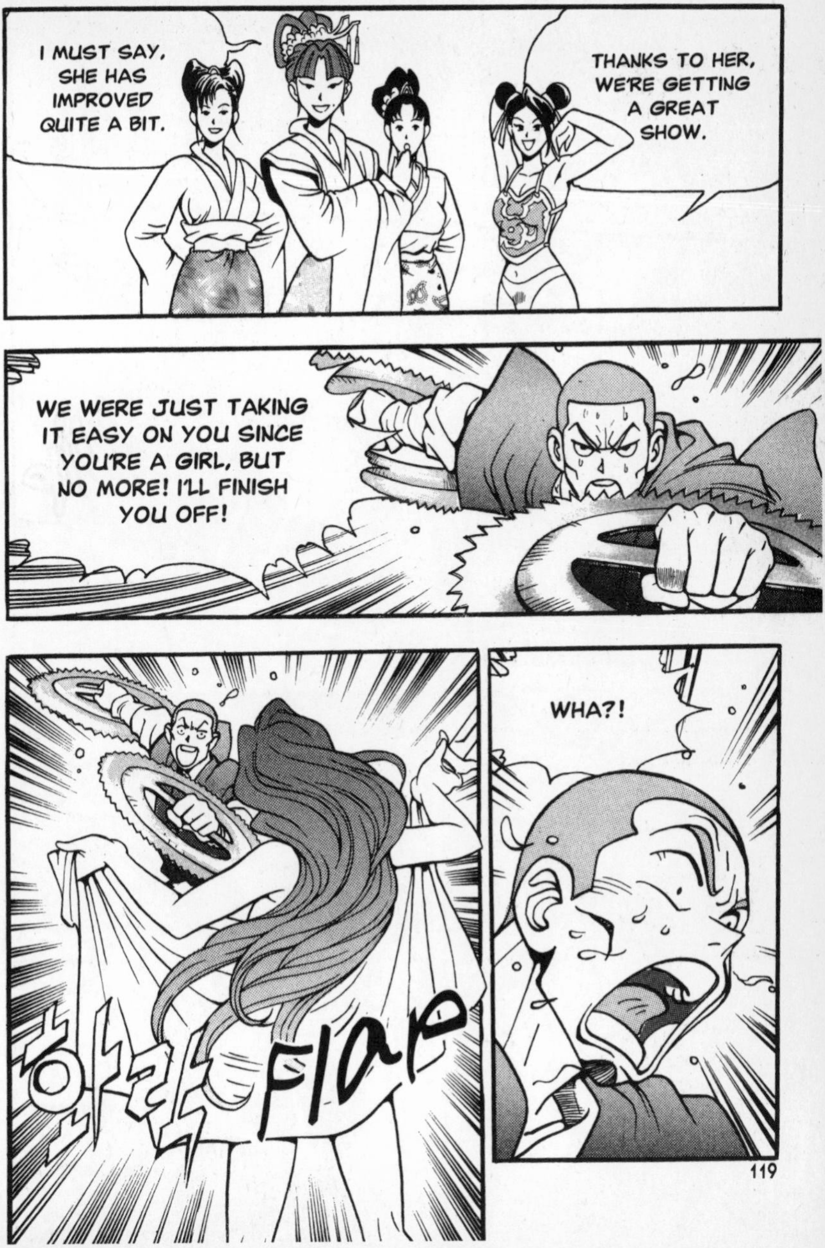
I MUST SAY, SHE HAS IMPROVED QUITE A BIT.
THANKS TO HER, WE'RE GETTING A GREAT SHOW.
WE WERE JUST TAKING IT EASY ON YOU SINCE YOU'RE A GIRL, BUT NO MORE! I'LL FINISH YOU OFF!
FLAP
WHA?!

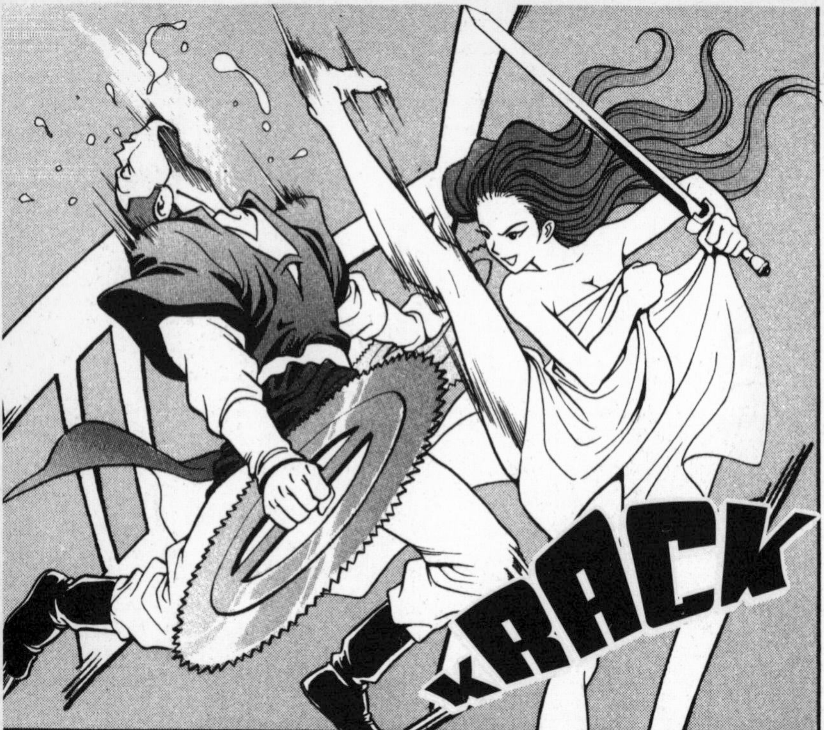
KRACK

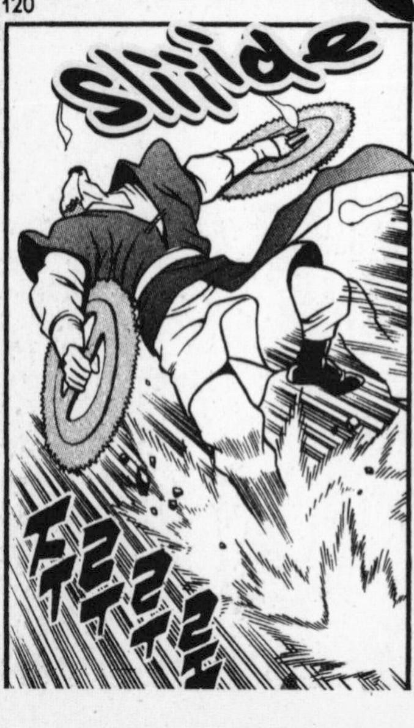
Sliide

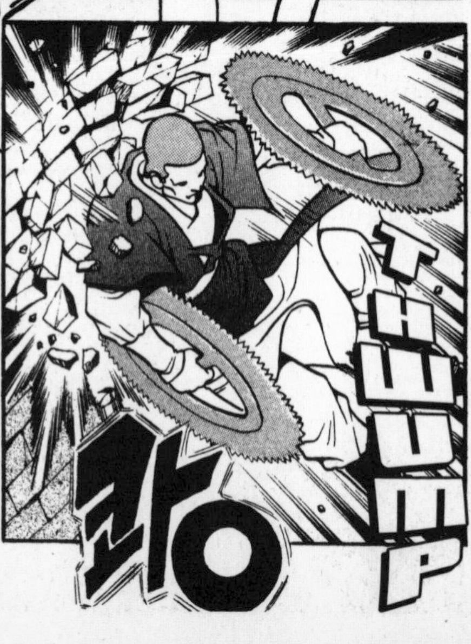
THUMP

FOUR BANDITS OF MIDLANDS HAVE COME ON THEIR OWN?

YES, MASTER.

LOOKS LIKE OUR REPUTATION HAS BEEN SPREAD ACROSS THE LAND.

HAVE THE BANDITS REVEALED THEIR **FOUR WHEEL FORMATION?**

NO, MASTER, THEY HAVEN'T.

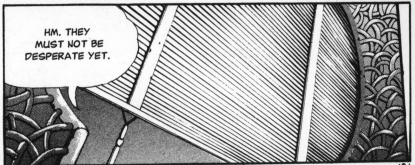

HM. THEY MUST NOT BE DESPERATE YET.

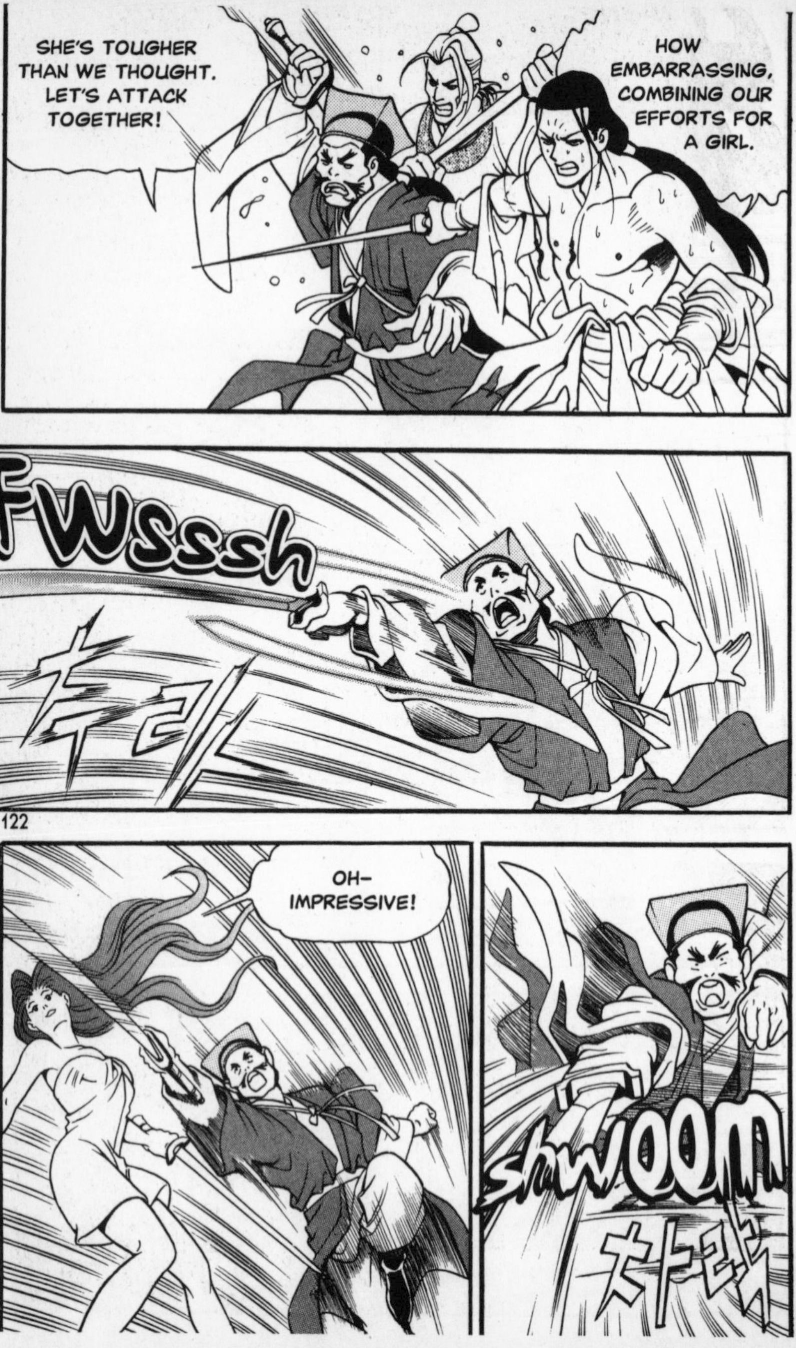
SHE'S TOUGHER THAN WE THOUGHT. LET'S ATTACK TOGETHER!
HOW EMBARRASSING, COMBINING OUR EFFORTS FOR A GIRL.
FWSSSH
OH- IMPRESSIVE!
SHWOOM

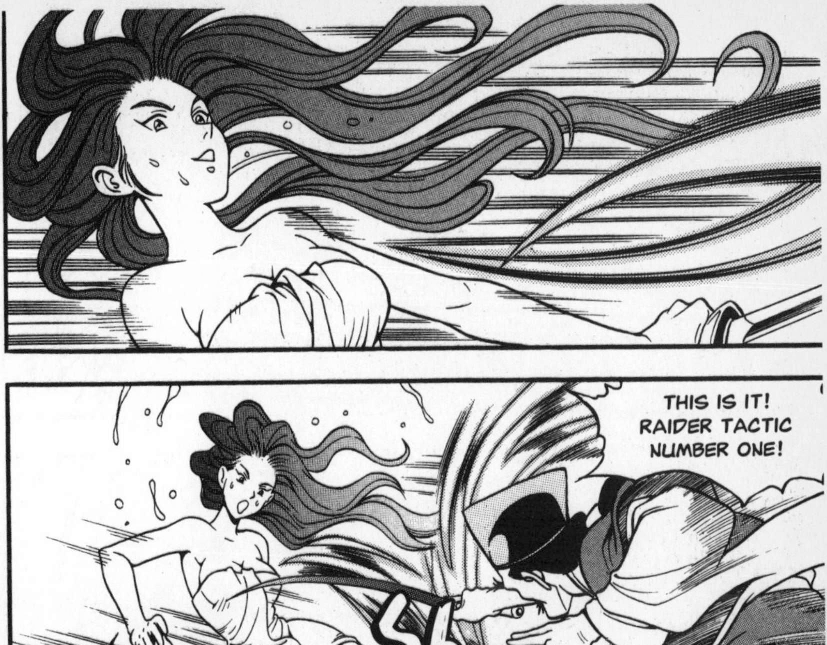
THIS IS IT!
RAIDER TACTIC
NUMBER ONE!
Shwack

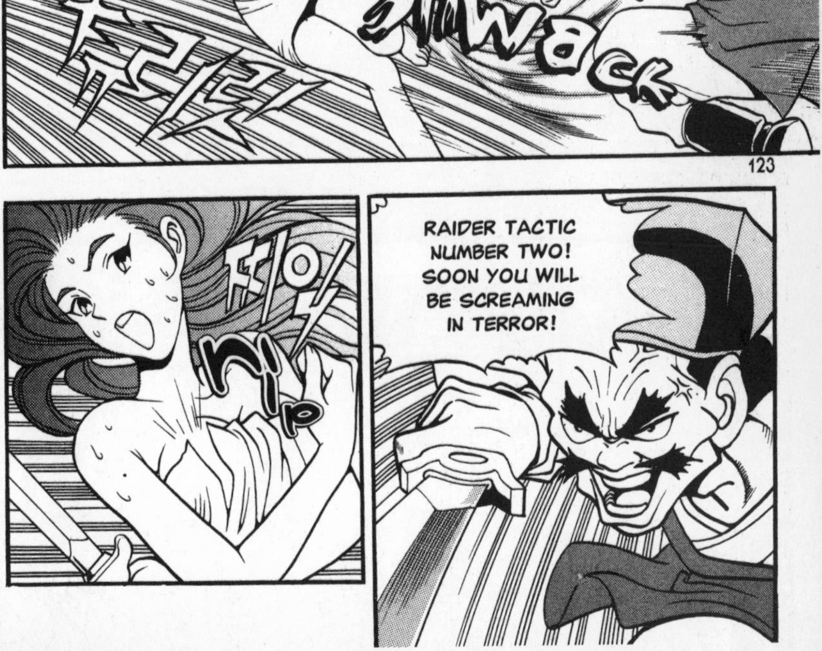
RAIDER TACTIC
NUMBER TWO!
SOON YOU WILL
BE SCREAMING
IN TERROR!

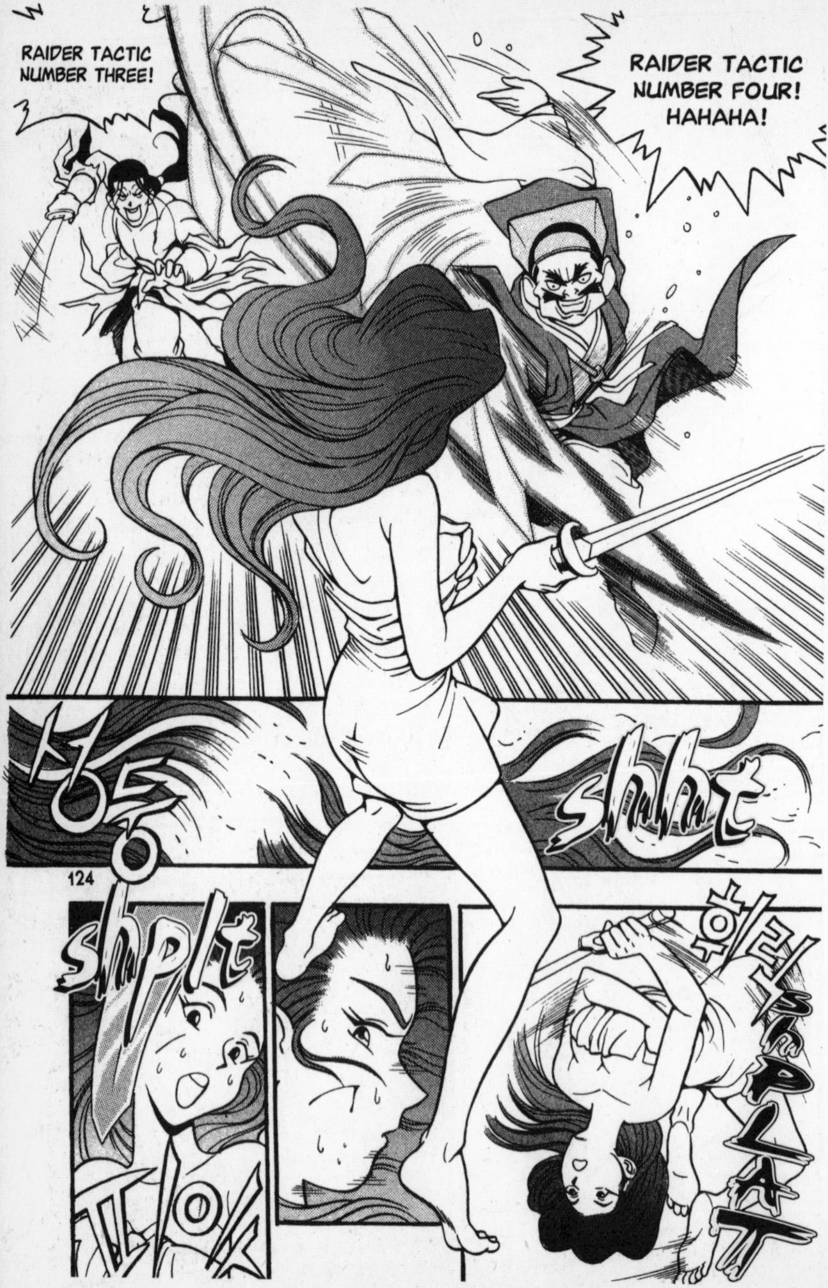
RAIDER TACTIC NUMBER THREE!
RAIDER TACTIC NUMBER FOUR! HAHAHA!
shhht
shplt

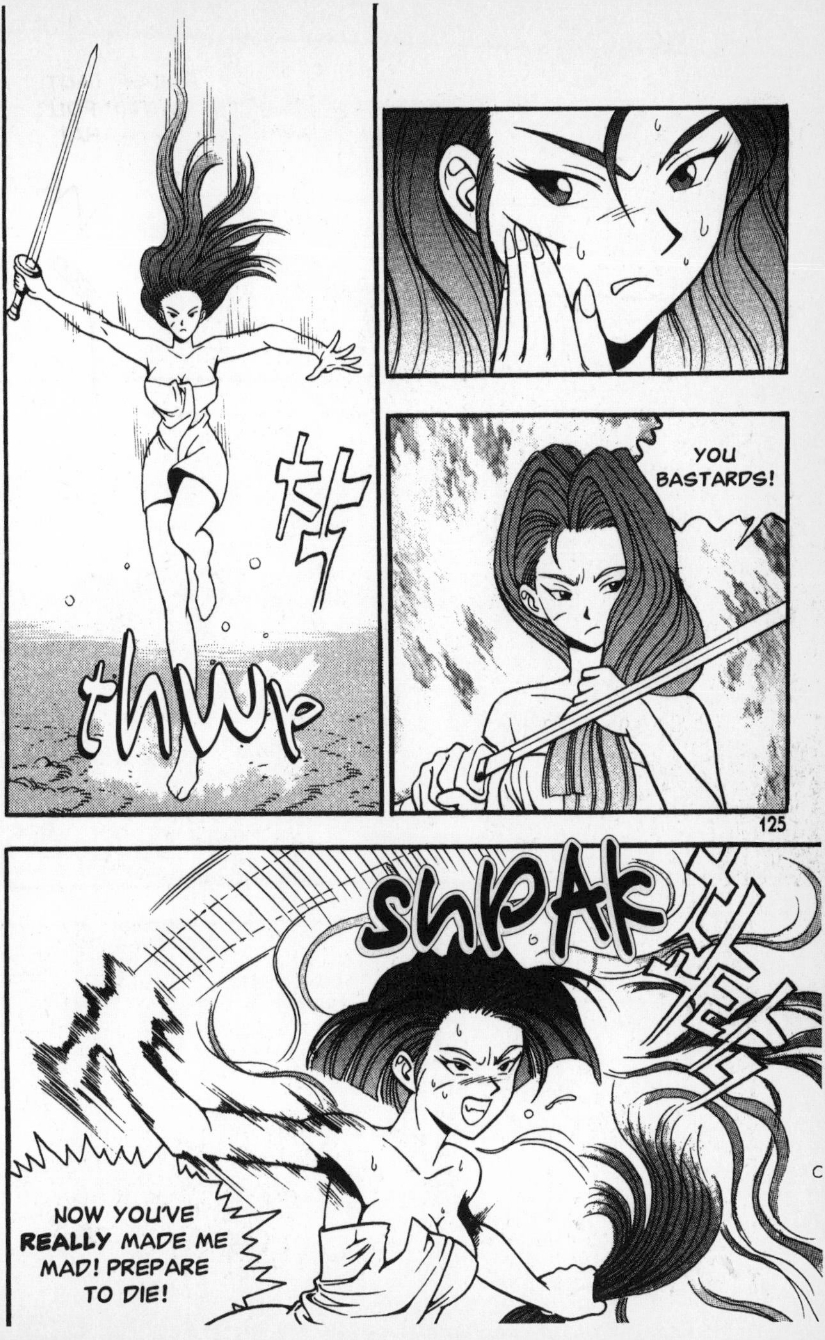
thwp
YOU BASTARDS!
shpak
NOW YOU'VE **REALLY** MADE ME MAD! PREPARE TO DIE!

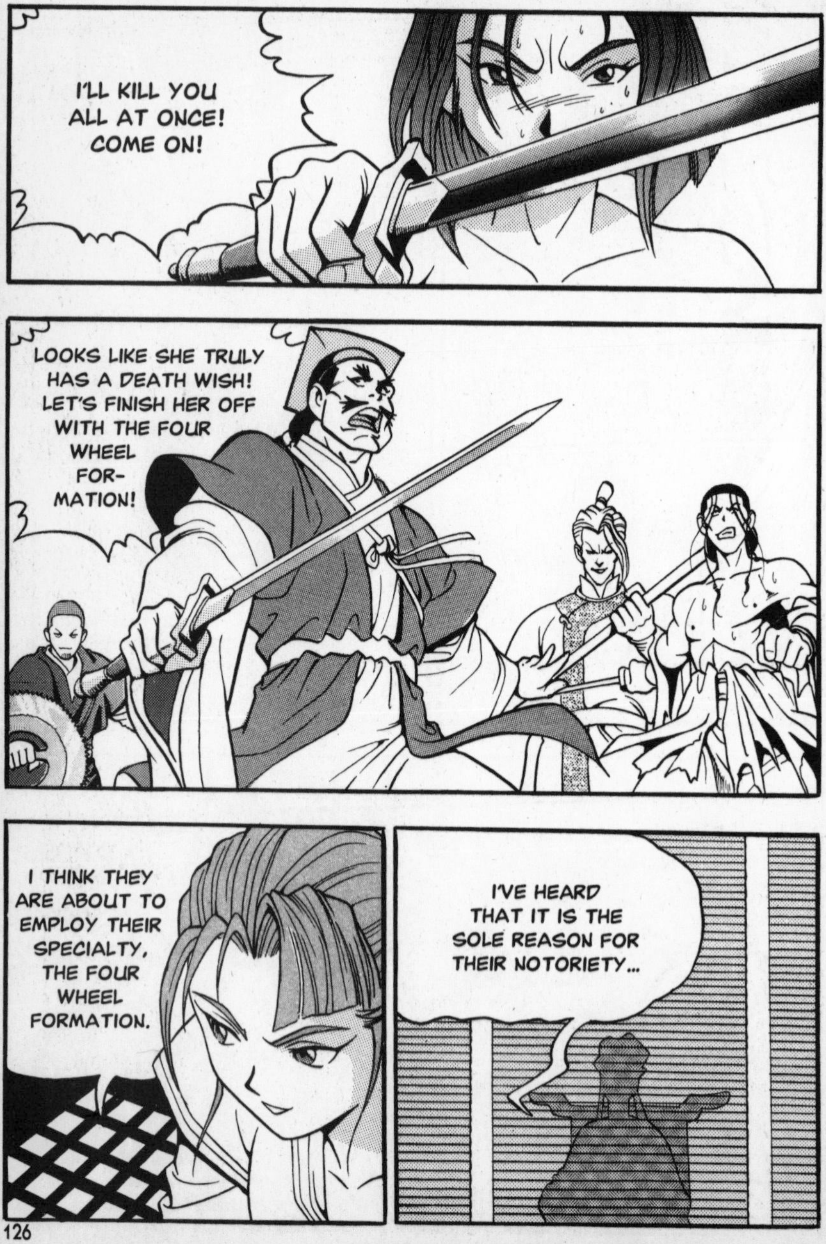
I'LL KILL YOU ALL AT ONCE! COME ON!
LOOKS LIKE SHE TRULY HAS A DEATH WISH! LET'S FINISH HER OFF WITH THE FOUR WHEEL FOR-MATION!
I THINK THEY ARE ABOUT TO EMPLOY THEIR SPECIALTY, THE FOUR WHEEL FORMATION.
I'VE HEARD THAT IT IS THE SOLE REASON FOR THEIR NOTORIETY...

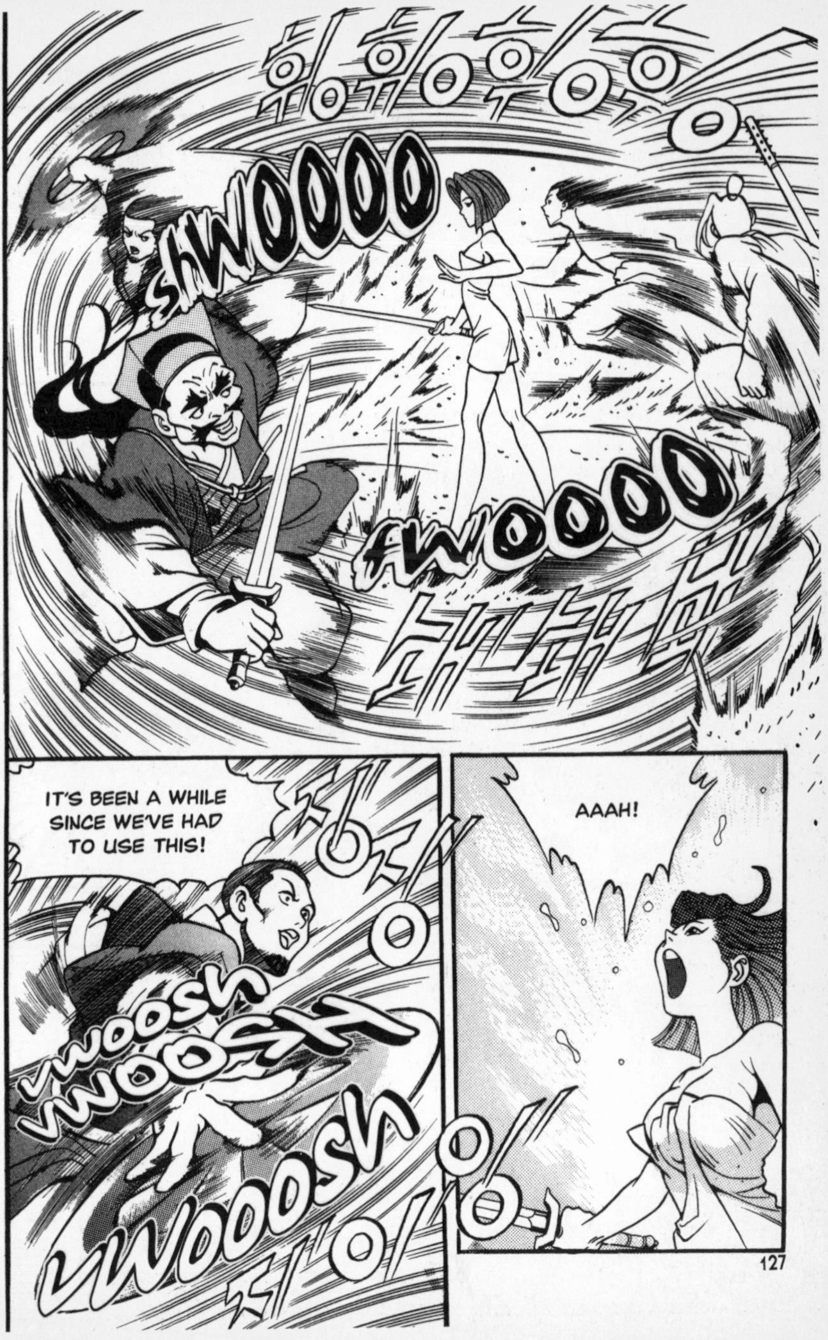
SHWOOOO
FWOOOO
IT'S BEEN A WHILE SINCE WE'VE HAD TO USE THIS!
WOOSH
WOOSH
WOOOOSH
AAAH!

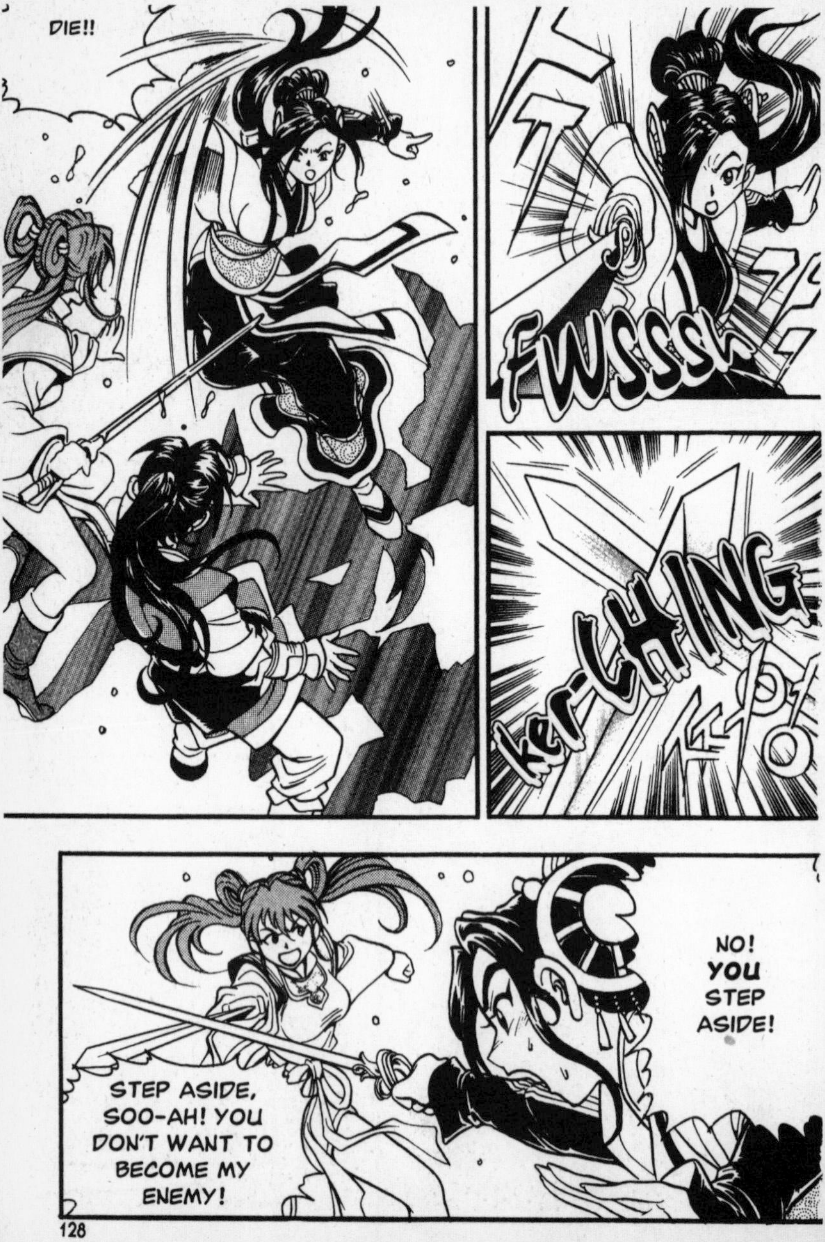
DIE!!
FWSSSH
ker-CHING
STEP ASIDE, SOO-AH! YOU DON'T WANT TO BECOME MY ENEMY!
NO! YOU STEP ASIDE!

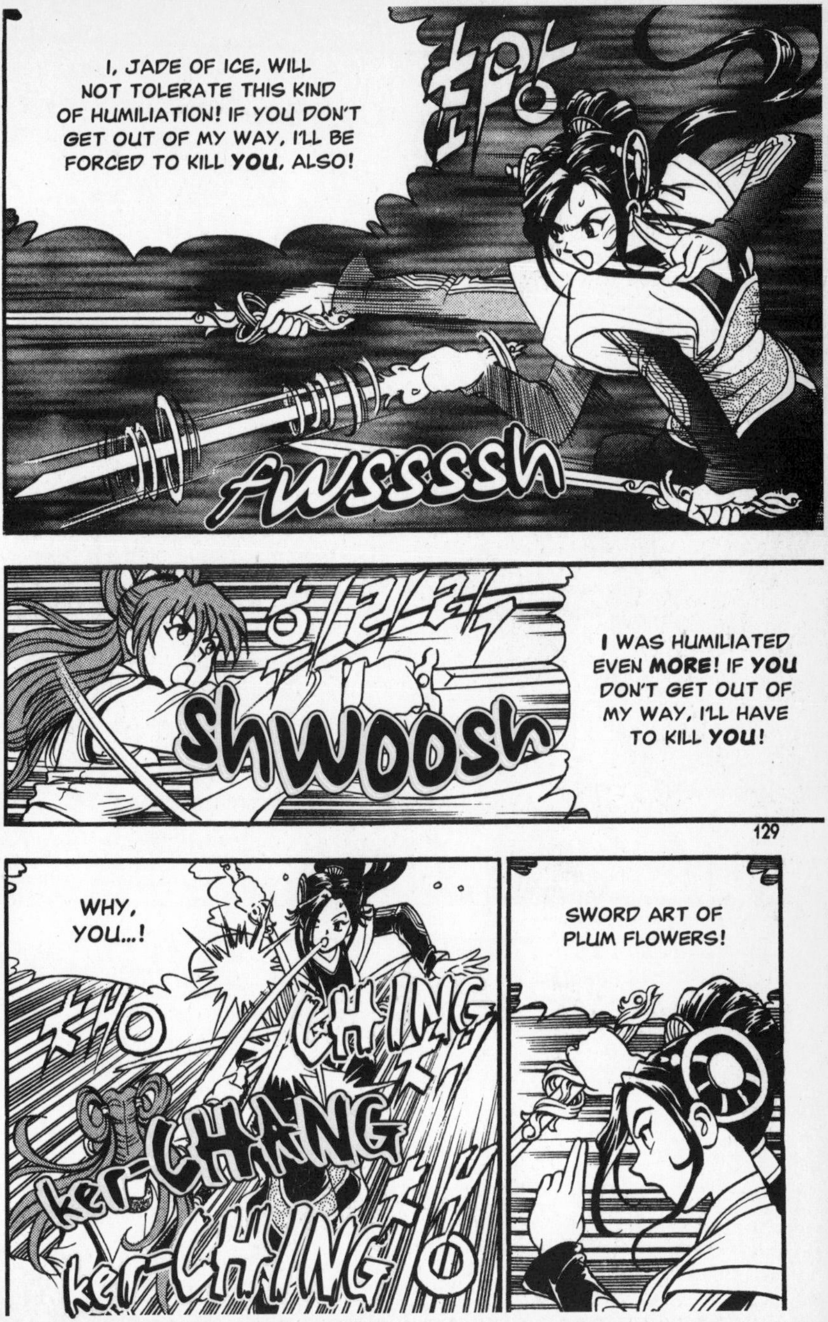
I, JADE OF ICE, WILL NOT TOLERATE THIS KIND OF HUMILIATION! IF YOU DON'T GET OUT OF MY WAY, I'LL BE FORCED TO KILL YOU, ALSO!
fwssssh
shwoosh
I WAS HUMILIATED EVEN MORE! IF YOU DON'T GET OUT OF MY WAY, I'LL HAVE TO KILL YOU!
WHY, YOU...!
CHING
ker-CHANG
ker-CHING
SWORD ART OF PLUM FLOWERS!

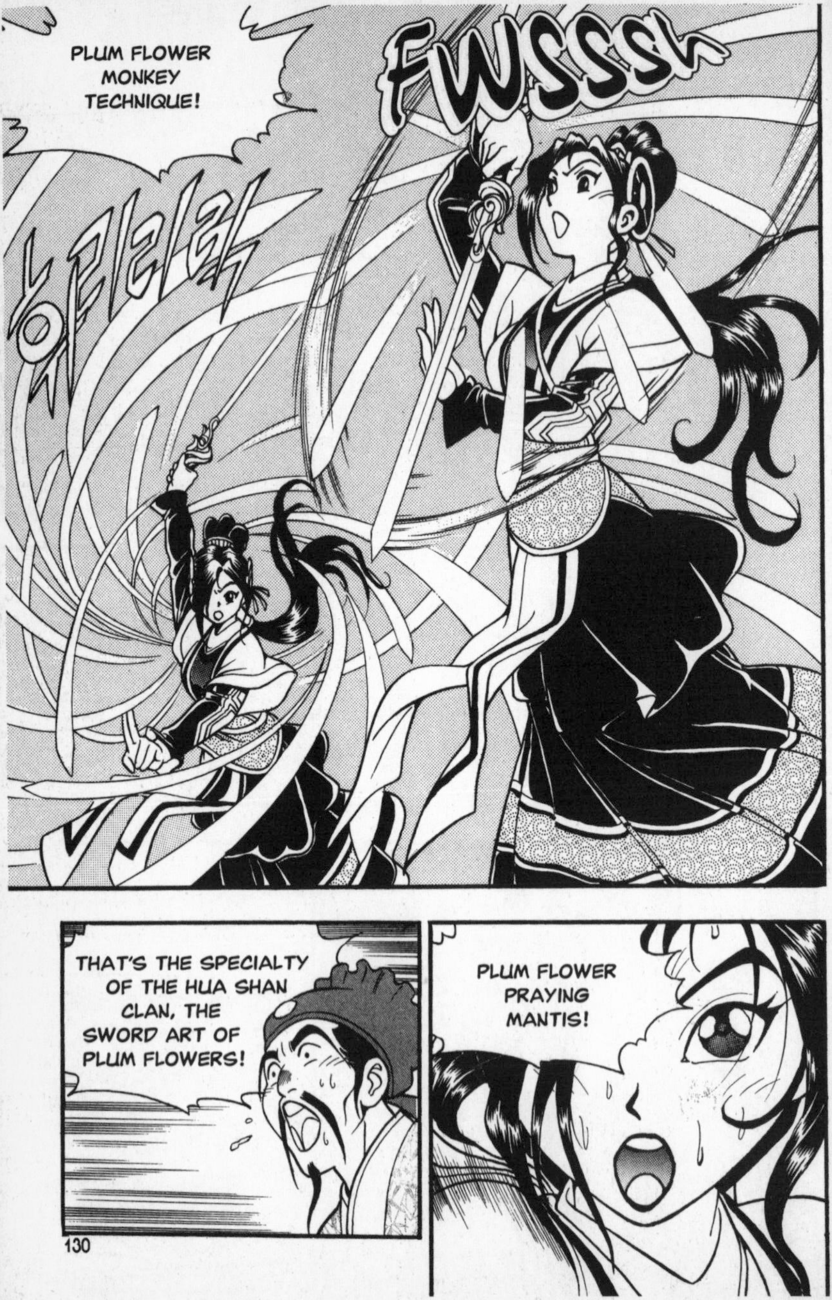
PLUM FLOWER MONKEY TECHNIQUE!
FWSSSH
THAT'S THE SPECIALTY OF THE HUA SHAN CLAN, THE SWORD ART OF PLUM FLOWERS!
PLUM FLOWER PRAYING MANTIS!

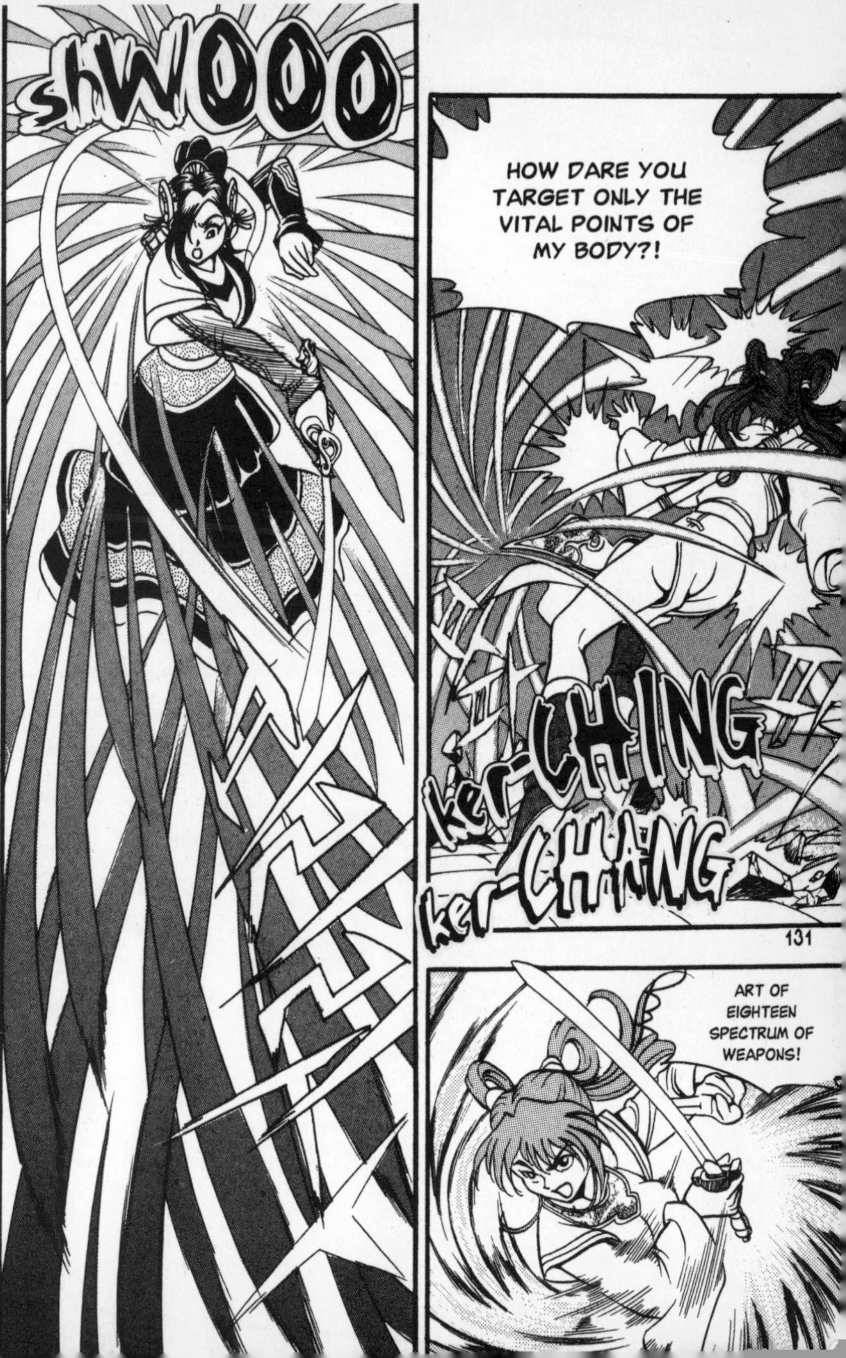
SHWOOO
HOW DARE YOU TARGET ONLY THE VITAL POINTS OF MY BODY?!
ker-CHING
ker-CHANG
ART OF EIGHTEEN SPECTRUM OF WEAPONS!

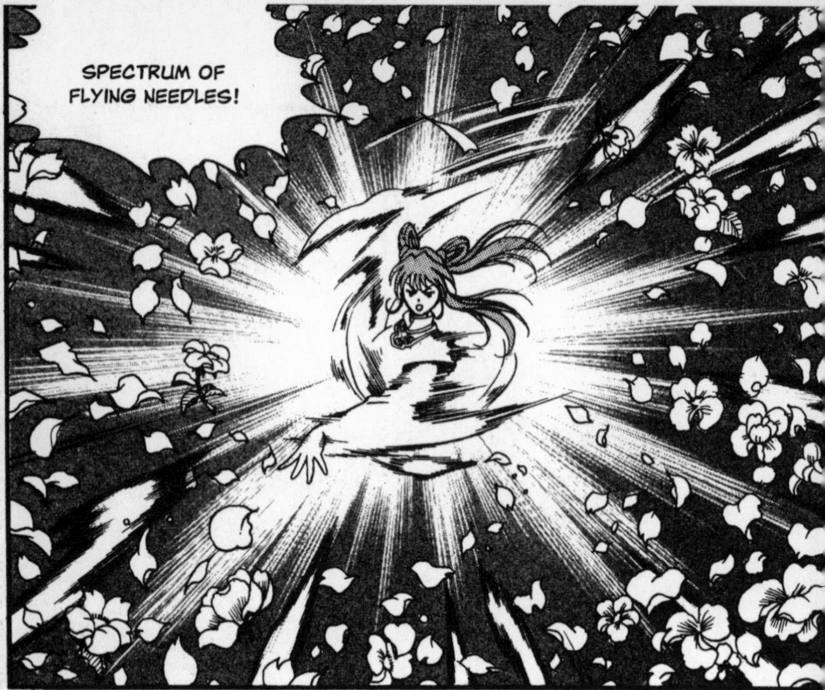
SPECTRUM OF
FLYING NEEDLES!

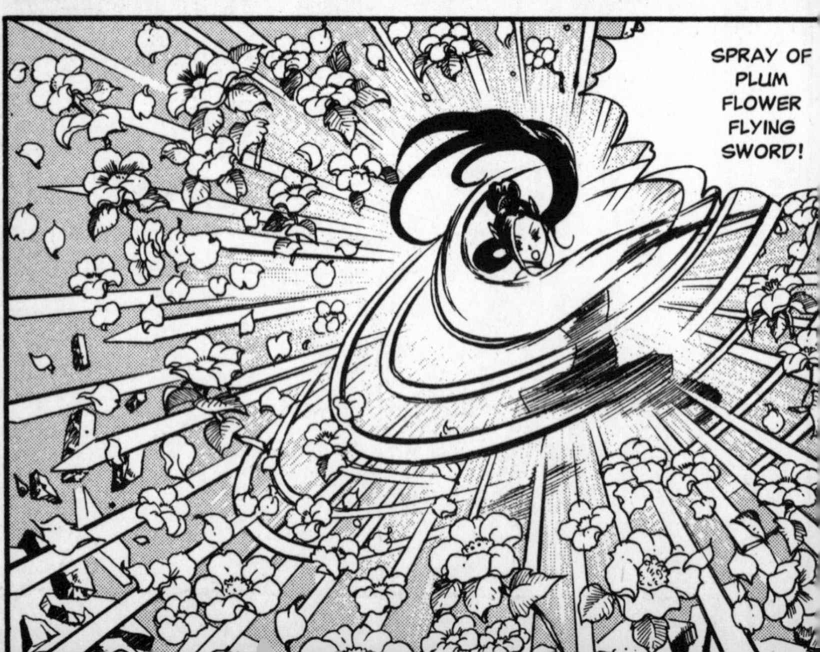
SPRAY OF
PLUM
FLOWER
FLYING
SWORD!

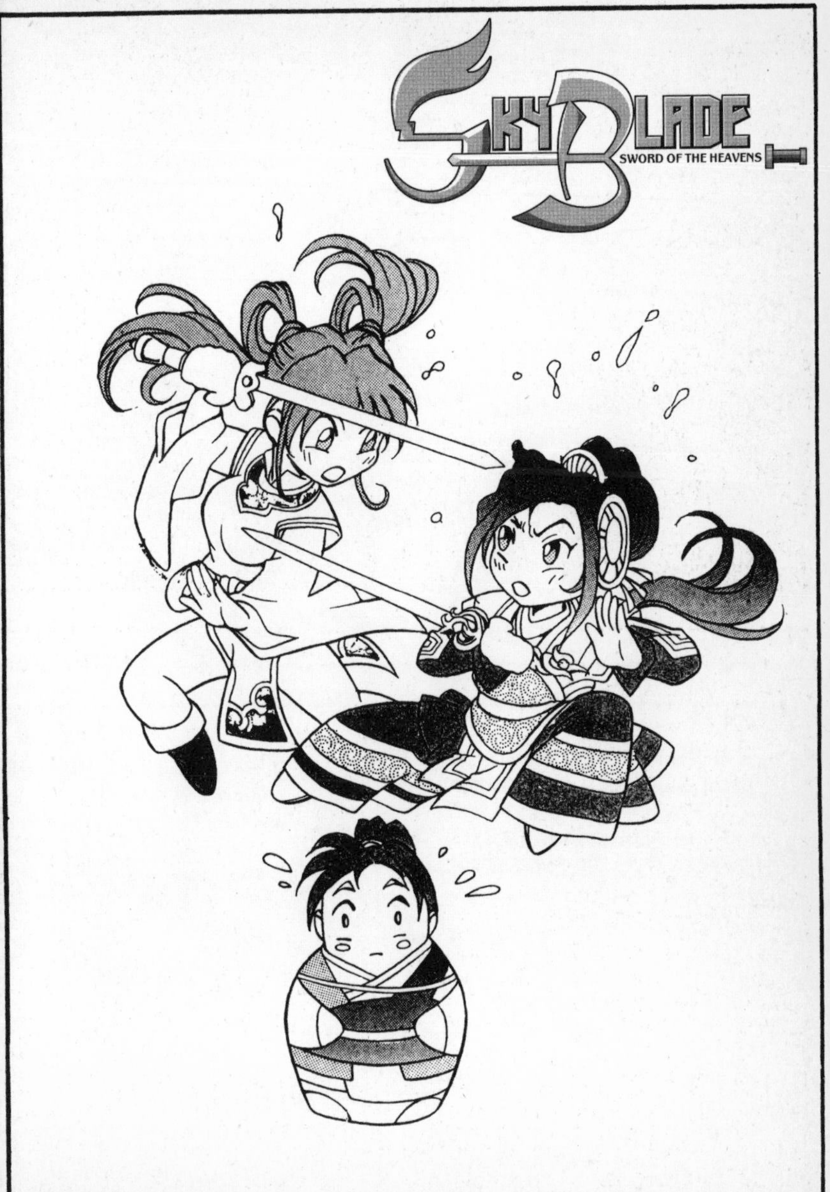
SKY BLADE
SWORD OF THE HEAVENS

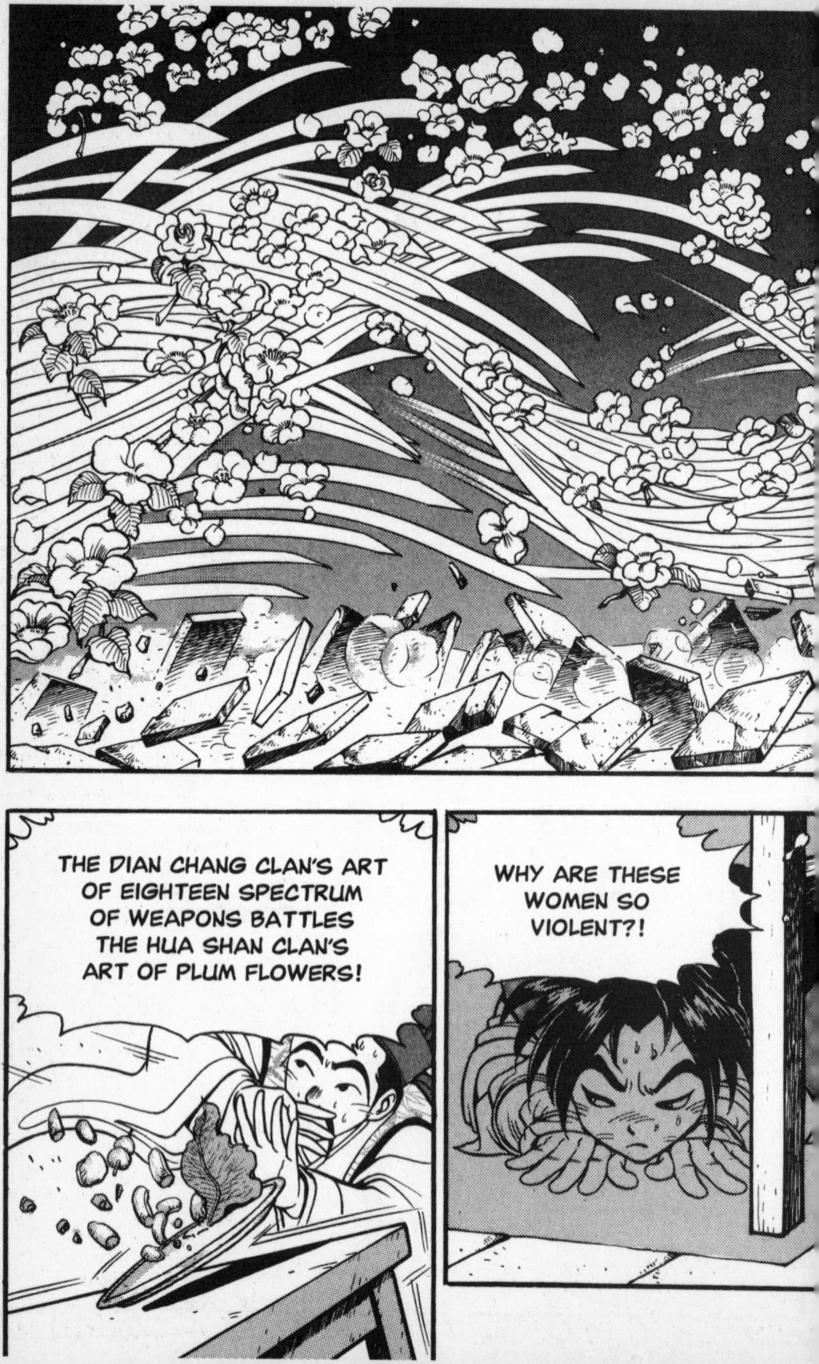
THE DIAN CHANG CLAN'S ART OF EIGHTEEN SPECTRUM OF WEAPONS BATTLES THE HUA SHAN CLAN'S ART OF PLUM FLOWERS!
WHY ARE THESE WOMEN SO VIOLENT?!

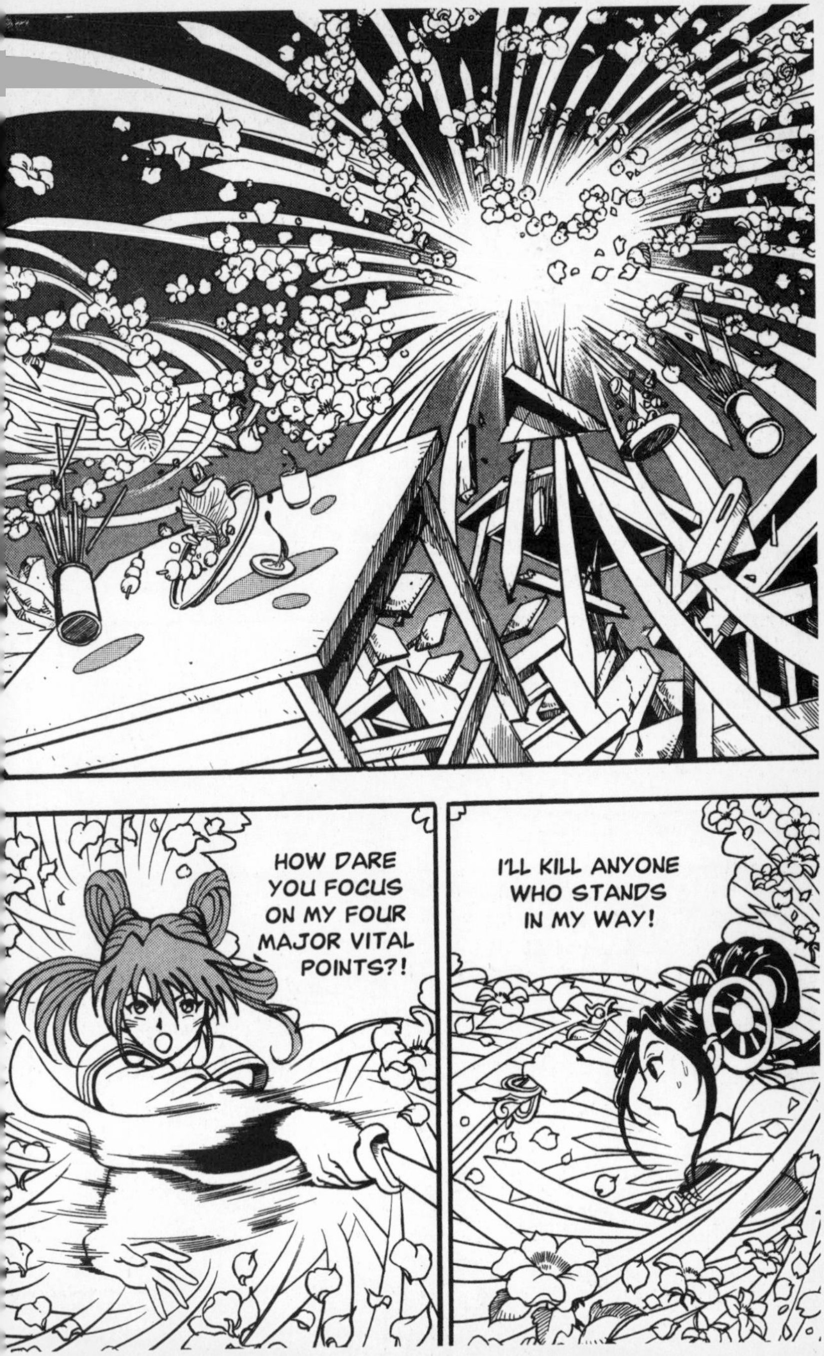
I'LL KILL ANYONE
WHO STANDS
IN MY WAY!
HOW DARE
YOU FOCUS
ON MY FOUR
MAJOR VITAL
POINTS?!

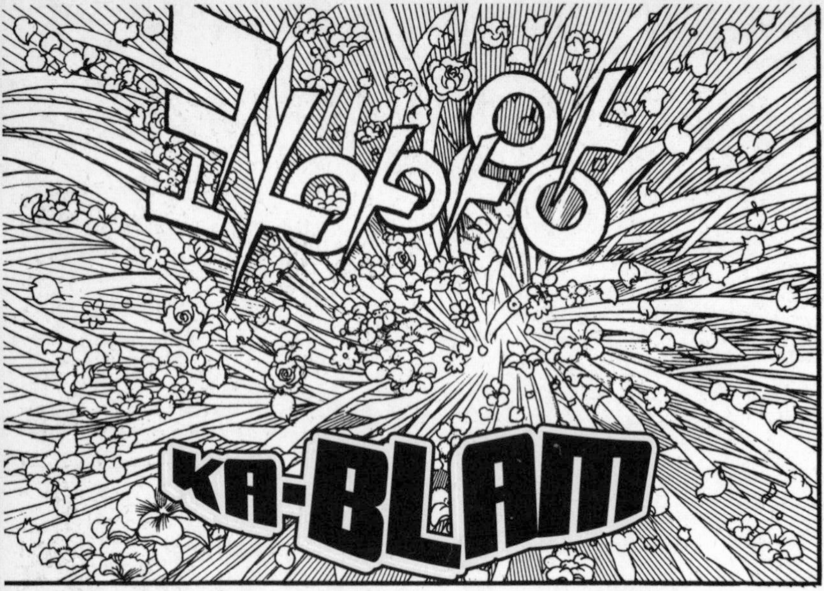
KA-BLAM

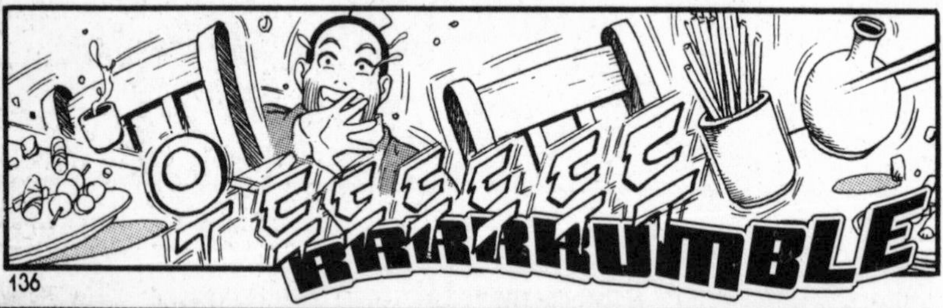
RRRRKUMBLE

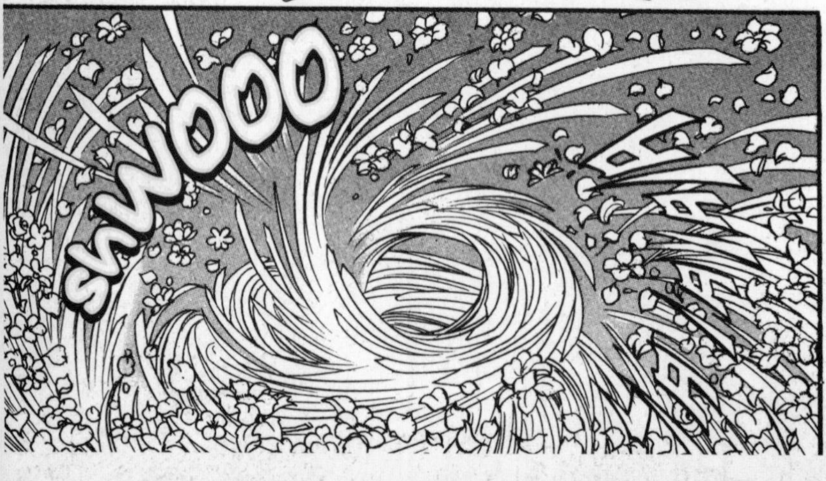
SHWOOO

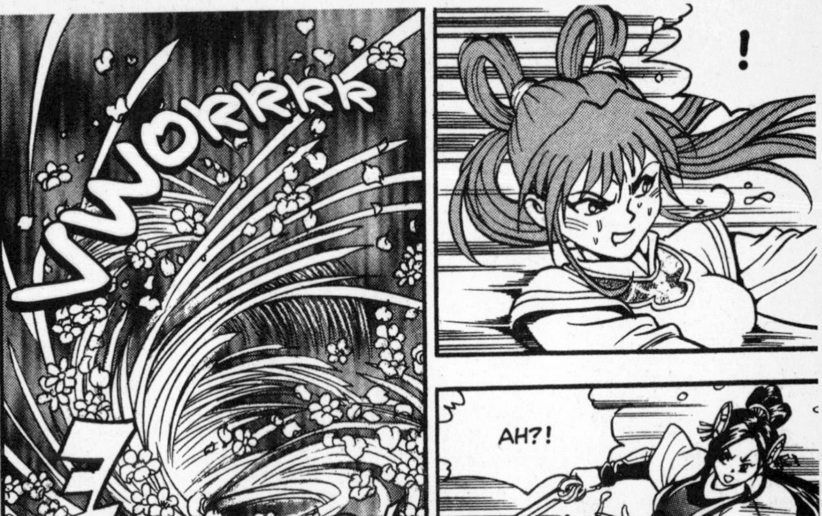

VWORRRR
!
AH?!

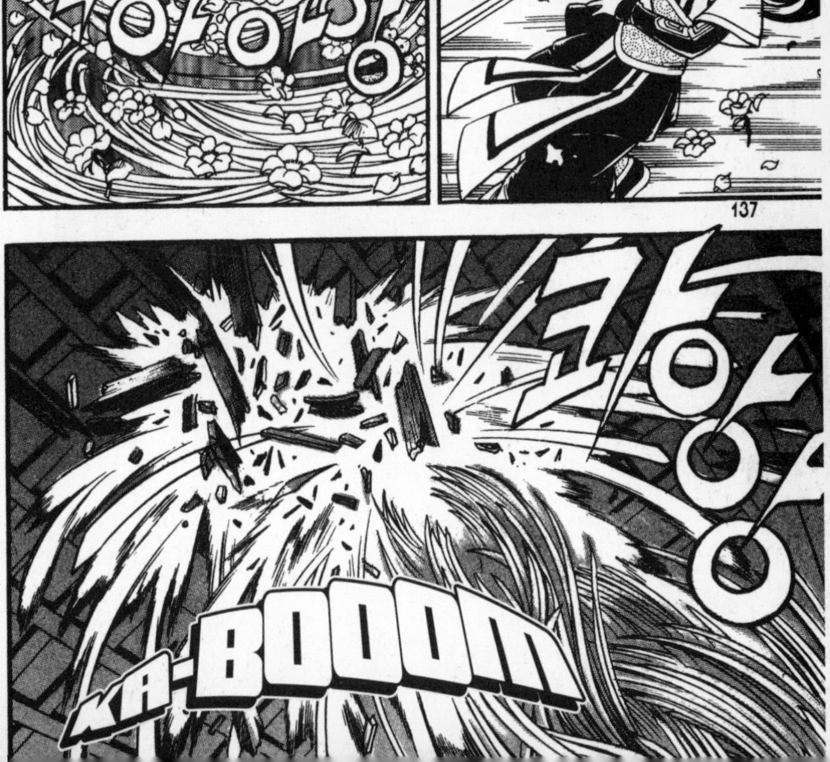

KA-BOOOM

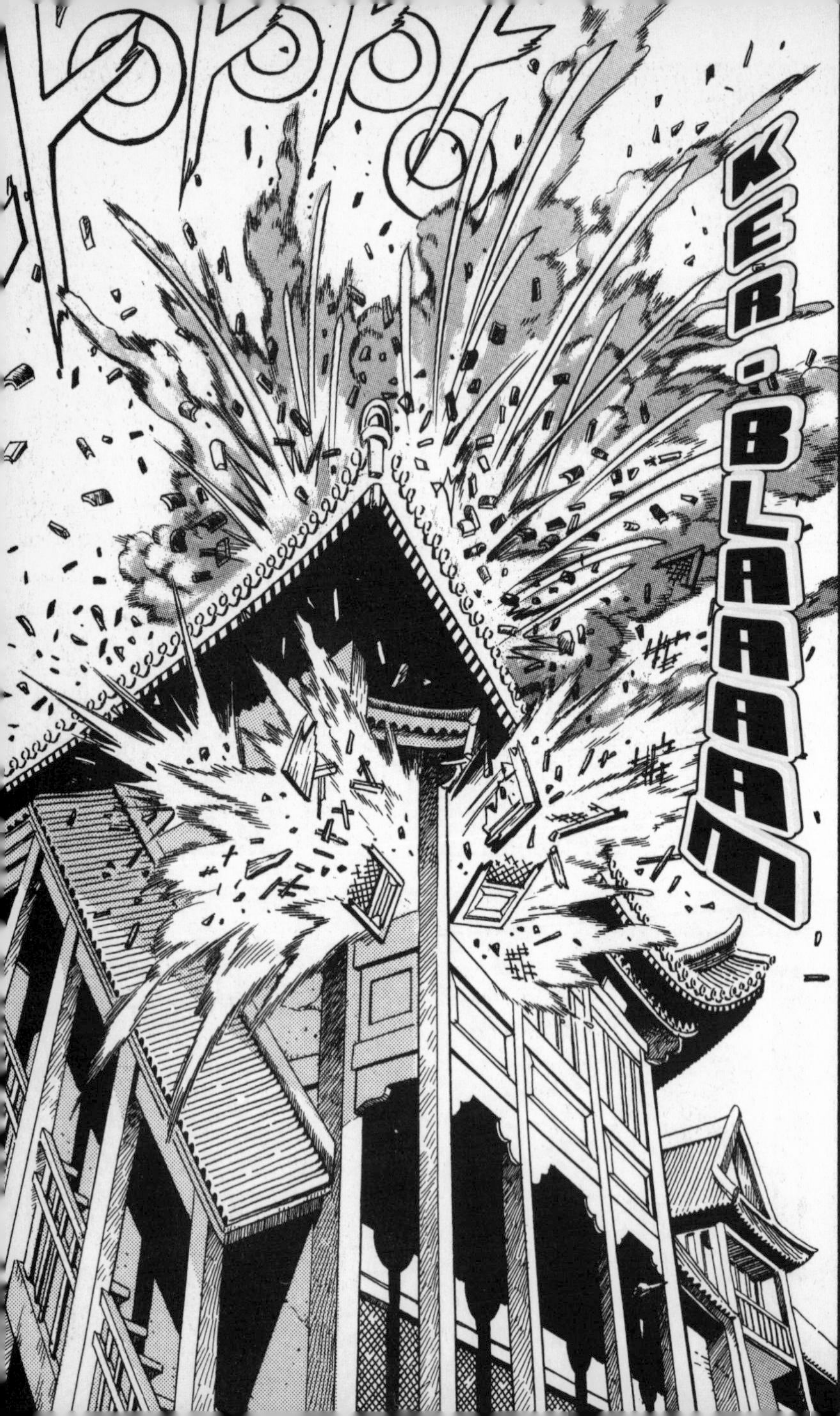
KER-BLAAAAM

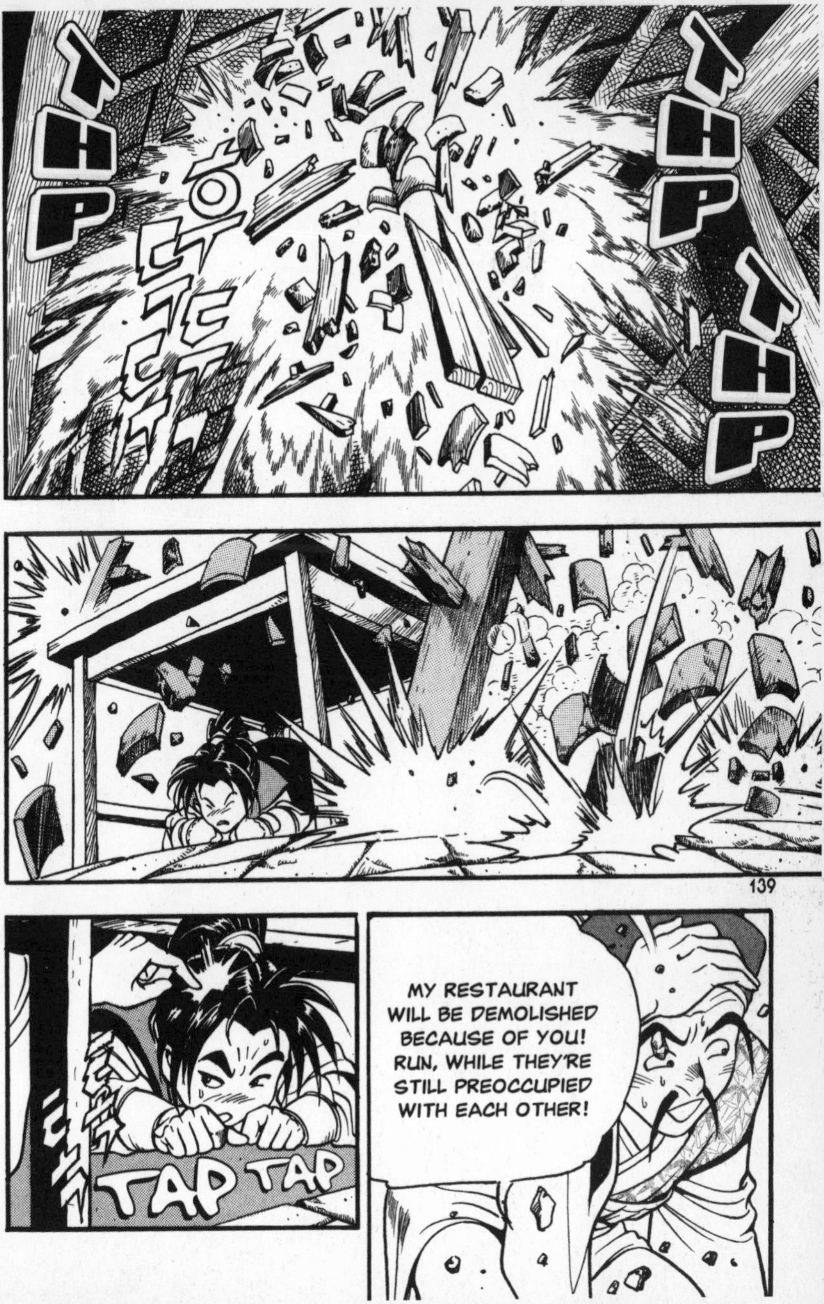
THP THP
THP
TAP TAP
MY RESTAURANT WILL BE DEMOLISHED BECAUSE OF YOU! RUN, WHILE THEY'RE STILL PREOCCUPIED WITH EACH OTHER!

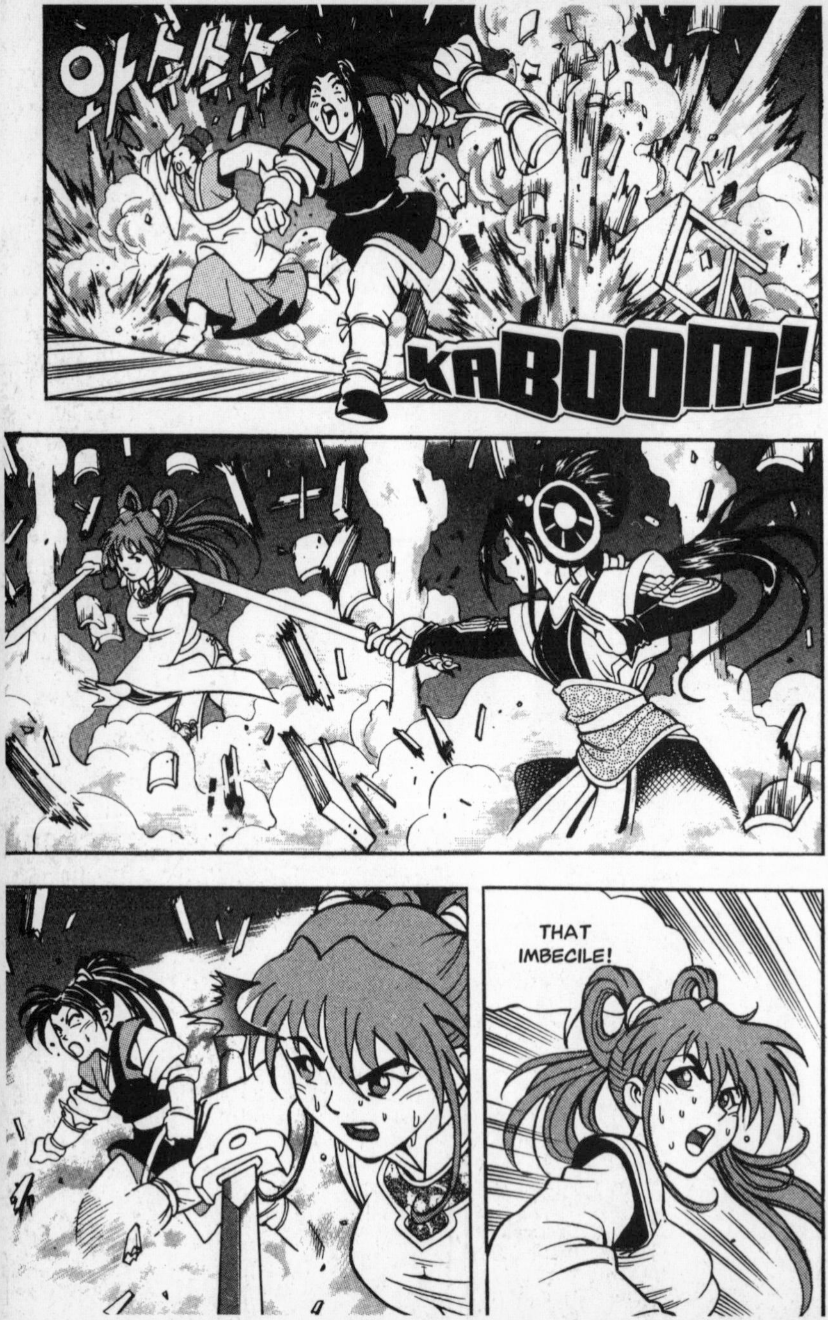
KABOOM!
THAT IMBECILE!

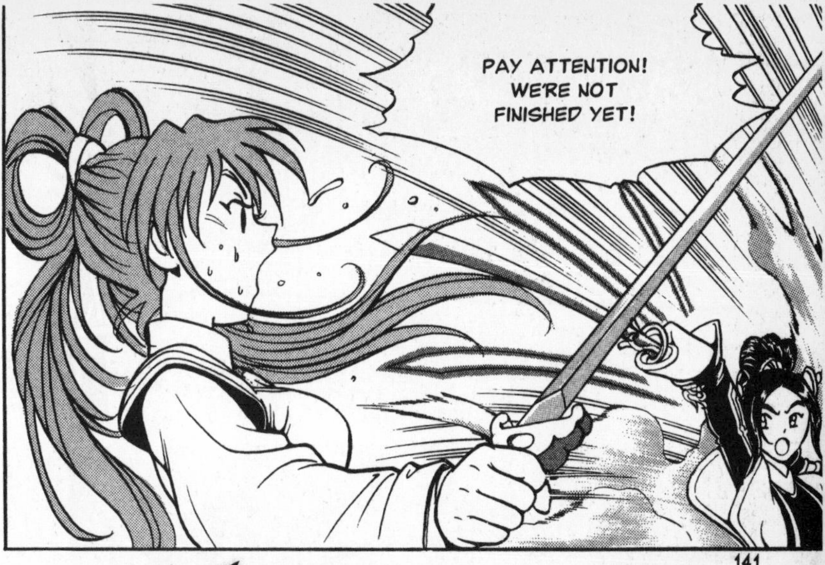
PAY ATTENTION! WE'RE NOT FINISHED YET!

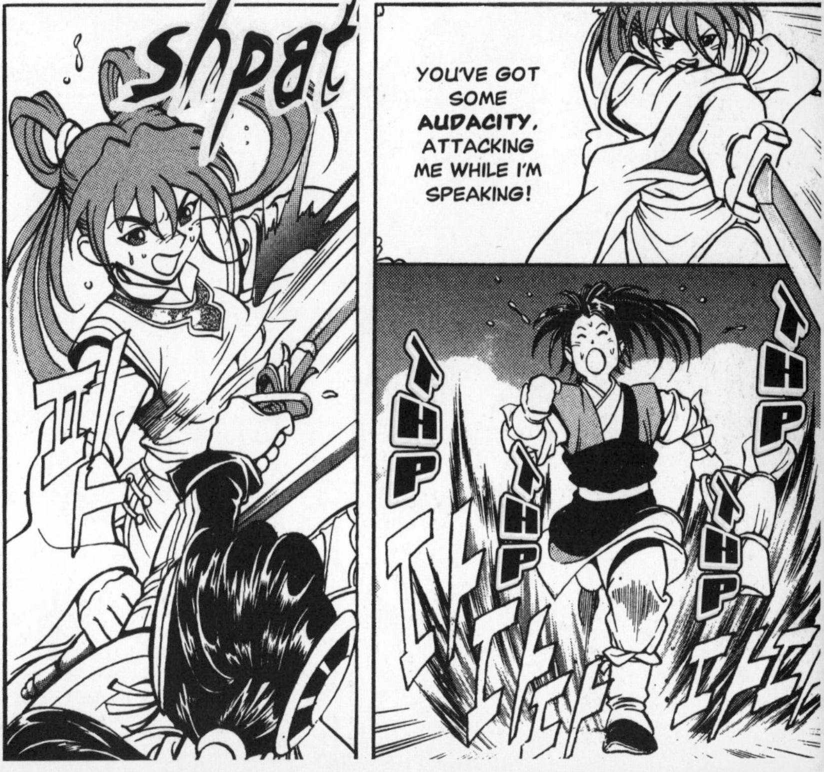
YOU'VE GOT SOME AUDACITY, ATTACKING ME WHILE I'M SPEAKING!
THP
THP
THP
THP
THP
shpat

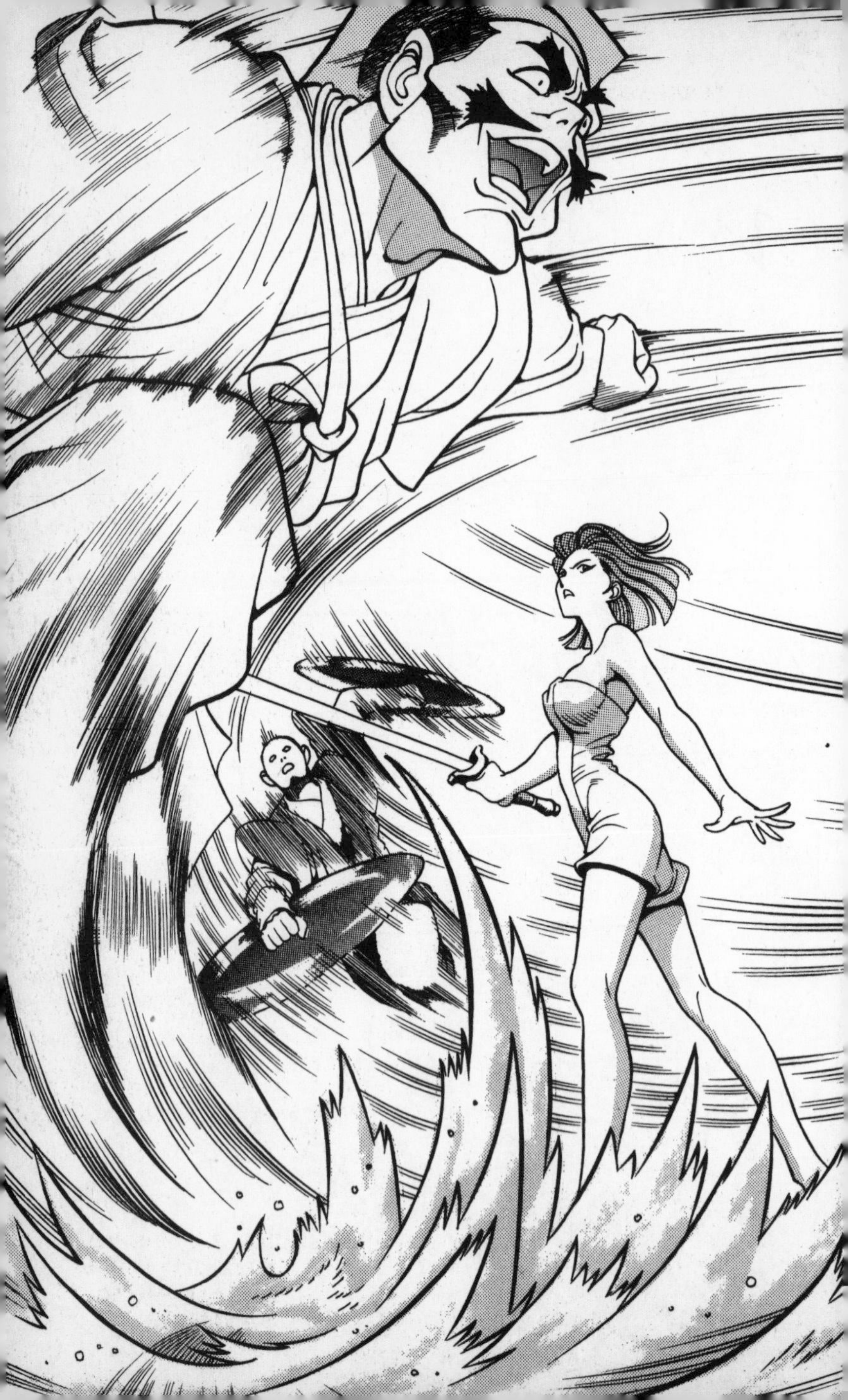

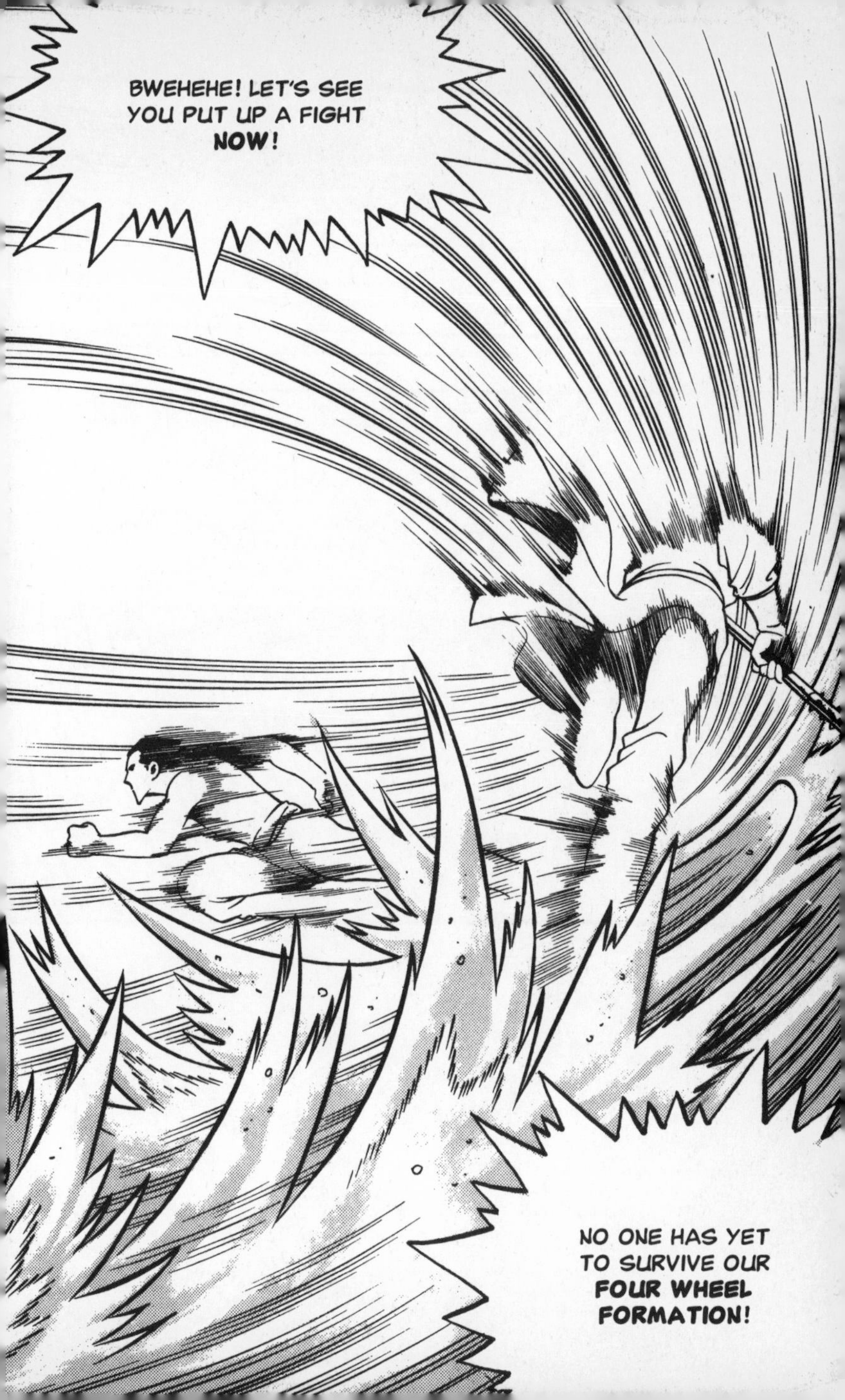
BWEHEHE! LET'S SEE YOU PUT UP A FIGHT **NOW**!
NO ONE HAS YET TO SURVIVE OUR **FOUR WHEEL FORMATION**!

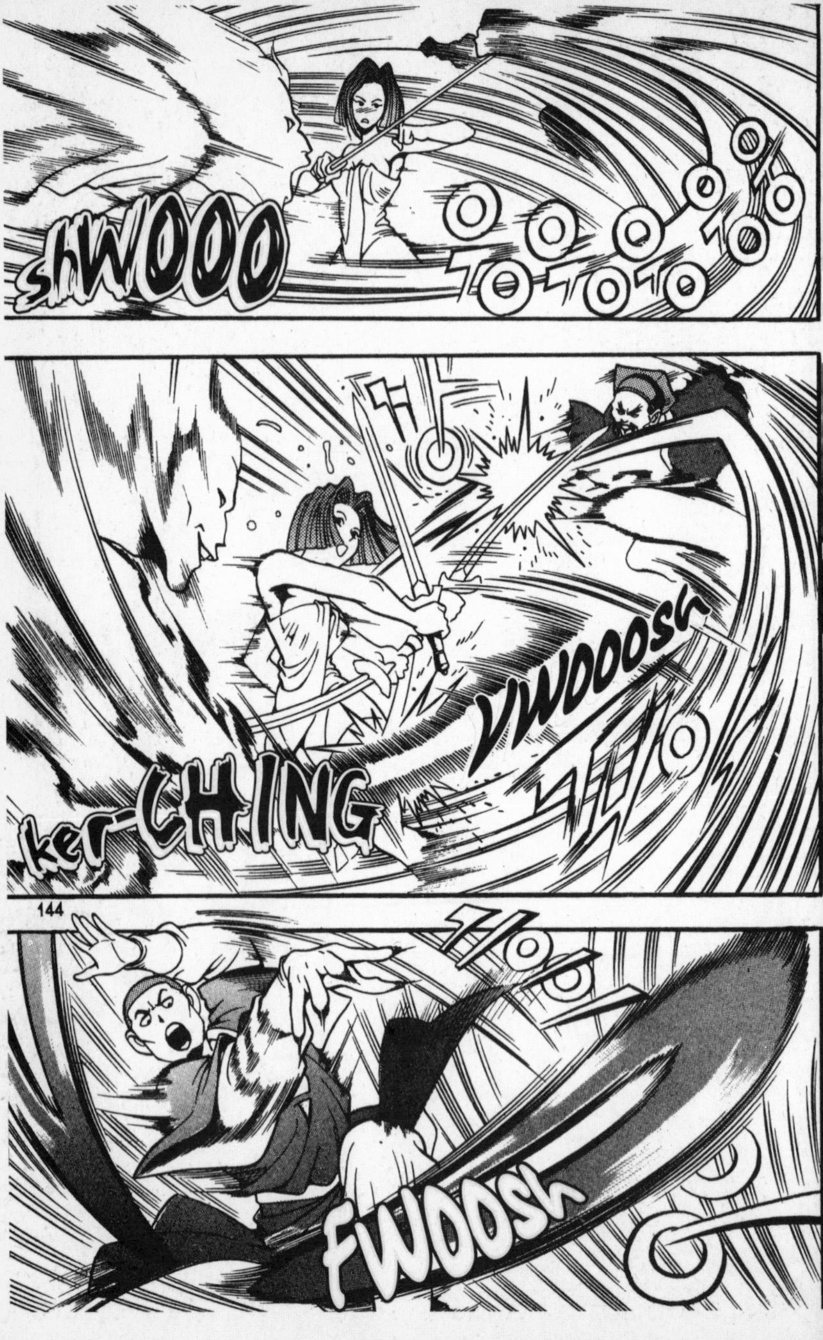
shWOOO
VWOOOSH
ker-CHING
FWOOSH

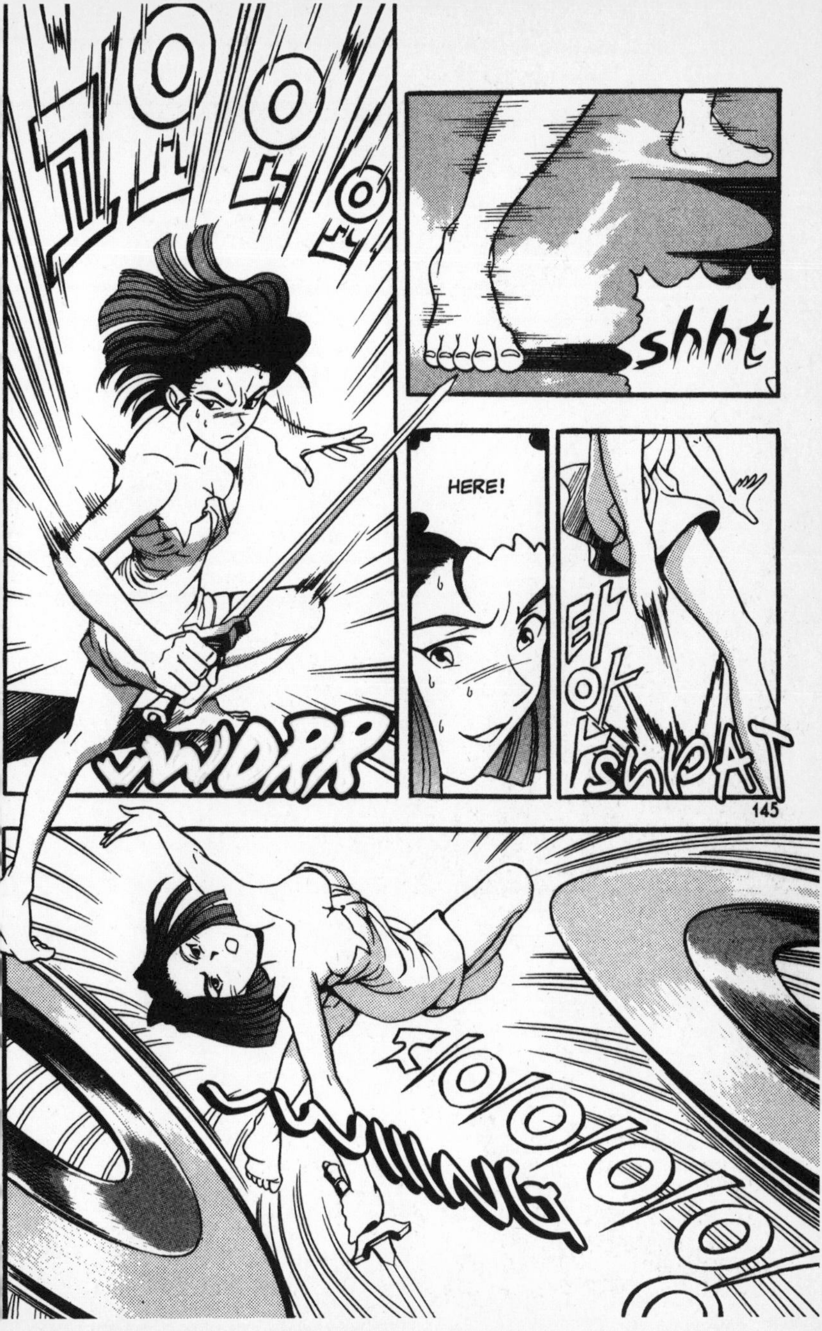
shht
HERE!
shPAT

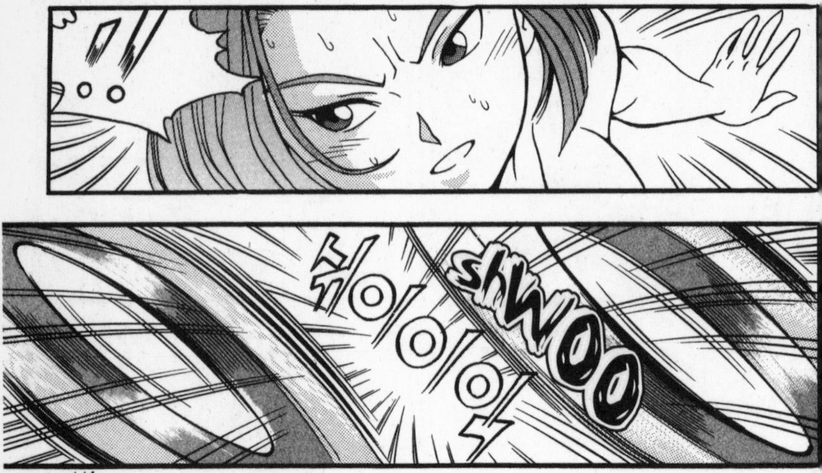
!...
HOOO!
SHWOO

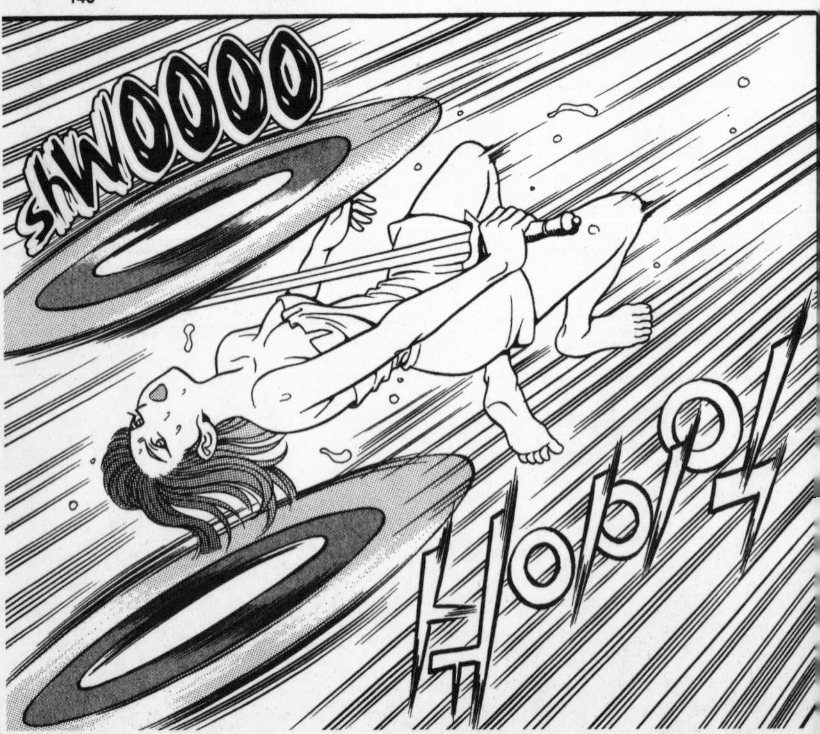
SHWOOOO
HOOO!

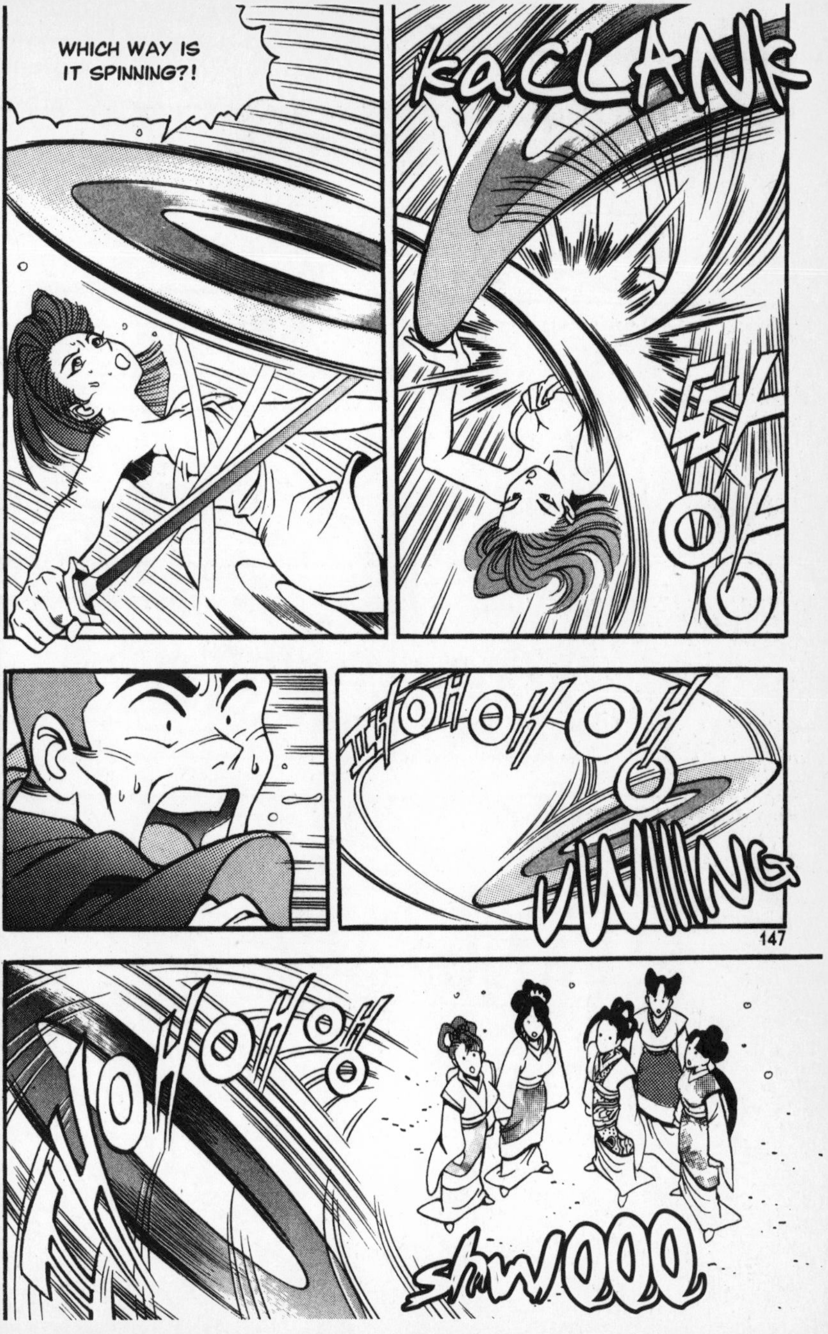
WHICH WAY IS IT SPINNING?!
kaCLANK
shwooo

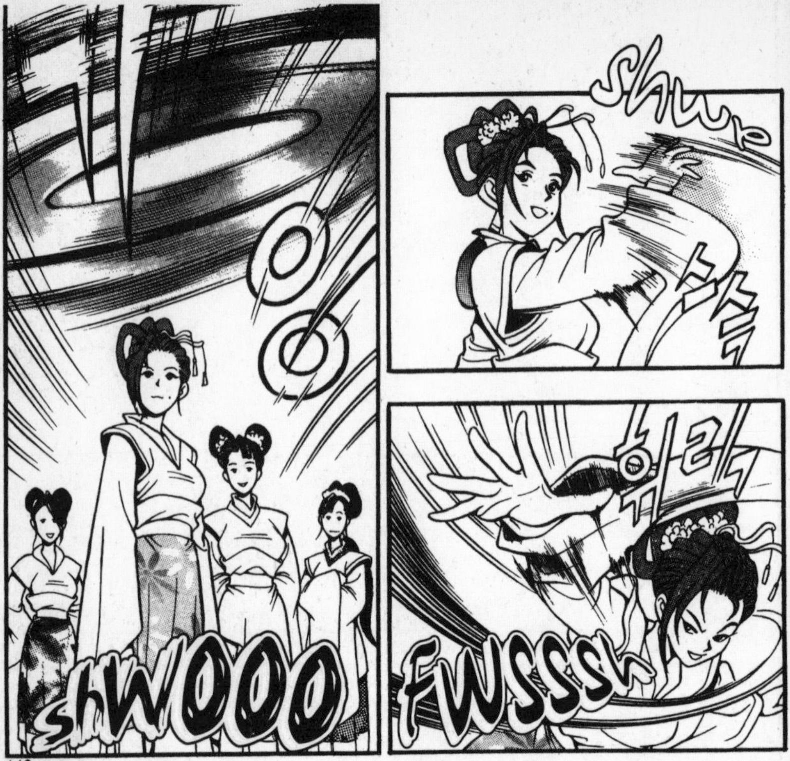
shWOOO
Shwe
FWSSSh

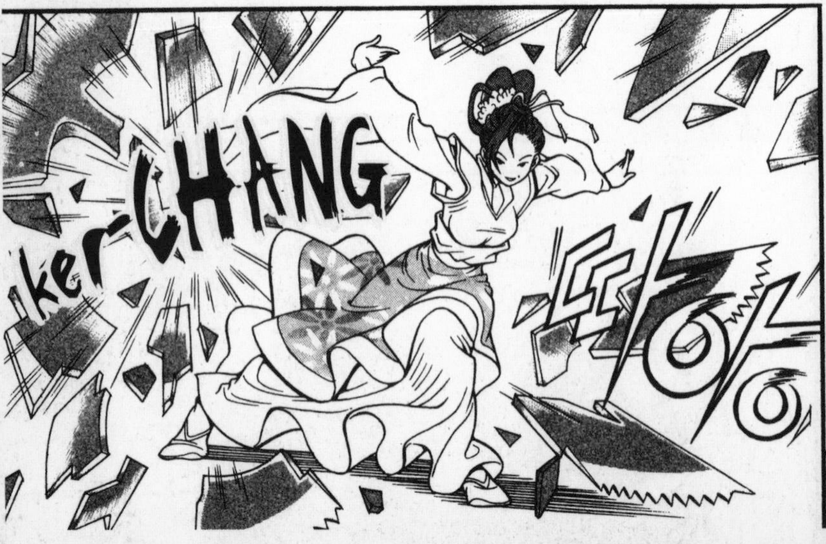
ker-CHANG

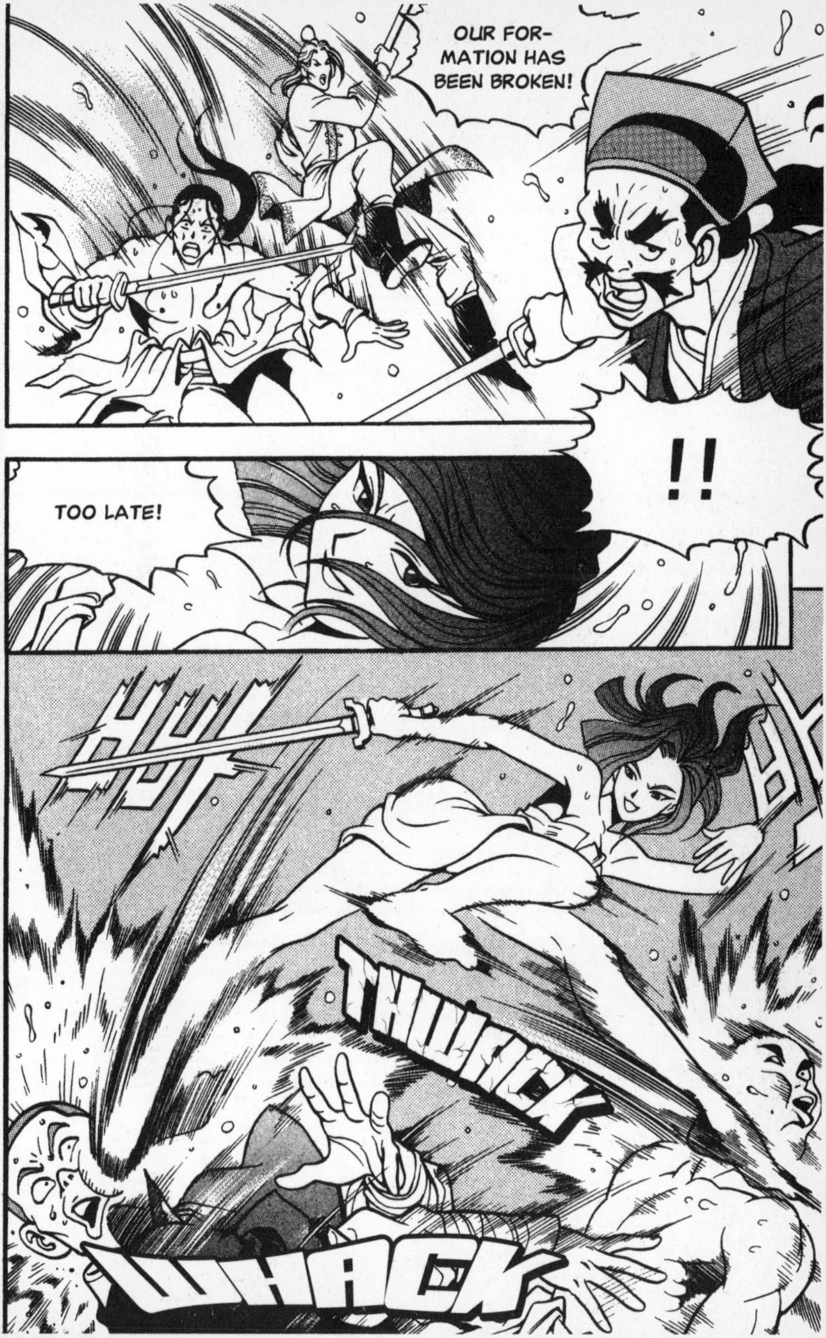
OUR FOR-MATION HAS BEEN BROKEN!
!!
TOO LATE!
THWACK
WHACK

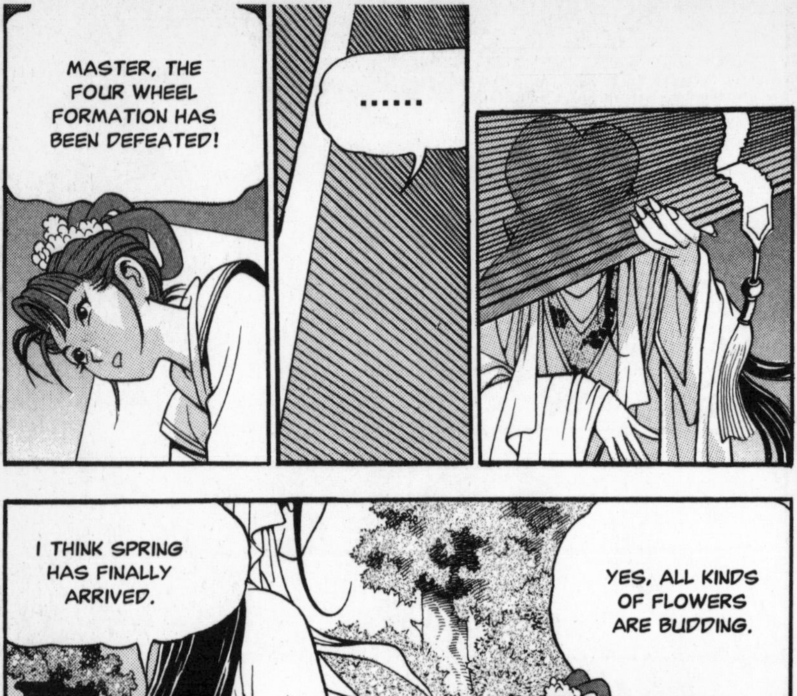
MASTER, THE FOUR WHEEL FORMATION HAS BEEN DEFEATED!
......
I THINK SPRING HAS FINALLY ARRIVED.
YES, ALL KINDS OF FLOWERS ARE BUDDING.

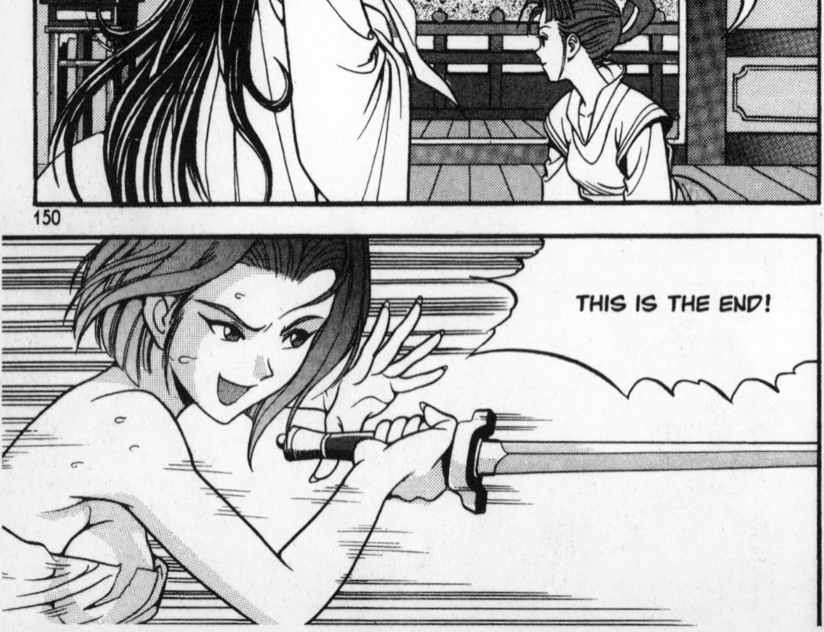
THIS IS THE END!

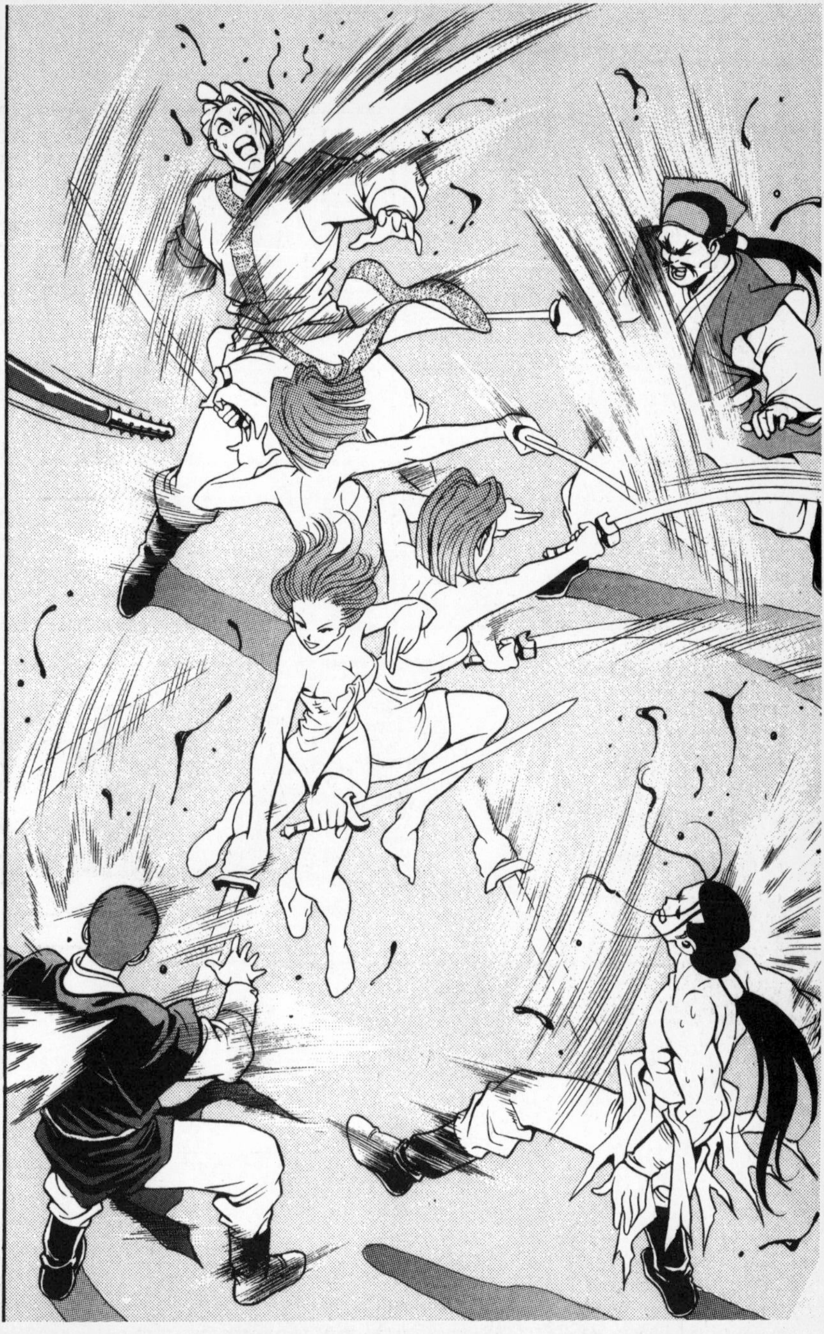

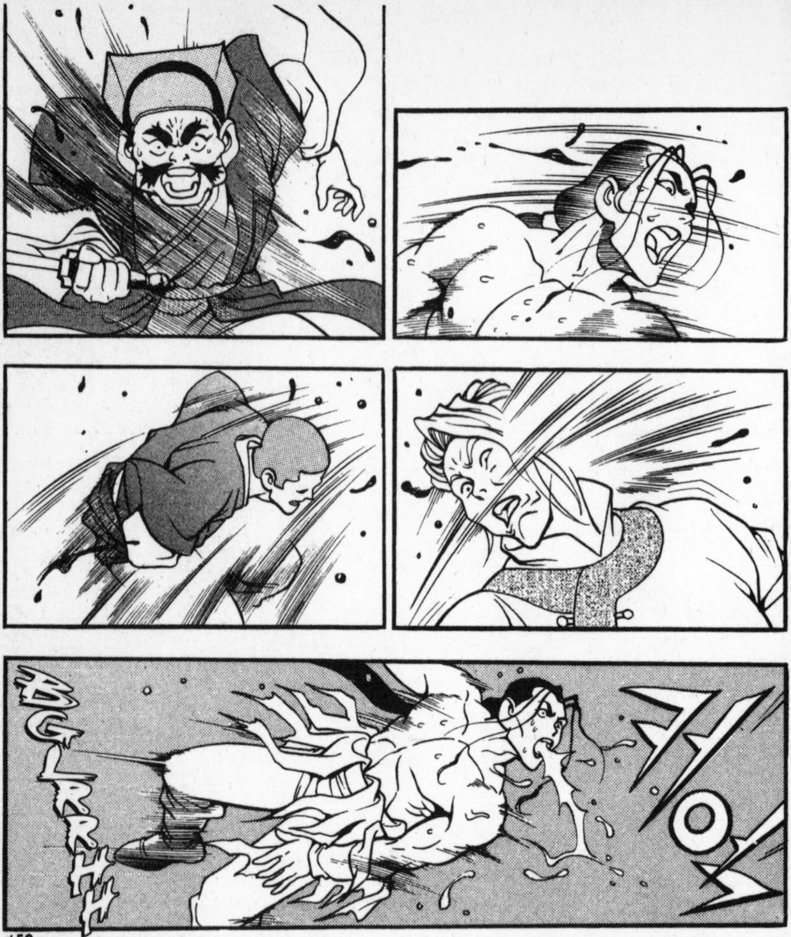
BGLRRHH

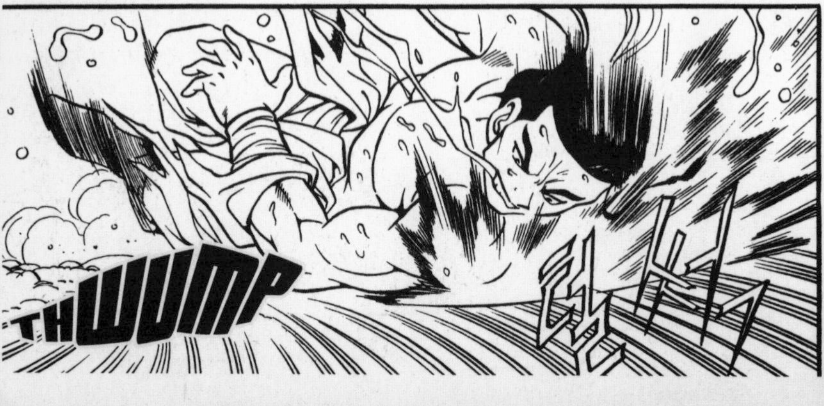
THWUMP

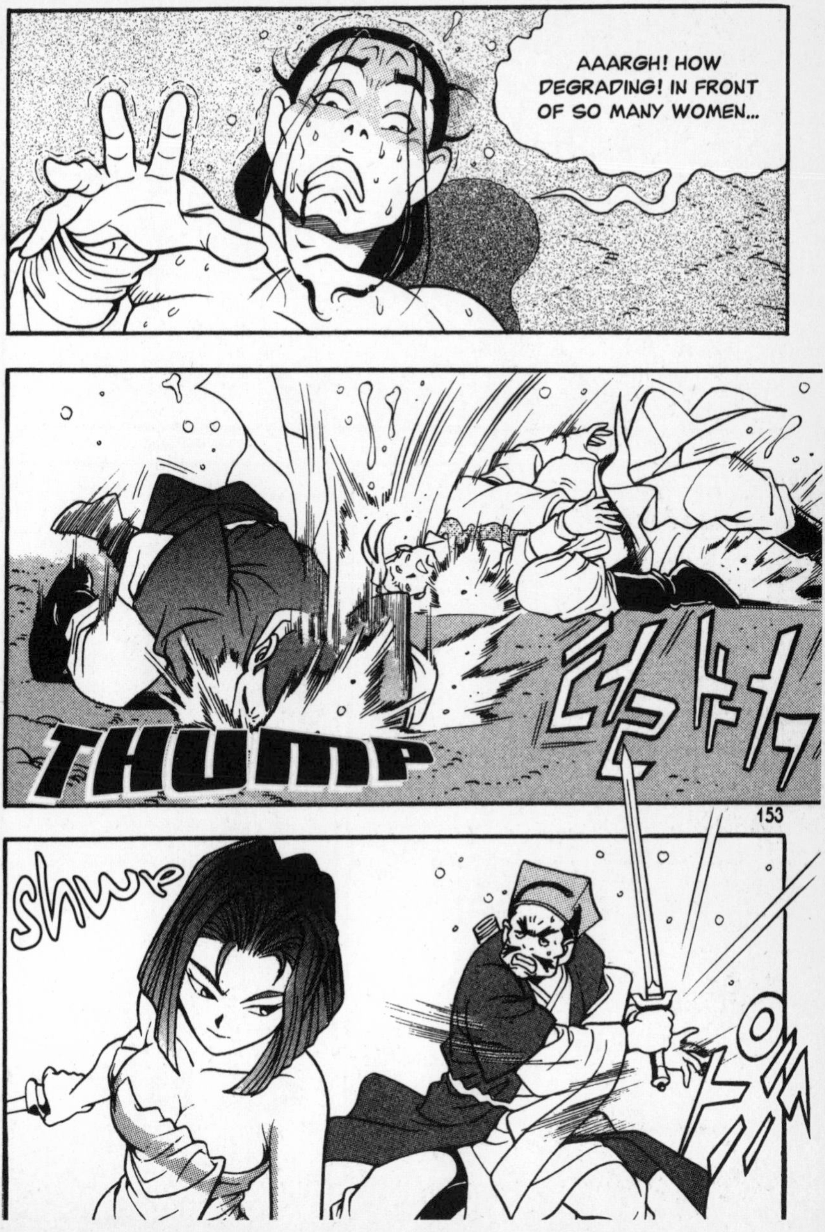
AAARGH! HOW DEGRADING! IN FRONT OF SO MANY WOMEN...
THUMP

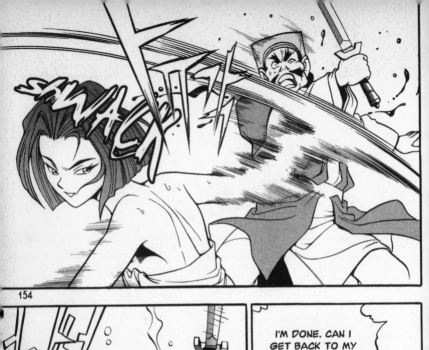

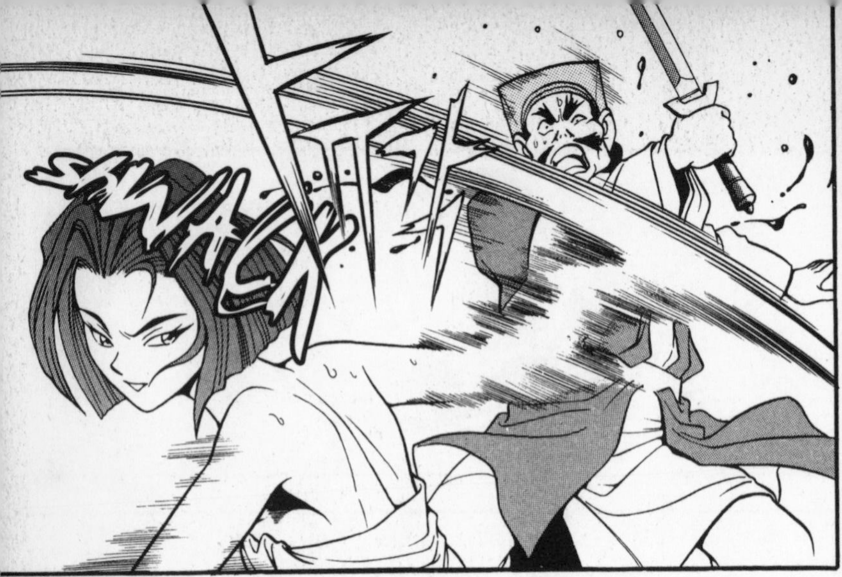
SHWACK

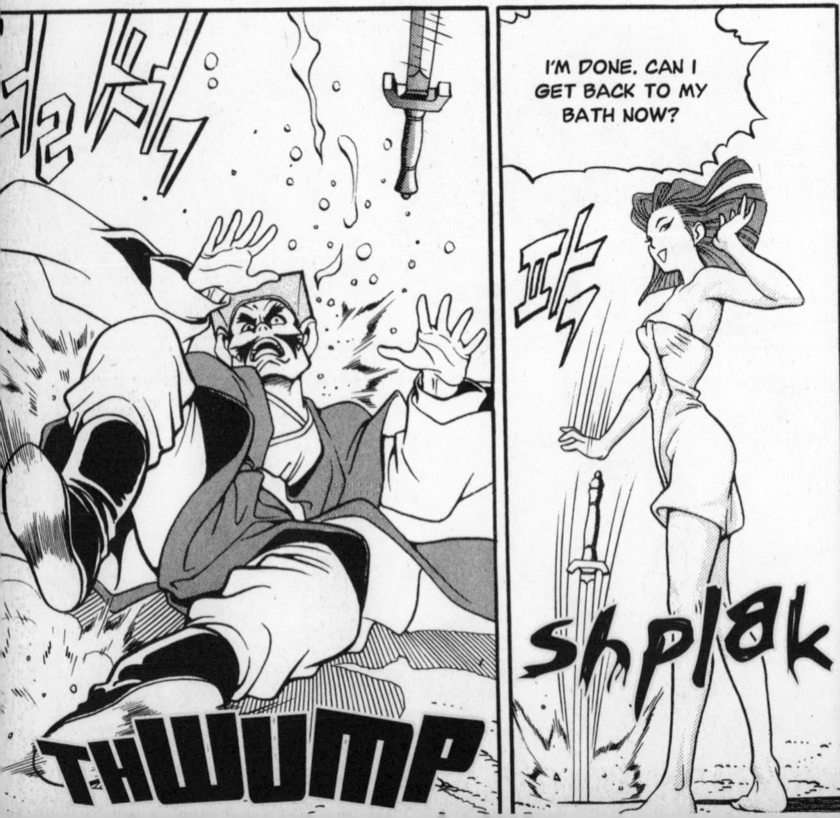
I'M DONE. CAN I GET BACK TO MY BATH NOW?
THWUMP
Shplak

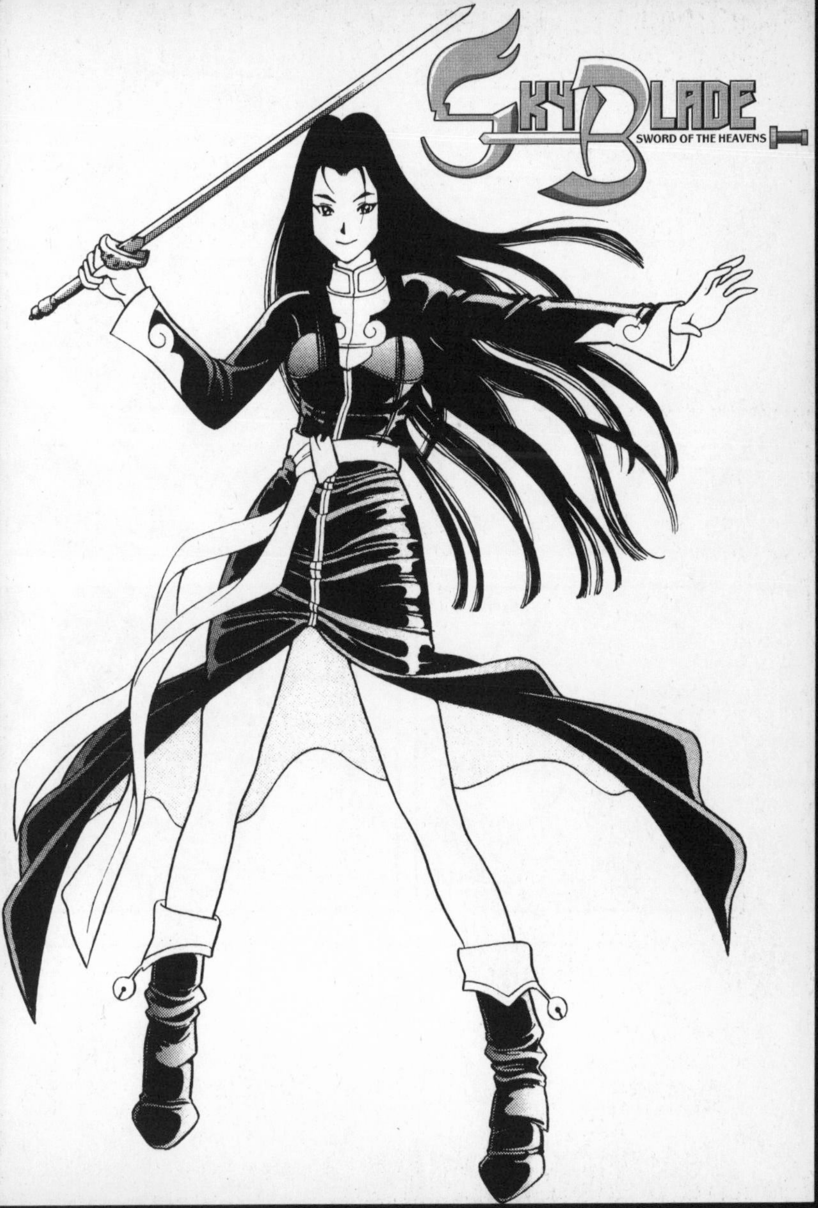
SKY BLADE
SWORD OF THE HEAVENS

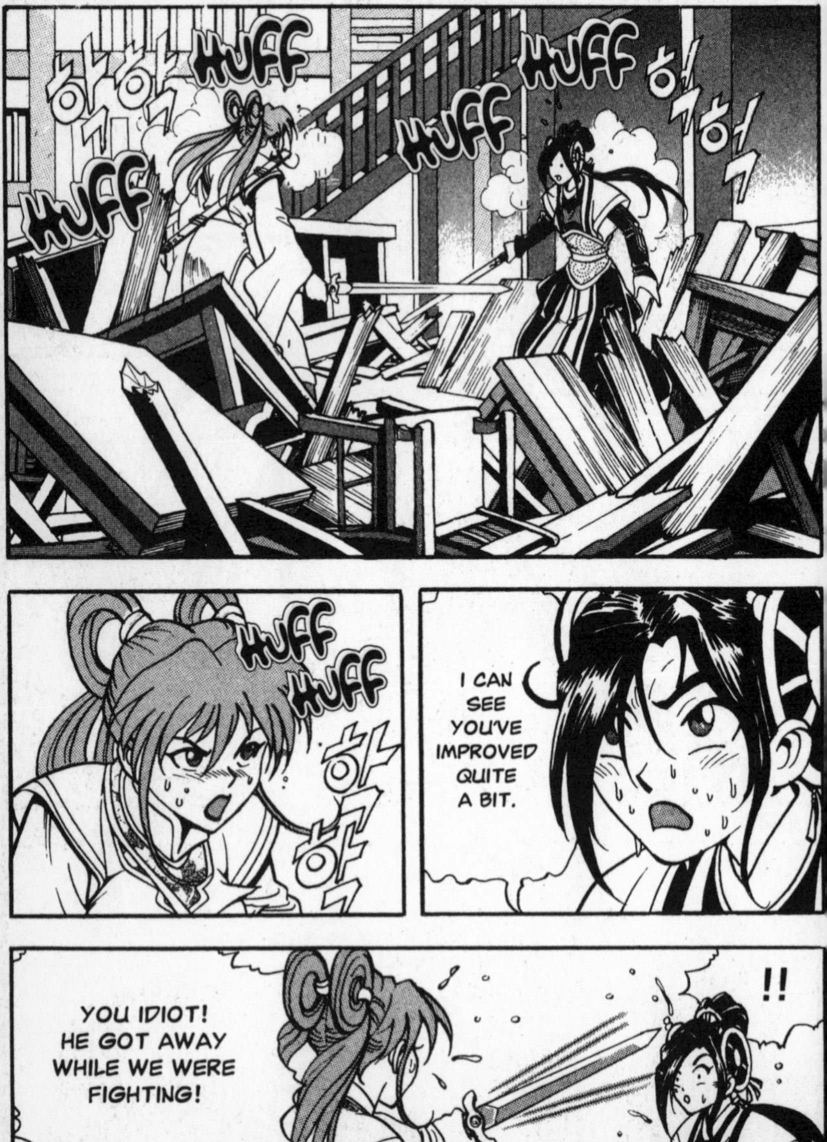
HUFF
HUFF
HUFF
HUFF
HUFF
HUFF
I CAN SEE YOU'VE IMPROVED QUITE A BIT.
YOU IDIOT! HE GOT AWAY WHILE WE WERE FIGHTING!
!!

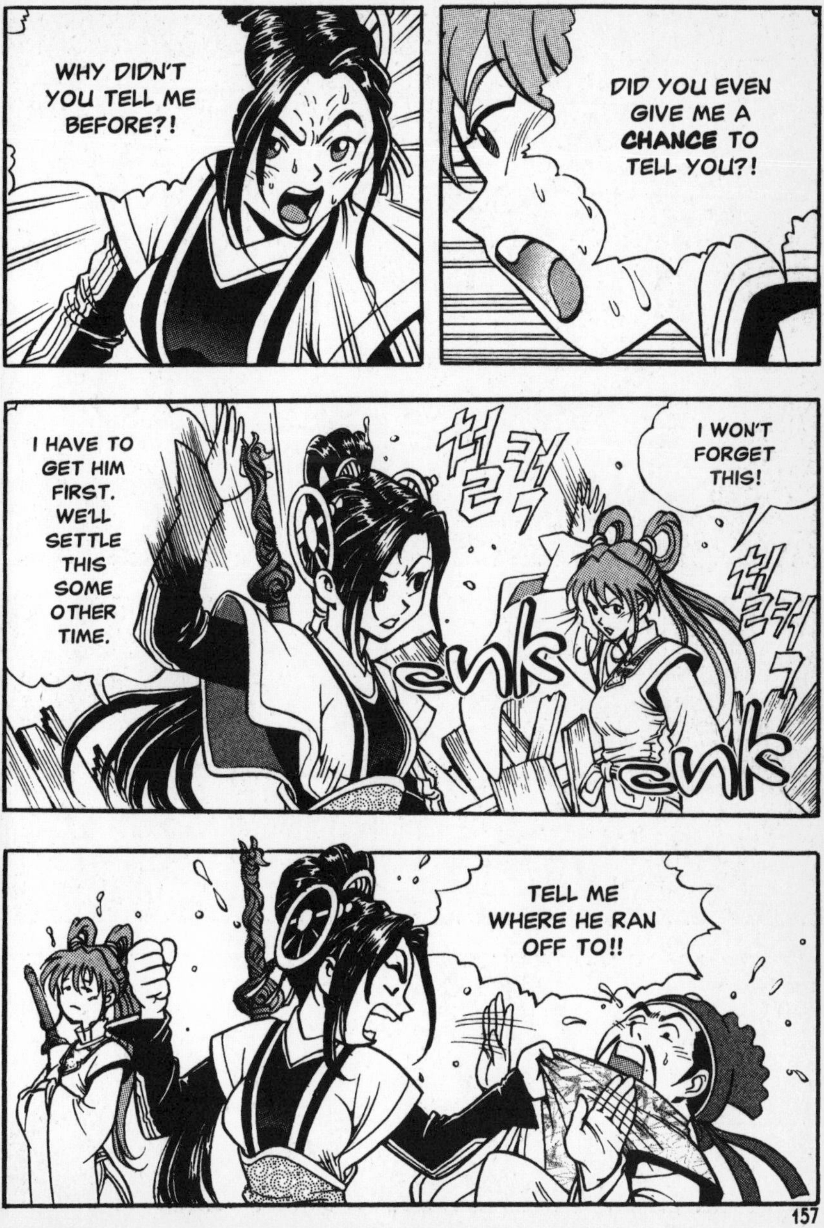
WHY DIDN'T YOU TELL ME BEFORE?!
DID YOU EVEN GIVE ME A **CHANCE** TO TELL YOU?!
I HAVE TO GET HIM FIRST. WE'LL SETTLE THIS SOME OTHER TIME.
철컥
cnk
I WON'T FORGET THIS!
철컥
cnk
TELL ME WHERE HE RAN OFF TO!!

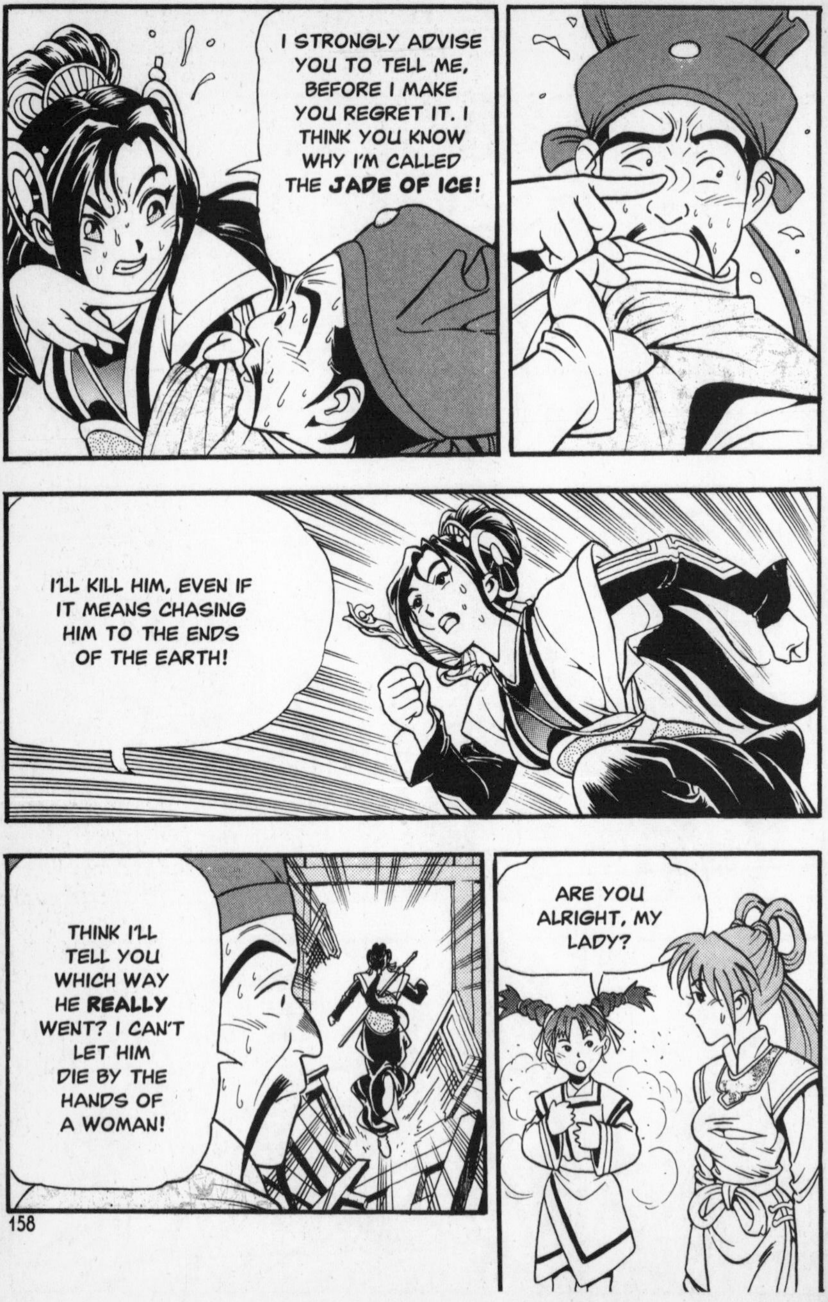
I STRONGLY ADVISE YOU TO TELL ME, BEFORE I MAKE YOU REGRET IT. I THINK YOU KNOW WHY I'M CALLED THE JADE OF ICE!
I'LL KILL HIM, EVEN IF IT MEANS CHASING HIM TO THE ENDS OF THE EARTH!
THINK I'LL TELL YOU WHICH WAY HE REALLY WENT? I CAN'T LET HIM DIE BY THE HANDS OF A WOMAN!
ARE YOU ALRIGHT, MY LADY?

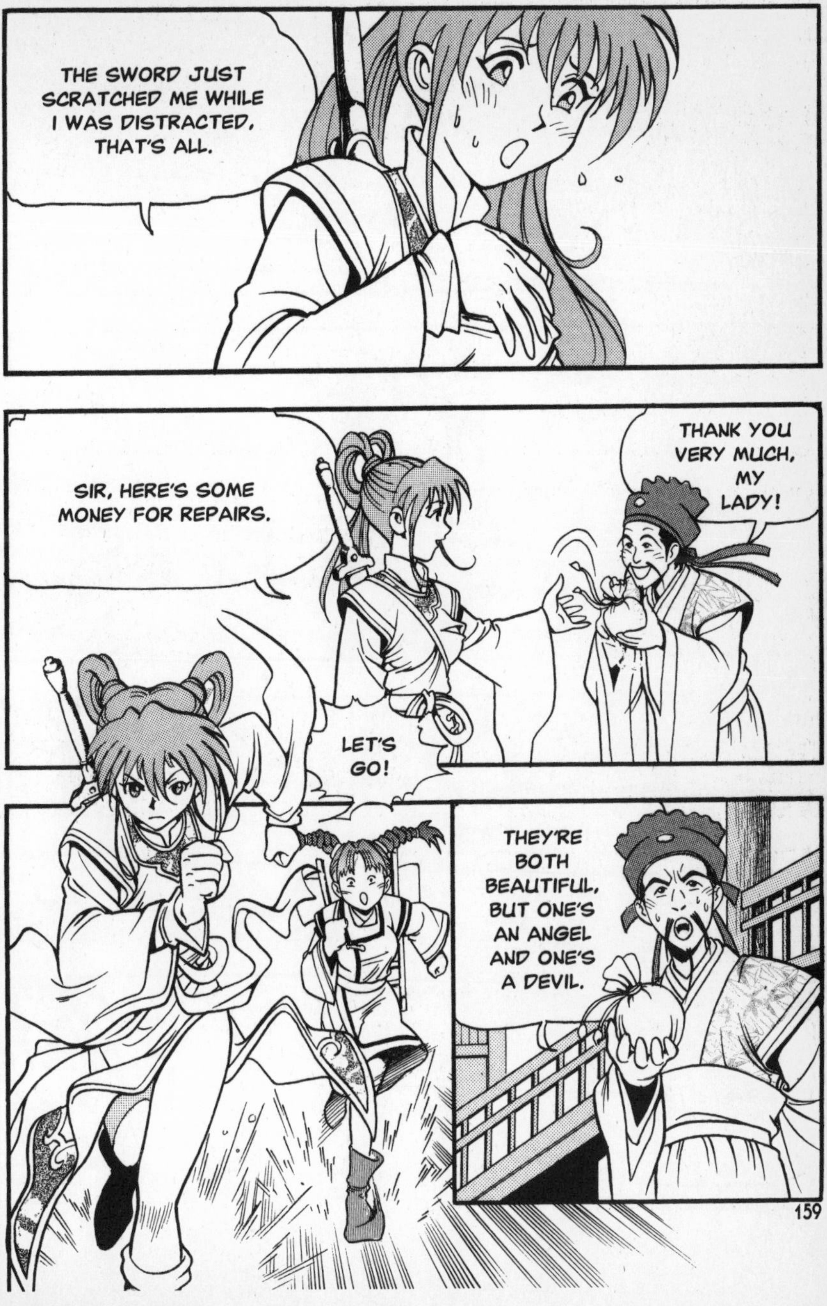
THE SWORD JUST SCRATCHED ME WHILE I WAS DISTRACTED, THAT'S ALL.
SIR, HERE'S SOME MONEY FOR REPAIRS.
THANK YOU VERY MUCH, MY LADY!
LET'S GO!
THEY'RE BOTH BEAUTIFUL, BUT ONE'S AN ANGEL AND ONE'S A DEVIL.

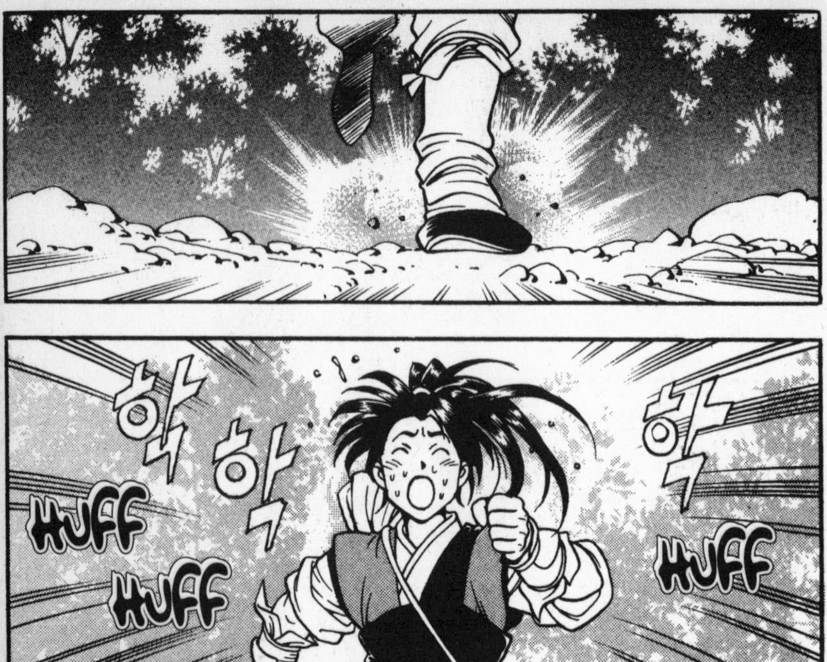
학
학
HUFF
HUFF
학
HUFF

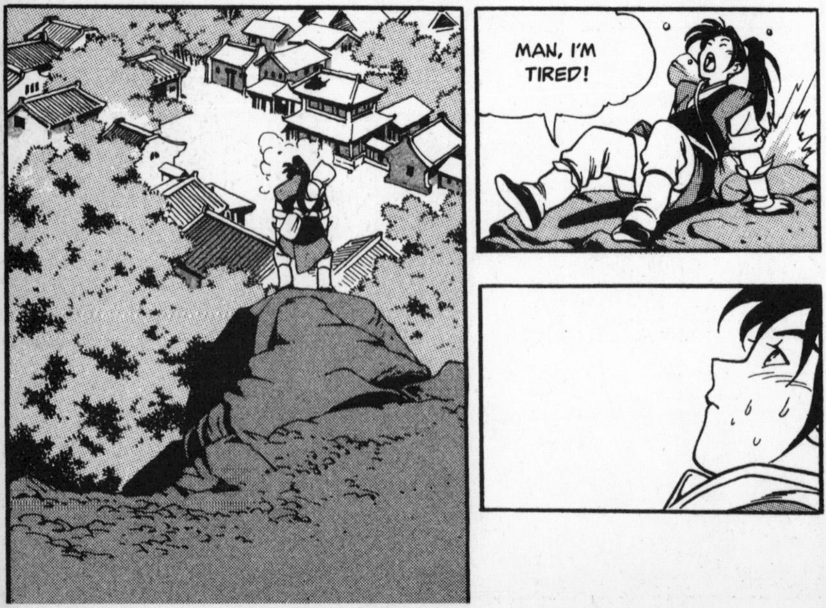
MAN, I'M TIRED!

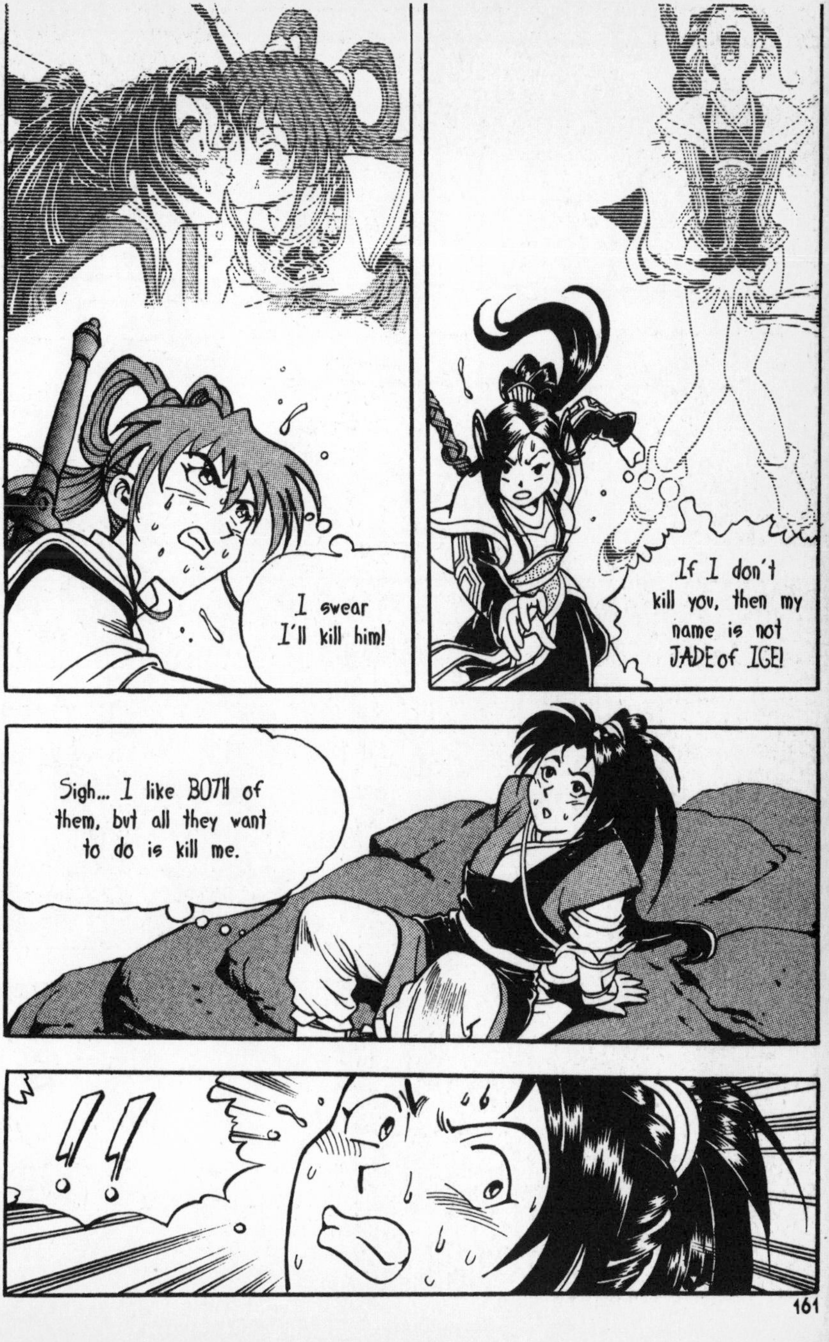
I swear I'll kill him!
If I don't kill you, then my name is not JADE of IGE!
Sigh... I like BOTH of them, but all they want to do is kill me.
!!

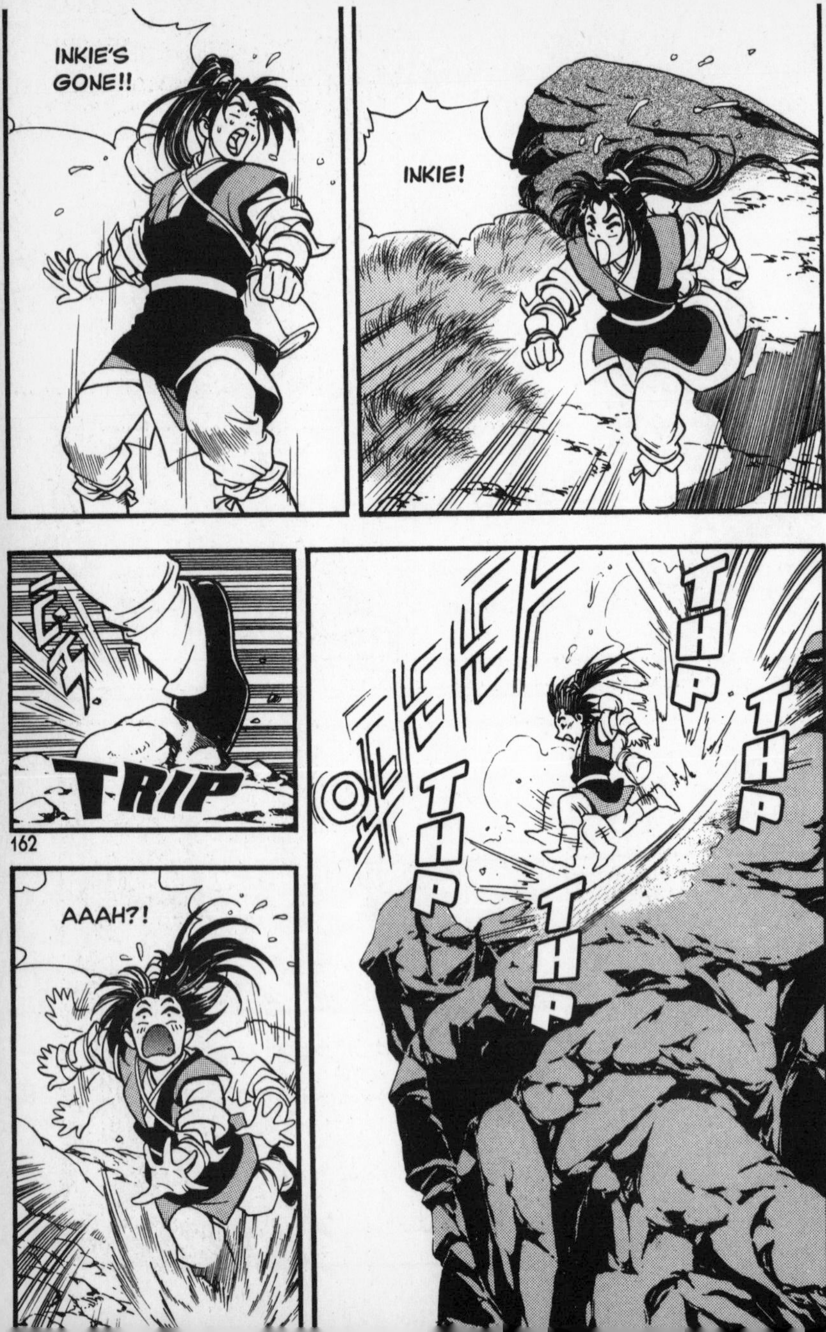
INKIE'S GONE!!
INKIE!
TRIP
THP THP
THP THP
THP THP
AAAH?!

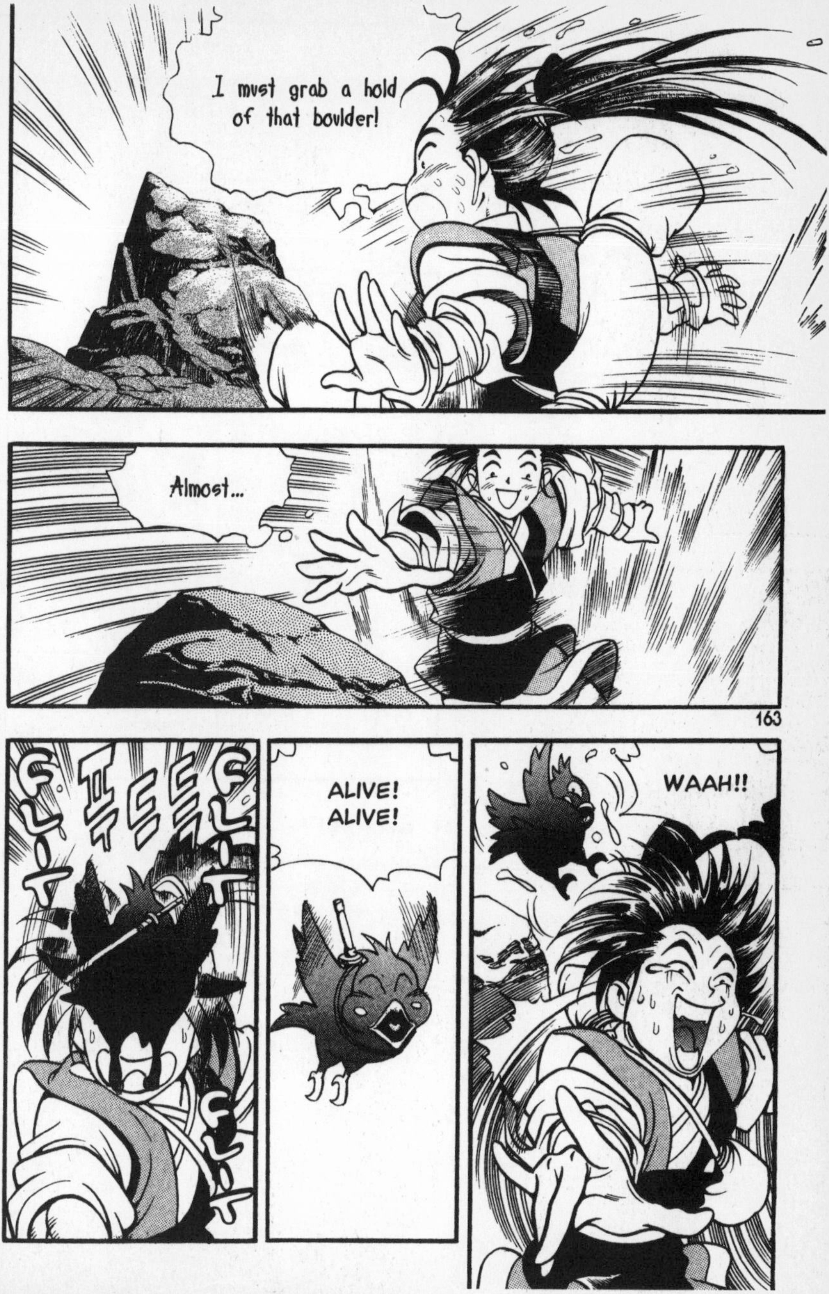
I must grab a hold of that boulder!
Almost...
FLIT
FLIT
FLIT
ALIVE! ALIVE!
WAAH!!

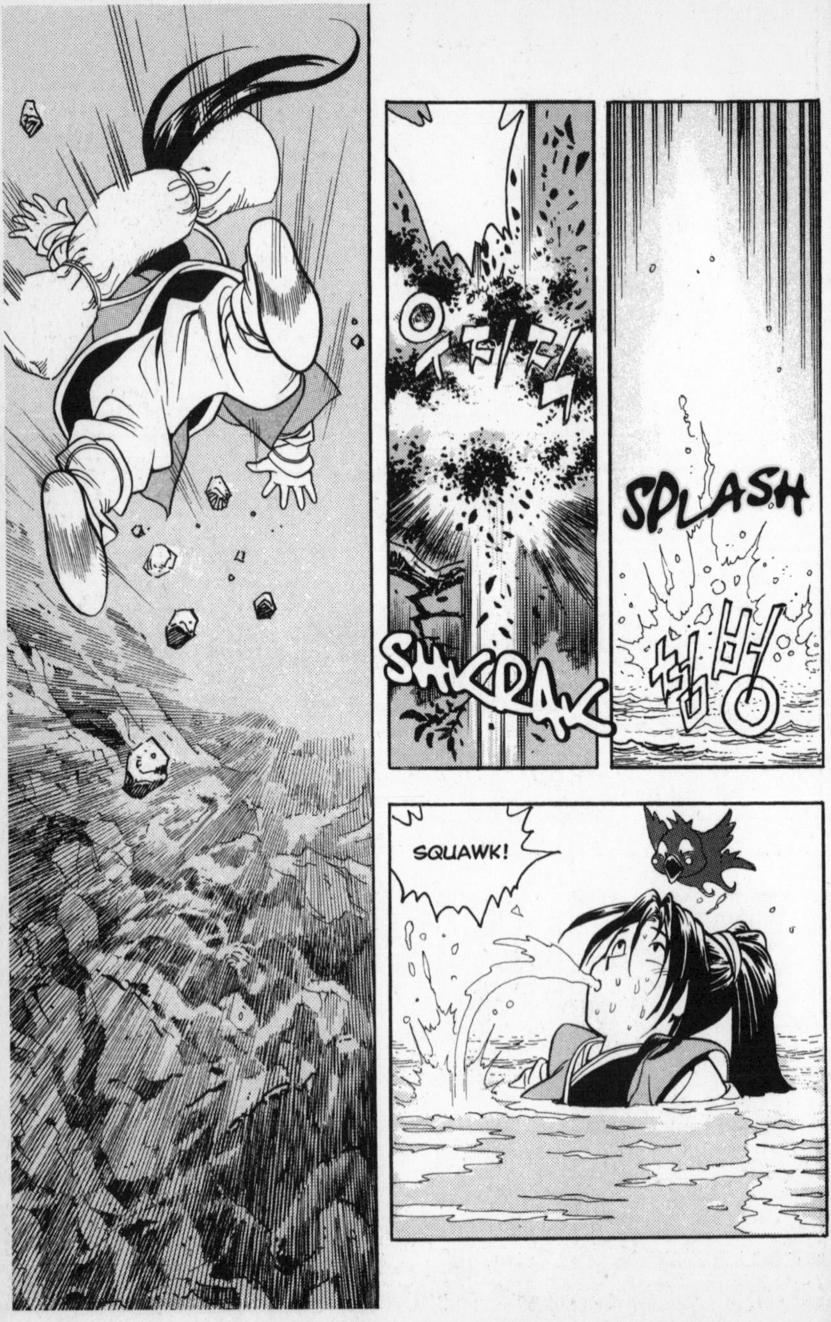
SHKRAK
SPLASH
SQUAWK!

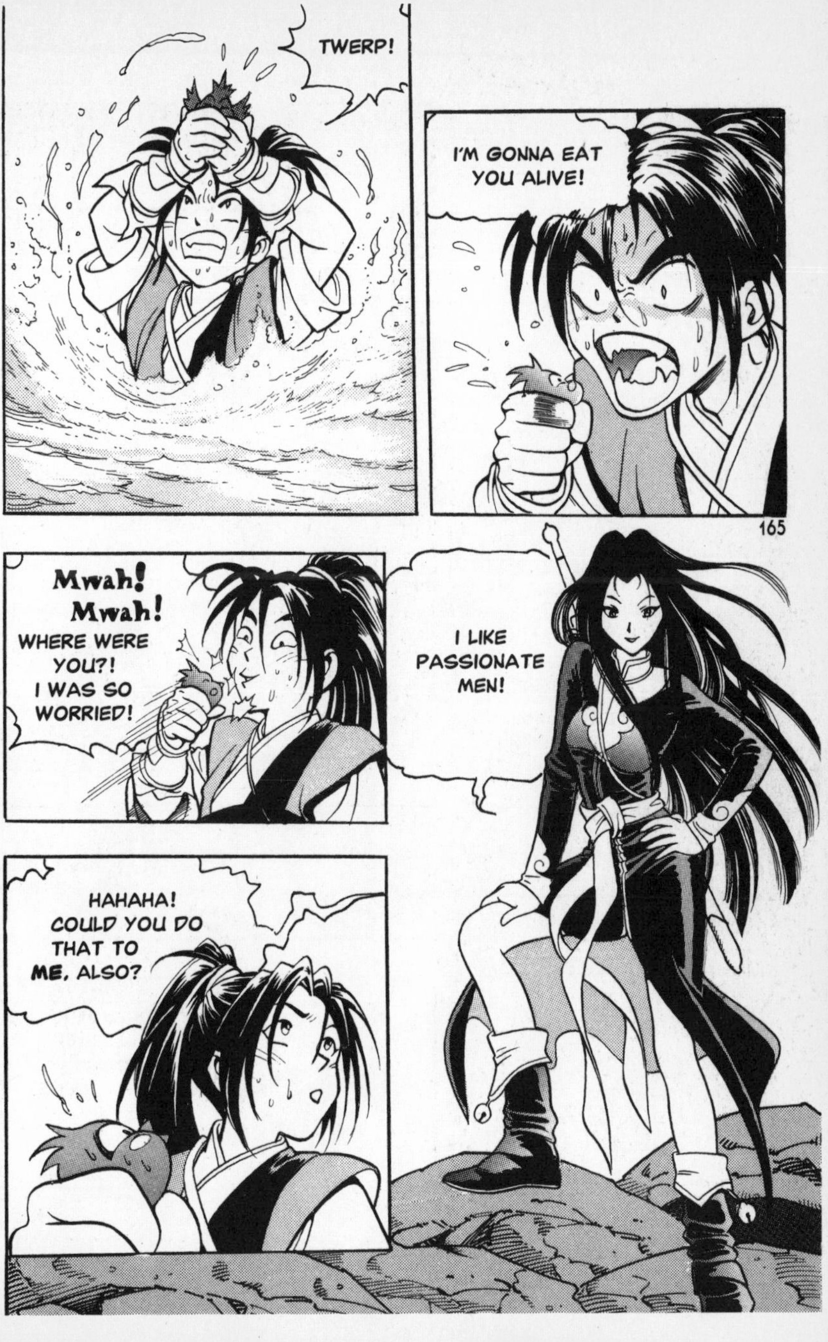
TWERP!
I'M GONNA EAT YOU ALIVE!
Mwah! Mwah!
WHERE WERE YOU?! I WAS SO WORRIED!
I LIKE PASSIONATE MEN!
HAHAHA! COULD YOU DO THAT TO ME, ALSO?

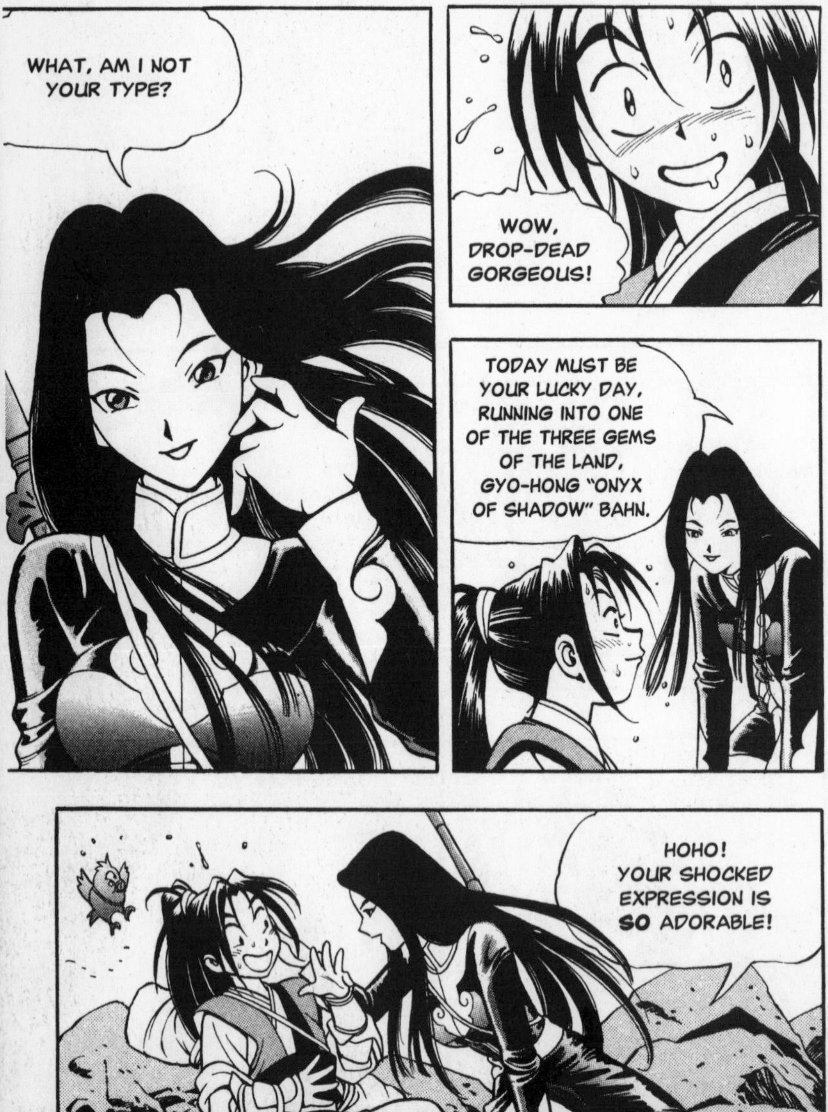
WHAT, AM I NOT YOUR TYPE?
WOW, DROP-DEAD GORGEOUS!
TODAY MUST BE YOUR LUCKY DAY, RUNNING INTO ONE OF THE THREE GEMS OF THE LAND, GYO-HONG "ONYX OF SHADOW" BAHN.
HOHO! YOUR SHOCKED EXPRESSION IS SO ADORABLE!

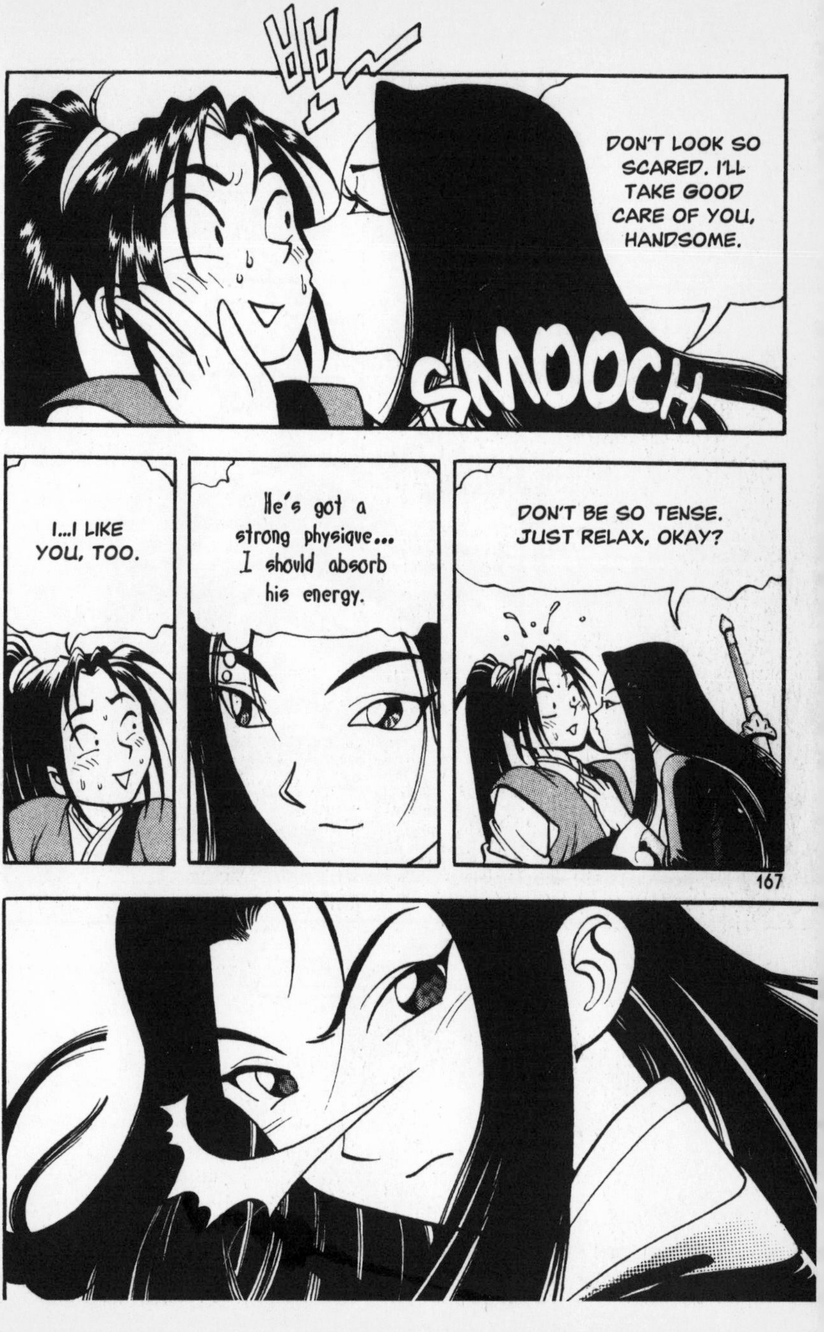
DON'T LOOK SO SCARED. I'LL TAKE GOOD CARE OF YOU, HANDSOME.
SMOOCH
DON'T BE SO TENSE. JUST RELAX, OKAY?
He's got a strong physique... I should absorb his energy.
I...I LIKE YOU, TOO.

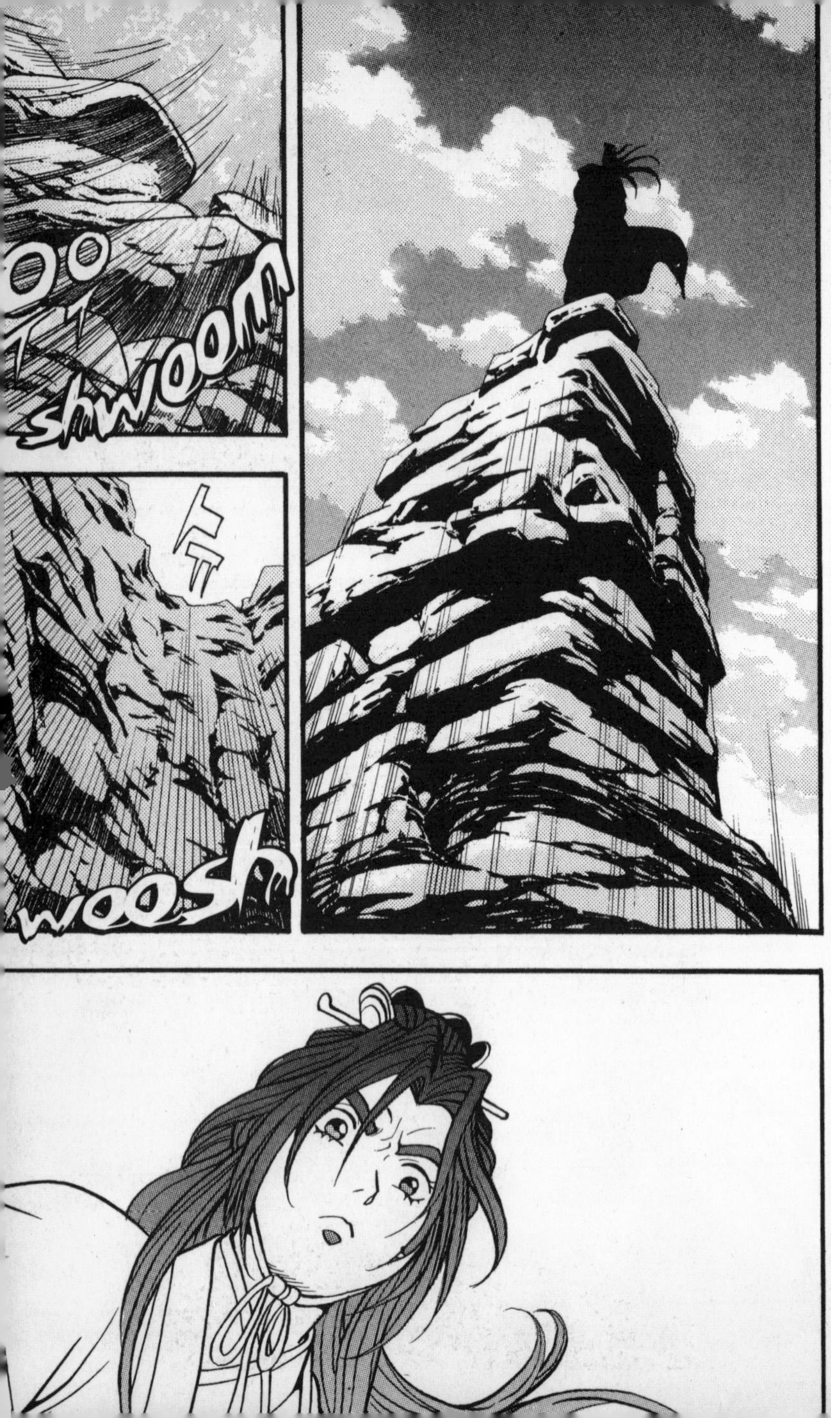
shwoom
woosh

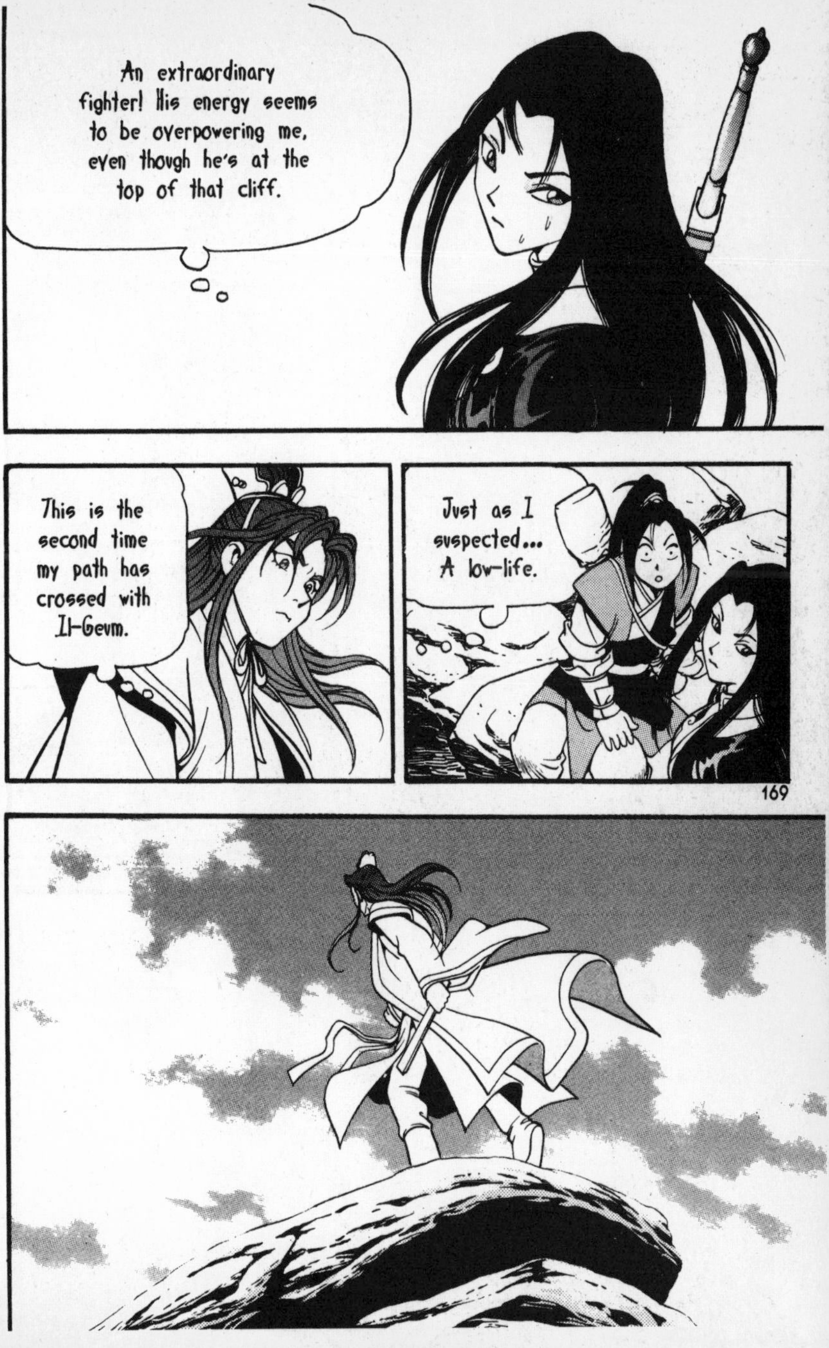
An extraordinary fighter! His energy seems to be overpowering me, even though he's at the top of that cliff.
This is the second time my path has crossed with Il-Geum.
Just as I suspected... A low-life.

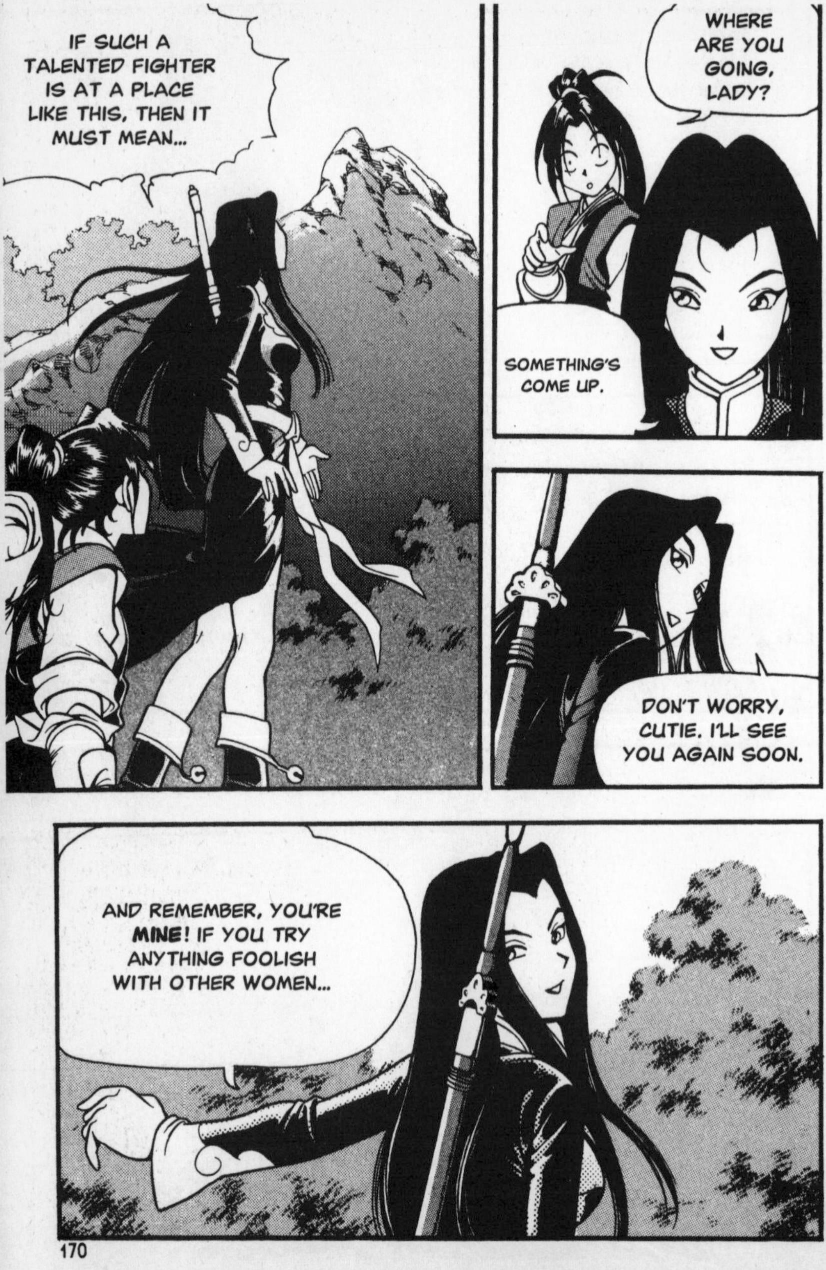
IF SUCH A TALENTED FIGHTER IS AT A PLACE LIKE THIS, THEN IT MUST MEAN...
WHERE ARE YOU GOING, LADY?
SOMETHING'S COME UP.
DON'T WORRY, CUTIE. I'LL SEE YOU AGAIN SOON.
AND REMEMBER, YOU'RE MINE! IF YOU TRY ANYTHING FOOLISH WITH OTHER WOMEN...

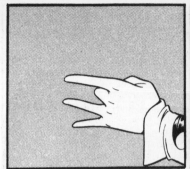

THEN I'LL PUT A HOLE THROUGH YOUR CHEST LIKE THAT TREE.

DUH...

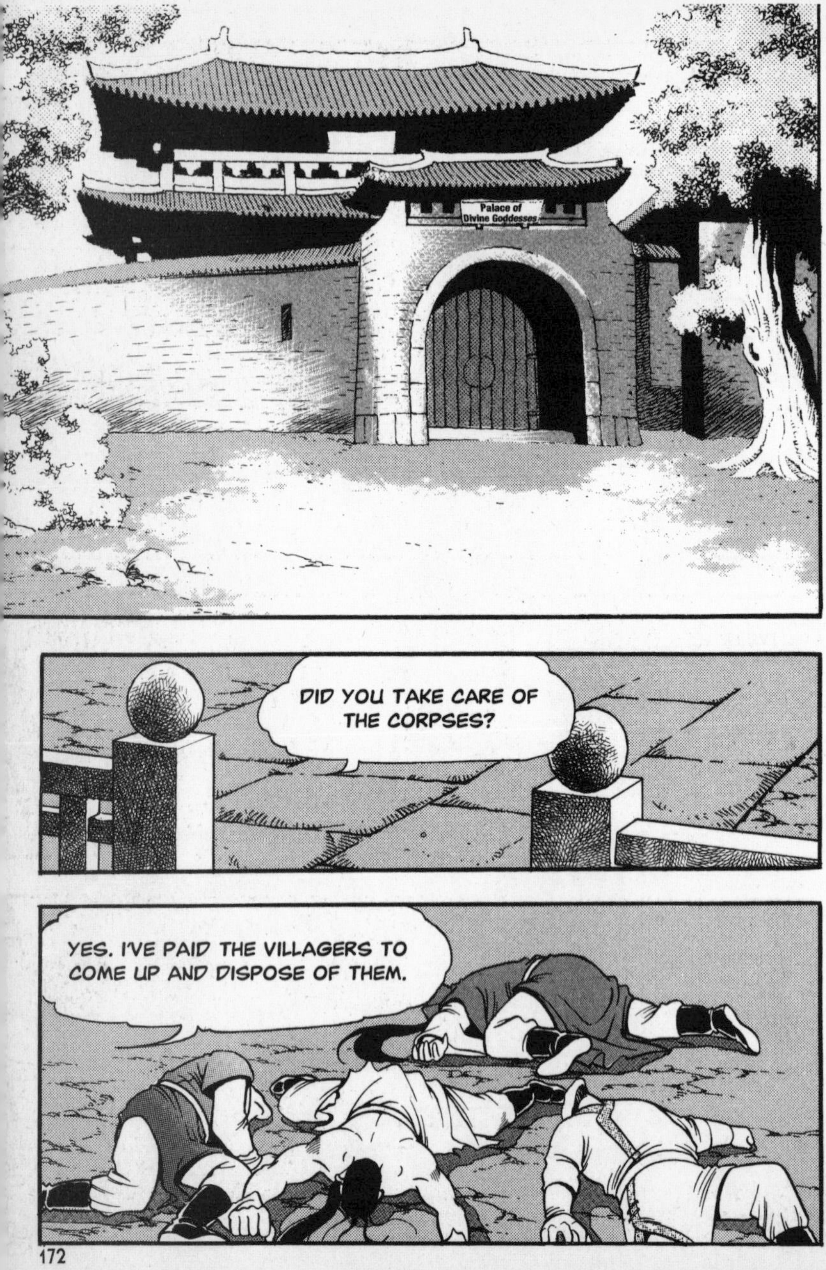
Palace of Divine Goddesses
DID YOU TAKE CARE OF THE CORPSES?
YES. I'VE PAID THE VILLAGERS TO COME UP AND DISPOSE OF THEM.

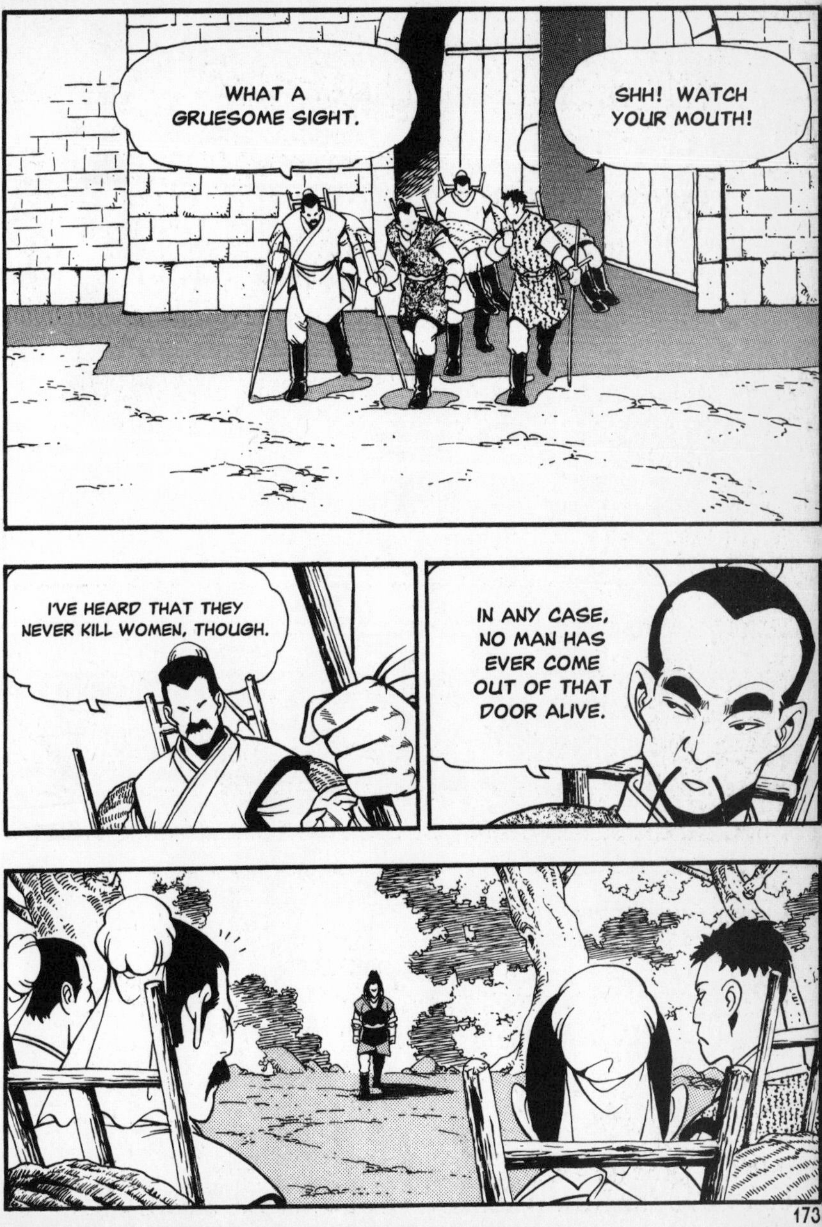
WHAT A GRUESOME SIGHT.
SHH! WATCH YOUR MOUTH!
I'VE HEARD THAT THEY NEVER KILL WOMEN, THOUGH.
IN ANY CASE, NO MAN HAS EVER COME OUT OF THAT DOOR ALIVE.

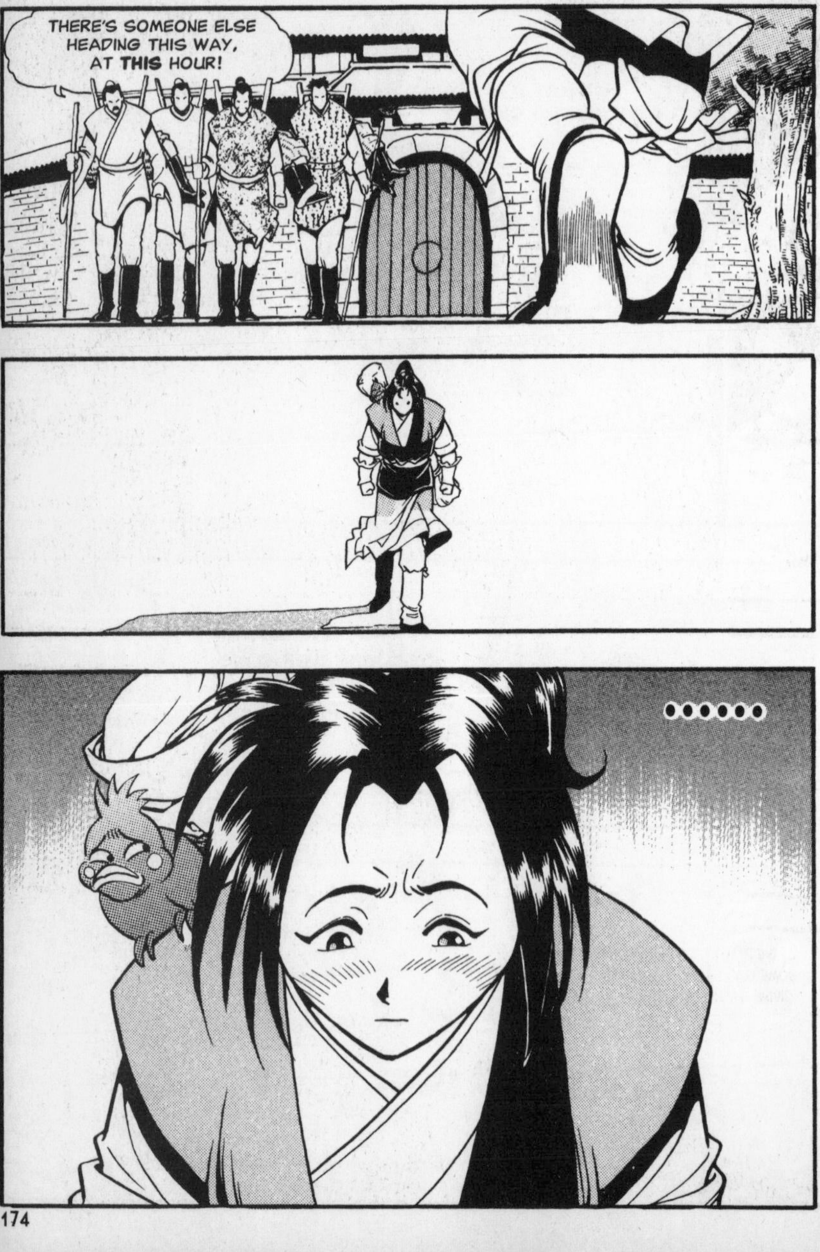
THERE'S SOMEONE ELSE HEADING THIS WAY, AT **THIS** HOUR!
••••••

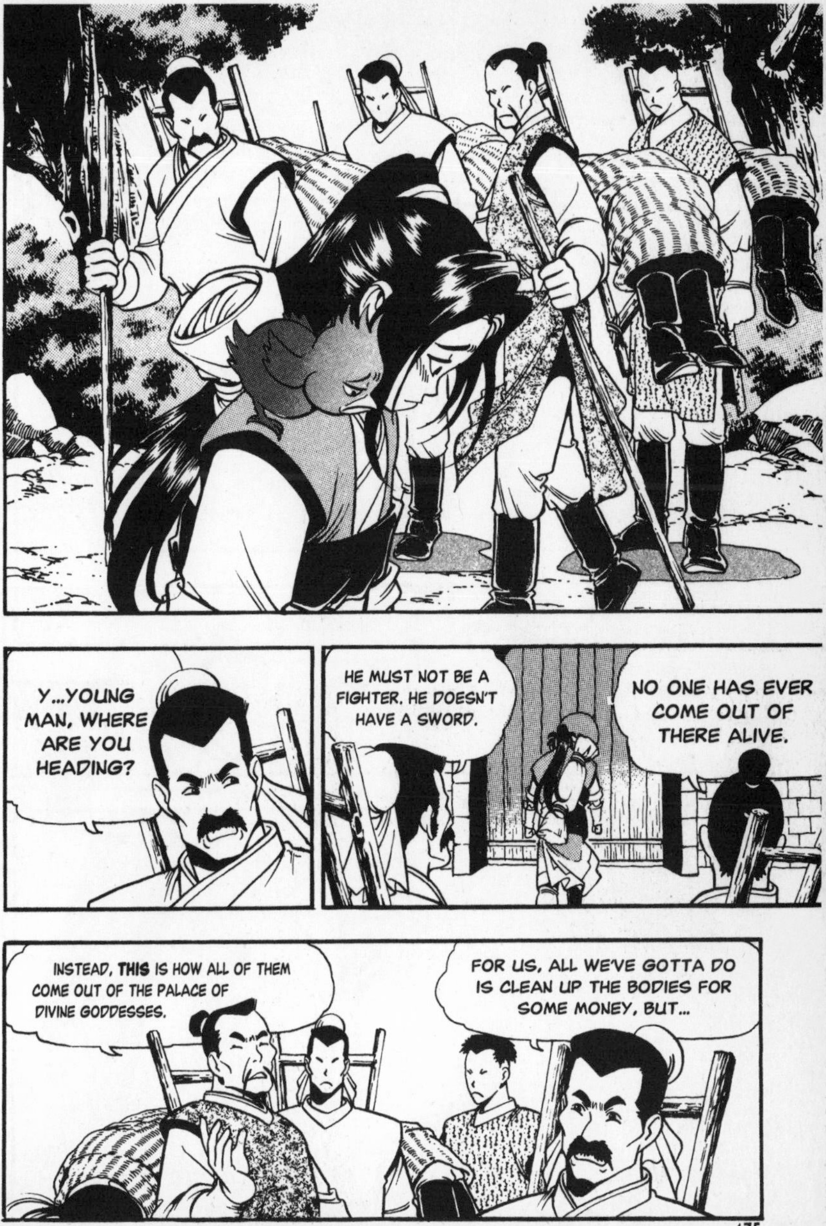
Y...YOUNG MAN, WHERE ARE YOU HEADING?
HE MUST NOT BE A FIGHTER. HE DOESN'T HAVE A SWORD.
NO ONE HAS EVER COME OUT OF THERE ALIVE.
INSTEAD, THIS IS HOW ALL OF THEM COME OUT OF THE PALACE OF DIVINE GODDESSES.
FOR US, ALL WE'VE GOTTA DO IS CLEAN UP THE BODIES FOR SOME MONEY, BUT...

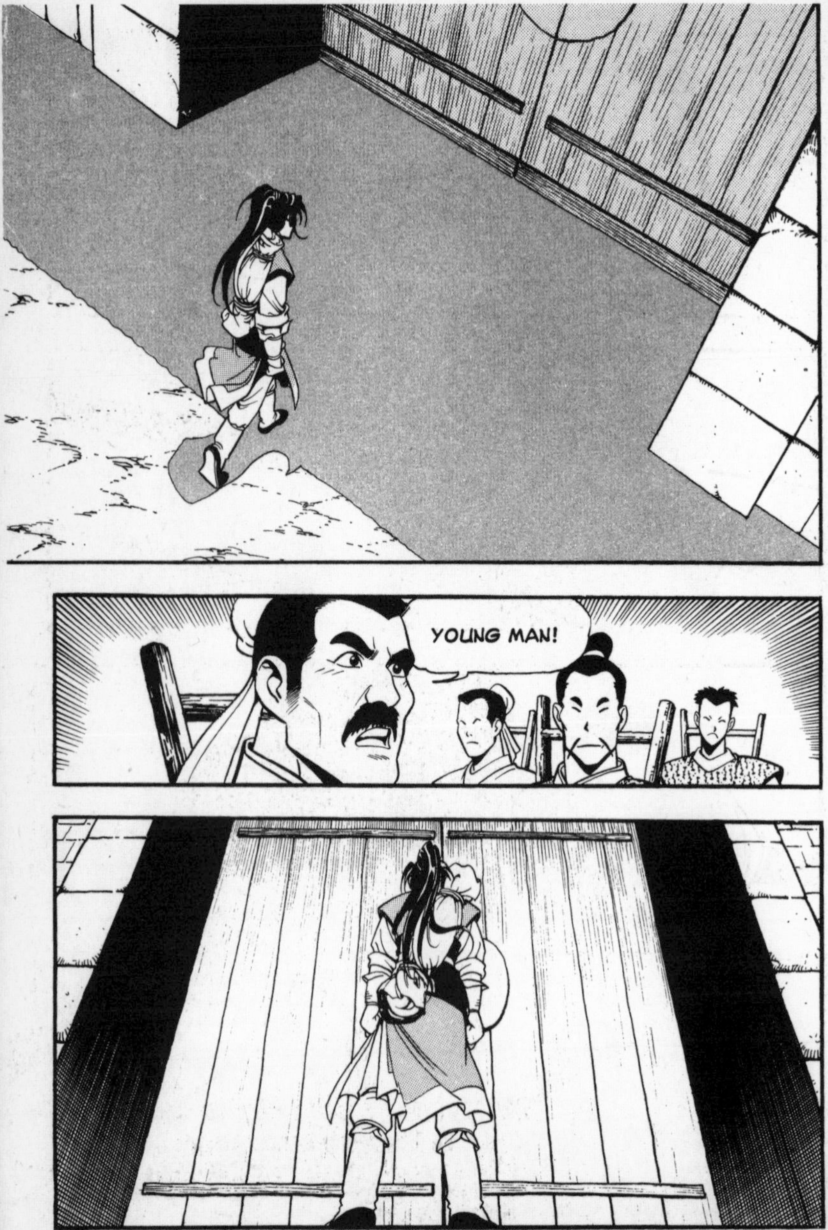
YOUNG MAN!

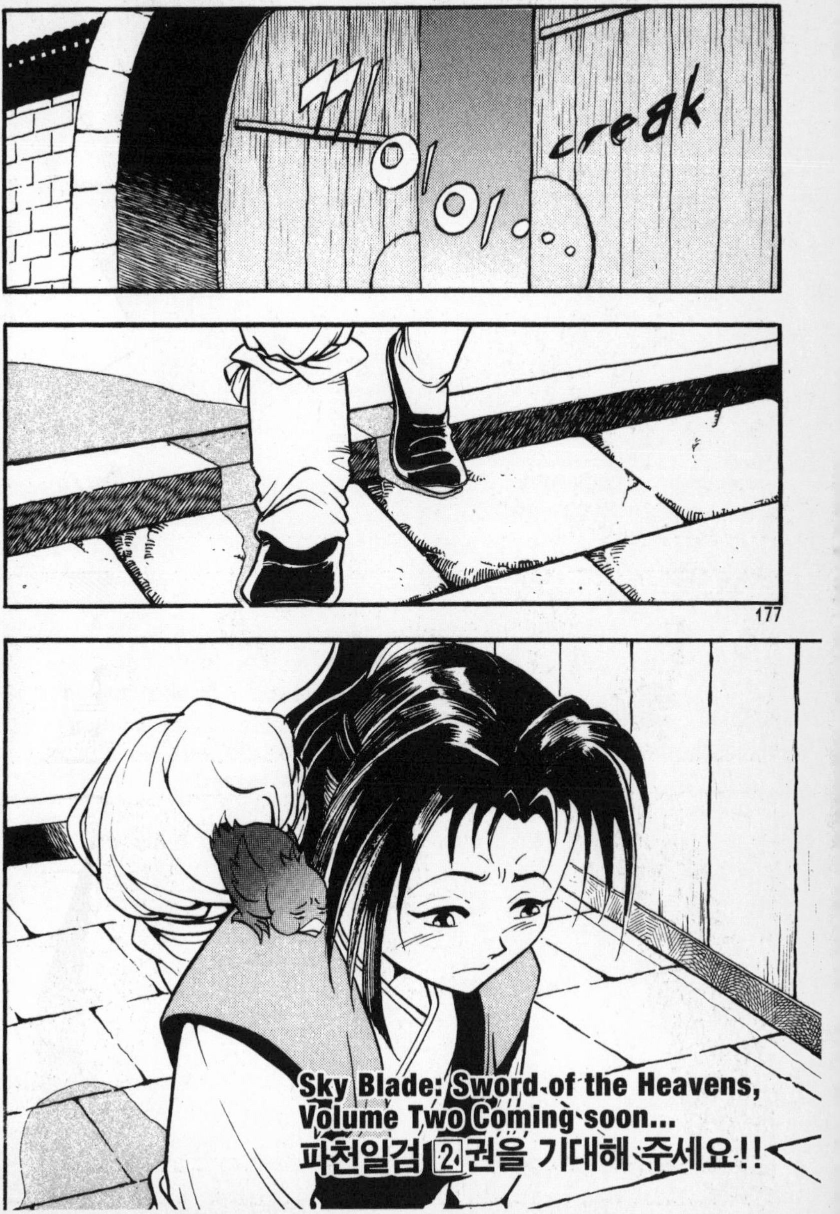
끼이이...
creak
Sky Blade: Sword of the Heavens,
Volume Two Coming soon...
파천일검 ②권을 기대해 주세요!!

LETTER FROM THE ADV MANGA TRANSLATION STAFF

Dear Reader,

On behalf of the ADV Manga translation team, thank you for purchasing an ADV book. We are enthusiastic and committed to our work, and strive to carry our enthusiasm over into the book you hold in your hands.

Our goal is to retain the true spirit of the original Korean book. While great care has been taken to render a true and accurate translation, some cultural or readability issues may require a line to be adapted for greater accessibility to our readers. At times, manhwa titles that include culturally-specific concepts will feature a "Translator's Notes" section, which explains noteworthy references to the original text.

We hope our commitment to a faithful translation is evident in every ADV book you purchase.

Sincerely,

Javier Lopez
Lead Translator

Jason An

Simon Jung

ADV Manga™

Jade of ice

The Divine Goddesses

THE TWIN devils OF NORTH & SOUTH

SKY BLADE
SWORD OF THE HEAVENS
2
Author: Hyun Kang-Suk
Illustrator: Ah Shin
ARTWORK SUBJECT TO CHANGE

Put them together and you've got **BIG TROUBLE for IL-GEUM!**

SKY BLADE
SWORD OF THE HEAVENS

ADV MANGA™

www.adv-manga.com

More Manga Monthly!

One's just not enough.

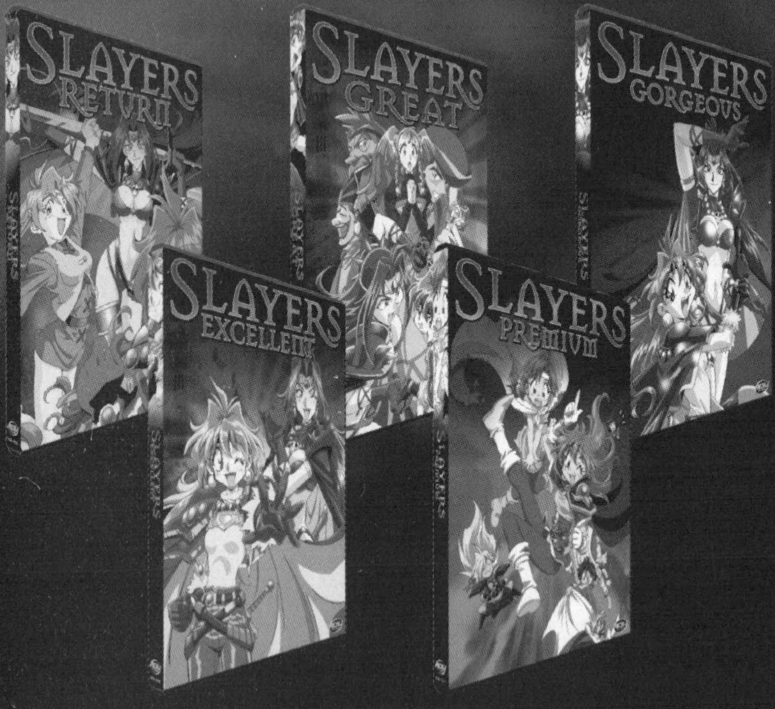
SLAYERS RETURN
SLAYERS GREAT
SLAYERS GORGEOUS
SLAYERS EXCELLENT
SLAYERS PREMIUM

MANGA SURVEY

PLEASE MAIL THE COMPLETED FORM TO: EDITOR – ADV MANGA
℅ A.D. Vision, Inc. 10114 W. Sam Houston Pkwy., Suite 200 Houston, TX 77099

Name:_____

Address:_____

City, State, Zip:_____

_____

E-Mail:_____

Male ☐   Female ☐   Age:_____

☐ **CHECK HERE IF YOU WOULD LIKE TO RECEIVE OTHER INFORMATION OR FUTURE OFFERS FROM ADV.**

All information provided will be used for internal purposes only. We promise not to sell or otherwise divulge your information.

1. Annual Household Income (*Check only one*)
☐ Under $25,000
☐ $25,000 to $50,000
☐ $50,000 to $75,000
☐ Over $75,000

2. How do you hear about new Manga releases? (*Check all that apply*)
☐ Browsing in Store   ☐ Magazine Ad
☐ Internet Reviews   ☐ Online Advertising
☐ Anime News Websites   ☐ Conventions
☐ Direct Email Campaigns   ☐ TV Advertising
☐ Online forums (message boards and chat rooms)
☐ Carrier pigeon
☐ Other:_____

3. Which magazines do you read? (*Check all that apply*)
☐ Wizard   ☐ YRB
☐ SPIN   ☐ EGM
☐ Animerica   ☐ Newtype USA
☐ Rolling Stone   ☐ SciFi
☐ Maxim   ☐ Starlog
☐ DC Comics   ☐ Wired
☐ URB   ☐ Vice
☐ Polygon   ☐ BPM
☐ Original Play Station Magazine ☐ I hate reading
☐ Entertainment Weekly   ☐ Other:_____

MSB/001

4. Have you visited the ADV Manga website?

- ☐ Yes
- ☐ No

5. Have you made any manga purchases online from the ADV website?

- ☐ Yes
- ☐ No

6. If you have visited the ADV Manga website, how would you rate your online experience?

- ☐ Excellent
- ☐ Good
- ☐ Average
- ☐ Poor

7. What genre of manga do you prefer?
(*Check all that apply*)

- ☐ adventure
- ☐ romance
- ☐ detective
- ☐ action
- ☐ horror
- ☐ sci-fi/fantasy
- ☐ sports
- ☐ comedy

8. How many manga titles have you purchased in the last 6 months?

- ☐ none
- ☐ 1-4
- ☐ 5-10
- ☐ 11+

9. Where do you make your manga purchases? (*Check all that apply*)

- ☐ comic store
- ☐ bookstore
- ☐ newsstand
- ☐ online
- ☐ other:________________
- ☐ department store
- ☐ grocery store
- ☐ video store
- ☐ video game store

10. Which bookstores do you usually make your manga purchases at?
(*Check all that apply*)

- ☐ Barnes & Noble
- ☐ Walden Books
- ☐ Suncoast
- ☐ Best Buy
- ☐ Amazon.com
- ☐ Borders
- ☐ Books-A-Million
- ☐ Toys "Я" Us
- ☐ Other bookstore:

____

11. What's your favorite anime/manga website? (*Check all that apply*)

- ☐ adv-manga.com
- ☐ advfilms.com
- ☐ rightstuf.com
- ☐ animenewsservice.com
- ☐ animenewsnetwork.com
- ☐ Other:________________
- ☐ animeondvd.com
- ☐ anipike.com
- ☐ animeonline.net
- ☐ planetanime.com
- ☐ animenation.com

All information provided will be used for internal purposes only. We promise not to sell or otherwise divulge your information.